SYSTEMS ARCHITECTING

Creating and Building Complex Systems

EBERHARDT RECHTIN

University of Southern California,
Los Angeles

PRENTICE HALL P T R, Englewood Cliffs, New Jersey 07632

Library of Congress Cataloging-in-Publication Data

Rechtin, Eberhardt.
    Systems architecting : creating and building complex systems /
  Eberhardt Rechtin.
        p.   cm.
    Includes bibliographical references and index.
    ISBN 0-13-880345-5
    1. Systems engineering.   I. Title.
  TA168.R37 1991
  C20'.001'1--dc20   90-49470
                                                          CIP

Editorial/production supervision
   and interior design: Rob DeGeorge
Cover design: Bruce Kenselaar
Prepress buyer: Kelly Behr
Manufacturing buyer: Susan Brunke

 © 1991 by Prentice Hall P T R
Prentice-Hall, Inc.
A Simon & Schuster Company
Englewood Cliffs, New Jersey 07632

The publisher offers discounts on this book when ordered
in bulk quantities. For more information, write:

   Special Sales/College Marketing
   Prentice-Hall, Inc.
   College Technical and Reference Division
   Englewood Cliffs, NJ 07632

Printed in the United States of America
10 9 8 7 6 5

ISBN 0-13-880345-5

PRENTICE-HALL INTERNATIONAL (UK) LIMITED, London
PRENTICE-HALL OF AUSTRALIA PTY. LIMITED, Sydney
PRENTICE-HALL CANADA INC., Toronto
PRENTICE-HALL HISPANOAMERICANA, S.A., Mexico
PRENTICE-HALL OF INDIA PRIVATE LIMITED, New Delhi
PRENTICE-HALL OF JAPAN, INC. Tokyo
SIMON & SCHUSTER ASIA PTE. LTD., Singapore
EDITORA PRENTICE-HALL DO BRASIL, LTDA., Rio de Janeiro

To Deedee, my beloved wife, partner,
patient advisor, and inspiration

CONTENTS

3 MODELING, SIMULATING, AND PROTOTYPING   52

4 THE ARCHITECT'S KIT OF TOOLS   75

PART TWO   CHALLENGES   **158**

11 THE CHALLENGE: BIOLOGICAL ARCHITECTURES AND INTELLIGENT BEHAVIOR 216

12 THE CHALLENGE: THE COMPLEX WORLD OF ECONOMICS AND PUBLIC POLICY 243

PREFACE

THE ORIGINS OF SYSTEMS ARCHITECTING

Architecting, the planning and building of structures, is as old as human societies and as modern as planning the exploration of the solar system. It arose in response to problems too complex to be solved by preestablished rules and procedures.

In the beginning of civilization, individuals made and built things by themselves. Later, groups built things collectively; specialization and craftsmanship began. Much later, it was recognized that still larger things could be built if some general principles were followed; engineering and science emerged.

Then, many thousands of years ago, city-states began public works of such technical and social complexity that engineering alone could not solve the resultant problems. Egyptians built canals and irrigation systems that not only exploited the Nile, but largely determined the economic status of the country. Phoenicians built maritime and naval fleets. The Greeks and Romans built cities, aqueducts, fortifications, and empire-spanning road systems. From these endeavors arose the first great architectures—civil, military, and naval.

Conceiving the great architectures required creative individuals capable of understanding and resolving problems of almost overwhelming complexity—the first great architects. Some, like Imhotep, the Egyptian, and Vitruvius, the Roman, we know from historical writings. Others, like Daedalus, the imprisoned architect of the Labyrinth of Crete, who achieved the impossible—escape by air—we know only by legend.

Building architects had to bring together structures, psychology, art, and aesthetics. Civil-works architects had to integrate structures, mechanics, politics, economics, geology, and hydrology. Naval architects combined structures, mechanics, hydrodynamics, aerodynamics, meteorology, economics, and military engineering. All had to accommodate the physical and social environment in which their efforts were undertaken. Systems architects do likewise, though their primary interests—as are those of this book—are primarily functional rather than aesthetic.

Architecting thus came into being as both a science and an art. The former is analysis-based, factual, logical, and deductive. The latter is synthesis-based, intuitive, judgmental, and inductive. Both are essential if modern systems architecting is to be complete.

It is the central premise of this text that similar historical developments are underway in aerospace, electrical, industrial, and other engineering fields. How do we know? First, we see it in the literature. The word "architecture" is now widely used in communications, space systems, computers, software, networks, and transportation systems—air, ground, and space. Second, if there are architectures, there must be architects to build them. Indeed there are, although they have gone under different names. They have been called configurators, chief engineers, chief designers, design team leaders, and advanced-systems engineers. But they are the architects, nonetheless.

Within the last few decades, there have been huge system architectural challenges—global air transportation, global communications, national and international space programs, the strategic deterrent—resulting in architectures of unprecedented size and scope. At the same time, there have been major challenges in architecting highly complex integrated circuits, software languages, and sensing systems.

The results have been the generation of new classes of *system* architects—aerospace architects, communications architects, computer architects, software architects, and manufacturing-process architects. It is no coincidence that these developments occured virtually simultaneously with major developments in the information sciences. Statistical information theory showed that optimum communication designs were possible. Switching and network theories led to vastly improved communications systems. Guidance and control introduced computer "smarts" to aerospace and transportation systems. Today, only a few decades after the advent of computers, it is rare to find any system, from household appliances to planetary explorers, that lacks some form of machine intelligence. The achievable performance of such systems is so much greater than that of their predecessors that completely new architectural forms are now called for. One can see this even in the oldest of the architectures, that of homes, which increasingly are becoming smart machines for living and enjoyment.

An even more recent impact of computers on architecture is in the rapidly increasing number of computer models of system elements. The architect now has tools and techniques undreamed of a few decades ago. A modern systems architect must be as proficient in the use of these mental tools as any skilled artisan is of the tools that aid his hands.

And, finally, mankind is passing into another era, one in which machines extend the human mind as they have long extended the human muscle and senses. The architectures of that extension will be as complex technically, psychologically, aesthetically, socially, and politically as any architectures yet attempted. In the early stages, it will be a matter of considering machine intelligence as an element in every systems architecture. Later, it will be the challenge of gaining acceptance for machine judgement as well as assistance in human affairs.

Less evident, perhaps, is whether systems architecting is, or should be, a recognized profession. For a profession to be recognized requires notable achievements, acknowledged practitioners, and an accredited course of study. As we shall see, achievements and practitioners abound in the newest engineering disciplines.

What now needs to be done is to establish a formal course of study. But what should it be? Fortunately, civil architects can give us some answers. From their experience, three elements are needed.

First, the potential systems architect should know the engineering fundamentals on which each architecture is based. As noted earlier, architecting is a consequence of system complexity. As complexity increases, the search for a "best" system by analytic comparison of all conceivable alternates becomes impractical. "Common sense," derived from specific engineering fundamentals and the experience of other architects, is needed to reduce the search to practical dimensions. It is not enough to know of Maxwell's, Navier-Stokes', or Newton's equations. One must also understand their engineering consequences.

Second, experience and judgment are necessary. Studies of many professions show that between formal education and field experience, about 10 years is required to be an acknowledged professional. Hands-on system problem solving is mandatory. In the earlier architectural fields, this is accomplished in "design studios." In the more recent engineering fields, the equivalent studios are specialized design laboratories well equipped with work stations. Such design laboratories are in the formative stage at several institutions.

And third, the architect needs to acquire the insights gained from experience in the design laboratories on the job. The purpose of this text is to help make gaining that experience more efficient by the presentation of *heuristics*—insights and lessons learned—developed over the last few decades in a wide spectrum of major systems.

The heuristics are in **bold type**, permitting rapid scanning and search, not only for the heuristics, but for the context from which they were derived. The text is designed for several kinds of readers: those who are or would be systems architects and those who work closely with them—clients, managers, systems engineers, builders, and users.

The perspective is that of an architect, that is, a focus on those features important at the *systems* level of fields that individually are the province of experts. Those features may well demand an in-depth knowledge of some fields, especially if new system-critical technologies are being introduced for the first time. The architect is *not* a generalist, but rather a systems-oriented specialist.

The text is organized in three parts. Part One presents the fundamentals of systems architecting from conceptual design to final operations. Part Two highlights the major challenges confronting systems architecting in the modern world. Part Three concerns the relationships between architecting and managing and the needs of each to understand the other.

Appendix A lists all the heuristics in the order in which they appear in the text, that is, in the order in which they are first useful in system implementation. Key words are in **bold type** to aid in quick search. Page numbers are given to place each heuristic in context.

Appendix B lists texts the author found useful as a foundation of a systems-architecture reference library.

The book in some ways resembles the architecting process itself. It attacks the complex problem—learning about architecting—in successive levels. The top level, the quick scan of the table of contents and the boldface heuristics in the text, defines the scope. The next level, reading individual chapters, adds structure through partitioning into separable subjects. Successive levels yield descriptive and prescriptive rules and procedures.

To aid in pursuing some subjects in still more detail than is practical in this book, each chapter ends with a recommended reading list, followed by still further suggestions for browsing. The intent here is to present windows on specialty worlds rather than definitive scholarly works.

Within the text itself, two kinds of credits are given. One kind, given in parentheses, for example, (Smith, 1978), refers to published materials given at chapter end or traceable through the Author Index. The second kind, given in square brackets, for example [Spinrad, 1989], recognizes the originators of key ideas from unpublished lectures or conversations with the author over the years.

TO USE THIS BOOK

For a quick scan, look at the Table of Contents, the Introduction to Part One, Chapter 1, and Appendix A.

For managers interested in establishing systems architecting as an essential function of their organizations, add the Introductions to Part Two and all of Part Three, written for just this purpose. For a greater level of detail, add Chapters 2, 3, 6, and 7, depending on interest.

For those who want to learn the fundamentals of systems architecting, Part One gives the essentials and most of the heuristics. The remaining heuristics can be found through Appendix A and the page numbers given there.

For those practicing or wanting to practice systems architecting, Part Two gives some of the most important present challenges, Part Three tells how managers might see the field, with Chapter 16 suggesting lines of research.

For those desiring to teach from this book, I would suggest a variation on the case study method. There are no case studies in this text, only diverse examples to illustrate central points. Yet it is important that the student follow the architecting process through a specific system. So, in my own classes I asked each student to choose a system of personal interest and to use it as a frame of reference—a context—to which the ideas in the text could be attached. The students, all graduate practicing systems engineers, chose systems as diverse as a particular spacecraft, a document handling system, a personal computer, a secure communication system, a new attraction for Disneyland, a robotic manufacturing system, and a national program for the manned exploration of Mars. In effect, each student developed a personal case study as the course progressed. A number were turned into first rate, publishable reports.

ACKNOWLEDGMENTS

Those to whom I and this book owe the most are my naval architect father, who introduced me to the ethos of architecting, to Drs. William H. Pickering and Frederick C. Lindvall, who introduced me to systems, to my professional associates, with whom I have shared great engineering adventures, and to Arthur Raymond and Bob Spinrad, on whose insights key sections of this book are based.

It is well said that to learn, teach. And from my graduate students, experienced systems engineers all, I have learned much: Michael Asato, Rob Carpenter, Michael R. Day, April Gillam, Kathrin Kjos, Jonathan Losk, Mark Maier, Scott McCarty, Matt Richards, and Marilee Wheaton are notable among many who expanded the fields of heuristics and systems architecting.

Personal thanks are certainly due to the faculty of the University of Southern California, who encouraged and supported the teaching and writing of *Systems Architecting*, especially Provost Cornelius J. Pings, Dean Leonard M. Silverman, and Professors Gerald Nadler, Larry G. Redekopp, E. Philip Muntz, Solomon W. Golomb, and Alan J. Rowe. Special thanks are due to Stephanie Chester for assistance in documenting the reference material. Latest in the sequence of helping associates, Michael Hays, executive editor, and Rob DeGeorge, production editor, have given me encouragement and assistance when most needed.

To all, my thanks.

Eberhardt Rechtin
University of Southern California

part one

Architecting Complex Systems

INTRODUCTION

Systems architecting combines the theory and engineering of systems with the theory and practice of architecting. Conventional architects, civil and naval, engage in the architecting of buildings and ships. Systems architects do the same, but for systems, particularly those in electronics, computers, communications, aircraft, spacecraft, and manufacturing plants.

A system is a collection of things working together to produce something greater. A system can be tangible like a skyscraper, airplane, or communication network, or intangible, like a computer software program or aircraft test program. The unique elements of a system are the relationships between its parts. A system has the further property that it is unbounded—each system is inherently a part of a still larger system.

The essence of architecting is structuring. Structuring can mean bringing form to function, bringing order out of apparent chaos, or converting the partially formed ideas of a client into a workable conceptual model. The key techniques are balancing the needs, fitting the interfaces, and compromising among the extremes.

The systems architect's task is to bring structure in the form of systems to an inherently ill-structured unbounded world of human needs, technology, economics, politics, engineering, and industrial practice.

Like the complex systems it addresses, architecting has many dimensions and can be described in many ways. As a highly creative human activity, it can be described in behavioral science terms. As a critical part of any complex system development, it can be described in functional terms. The architect, as a member of a project organization, can also be described in relational terms, that is, what does the architect *do* for the project and with whom are the key relations?

But perhaps the easiest description of architecting is one long used in engineering and science—a retrace of its history with a few diagrams to help. From this history, we can see why and when architecting appears in the flow of system development and acquisition. And from that, we can see why and how the architect operates.

Any project, whether to build a hut or a spacecraft, begins with a potential user, a perceived need, and a set of resources—human and physical. Examined in the long history of projects, most projects begin as an evolutionary adaptation of some existing structure.

In simple adaptations, the purposes and hence the *concept* of the structure (a house, an airplane, a software application) is so well understood as to be self-evident. The steps are only to build and operate it. Diagramatically:

The diagram deliberately has no arrows in it—there can be backward flow, or feedback, as well as forward flow. For example, to build something practical may require modifying the original perceptions of needs and resources. Based on operational experience, a system may have to be rebuilt for simpler maintenance. New operational needs may call for a whole new start.

The first complication in this straightforward process occurs when a new *kind* of structure is required—along similar conceptual lines, but requiring new principles and technologies.

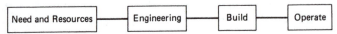

As the structures become more complicated, the project flow becomes more complicated as well.

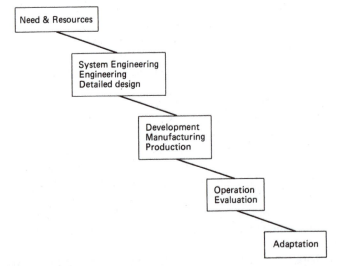

From its shape, this flow diagram is often called "the waterfall." Typically, different groups carry out the different functions, with systems engineers charged with making the elements of the structure fit each other at what are called interfaces. Hence the term, "interface engineering," or "integration," as the core of the systems engineer's job.

With minor variations, the waterfall accurately characterizes the flow of many system projects. It is built into government system acquisition programs. Its terminology has become a part of the language.

But, for complex systems in today's world, the conventional waterfall lacks several critical elements that have had major impacts on system success or failure.

The most conspicuous of these have been social and political factors. Public and individual perceptions, rational or not, have powerful effects on the progress and perceived success or failure of complex systems. One need only mention nuclear power plants, manned space exploration, supersonic aircraft, the military-industrial complex, unpredictable government funding, or government data bases to appreciate the new kinds of problems system builders must consider.

Becoming more and more evident is the need for higher and higher quality and reliability as systems become more complex. The public and most individuals are willing to accept failure rates of once every few years. The catch is that this rate applies to all products or systems, regardless of complexity. Thus, as the number of elements and interfaces increases, the reliability of each element must increase if the system failure rate is not to increase. An element good enough in a simple system may be unacceptable in a more complex one. Upgrading the elements usually means redesign, reengineering, more disciplined manufacturing, and more careful testing of almost every element. Similarly stringent demands are made by safety and survivability as system complexity increases.

Given all these dimensions of architecting, it is not readily apparent how to create a satisfactory, much less an optimum, system. A technical optimum may not be a political or economic one, or vice versa.

For some architectures, it may be sufficient to conceive a few alternates and choose the best among them. But what happens when analyzing all possible alternates becomes impractical? These questions have occupied the minds of thoughtful architects in all fields for some time. Indeed, writings on the subject date back at least as far as the Romans. A recent group to become interested, information-systems theorists, has, perhaps not surprisingly, produced some of the most illuminating answers. Still more recently, behavioral and cognitive (knowledge) scientists have contributed powerful insights based on new understandings of intelligent behavior in humans and machines. Part of the reason for the new insights from these particular groups is that the systems with which they are involved are abstract products built almost solely out of human thought instead of by human hands.

One result of the increasing importance of social, political, quality, reliability, and other "real world" factors has been an increased awareness of the need for system architecting—and for system architects. As might be expected, the core of architecting is in system conceptualization. But, a key test of architecting is a successful certification to the client that the desired product has been produced. And final judgment comes only with operational evaluations by the client, one's peers, and the public. The chapters in Part One, as one way of organizing the subject of architecting, follow this life cycle, highlighting the lessons learned along the way.

Architecting usually begins with generating an abstract mental or paper description—a model—of the system and its environment. There will be many steps and perhaps many years between this abstraction and the final evaluation. And well before that evaluation is completed, the system will encounter "the real world." Lack of awareness that the real world can be quite different from the architect's conceptual model of it has punished many an otherwise rational architecture. Assumptions will be tested and perhaps found wanting. Theories, ideas, and designs will be tested. To complicate the architect's problems, the world in which the system will have to exist will probably change while the system is being built.

Adding these complicating factors to the conventional waterfall results in the expanded waterfall shown in the figure. Social, political, reliability, and real world elements have been connected to the main flow with lines whose widths

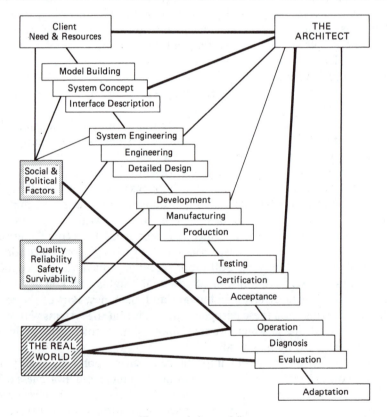

The expanded waterfall.

indicate the strength of the connection. And, finally, the architect has been placed in the figure to show where and to what degree architecting plays a role in the project flow.

This figure thus provides a structure, an architecture if you will, of Part One of this text. The chapters begin with history, concentrate on the conceptual phase, flow down the same waterfall, and take excursions into the shaded elements, much as the architect would during the project's life cycle. As the figure implies, the architect, in time and position, does not see the real world until late and then only indirectly as it impacts the system and its waterfall. It is the nature of the business. The experienced architect, however, will have had all these steps, excursions, and pitfalls in mind from the beginning, or else the system and its users will suffer.

The position of the architect, both in the figure and in practice, tends to be to one side rather than in the direct command flow. But not always, as Chapter 1 indicates. In any case, the connection with the client needs to be so strong that the architect is often—and best—considered as the client's agent, even if employed by the builder or a third party.

Running through all the chapters are some important threads—complexity and reliability; synthesis and analysis; modeling; the importance of computers as design aids for, and elements in, systems; the role of the architect in each phase of system development; and the relationships with the customer, systems engineer, and builder.

The threads are strong enough that almost any one of them could have replaced the waterfall as the central theme, with the waterfall as another thread. Some readers may even prefer following a particular thread, providing a still different perspective of the intertwining fabric of architecting.

Part One can be read in several ways. For those interested in a quick scan, read the Table of Contents and browse through the heuristics in Appendix A. To appreciate the scope of architecting, leaf through the text, stopping at interesting **boldface** heuristics and read the material in the vicinity. For deeper understanding, read the chapters and scan the references for subjects of interest.

Appendix B lists some of the most relevant textbooks for those interested in establishing their own or an institutional library on systems architecting.

1

THE SYSTEMS ARCHITECT

The ideal architect should be a man of letters, a skillful draftsman, a mathematician, familiar with historical studies, a diligent student of philosphy, acquainted with music; not ignorant of medicine, learned in the responses of jurisconsults, familiar with astronomy and astronomical calculations.—Vitruvius, 25 B.C. (Vitruvius/Morgan (tr.), 1960)

We begin with a short look at the long and honorable history of civil architects and their architectures. It is a history being repeated in decades instead of centuries in the new fields of communications, aerospace, computers, information sciences, and related engineering disciplines. As was the case with civil and naval architects before them, the new architects emerged when engineering problems became too complex to be solved by analysis alone. In today's parlance, single-variable optimization and multivariable trade-offs, while necessary, were not sufficient. When the problems included technology, economics, policy, politics, and psychology, striving for deterministic, much less optimum, solutions became a waste of time and energy. A different, more intuitive, approach was needed if satisfactory solutions were to be found within a reasonable time and cost. The historical, and still valid, approach was architecting—that combination of arts and sciences that specifies the functions to be performed and describes the system to be built.

THE EMERGENCE OF THE SYSTEMS ARCHITECT

Complexity, for all the difficulties it introduces, is part and parcel of progress. A manual laborer can build a simple shelter all alone. A team of craftsmen can build a conventional house in a known environment. But to build still more complex structures requires engineering, that is, the application of scientific and mathematical principles.

Providing the structure is well conceived and specified, engineers can design and builders can implement it with high confidence. Subsystems can be identified, their problems solved, and the whole assembled to the customer's satisfaction. To do so may require engineering specialties of great sophistication—hydraulics, aerodynamics, statistics, electronics, mechanics, information processing—but the engineers can almost always guarantee satisfaction if not absolute success.

But engineering, too, has its limits. They are encountered when a system contains more than a handful of subsystems. To understand why, it is necessary to define a *system* more precisely.

A system is defined here as a set of different elements so connected or related as to perform a unique function not performable by the elements alone. The most important and distinguishing characteristic of a system, therefore, is the *relationships among the elements*. To illustrate this, imagine that your automobile was completely disassembled and laid out on your driveway. All the elements individually would be just as before, all in working order. But you would have no transportation. Transportation, the unique system function, only exists when all the elements are connected together and function as a whole. Furthermore, the automotive system must be able to comply with regulations, operate on available roads, be energized with available fuels, perform reliably, and be attractive enough for you to purchase it in the first place. Your automobile, thus, must not only have internally compatible subsystems, it must be compatible with outside elements as well. Clearly, interrelationships are both the strength and the weakness of a system. They are responsible for its unique function on the one hand and its unavoidable complexity on the other.

Serious difficulties arise when the number and nature of the elements result in so many complex interfaces that what one subsystem does to the rest is no longer as simple as single inputs and outputs. Then the relationships between function and form break down. The needs of the client are likely to prove mutually inconsistent. The impact on the environment may be difficult to assess. Information may be lacking or unavailable on operating conditions. New technologies may look promising, but their risks will not yet be known. A satisfactory resolution of such a situation is unlikely to come solely from scientific and engineering principles, equations, algorithms, and techniques.

This level of system complexity arose early in civil structures, many thousands of years ago in the planning and building of Egypt's irrigation system. That system needed astronomy to predict the flow times of the Nile, arithmetic to allocate water and farm products, hydraulics to assure proper water flow, and geometry for surveying and construction. The system, in addition, had to be compatible with effective public administration, politics, religion, and law. To be a "canal builder" was a mark of distinction. Its architects formed a virtual dynasty. Its officials were at the highest levels; at least one became a prime minister. Its successful implementation undoubtedly led to the expansion of Egypt to include most of the Nile River valley. The nationwide irrigation system no doubt ranked in importance with defense.

By the time of the Greeks, naval and military architecting were being practiced, though not explicitly recognized as such, generated by the technological and sociopolitical complexities of ships, weapons, and defenses. By 25 B.C., architecture was well understood as a combination of engineering, liberal arts, and creative genius. Marcus Vitruvius Pollio, ''Vitruvius,'' one of the greatest of Roman architects, wrote a 10-volume work on the subject—its educational requirements, its basic principles, environmental considerations, city planning, social structure considerations, mechanics, properties of materials, aesthetics, acoustics, surveying, water systems, astronomy, siege machines, pumps, and construction machinery. It is still a valued reference, available in paperback.

Later architects further extended Vitruvius' principles to still greater structures and more and more advanced engineering. By the 1600s, the need to do architecting was generally appreciated. By the 1800s architecture had become a recognized profession. Schools of architecture were established throughout Europe. The first schools of architecture were established in the United States just after the Civil War (MIT in 1865; Cornell in 1871) and proliferated thereafter.

By remarkable coincidence, the late 1800s saw the beginnings of the new fields of electrical and aeronautical engineering. In decades instead of centuries, these fields advanced from the craftsman through advanced engineering phases. Complexity reached unprecedented levels.

For millenia, man had attempted to fly. (Mythology gives Daedalus the first credits, though Daedalus and Icarus more likely used kites than wings to escape the labyrinth.) Primitive gliders had evolved by the late 1800s.

But the true solution to the manned-flight problem would need an integrated combination of efficient engines, airfoil design, new structural materials, and, most important to the final success, a sure means of control. The Wright brothers combined all these, tested the ideas in their own primitive but instrumented wind tunnel, architected a system solution, and performed a careful series of flight tests. The public image of a couple of bicycle mechanics inventing a ''new flying machine'' in their garage is quite wrong.

The history of rocketry followed a similar course. The Chinese invented a simple rocket nozzle and an energetic but controllable propellant satisfactory for small-scale fireworks. Thousands of years were to pass before rockets were more than unguided missiles. They were useful more to terrorize enemy troops than to create major damage. Their aerodynamics, much less their control, was little understood.

The Germans and Americans, only 50 or so years ago, finally produced true launch vehicles capable of great ranges and accuracies. The early vehicles were plagued with rocket engine instability. Catastrophic explosions were common, high-performance engines being a confined, violent, but controlled conflagration in any case. Once that hurdle was passed, the next problems were with complex propulsion-*system* failures—violent vertical oscillations of the whole vehicle, the so-called Pogo effect, finally traced to interactions of fuel, tankage, plumbing, pumps, and structure. Guidance and control solutions came slowly. There were debates over position feedback, force feedback, control-surface location, instrument type, instrument location, and the "rubber structure." Vibration, particularly of sensitive mechanical, electrical, and electronic devices, became an overriding concern. More recently, with the advent of huge engines, acoustics has begun playing a dominant role in vehicle and payload design.

Remarkably sophisticated communication systems have also been around for millenia. Some of them have evolved into highly effective networks. The Romans had an effective optical network using spaced towers that allowed them to communicate to the edge of their empire, the British Isles. But it was not until the late 1800s that technology and experimentation made electrical, and then radio, communications possible.

An extensive body of telecommunications theory has been developed, permitting prediction of communications possibilities—and the technology that would be required for them—well ahead of time. Point-to-point communications developed rapidly, but it was apparent that with increasing demand, simply replicating point-to-point links would not suffice. The system solution, epitomized by the now-dismembered Bell System network, consisted of automatic switches, hierarchical multiplexing signal protocols, multiple-homing interconnected central nodes, and very strong configuration control.

The Bell System solution accommodated unforeseen technologies (satellite links, transistors, integrated circuits, optical fibers, etc.) rapidly and easily, producing a steadily improving capability with minimal disruption. Built into the architecture was an expensed research effort that continuously paid for itself in increased communications capability, lower cost per minute, and increased revenues. It remains one of the finest system architectures in the world, although its original social purpose of price related to need has been supplanted by price tied to link cost.

Information systems, too, have a long history. But they have advanced more in a shorter period than any other system, driven by a technology that offers unprecedented rates of progress in computation, information storage and retrieval, and system architectures. More than any other modern field, even communications, the term "architecture" is widely understood and used for what it is—a top-down description of the structure of the system. Information systems have a special property. Although the hardware of computers is still very important in providing new options, the key "structure" that is being built is generally software—a pure product of the mind, almost instant in applicability. Earlier architectures copied and then enhanced man's actuators (hands, arms, legs, and muscles) and sensors (eyes, ears, chemical detection, touch).

Information (knowledge) architectures now routinely emulate, and soon will far extend, selected functions of the brain.

The proliferation of information system architectures, as we shall see, is accelerating. As a result, some of the newest approaches to architecting have come from information systems as the conventional approaches to searching for solution—trial, error, and analysis—prove inadequate.

Just as craftsmen initially did engineering, so engineers initially did architecting. Specialization came later. Systems architects in the new fields have come into being for the same reasons as civil and naval architects. Indeed, the history of systems architecture itself is following the history of classical architecture, only much more rapidly. As was the case with the earlier architects, the new architects were seldom recognized for what they were, the function of architecting was not made an explicit part of system acquisition, and formal education was late in arriving.

But the contributions of the new architects have been remarkable. Here are but a few of the better-known architects and their products:

- John K. ("Jack") Northrop, Arthur Raymond, and the Douglas Aircraft DC-3 series
- Clarence L. ("Kelly") Johnson and the Lockheed P-38, U-2, and SR-71
- Harry Hillaker and the General Dynamics F-16
- Wernher von Braun and the Redstone/Jupiter/Saturn space launchers
- Simon Ramo, Bernard A. Schriever, and the Air Force ICBM program
- Hyman Rickover and the Navy Nautilus nuclear submarine
- Harold A. Rosen, Thomas Hutspeth, Donald Williams, and the Hughes spinning geosynchronous communication satellite series
- Eberhardt Rechtin, Walter K. Victor, Robertson Stevens, and the NASA/JPL deep-space communication and radionavigation systems
- Maxime A. Faget, Robert R. Gilruth, and the Apollo lunar vehicles
- Paul McCready and the Gossamer ultralight aircraft series
- Frederick P. Brooks, Jr., Gene Amdahl and Gerrit A. Blaauw, and the IBM 360 operating system
- The Xerox PARC group of the 1970s and SMALLTALK
- Seymour Cray and the Cray supercomputer series
- Steven Jobs and the Apple™ Macintosh™ PCs
- Joel S. Birnbaum and the RISC architecture

There have been many others—those responsible for ARPANET, ETHERNET™, INTELSATs, the USAF Space-Ground Link Subsystem, FLEETSATCOM, the Defense Satellite Communication Systems, weather satellites, LANDSAT, the Boeing 707 series, new software languages, space launch vehicles, manufacturing complexes, and the like.

As individuals, or as members of very small teams, these were architects who took a global view and matched concepts to it. Some, but not all, were also brilliant engineers. Some, but not all, were also marvelous managers. But all were true architects in the classical definition of the term. In due time, just as with naval architects, they will be recognized as the aerospace, communications, software, and industrial architects that they are and were.

Early recognition of the successful new architects would be valuable on several counts. But far more important would be an explicit recognition by government and industry of the function of architecting as demonstrated by those architects.

Why is the recognition of architecting important? Civil architects provide a ready and hard-learned answer. With inadequate architecting, major architectural errors occur. An ICBM system was built without a confirmed basing mode. An ABM system was begun without a solution, not necessarily technical, to offensive saturation. A space launch system was built with an inadequate consideration of the overall launch fleet problem. Communication networks were dismantled into competing subnetworks. Aircrafts were built that were obsolete on arrival. Software languages were constructed that were overly sensitive to human error, mismatching the applications and communicating poorly with the human mind. Manufacturing plants were built without future flexibility in the new, and necessarily more complex, manufacturing world.

The architecting problems in manufacturing systems are particularly important today. A clear trend is underway in manufacturing that has already occurred in agriculture. Agriculture used to employ the majority of the American population. It now employs a few percent, a more than twentyfold increase in productivity over 100 years, or about 3% per year compounded. The same trend is apparent in manufacturing. Under the steady pressure of competition, it is likely to continue.

The results of this trend over the career span of today's engineering students are likely to be even more dramatic than in agriculture. From an engineer's perspective, flexibility, tight process control, well-instrumented feedback reporting, far more reliable components, efficient inventory systems, and worldwide distribution systems will all be critical. The new manufactured products will be more complex and much "smarter." The modern automobile and modern appliances are familiar examples. Clearly, unless production lines are well architected, their useful lives will be unprofitably short.

THE ROLE OF THE ARCHITECT

The classical definition of the architectural process, architecting, is "the planning and building of structures." If "structures" is used in a broader sense to include configurations, frameworks, and networks—*systems* if you will—then systems architecting is planning and building systems.

The definition of architecting, in either classical or modified form, clearly overlaps that of engineering. It is unavoidable. That overlap is recognized in such terms as architect–engineer, systems engineer, designer, chief engineer, and airplane "configurator." But distinguishing between architecting and engineering is important if the architecting function is to be effective. Two distinctions are particularly important—function versus form and complexity versus specificity. But, first, some historical background.

The architecting-versus-engineering question is not a new one. It goes back at least as far as Vitruvius, who distinguished between ratiocinatio and fabbrica (roughly, theory and practice) and who maintained that the union of the two is the essence of architecture. Until relatively recently, no clear-cut distinction was made between architecting, engineering, and planning. Architecting was sometimes done by mathematicians (Archimedes), exceptional client–emperors (Hadrian), artists (Raphael and Michelangelo), and scientists (da Vinci).

There are, even today, elements of craftsmanship, mathematics, art, and science in the practice of architecture. The coming together of all these bodies of knowledge (and their practitioners) produced, as one might expect, technical, judgmental, and professional conflicts. The resolution of the conflicts slowly became recognized as an important function of the architect.

The architect became one who could make all the pieces fit. In today's parlance, the architect became an integrator. By the Renaissance, a good architecture was seen as one where all the pieces were in harmony. In today's terms, good architectures were generally derived from compatible pieces, that is, they were system engineered.

More recently, architects began to appreciate that still better architectures might be based on complete submission of the individual parts to the purpose or function of the whole. "Form follows function" became a guiding principle.

As a result, architectures began to be designed—architected—from the top down, driven by the *function,* instead of the *form,* of the system. In short, "system engineering is form-based and system architecting is function-based" [Hillaker, 1989, at USC].*

The second important distinction between architecting and engineering, described earlier, is in the complexity of the problems each must solve.

To be more quantitative, if each of n variables interacts with each of the others, the number of interactions will be on the order of $n(n-1)/2$. Engineers, with deterministic techniques, have typically been able to handle 5–10 such variables, or perhaps 10–50 interactions, by careful attention to the most important ones. Successful architectures, consequently, evolve slowly. Completely new

---

*The square brackets [ ] indicate credits for ideas expressed to the author in unpublished lectures or conversations. USC is the University of Southern California.

problems can arise with the addition of only one more variable (e.g., one new variable adds 15 to 25 more interactions in the preceding example).

But it is not uncommon for complex systems to contain dozens if not hundreds of possible variables and hundreds of interactions. Aircraft, spacecraft, communication networks, transportation systems, production lines, simulators, and test facilities fall in this range of complexity. The architect's problem is to reduce this complexity to a manageable degree, specifically to the point where the powerful techniques of engineering analysis can be brought to bear. The "nice-to-have" functions have to be separated from the essential ones. Choices have to be made of which set of variables should be considered first and over what range. Constraints have to be applied to keep the possible "solutions" within realistic bounds. And the result has to be one or more well-specified well-described possible systems. It is at this point that efficient systems engineering can begin.

The architect, therefore, is not a "general engineer," but a specialist in reducing complexity, uncertainty, and ambiguity to workable concepts. The systems engineer, in contrast, is the master of making feasible concepts work.

Another, more pragmatic, way of distinguishing architecting from engineering is by the tasks typically performed.

Architecting is working *for* a client and *with* a builder, helping determine the preferred architecture, that is, helping determine relative requirement priorities, acceptable performance, cost, and schedule—taking into account such factors as technology risk, projected market size, likely competitive moves, economic trends, political regulatory requirements, project organization, and the appropriate "illities" (availability, operability, manufacturability, survivability, etc.). Toward the end of the project, architecting is also certifying completion and satisfactory operation of the system.

Engineering is working *with* an architect and *for* a builder, applying the best engineering practices to assure compliance at the system level with the designated architecture and with applicable specifications, standards, and contracts. Toward the end of the project, engineering is certifying such compliance.

Clearly, single individuals can perform combinations of these tasks, for example, the client–architect, the architect–engineer, the system engineer, and the architect–builder. For small projects, the engineer may be the architect, system architect, and construction supervisor. Certainly, both engineers and architects have mutual interests in well-fitting interfaces and in system success.

Nonetheless, the architect tends to concentrate on concepts, synthesis, top-level specifications, nontechnical as well as technical interfaces, and mission success. The engineer tends to concentrate on defined subsystem interfaces, analysis, and performance to specification. Because success depends both on a realizable architecture and on successful implementation of it, the architect and the engineer necessarily share responsibility for each other's success.

Another difference—the number of architects is small compared to the number of engineers. Part of the reason is that architectures tend to be the product of a single mind, or of a small team, in the interests of the integrity of the architectural construct. And part of the reason is that the efficient architect necessarily concentrates only on the interfaces that most affect the functioning of the system as a whole. Engineers are responsible for integrating and managing all interfaces before the job is complete. Hence, a relatively larger number of systems engineers is needed to manage, or at least be concerned with, each and every interface.

There is one area where engineering and architecting are very similar—ethical principles. The codes of ethics of engineering and of architecture, as published by their societies, are virtually identical. Objectivity, integrity, competence, regard for the public welfare, fairness in dealing with employees and clients, confidentiality, and honest recognition of contributions are common to both. The differences, when they occur, stem from the different relationships that the engineer and the architect have with the client, builder, and public. The engineer, for example, is more likely to face dilemmas related to profit; the architect, dilemmas related to confidentiality. The architect must be trusted both by the client and by the builder, their natural conflicts of interest notwithstanding. If not, critical information will be withheld. Options will not be proposed. Yet premature disclosure can be harmful, too. The dividing line between confidentiality and coverup can be a matter of perception. In the architect's world of complexity, uncertainty, and ambiguity, following ethical principles can be more difficult than in the more structured one of the engineer.

THE PROCESS OF ARCHITECTING

Without question, the architect's greatest impact comes during concept formulation and preliminary design. It is a time of great creativity. Yet creativity is one of the least understood of human activities. To many people, it is something mysterious, magical, unfathomable, neither inherited nor learned—and, hence, inherently unteachable. If this were so, then the most important parts of architecting would be matters of chance. But this cannot be so. If it were, then experience and judgment would not count, and clearly they do. The challenge of the importance, and yet the lack of understanding, of creativity has intrigued many a philosopher and architect over the centuries. The result is a fascinating body of speculation, factual research, and theory.

The Normative (Pronouncement) Methodology

The earliest methods of architecting were based on the respected value judgments of prominent and successful architects. These architects, faced with the problem of instructing subordinates and justifying their approaches to others, pronounced what was good architecture and how to achieve it. Their pronoucements were prescriptions for action. Do this. Don't do that. "Schools" of architecture came into being. In civil architecture, famed architects from Vitruvius to Frank Lloyd Wright prescribed rules in great detail.

This judgmental, experiential, approach to architecting is usually called the "normative" theory of architecting. It is based on perceptions of good, bad, right, and wrong (Nadler, 1981).* Its rules are laden with values of the creator (Lang, 1987). A more descriptive name might be the Pronouncement Theory. The better the architect, the better the results, of course. And it does make the job of the subordinates and followers easier. It does reduce uncertainty. But the rules can become dogma, and innovation suppressed.

A weakness of the normative method is that, like any dictated methodology, the more detailed its rules become in the interests of defining what is good and what is bad, the more difficult it becomes to be generally applicable or internally consistent. For example, Blaauw (1972) judged the principles of good information systems architecture to be

1. consistency
2. orthogonality (elements relatively independent of each other)
3. propriety (proper to functions, no unnecessary function)
4. parsimony (no functional redundancy in different forms)
5. transparency (functions introduced in implementation not imposed on the user)
6. generality (multipurpose)
7. open-endedness (alternate uses of needed function)
8. completeness (in solving needs and desires of user)

Although individually each principle might be worthwhile, the list as a whole, if applied to ultrareliable spacecraft computers or to neural networks, proves to be inconsistent both internally and with system needs. Then, too, time and clients' needs change. And new normative principles have to be created.

The Rational (Procedural) Method

The difficulties with the pronouncement approach led to the rational method. In contrast with the former, which specifies the end solution, the latter focuses on the *procedures* by which solutions can be found. Its most powerful tools are mathematical—set theory, probability theory, vector algebra, predicate calculus, algorithms, and problem-solving methodologies. To illustrate the approach: two of the primary tools, forward and backward "chaining," are to start stepping from the problem toward the solution and to start stepping from a few likely solutions toward the problem. The hope is to meet somewhere in

*Textbook citations not found at chapter end may be found in Appendix B.

between. A typical step is the logical sequence, If . . . then . . . or else. . . . Filling in the blanks may not be easy, but it is considerably better than trying to bridge the whole gap from problem to solution in one jump.

A version of the rational theory is general systems theory (GST). It began in the late 1940s when systems theory, statistical optimization, and cybernetics were just beginning. Its earliest and most famous proponent was Norbert Weiner, a mathematician. It was hoped then that "the systems approach" might solve many of the world's most serious system problems. As with Shannon's information theory, systems theory has led to new ways of thinking about problems. Its premise is that systems, as constructs of related elements, can be studied in the abstract, independent of their context (e.g., software, launch vehicles, communication networks). It is an idea not too dissimilar to that of pure mathematics, the processing of numbers independent of their meaning. If so, then solutions could be found for system problems caused by the system's *form* (relationships) rather than by the system's function (context). Specific systems would be "mapped" into general systems, the general system problems solved, and then remapped back into the specific systems.

The history to date of general system problem solvers (GSPS) has been mixed. Some general and often useful statements *can* be made. But before getting very deep into a complex system problem, assumptions and contraints have to be applied that are strongly context-dependent. More importantly, perhaps, the GSPS requires a structure on which to operate, and yet structuring is the name of the game in conceptual design. In addition, not all relationships are quantifiable or of equal importance. As is discussed in the next chapter, $2 + 2$ does not always equal 4 in systems work. But when it does, general system problem solvers have a role to play.

Underlying the rational theory is the premise that problem solving is inherently procedural, that is, it consists of relatively simple logical steps operating on an extensive memory base. In this approach, the architect aims at acquiring, developing, and learning how to use sets of procedures to tackle system problems. It is at the heart of system engineering.

This procedural premise is based, to some extent, on drawing analogies between computers and human minds. Indeed, the rational theory was generated in large part by cognitive (knowledge), information, and behavioral scientists applying the scientific method to the study of how humans solve problems.

It is certainly true that in a number of critical ways, human thought resembles the functioning of computers (or vice versa if you prefer). Human memory, like some computerized data bases, is organized in related, or associated, "chunks." These chunks are used to drastically narrow the search for a solution when the number of possible options is otherwise overwhelming ("extracomputational"). The classic example is playing chess, a deterministic game with an almost infinite number of possible moves. Like computers, the brain has both short- and long-term memory and can carry out sequences of logical steps.

By combining these empirical facts, it was proposed (Simon, 1969) that the human brain's apparent complexity is the result not of a complex architecture, but rather of the mass of experiential information contained in the brain's memory. If this were true, then the *process* of problem solving and/or architecting presumably would be found to be a series of rational, if not necessarily optimum, steps operating on an established data base. And human architecting would be seen, at its fundamental level, not to be "intuitive," but to be mechanistic. These speculations, understandably, were and are controversial. As it has turned out, the human mind has several different ways of thinking, only one of which is logical and rational, and architecting at times uses them all.

In particular, it is known from experiment that humans solve extracomputational problems of great complexity with little apparent difficulty. Some of these problems are downright "wicked." Wicked problems, by definition, never even reach a proper formulation of goals, much less of functions and forms. One could say that wicked problems represent a situation looking for a resolution rather than a function seeking a form.

Optimum resolutions are unreachable if the goals cannot be determined or even prioritized. Yet human minds demonstrably resolve such situations. Architects, in particular, are expected to do so.

The mind also exhibits another characteristic, but nonrational, behavior: the "pause to reflect," or a "review of the bidding." It occurs just after conceiving a solution, but before proceeding with implementing it. Presumably, if conceiving a solution, were based on rational facts alone, implementing it would be automatic. This pause apparently is particularly characteristic of the more successful architects and "expert experts." Curiously, it may also exist at a very basic level. Researchers report that mice do the same thing when confronted with choices in a maze. So far, at least, rational theories do not account for these apparently basic capabilities of biological intelligence. The hope of their developers, of course, is that the theories will do so in due course.

Putting these speculations to one side, the rational method is nonetheless a notable improvement on the normative one. It is less value laden. It adjusts more easily to changes in the problem and environment. It explicitly recognizes complexity and attempts to deal with it in a rational way. But it cannot be completely value-free; someone has to decide what the underlying assumptions and axioms should be. And although its rules are easy to teach and follow, it does require more expertise by the practitioner than does following pronouncements.

The Argumentative Approach

Another perception of architecting is that achitecting is a learning and arguing (dialectic) process, with a number of participants entering the process at various times, contributing new problems, new possibilities, and new options (Lang, 1987, p. 43). One of its several versions is brainstorming. It has special utility in evolving sociopolitical situations. But it can be difficult to control, with the original objectives being lost in the process and dramatic ideas driving out more reasoned ones, that is, too many cooks can spoil the soup and too many special interests can stall the process. Its use in architecting has been small.

THE HEURISTIC APPROACH

> Heuristic search . . . is in fact the principal engine for human problem solving. (Simon, 1981, p. 56)

Which brings us to the most recent effort to describe architecting, especially that of complex systems: *heuristic reasoning,* or heuristics. Because it particularly aids in conceptual design and because it provides the foundation for this book, it is discussed in some detail. The heuristic approach has some of its origins in the pronouncement and rational approaches.

Its central ideas, however, come from asking architects what they do when confronted with highly complex problems. The skilled architect and designer most likely would answer, "*Just use common sense.*" It is a proper, if not very precise, answer. It requires some expansion.

First, a better expression than "common sense" is *contextual* sense—a knowledge of what is reasonable within a given context. Practicing architects through education, experience, and examples accumulate a considerable body of contextual sense by the time they are entrusted with solving a system-level problem—typically 10 years.

Second, and equally important, architects know how to use that accumulated common sense. Like master chess players that have memorized 50,000 patterns of pieces on the chess board and "instinctively" make a sound move, architects have insights, lessons learned, rules of thumb, and the like that consciously or unconsciously are brought to bear on complex problems.

Heuristics can be defined in several ways, with the most easily understood definition dependent on the reader's background. For example:

- For those of a theoretical bent: as specific problem-structuring devices, ranging from decision rules to a variety of analogies, analogs, and models used to guide the search for solutions (Rowe, 1987, p. 75).
- For general pragmatists: as widely accepted qualitative statements that, as judged from examples, add structure to ill-defined situations.
- For managers: as commonly accepted insights, gained from experience, that bring order out of apparent chaos.
- For engineers: as statements of common, or contextual, sense that aid in concept development, problem solving, decision making, or judgments.

Different words are used, but they all mean essentially the same thing. Heuristics differ from an individual's pronouncements by being subjects of a general consensus. They differ from scientific laws by being more qualitative, more suggestive, and usually less amenable to replicable measurement. They differ from mathematical statements in being inductive instead of deductive, that is, they are generalizations from specific examples, not conclusions derivable from general principles.

A powerful heuristic has several properties. The opposite statement from a specific heuristic does *not* make sense or leads to failure. If both a proposed heuristic and its opposite can be shown to make sense, depending only on the examples chosen, then neither is a valid general heuristic. Putting it another way, the fewer conditional ("if") statements in a heuristic, the stronger, broader, and more complete it is.

Heuristics generally come in two forms. The first is **descriptive** (what is the situation) and the second one is **prescriptive** (what to do about it). The more succinct and even humorous the heuristic, the more easily it is remembered. A well-known descriptive heuristic is

Murphy's Law, If anything can go wrong it will.

A matching prescriptive one is the **KISS** heuristic,

Keep It Simple, Stupid.

KISS is sometimes stated as the three rules for achieving successful system performance:

Simplify. Simplify. Simplify.

Both are variations on Occam's Razor:

The simplest solution is usually the correct one.

All these heuristics deal with complexity directly. **Murphy's** describes a warning and **KISS** prescribes a response. All are powerful messages to an architect concerned with highly reliable, but unquantifiably complex, systems.

Heuristics have much in common with the rational approach. Both are based on experience. Both seek satisfactory, rather than necessarily optimum solutions. Both have **prescriptive** (procedural) elements, for example, chaining and KISS. Indeed, many of the rules and algorithms in the rational approach are labeled as heuristics by their authors. Generally, however, few **descriptive** heuristics are found in the rational approach. Many are found in the heuristic approach.

There is also some commonality with the pronouncement approach. Both provide guidelines originating in an individual's experience. Some of the pronouncements of successful architects no doubt were originally based on empirically validated heuristics. But there is a major difference. With pronouncements as instructions, a solution consonant with those pronouncements is almost guaranteed. But heuristics *of themselves* provide no guarantee that a particular approach will work well, much less optimally. Heuristics help define the territory ahead and offer some guidelines on how to proceed. Whether they are sensible or not depends upon the context—and it is the architect's business to know that context well.

Considering the ill-structured nature of the problems the architect often faces, heuristics can serve the architect well, particularly if used collectively and early. As Michael R. Day (1988) observed in studying the Defense Satellite Communication System, a decision which simultaneously satisfies several heuristics is stronger than one using any single one. And Rob Carpenter (1989) found that for antisubmarine warfare systems, an approach that seemed best was to use heuristics to stimulate ideas followed by rational methods to refine and evaluate them.

Other studies showed that many heuristics apply not just to the conceptual phase, but throughout the project waterfall as well.

Designers have also found that heuristics can aid in the rapid reduction of the number of design possibilities from tens or hundreds to a manageable handful—impractical by purely rational analysis. They also can

- be reminders of past situations of a similar or analogous type,
- help evaluate architectural choices,
- act as sanity checks and first-order assessments, and
- act as teaching aids, as in this book, and
- pass on hard-won lessons learned to the next generation, particularly when the fields, like aerospace and electronics, are in the rapid learning phase.

But heuristics are not error-free as Alan Rowe (1988) points out. Depending on the context, some assumptions may be inconsistent and the supporting data may be inappropriate. Based as they are on past experience, heuristics can be weak in predicting chance events; on the other hand, *no* approach does well on that score.

Heuristics, in short, need to be used with a mind open to later facts and circumstances. They need to be challenged from time to time. They are not immutable. But they are far better than guesswork or uninformed hunches.

Which brings us to the heuristics to follow in this text. Many of them are "new" in the sense of not having been stated in this particular form before. How then can a "new" heuristic be tested for validity? There are several ways. The best would probably be a disciplined research inquiry into a statistically significant number of architects' experiences to test the proposed heuristic in a specified context. Few such tests have been done for any heuristic. The test used in this text is, therefore, an expedient one. First, they follow the previously stated criteria for a strong heuristic. Second, they are consistent with the author's 40 years of experience—or they wouldn't be here at all. Third, a good heuristic, when presented to a professional in the business, generates a particular (and unconscious) response—a couple of nods of the head and a discourse on the individual's own experiences. A further test was to present the heuristics for study and comment to a special group of students: more than 50 graduate engineers working as system engineers in the Southern California aerospace and electronics industries. If a heuristic passed such scrutiny, it stood for the time being. The invitation to the reader is to augment, to better articulate, or to modify the heuristics in this text in the reader's own context. Only then will they become part of the reader's common sense.

A QUICK COMPARISON OF ARCHITECTING METHODOLOGIES

Table 1–1 summarizes the previous discussion. A quick glance shows that the sharpest differences are between the normative (N) and the rational (R) approaches, with the heuristic being closer to the rational, but with a few notable differences. The heuristic is more pragmatic, contextual, and deliberative, but

TABLE 1–1 Comparison of Design Methodologies

Parameter	Nature of Parameter[a]					
Value set	Subjective	N	Objective	R	Pragmatic	H
Reasoning	Inductive	N, H	Deductive	R		
Data base	Examples	N, H	Facts	R		
Nature of problem	Structured	N, R	Ill-structured	R, H	Wicked	H
Problem definition	Explicit	N	Implicit	R, H		
System goal	Optimize	N	Satisfy	R, H		
Nature of the rules	Rigid	N	Algorithmic	R	Contextual	H
Dependence on practitioner	Independent	N	Dependent	R, H		
Required expertise	Novice	N	Graduate	R	Expert	H
Problem-solving procedure	Instruction	N	Calculative	R	Deliberative	H
Evaluating multiple options	Poor	N	Good	R	Helpful	H
Handling sociopolitical issues	Poor	N, R	Helpful	H		
Validity and verification of solution	Assured	N, R	Limited	H		
Replicability of solution	Exactly	N, R	Approximate	H		

[a]N = normative, R = rational, and H = heuristic.

Source: Rechtin, 1989. The primary conclusion is that the suitability of a methodology depends on project type, phase, purpose, client, and environment.

requires more experience and judgment than either the normative or the rational (Kjos, 1988).

If the problems are well defined, the rules are clear, the choices are few, and the sociopolitical issues are straightforward, then the by-the-book normative approach is best. Its problems can be solved and verified by someone with limited experience. This situation is common in a project well underway.

If none of these conditions is satisfied, the heuristic approach is best, but an optimum verifiable solution to such situations should not be expected. These conditions are typical in the earliest stages of a project and when unexpected events—technology breakdowns, sociopolitical disputes, no-win choices, or responding to the notorious "unknown unknowns"—cause major disruptions in normal project flow.

The rational approach, positioned between the other two, does best when the conditions are reasonably stable and understood, that is, in system engineering and subsystem design. It can make clear choices between defined alternatives and provide certifiable proof of performance. Reaching and maintaining that approach is, indeed, one of the objectives of heuristic methodology.

Regardless of which approach is taken and when, there is general agreement that architecting is a wondrous product of the human mind. The better the architect understands its methodological foundations, the better the results.

THE ARCHITECT AND THE ARCHITECTURAL TEAM

Conceptual design of complex systems severely stresses the best capabilities of the human mind. And yet it can be argued that the problems of complex systems are so multidimensional that keeping all the interrelationships straight can only be done within a single mind—and certainly not by a committee. As Robert J. Spinrad puts it, the only place that there is enough bandwidth between all the rational and arational factors in a system design is between the two halves of a single brain.

It certainly has been demonstrated that if the conceptual process is controlled by what Frederick P. Brooks calls a "chief architect," it can produce dramatic results. Brooks (1982), Spinrad (1988) and others believe with justification that **the greatest architectures are the product of a single mind** or at least of a very small, carefully structured team. In Spinrad's (1988) perception, architecting is

1. Top-level design—functional, physical, and operational, the partitioning of which can be very important (the "what").
2. Creative, *obsessive,* juggling of requirements, constraints, technology, costs, and standards (the "how").
3. Creating an enduring base for growth and change (the "why").

This perception of architecting was created in the fiercely competitive cal-
dron of personal computer and copier development. Otherwise desireable functions conflict with each other. Standards conflict with sustainable commercial
advantage. "Good" is determined by a customer base undeterminable beforehand. Not only are there many variables, there are no simple tradeoffs. In this
world, Spinrad continues, "a lot of right brain 'reasoning' goes on—a kind of
gestalt process. Critical choices are often a matter of 'architectural taste.' "

This strongly person-oriented perspective is especially noteworthy coming
from Brooks and Spinrad, both from very large organizations, IBM and Xerox,
respectively, where large development teams are the norm. It would seem to
argue that architecting needs to be a separable and special activity in the development process. Brooks notes even further that if a software development is in
[design] trouble, adding more people *increases* the time to completion. Hence
the title of his book, *The Mythical Man-Month*. This result differs sharply from
what would be predicted by rational theory in which more parallel effort (e.g.,
in computers) shortens the solution time. But, then, neither Brooks nor Spinrad
were talking about structured computerlike problems. They were talking about
the conceptual phases of architecting.

THE EDUCATION OF A SYSTEMS ARCHITECT

Civil, naval, and military architecture are each built upon specific engineering
foundations, as are aerospace, communications, and other systems architectures. From these come the essential understandings of what is possible. But to
these must be added a systems perspective, judgment, architectural "taste,"
and common sense. How, then, can architecting be *taught?* Where to begin?

A reasonable place to start is with classical architecture. Classical architecture, in addition to being a source of architectural theories and some of the
best heuristics, can also suggest proven techniques for educating the new brands
of architects. In return, the new architectures provide new cases and technologies for study in the classical approach, especially in smart systems and software.

Business administration is also a source of ideas, particularly in those
areas closely related to architecting, management, and decision theory. However, unlike business managers who can manage (almost) any business independent of the product of that business, there is probably no such thing as a
"generic" systems architect—one who can architect anything from a launch vehicle to a new software language.

The engineering architect can only go so far with management and decision theories. Past that point, a knowledge of the underlying disciplines (structures and mechanics for the civil architect; aeronautics, astronautics,
electronics, and computers for others; etc.) is essential in separating the essential from the merely important.

Thus, one of the most important questions in architectural education is just how to integrate the underlying disciplines with the rest of an architect's education. It is not a new question. (See Stubbs, 1987, for a debate on the subject by nine civil architecture educators.)

If lessons learned in the schools of engineering, architecture, and business administration about designing, architecting, and managing are condensed, their collective minimum essentials seem to be as follows:

- A knowledge of the theory and practice of systems architecting to help the architect become efficient in gaining practical experience and judgment.
- Experience in a design studio (laboratory) to integrate technology and architecture to help the architect become proficient in applying the best engineering and architectural principles.

This text is aimed at the first of these essentials. It is intended to be complementary to the second.

SUMMARY

System architectures and architects are now emerging in the complex fields of communications, information processing, aerospace, and the manufacturing industries. As with their civil, naval, and military predecessors, the systems architects are specialists in complexity within the context of an underlying engineering discipline. The architect is of most value when system complexity exceeds the level where synthesis can be accomplished by multiple analyses. A primary tool of the efficient architect is common (contextual) sense, often articulated as heuristics.

RECOMMENDED READING

BROOKS, FREDERICK P., JR. (1982). *The Mythical Man-Month, Essays on Software Engineering.* Reading, MA: Addison-Wesley. A classic in the software architecture field, it is well worth reading for nonsoftware engineers as well. It contains some serious as well as half-humorous heuristics. Read the entire book. It's fun and not that long.

CHIGNELL, MARK H., D. CHOL, J. G. PETERSON, and G. NADLER. (1987). *The Validity of Rational Approaches to Conceptual Design,* Report No. CH2503-1/87/0000-0995. New York: IEEE. The report argues that the rational theory of design applies better to the partitioning and realization phases of design than to the earliest conceptual phase by noting the value of purpose expansion, not addressed in rational theory, in conception.

GENESERETH, MICHAEL R., and N. J. NILSSON. (1987). *Logical Foundations of Artificial Intelligence.* Los Altos, CA: Morgan Kaufmann. This is quite a mathematical text on the logical foundations of the rational theory of intelligence, emphasizing the use of predicate calculus. As stated in the Preface to the book, "This book rests on two main assumptions. First, scientific and engineering progress in a discipline requires the invention and use of appropriate mathematical apparatus with which to express and unify good ideas. Second, symbolic logic forms a most important part of the mathematics of Artificial Intelligence."

KLIR, G. J. (1985). *Architecture of Systems Problem Solving*. New York: Plenum. This is a recent GSPS text. Providing insights into system characteristics and complexity, it is for the mathematically and operations research inclined.

KOSTOF, SPIRO. (1977). *The Architect*. New York: Oxford University Press. Read especially the first three chapters. It is the millenia-long history of the profession of architecting.

LANG, JON. (1987). *Creating Architectural Theory, The Role of the Behavioral Sciences in Environmental Design*. New York: Van Nostrand Reinhold. Presents the theories of design, from the intuitive through the rational (e.g., Simon's), the argumentitive (many participants), and the learning (iterative) formulations. See especially Chapters 4-7, pp. 37-72.

NADLER, GERALD. November/December 1985). "Systems Methodology and Design." *IEEE Transactions on Systems, Man and Cybernetics* SMC-15, 6, 685-97. Gives the wider perspective of solving system-level design problems and, in particular, the differences between conventional methodology and systems methodology. Extensive reference list. See especially Part Two, pp. 61-108.

PEARL, JUDEA. (1984). *Heuristics, Intelligent Search Strategies for Computer Problem Solving*. Reading, MA: Addison-Wesley. This is a text based on the results of the UCLA Cognitive Systems Laboratory in probabilistic problem-solving methods using prescriptive heuristics, for example, backtracking, chaining, best first, and hill climbing. It discusses how heuristics are discovered (by relaxing constraints to reach simplified models), how errors affect an heuristic search strategy, and game playing. It provides an extension of rational theory in the direction of probablistically provable intuition. The problems considered in the text are all well-defined; their complexity comes from a plethora of possible moves, for example, chess, games, etc.

PEÑA, WILLIAM. (1977). *Problem Seeking, An Architectural Programming Primer*. New York: Cahners Books. The book addresses the principles and techniques of architecting that precede design (called "programming" by Peña), which is roughly equivalent to problem definition. It contains five steps: (1) establish goals, (2) collect and analyze facts, (3) uncover and test concepts, (4) determine needs, and (5) state the problem. And it concerns four major considerations: function, form, economy, and time. The book emphasizes client–architect relationship and the iterative nature of seeking the (real) problem for the designers to solve.

RAYMOND, ARTHUR. (1951). *The Well Tempered Aircraft*. London: Royal Aeronautical Society. This is a classic paper in aerospace architecting by the chief engineer of the DC-3 airplane, the first airliner that let commercial airlines make a profit on passenger traffic. Its principles and heuristics still hold four decades later.

ROWE, ALAN J. (1988). *The Meta Logic of Cognitively Based Heuristics*. Los Angeles: U.S.C., School of Business Administration. The relationship of heuristics to the cognitive (thinking) processes of the human mind is presented. It is a valuable summary of recent thought on the nature and use of heuristics in human problem solving.

ROWE, P. G. (1987). *Design Thinking*. Cambridge, MA: The MIT Press. The book is a slightly different perspective from Lang's, again by an architect–professor, on the theories of design, in this case, elaborating more on the heuristic approach. See Chapter 2, pp. 39–113, for the procedural approach and scan Chapter 3 for the normative approach to civil architecture.

RUBINSTEIN, MOSHE F. (1975). *Patterns of Problem Solving.* Englewood Cliffs, NJ: Prentice Hall, pp. 19–21. The book is from a well-known UCLA course on solving conceptual problems. It categorizes human thought processes in solution formulation as:

"1. Work forwards and backwards

2. Generalize of specialize

3. Explore multiple directions based on partial evidence

4. Form stable substructures

5. Use analogies and metaphors

6. Follow your emotions."

(Adapted by permission of Prentice Hall, Inc.) These processes apply both to individual and group creativity. Recognizing the latter, one might add a seventh: bounce your ideas off others. It includes chapters on problem solving, language and communication, computers, probability and the will to doubt, and models and values. The book should be in every architect's library. It is excellent material for Chapter 3 of this book.

SPINRAD, ROBERT. (October 1988). *Lecture at the University of Southern California.* Los Angeles (unpublished).

STUBBS, M. STEPHANIE. (August 1987). "Technical Education of Architects." *Architecture* 76, 8, 73–77. Nine architectural educators present their views on the integration of technical education into the design studio and offer some alternative approaches toward accomplishing this goal.

VITRUVIUS. (1960). *The Ten Books on Architecture,* (original 25 B.C.) translated by Morris Hicky Morgan. New York: Dover. This book is easily scanned. It is notable for its breadth of view, even 2000 years ago. See Table of Contents, Book I, Chapter II; Book IX, Introduction; Book X, Chapter XVI. It presents the normative approach.

TO BROWSE, DEPENDING ON INTERESTS

ALLEN, FREDERICK. (Fall 1988). "The Letter that Changed the Way We Fly." *Invention & Technology,* This is the story of how the DC-3 came into being.

American Institute of Aeronautics and Astronautics. (1978). *AIAA Code of Ethics.* New York: American Institute of Aeronautics and Astronautics.

BEAM, WALTER R. (1989). *Adapting Software Development Policies to Modern Technology.* Washington, DC: National Academy Press. The book concludes that the conventional waterfall model of system acquisition is deficient for *unprecedented* systems and that very high-level languages are increasingly needed. It also notes that software now controls the operations of major (Air Force) systems, whereas 10 years ago it did not.

BLAAUW, G. A., VON. (1972). "Computer Architecture." *Electronische Reckenanlagen* **14**, 4, 154–159.

BOOTON, RICHARD C., JR., and S. RAMO. (July 1984). "The Development of Systems Engineering." *IEEE Transactions on Aerospace and Electronic Systems* **AES-20**, 4, 306–9. This book presents the development of systems engineering as seen by two of its most illustrious practioners in the U.S. intercontinental ballistic missile program. It states that [in the ICBM context] systems engineers create the architecture of the system, define the criteria for its evaluation, and perform trade-off studies for optimization of the subsystem characteristics, with the principal tool being the computer.

CANTY, DONALD. (September 1963). "What Architects Do and How to Pay Them." *Architectural Forum* **119**, 92–95.

CARPENTER, ROBERT. (1989). *Design Approaches and ADI ASW.* Unpublished graduate report, University of Southern California, Los Angeles.

DAY, MICHAEL R. (1988). *Evidence of Heuristics in DSCS History.* Unpublished graduate report, University of Southern California, Los Angeles.

GAJSKI, D. D., V. M. MILUTINOVIĆ, H. J. SIEGEL, and B. P. FURHT. (1987). *Computer Architecture.* Washington, DC: The Computer Society of the IEEE. A collection of the best writings on the subject during the last decade.

GELL-MANN, MURRAY. (Spring 1988). "Simplicity and Complexity in the Description of Nature." *Engineering & Science,* **LI**, 3, 2–9. A physicist looks at simplicity (of scientific theorems), at apparent complexity (fractals), at chaos (nonlinear recursives), and at adaptive complex systems. This book is of general interest and for philosophical readers.

KJOS, KATHRIN. (1988). *Comparative Analysis of Normative, Rational and Heuristic Theories of Design.* Unpublished graduate report, University of Southern California, Los Angeles.

RECHTIN, EBERHARDT, (Ed.). (1989). "A Collection of Papers on Systems Architecting." Unpublished graduate reports by 11 graduate students, University of Southern California, Los Angeles.

SPINRAD, ROBERT J. (1988). *Systems Architecture.* Vuegraphs accompanying a lecture to the University of Southern California. Unpublished. Three parts: What is Architecture? What are the characteristics of a good architecture? What are the major document-processing architectural issues? This was a particularly perceptive discussion of the theory and practice of architecting.

WEINBERG, GERALD M. (1988). *Rethinking Systems Analysis and Design.* New York: Dorset House. See especially Chapters I, II, V, and VI.

2

ON BOUNDARIES
AND INTERFACES

Systems engineering is a branch of engineering that "concentrates on the design and application of the whole as distinct from the parts . . . looking at a problem in its entirety, taking into account all the facets and all the variables and relating the social to the technological aspects." (Simon Ramo 1973)

The first imperative of architecting, even before any discussions with a client, is to understand the unique nature of complex systems. Approaching systems simply as one more design problem or one more product to be invented can be a serious mistake.

"Systems" mean different things to different people. For our purposes here, the definition of "system" has two parts:

1. A system is a complex set of dissimilar elements or parts so connected or related as to form an organic whole.
2. The whole is greater in some sense than the sum of the parts, that is, the system has properties beyond those of the parts. Indeed, the purpose of building systems is to gain those properties.

Example:

From Chapter 1: the system function of an assembled automobile is transportation, unavailable from the parts separately.

Example:

The human body has many parts. But only as a system can a human being walk, breathe, talk, or live.

Example:

One of the most famous aeronautical systems is the DC-3, a Douglas Aircraft airliner designed and built in the late 1930s and still in service. As Arthur Raymond, its chief engineer, describes it, the DC-3 consisted of largely available parts—airfoil shapes from NACA (National Advisory Committee on Aeronautics), commercially available engines, a monocoque (shell) fuselage demonstrated by others, including the Boeing Company, and commercially available controls. The client had specified three engines, concerned that the airliner be able to fly safely with one engine inoperative. But with two engines on the wings, the third engine would have to be on the nose of the aircraft. Located there, the third engine would obscure the pilot's vision and transmit engine vibration and noise directly into the cabin—to the considerable discomfort of the passengers. Deleting that engine would clearly be advantageous, but then the safety problem had to be solved. Improved aerodynamics, a slightly swept-back wing configuration, special control surfaces, retractable landing gear, and better engines provided the solution. The resultant airliner demonstrated the necessary engine-out capability. In a short time, accelerated by World War II, the DC-3 was in worldwide service. When asked what had really been achieved—after all, the parts were available or readily modified—Raymond modestly answered, "Well, we produced the first airliner that let the airlines make a profit . . . . " The architectural achievement that revolutionized air travel was a *system-level* breakthrough, produced by combining elements in a special way to achieve system goals.

The only thing added to the parts to make the whole greater than its parts is the interrelationships among them. Thus,

Relationships among the elements are what give systems their added value.

From this, it follows that

The greatest leverage in system architecting is at the interfaces.

Example:

From management: in typical system procurement, subsystems are built by separate subcontractors, each of which endeavors to produce good products within specifications stated by the client or prime contractor. The subcontractors clearly know the most about the core of their assigned subsystems and less about their periphery over which, in any case, they have less control. Hence, the system architect at the prime-contractor or client level can be most effective by helping define and control the interfaces.

Example:

The guidance and control element of aerospace systems has more interfaces with other subsystems than does any other part of the system. It interfaces with propulsion, structures, vehicle dynamics, navigation, actuators, and external command. As such, its design largely determines system accuracy, stability, and response to environment.

Example:

One of the most important human systems, though rarely thought of as an engineering problem, is the family unit. Like other systems, this one has failures from time to time. Professional therapy may be called for to restore the family system to functional health. It is a demonstrably successful principle in family therapy (Minushin, 1974, 1981) that the therapist concentrate not on the individuals, but on the relationships between them. Individuals, like engineering elements, cannot be changed easily, but how individuals function in relation to each other can be. In engineering terms, the interfaces need to be identified, defined, and made functional.

Is the interface-leverage heuristic always true? No. Can exceptions be found? Yes. Sometimes the architect does have to expend more effort on one element than on all the rest. But then the architect becomes instead a specialist, at least for a while. There can indeed be architectural leverage in working on individual system elements, *but the rationale should be to produce needed system-level results.* Improving an element by a factor of 10 for a net system gain of 1% is inefficient at best, though that approach occasionally has to be used. Spacecraft engineers sometimes find themselves in such a position when fighting the expensive battle to cut a few pounds off the spacecraft weight. It is clearly preferable to look for 10% changes, like Art Raymond, in the elements that will improve the system as a whole by a factor of 10.

In the early 1960s, Christopher Alexander (1964) proposed that a good architecture was one with a minimum number of "mis-fits" among the system elements. In other words, the misfits distinguished poor from good architectures, and, therefore, the fewer the better. The minimum misfit criterion is perhaps most valuable in suggesting to the architect how to begin the design of a typical system's many interfaces:

The efficient architect, using contextual sense, looks for the likely misfits and designs the architecture so as to eliminate or minimize them.

Now there is no guarantee that this heuristic, nor any other, will produce the best possible result. There may be many different combinations of (modified) function and (alternate) form that will yield a somewhat lower number of misfits. But, with a reasonable configuration having a small number of misfits, the result should be satisfactory.

Using the misfit heuristic takes some care. Deciding on what is and what is not likely to be takes judgment. In so deciding, it is important to understand Alexander's rather broad definition of a misfit: "Any state of affairs in the ensemble which derives from the interaction between form and context, and causes stress in the ensemble" (Alexander, 1964).

This definition requires looking not only at the individual interfaces one by one, but at the whole "state of affairs in the ensemble." It is not unusual for one element to affect another indirectly through a third element or through an unexpected path. Finding likely misfits can be tedious and may well be incomplete. Reducing misfits may require restructuring the *problem* as well as the configuration. The DC-3 architects did so in changing the client-specified third engine requirement to the more basic one of flight safety, resulting in the superior two-engine configuration.

The focus on misfits is not so much that the architect ignores the rest of the presumably good fits—to do so would be dangerous—but that they are left to later at the next, more detailed, level of design. Obviously, the best architects are those with the contextual judgment to spot the most likely and important misfits. There unquestionably is an element of risk here to both the system and the architect should a critical misfit be missed!

As a new system proves itself, gains acceptance, and matures, the role of the systems architect diminishes, as it should. The design effort shifts to the systems engineers. The systems architect becomes the client's system advisor, focusing on the client's interests and objectives, checking trade-off decisions and advising during system acceptance.

However, when markets, political conditions, requirements, complexity, and/or technologies change sharply—as happens increasingly today—the problems to be solved again become architectural. Steady evolution proves inadequate to the challenge. There are too many new external relationships and too many resultant adjustments to continue business as usual in the new environment. Development could be stifled and potential system gains could too easily be delayed or denied.

For example, DC-3's opened up air travel, but required a whole new infrastructure of airports to be built in support. Jet aircraft made global air transportation practical, but only to countries and cities where very large airports could be financed and built. Satellites added new possibilities for communications and surveillance, but required specialized launch vehicles, launch bases, and ground stations. All required major qualitative changes in the larger system architecture.

Major changes like these dramatize, like nothing else can, another basic characteristic of systems—they are inherently unbounded.

THE UNBOUNDED NATURE OF SYSTEMS

Virtually every system has subsystems. Even the simplest element is further divisible. At the same time, every system is part of a larger system, embedded in a still larger context. Figures 2–1 and 2–2 illustrate the point graphically in two different system topologies—nested and overlapping. The system labeling, incidentally, is the familiar one used in report outlines, themselves nested systems of systems.

Unboundedness is strikingly illustrated by a seemingly simple design problem given to civil architecture students, the common water faucet. To design the

SYSTEM I, The Outside World

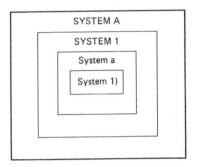

Figure 2–1. Nested systems.

faucet requires knowing for which room. A bathroom faucet, a kitchen faucet, a hallway drinking fountain, and an outdoor hose connection are not the same. To design the faucet also requires knowing for which building, for which town, for what kinds of people, and so on. Nor is the faucet itself indivisible. It has interrelated characteristics of appearance, corrosion, lifetime, cost, and feel. The faucet has still other dimensions, for example, as an element in water management, waste management, and conservation of the environment—all changing with time and predictable population demographics. This last dimension is not a trivial one—faucet restrictors could be made mandatory to help assure adequate water for cities and farms while preserving scenic lakes and rivers.

The larger world frequently imposes serious limitations on new system designs. New and apparently revolutionary technologies are all too often limited in their impact when they are incorporated into complex systems. Laser communication links between satellites encountered major system problems when they were mounted on insufficiently stable satellite platforms. New rocket en-

SYSTEM I, The Outside World

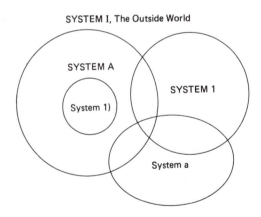

Figure 2–2. Overlapping systems.

gines were jolted by pressure waves reflected from the launch pad and by violent "pogo-stick" heaving due to propellant system instabilities. The famed around-the-world Voyager aircraft had at least as many ergonomic problems as those involving aerodynamics, structures, and materials.

ARCHITECTING AND THE SOCIOPOLITICAL WORLD

Even greater unboundedness occurs in communication networks, signal processing, computer software, manufacturing plants, aircraft, and space vehicles. Nowhere is this more evident than in defense systems.

The MX (Peacekeeper) ICBM is an instructive example. The MX began as a straightforward, if complex, program:

- Of which the MX was a subsystem
- To modernize (in many ways with many technologies)
- One element of the strategic offense (out of a triad)
- To deliver many maneuvering warheads (military strategy)
- To counter ABM defenses built by the Soviets
- As projected by the U.S. intelligence system
- More accurately (political decision)
- Under better control (battle management and communications)
- And at a lesser cost (defense budget limitation)

The MX has been eminently successful in accomplishing this task. However, it is also a major element in arms control deliberations. It has been affected in major ways by international agreements and by the domestic issue of basing. On that last rock this otherwise remarkable program has been foundering. As the expression goes, locating the MX bases in the continental United States is fine, but "not in my backyard."

The MX is by no means the only example of the impact of "outside" sociopolitical systems. Examples are plentiful in nuclear energy, space exploration, heavy industry, and civil aviation.

In such cases, sociologists have learned that often it is not *what you* do but *how* you do it that is most important. *How* you introduce a system can strongly affect system design. Structural design may be constrained by the need to use local materials and labor. The achievable privacy of communications across national boundaries can be affected if local governments claim the right to monitor it. More often than not, the "how to do it" is a belated add-on to system design, sometimes voluntary and often involuntary. If early and voluntary, the client and architect usually maintain the initiative. If later and involuntary, the initiative passes to the opposition.

On the other hand, deliberately involving people who will be affected by the system can *solve* problems as well as create them.

Example:

Worldwide operations, such as those of international airlines and communication networks, in which high standards of performance are critical, have long been best carried out by assigning the local nationals the greatest possible responsibility. The result is cooperative competition to be the best in the system. The NASA/JPL Deep Space Network, a very high-performance network of stations around the world, has long been operated by Americans, South Africans, Australians, and Spaniards, each in charge of their own stations. With each station striving to be the best, network performance has been achieved within a fraction of a decibel of that promised. National pride can indeed be a critical element in a system's architecture and essential for its success.

A crucial element in the sociopolitical world is public relations and the media. Success or failure is a matter of perception, and the media can strongly influence that perception. The lesson, well known to the media and learned painfully by many projects, is

Success is defined by the beholder, not by the architect.

Example:

Whatever the architects' definition of success of the Apollo lunar flight might have been, the addition of real-time television, not originally planned and indeed strongly opposed in some quarters, considerably increased the perceived success. It enabled the world audience to be present at virtually the instant of the first human foot stepping on lunar soil. In that instant, Apollo succeeded. Equally important, failure was being second to the Soviet Union—*not* as suffering loss of life, painful as that loss later became.

Example:

In contrast, Shuttle success was initially defined as routine, safe, cost-effective access to space, almost literally the friendly skies of NASA. By definition, its reusable vehicles would require no replacements and could be fully booked. Failure, almost by definition, was anything less. As a consequence, the *Challenger* loss, instead of being perceived as a regrettable accident of a revolutionary aircraft manned by military test pilots became perceived, through prior NASA claims and subsequent media action, as a nationwide human tragedy and a financial debacle.

Example:

The architects of the DC-3 clearly understood that it was the *passengers* who would define its success or failure. Only they would determine whether flying was other than an ordeal, whether flying was better than other modes of travel, and whether the budding TWA airline could charge a profitable fare.

Example:

It was a great product, but the company went bankrupt.

Example:

The operation was a success, but the patient died.

Example:

The ARPANET was architected as an interactive computer exchange, but the users liked it much better for electronic mail.

Example:

A number of military systems, designed for one purpose, found their most effective use elsewhere. A likely reason for this result will be discussed in the chapter on purposeful opposition, Chapter 9.

Success and failure, then, are not simple things easily defined. What may look like success from one perspective, may look like failure from another. Success and failure are not easily bounded and circumscribed.

THE LIMITATIONS OF THE SCIENTIFIC METHOD IN ARCHITECTING

Granted that complex systems are unbounded, why is this so important to the systems architect? It is important because solving complex system problems, the architect's stock in trade, can require techniques beyond and even counter to well-established scientific and engineering methodology. Using only the latter may result in no solutions at all.

The scientific method is to start with measurements, to describe with theories, to predict based on those theories, and then to confirm or deny them with measurements replicable by others. Scientific truth, at its core, is predictable repeatable measurements. To paraphrase the famed scientist, Lord Kelvin, if it can't be measured, it's not science.

But in complex systems, never built before, meaningful measurements may be impossible or impractical. For example, how can an architect certify by prior measurement that a system using state-of-the-art components will exhibit low failure rates and a very long life? In other systems, making measurements so disturbs the system that the results are ambiguous if not meaningless. The Hawthorne effect is a classical example. In that famous Bell System experiment, an attempt to determine the best lighting conditions for a group of employees, worker performance improved regardless of what changes were made. Either more or less light improved productivity, no matter what the then-present light level was. The cause was finally traced to employees favorably responding to the unusual attention paid to them. As for replication of measurements and results, few systems situations are replicable either later or by others. Too many elements change with time and circumstance.

Quantification in the systems world can be deceptive if not irrelevant. To give a simple example: in this world, 1 + 1 is not necessarily 2. If the two things are exactly the same and do not interact, then 2 may be the correct sum. But, if they interact, another element has been added that may have a positive or negative effect on the total. (Indeed, systems are *supposed* to achieve more than the sum of the parts.) The result could be 3 or it could be 0; one could make the argument that it could be less than 0 or more than 3 or anywhere in between.

Or, as complexity increases, a previously stable linear system can abruptly go unstable and nonlinear. M. R. Gardner and W. R. Ashby (KLIR 1985 p. 21) showed that under carefully stated conditions, linear systems of 10 or more elements went unstable if their interactions were more than about 13% of the total possible ones. Although the specific percentage may be of more academic than practical interest, it does give a warning of trouble ahead if there are too many major interactions between elements.

There is a natural propensity among those trained in the scientific method to draw exclusionary boundaries, to exclude part of the larger problem in the interest of defining a solvable problem. There is a folk theorem in engineering that says if you can't solve the whole problem, then at least solve half of it. A systems architect would be the first to object. At the very least, the effects on and from the rest of the elements need to be understood before proceeding.

Psychologists recognize a similar exclusionary tendency in "group think." In group think, there is a deliberate, if undeclared, effort to exclude any and all information that contradicts the group's closed set of assumptions. "What if . . . " questions are shoved aside. Potentially disastrous conditions are declared low-risk. The status quo is considered immutable. Clearly, in the unbounded world of complex systems, exclusionary boundaries can be treacherous.

However, there is one area where science, engineering, and architecting are close to identical. All are initially confronted with situations of great apparent complexity. And all try to structure and simplify their problems.

In science, the search is for the simplest explanation (Occam's Razor), though, as Einstein warns, "not for one that is *too* simple." The search is for underlying principles and closed-form solutions. Because closed-form solutions require closed boundaries, a common first step in science and engineering problem-solving methodology is to define and bound the problem. Solutions within the boundaries are then sought and usually found. Maxwell's electromagnetic equations, for example, are such that given the boundary conditions, in principle, almost any electromagnetic radiation problem can be solved.

In engineering, the search is for prepackaged partial solutions—principles, dimensionless parameters, charts, tables, and techniques—that yield the right answer as simply as possible to the engineer's well-defined bounded problem. Failing that, the engineer uses experimentation, successive trial and error, and evolutionary design.

In architecting, the search is for a structure (an architecture) that will produce a satisfactory solution in a reasonably simple fashion. The architect recognizes that the system remains unbounded. That fact is explicitly acknowledged in *open* architectures—architectures readily adapted to respond to changing external events and conditions. Thus, all three, the scientist, engineer and architect, follow the heuristic: **Simplify, simplify, simplify.**

WHEN IS A BOUNDARY NOT A BOUNDARY?

To this point, boundaries have been treated as if each element was a definable entity. In other words, lines could be drawn between elements or, more generally, a single surface could enclose each element. But this is not always the case. For example, most elements have a set of characteristics—technical function, geographical location, user community, and so forth. Depending on which characteristic is chosen, like elements would be grouped differently. All those in the United States might be one group, or all those produced by the same company, or all those providing a particular service worldwide. The boundaries seen by each element would depend upon which group the element was in. More generally, boundaries can be uncertain or describable only in statistical terms, and those terms may depend on what further information is available. For example, conventional Wiener filtering distinguishes signals from noise only by their spectral content, a relatively imprecise determinant. But *phase* content can be an overriding characteristic of either or both signal and noise. A flat noise spectrum can be produced by either easily rejected randomly timed impulses or by a pernicious randomly varying continuous wave. Similarly, the spectral content of a square wave and that of the same combination of tones with a different phase relationship between them are alike, yet their wave shapes are very different. The effectiveness of Wiener filter theory is thus limited by uncertainties in the waveform coherence of the signal and interference.

A more general kind of uncertainty, formally expressible in Fuzzy Set Theory, is qualitative reasoning in which indefinite terms such as *large, small, too fast, about right,* and *enough* are used as criteria. Systems designed to such criteria, instead of exhibiting close continuous control, tend to be "softer" throughout the normal range of operation and come into play only when system performance strays toward the fuzzily described boundaries. The system is then nudged back again—a gentle limit-switchlike action. A Japanese subway system successfully uses such a system design to produce a more comfortable ride at operational speeds.

Other examples of ill-defined boundaries are as follows:

Example:

The conventional organization chart gives the impression of clean relationships among the units. Yet seldom are the charters of the units nor the perceptions of the participants that clear, nor is the rationale for the partitioning either explicit or permanent.

Example:

Some of the most complex interface regions are at physical surfaces, for example, at the surface of the sea, in wind-shear zones, in boundary-layer air flow over wings, and in diffuse boundaries in integrated circuits. For example, noting that airfoils are shaped with the thicker edge in front, an aerodynamicist recently proposed that perhaps racing yachts were designed incorrectly. An experiment indeed showed that drag was less if the boat were towed backward instead of forward. This is true enough in calm seas. Indeed, *under* the water, the bows of some ships look like a blunt airfoil, but not at the surface and not for rough seas. And automobile designers have found that one of the best aerodynamic shapes is a forward-pointing ground-hugging wedge and *not* an airfoil—automobiles, after all, should stay at the boundary of air and road and not take off like an airplane.

Example:

One of the most difficult of aerodynamic problems is that of flutter control, where active controls, structures, surfaces, and aerodynamic nonlinearities come together and interact in transonic flow fields (Ashley, 1988). Describing this region, much less defining the multiple interfaces analytically to a point where stable control can be achieved, has been a challenge for many decades.

Example:

Historians have remarked that one of the more serious social consequences of European colonization was the drawing of maps showing national boundaries. Up to the time of colonization, the political structure had been that of city-states in which authority of the state decreased with distance from the city. Midway between the cities, their authorities were the least. Typically, mountainous regions or wide rivers provided geographical separation, leading to mountain people and river people who owed little allegiance to the cities. Boundaries had little meaning. With the drawing of maps and line boundaries, authority was abruptly made absolute and total right up to the line on the map. Distance no longer separated the states and new kinds of wars resulted. Great suffering was imposed on the mountain and river people as each state demanded their absolute allegiance. The most striking example was in Southeast Asia, but Africa has been similarly disrupted. Nor is Europe itself immune. More than one European country is, in actuality, a transition zone between two or more sharply different, often conflicting, nationalities threatening to tear the transition nation apart. For better or worse, the world seems to lack a stable social structure for dealing with fuzzy boundaries and gray areas.

It is a naïve architect who arbitrarily draws lines through such regions or characterizes them as simple one-on-one interfaces. If lines must be drawn, then alternate lines should be studied for their sensitivity to specific location before making the choice. Each will produce a different architecture, different interfaces, and generally different performance.

A COMMENT ON THE "ILLITIES"

Commentaries on the procurement of complex systems are rife with condemnation of the "illities": reliability, affordability, maintainability, availability, accountability, and the like. The illities are condemned as extraneous, as unnecessary gold plating, and as superfluous paperwork, adding to program cost and micromanagement.

The architect should know better. The illities are the imperatives of the external world as expressed at the boundaries with the internal world of the system. Reliability is the imperative of the user, affordability that of the client, maintainability that of the operator, and accountability that of the auditor. Disparaging the illities is no help.

Unfortunately, the external world also views an illity—technical feasib*ility*—in a similar light, as a problem that the architects and engineers are contracted to solve within the external world's stated imperatives.

It is no wonder that there is friction and heat at the illity boundaries and that architects spend an inordinate amount of time there putting out the fires.

AGGREGATING AND PARTITIONING

Given the complexity and unboundedness of systems, how can the architect impose some order, some structure—in short, an architecture—where little structure seems present? A favored approach is to divide, or partition, the original problem into smaller problems, each of which is more readily solved than the original one. The formal name for this approach is reductionism.

But arbitrary partitioning into large numbers of subproblems (and, consequently, subsystems) can be a serious mistake. Slicing Figure 2–1 down through the middle and assigning each half to a different organization would create chaos. Or dividing Figure 2–2 into every little piece, some of which are parts of three or more subsystems, would make integration far more difficult than necessary.

Instead, two architecting processes need to be carried out together—partitioning and aggregating. Contrary to what might be thought, the first step in structuring is usually aggregating—collecting or clustering closely related functions or requirements together—rather than partitioning. There is no easy rule of thumb for how much aggregating to do. But studies of organizational span of control, of interdisciplinary combinations, and of human abilities to handle limited numbers of things simultaneously suggest that there should not be more than a handful of elements at any one system level. Too much detail or too much partitioning and the number of possibilities escalates out of control. Nor should there be so few that all the critical problems are buried out of sight within the clusters. Too little detail in some areas and system-critical functions may be handled badly or missed entirely.

All things considered, the top-level design—the primary architectural one—should probably consist of half a dozen or so elements. Whatever the particular choice, architects have learned through hard experience that

Choosing the appropriate aggregation of functions is critical in the design of systems.

The aggregation of functions often suggests a structure, or architecture, for the system itself. This matching of functional and subsystem elements works best when the elements can be consolidated in one location, in one environment, and in one kind of equipment.

If location, environment, and equipment factors are quite different, it might be wise to consider several different aggregations. System-level difficulties can be anticipated whenever function and form are structurally different, that is, whenever they are aggregated and partitioned differently.

Example:

Space Station Freedom consists of four or more major habitable modules and two long booms. All are interlaced with electrical, hydraulic, propulsion, thermal-control, life-support, communication, and other functional subsystems essential for operation of the station as a whole. The station must be able to survive if any of the modules are disabled. The system architecture, in effect, is a complex matrix with many intermodule interconnections. The architectural solution that has been adopted is to cluster by system function and solve the inherent physical partitioning problems by the design of the nodes interconnecting the modules.

Example:

Consider the problem, posed by Robert Spinrad, of designing a "simple" document-processing system. How and where should documents be compressed and decompressed, stored and retrieved, copied and read, transmitted and received? Should functions be centralized or distributed? At each node or only at the periphery? In the copiers or in the computers? The system might be configured by functional, physical, or geographical clusters, or combinations thereof. As one crucial consequence, the communication links among the elements could take many different forms. To complicate the issues further, different customers will prefer different system configurations. Most customers sooner or later will want the system to grow, but different customers will want growth in different directions. To cap it off, as Spinrad puts it, "The most important thing in architecting is not to make a serious blunder because you and your successors will have to live with it, and be cursed for it, for 20–30 years." Yet, it is not readily apparent which kind of clustering is best! The likely solution is to use the results of customer trials during the design phase.

Thus, much as one might desire it otherwise, it is not always practical to match the functional and physical (form) structures of a system. Hence, the relatively mild heuristic, applicable to both aggregating and partitioning:

> **Except for good and sufficient reasons, functional and physical structuring should match.**

We now focus on the determination of the major interfaces, the nature and location of which depends on how the structuring is done. There are choices to be made.

A house can be partitioned into rooms, into support subsystems (plumbing, electricity, heating, communications) that are distributed through the rooms, or by function—living, working, entertaining. A communication network can be divided geographically, by function, by user groups, or by competitors. A global surveillance mission can be assigned by satellite, aircraft, by land transport, or fixed stations; by government agency or service; by spectral coverage (visible, infrared, radar, radio); or by target.

Engineers, trained in the use of block diagrams, commonly think of partitioning in terms of connected blocks on a two-dimensional chart. But multidimensional systems, from the examples just given, typically require multiple connected layers—a treacherous source of hidden interface misfits.

Clearly, some partitioning is better than others. An arbitrary slice through a tightly integrated subsystem, through a fuzzy region, or through some critical blocks in a block diagram will create too many likely misfits, too many complex interfaces, and too many interactions. Various authors and design teams consequently have developed essentially the same partitioning heuristic:

> **In partitioning, choose the elements so that they are as independent as possible, that is, elements with low external complexity and high internal complexity.** (Alexander, 1964)

Or

> **In partitioning a distributed system, choose a configuration in which local activity is high speed and global activity is slow change.** (Courtois, 1985)

Or

> **In partitioning a system into subsystems, choose a configuration with minimal communications between the subsystems.** * (For example, aerospace, communication network, and software systems.)

Or

> **Don't partition by slicing through regions where high rates of information exchange are required.** (For example, computers.)

("Communications" is used here as shorthand for interrelationships, connections, interplay, information flow, etc. "Minimal" is, of course, relative; when applied to subsubsystems, it necessarily changes scale.)

An important corollary is that interfaces should isolate the elements such that only a few critical external events can change or disturb the inner workings. This semiisolation helps maintain internal stability and the flexibility needed to adapt to internal needs. It produces appropriate responses to an uncertain exter-

---

*As with most heuristics, this one has a major exception: massively parallel neural networks—but they are exceptional in many ways as will be seen in Chapter 11.

nal environment without suffering undue interference from it. The resultant heuristic, a variation of **minimum communications,** is, thus:

Design the elements to make their performance as insensitive to unknown or uncontrollable external influences as practical.

If partitioning is done accordingly, then many elements can be separately developed during conceptual design. Once the overall system design has been stabilized, it may be possible to reaggregate the separated elements and simplify the overall structure.

The minimal communications heuristic has application in many fields—integrated-circuit chip design, organization charts, traffic control, and spacecraft design. It is aimed at achieving good system performance with as little difficulty as possible. It does not necessarily result in, say, minimum weight or minimum power consumption. But, in a practical sense, it might—system problems are notorious for adding unexpected weight and power to accommodate interface problems.

Example:

Up to the time that President Kennedy proposed the Apollo program to go to the moon and back by the end of the 1960 decade, the generally accepted flight configuration (von Braun in 1956 and the Soviet Union as declared in 1990) included launch vehicles to go from the Earth to low Earth orbit, assembly there of a spacecraft to go to the moon and return to earth orbit, and then return to the Earth's surface in a specialized reentry vehicle. A space station would probably be needed in such an architecture for safe rendezvous, assembly, and reentry. Meeting the President's schedule from a standing start within nine years seemed unlikely. The previously accepted architecture was too complex with too many interdependencies. The solution was a radically different architecture, one in which the only rendezvous operations would be in lunar orbit by a Lunar Excursion Module mating with a Lunar Orbiting Module. However, that architectural decision, undoubtedly the best for Apollo, postponed an American space station for at least two decades, a trade-off still debated years later.

Example:

The question arose in a recent spacecraft design: Should the onboard computer configuration be centralized or distributed into the spacecraft subsystems (guidance, telemetry, etc.)? Centralizing meant less weight, less power, and more efficient redundancy. But a distributed computing configuration allowed the separate testing of subcontracted subsystems as functional units; without such capability, they could not be. But as such, they were much more likely to work when assembled into the larger system. Responsibilities were clearer. Equally important, the interactions between the subsystem subcontractors were fewer. The distributed system was chosen and worked well.

Example:

Some years ago, a satellite communications service was proposed that would connect the divisions of major corporations with very wide-band communications. The market turned out to be appreciably less than anticipated. Evidently, divisions in a geographi-cally distributed corporation tend to be relatively autonomous. Their interdivisional communication needs were few.

Example:

In defense communications, the more communications capacity required between ele-ments (units in an army, parts of a satellite communication network, etc.), the more vulnerable are the links to external interference, and, hence, the more vulnerable are the military units they support.

The last example, however, shows a clear case of conflicting requirements between capability and vulnerability. A central purpose of communications to the units is command and control. For better or worse, the amount of command and control needed in today's complex military–political world is steadily in-creasing. Hence, reducing communications to reduce its vulnerability might de-crease the unit's overall effectiveness.

This conflict is illustrative of a more general one, the conflict between the needs of a system (the military organization) and the needs of an element (com-munications) that supports it. In this case, an otherwise desirable communica-tions architecture did not fit the command and control system it was to support.

This leads to a widely applicable variation of the misfit criterion:

The architecture of a support element must fit that of the system which it supports.

The simplest fit is probably two overlaid identical architectures, for example, an information-network diagram that matches an organization chart. Less de-manding are architectures that match just at selected interfaces, for example, "gateways" in international communications and I/O (input/output) devices at computer terminals.

A technique particularly applicable to shared communications and com-puter support systems is what might be called a "virtual match," in which a more general architecture is so operated as to appear to the user as a dedicated network, available on demand. Generally speaking, such networks can be made much less vulnerable, through alternate routing and other means, than single point-to-point linkages.

Matching a system with its environment requires that the latter be reason-ably well defined if the overall system is to be partitioned into workable subsys-tems. The difficulty is that the environment has many elements—thermal and acoustic conditions, social and political pressures, etc.—that pervasively pene-trate many system subsystems. The choice of what is "inside" the system and what is "outside" in the environment can be one of the most difficult and criti-cal decisions in systems architecting.

Even after the best partitioning, some of the resulting elements will be found to have unanticipated problems in achieving intended performance, cost, or schedule, making it necessary to repartition, transferring a particularly difficult subsystem problem to another subsystem where it may be more tractable. For example, the structural stability problems of aerospace vehicles are more than a structures problem; they can be affected by the control subsystem and vice versa. Antenna-size problems can be reduced with more efficient signal coding. Bidirectional laser-link matchup can be a problem assigned either to platform stability or to laser search patterns or to both.

In many cases, the system architect is the only one in a position to recommend the appropriate transfer. But there can be resistance to the change. Subsystem designers tend to want to solve their own assigned problems, no matter how difficult. This is understandable and very human. The architect's approach must be equally human—establish from the very first a climate of mutual respect and understanding.

EXPAND THE PROBLEM

Another approach to system unboundedness is to take *advantage* of it. Expand the system boundaries. *Expand the problem.* Add more purposes and functions. Try expansionism rather than reductionism. Narrowly bounded systems can be so rigidly contained that freedom of action is limited. In the complex system world, with its ever-expanding boundaries, there may be more options. Within the original narrow boundaries, there may be too many requirements and constraints and too few variables with which to satisfy them. Expanding the boundaries (e.g., the purposes and functions) may add more variables than constraints, making the larger problem solvable.

Example:

An instrument manufacturer, which produced its own integrated circuits, perceived a problem in the cost of those circuits until it was realized that the profits produced by those circuits in the end instruments greatly exceeded the "excessive" costs. Far more important to profit was control of the design of the integrated circuits in assuring the performance and timeliness of the final product. Contrast this result with that at a company for which the integrated circuit was the end product. In the first case, a 20% difference in integrated-circuit cost made less than a 1% difference in product cost, but could affect sales dramatically. In the second case, a 20% difference in cost translated directly to the bottom line.

Example:

Adding additional purposes for a system has often increased its sponsorship to a level where the system was practical to undertake. This certainly has been the case in some government programs (e.g., space, defense, civil works, and big science), where economic betterment in selected areas generated enough votes to assure the necessary appropriations.

But adding purposes to gain support is a risky business. The added purposes can conflict with the original ones, adding otherwise unnecessary complexity and integration cost. The temptation to add purposes at marginal cost is strong, an action often followed by broken promises later when cost-reduction efforts force marginal customers to pay much more or leave, hence the cautioned heuristic:

Sometimes, but not always, the way to solve a difficult problem is to expand it.

CHALLENGE THE REQUIREMENTS

Another approach to reduce complexity is to challenge extreme requirements— those that during system architecting increasingly drive not only the design of the system as a whole, but of many of its elements. Efforts to satisfy an extreme requirement usually create complexity internal to the system, complexity that a reduced requirement might eliminate. In that elimination, reliability would probably increase. Cost would probably be reduced. Systems engineering could be simplified. The system as a whole would improve.

Example:

In the highly successful FLEETSATCOM project, design had barely begun when it became all too apparent to the contractor, TRW, that the satellite would become the most complex one yet built. Yet the function to be performed was itself not that difficult— simple turnaround ("bent-pipe") relaying of UHF communications. TRW immediately flagged the problem, requirements were changed, and the complexity dropped dramatically. One result was that the satellites have lasted more than twice as long in orbit as any designer would have predicted.

Example:

But not all situations turn out as well. A satellite program was due to be updated after particularly successful initial operations. The existing satellites were relatively simple and had demonstrated that the assigned mission could be performed at modest cost and weight. But a critical decision was made. It was decided at the client–architect level that a presumably useful additional function could be performed if the pointing accuracy of the satellite were improved by a factor of 10. But that decision led to requirements for more precision, more stability, and more mechanical interactions among the subsystems. The simple satellite became more complex. As a result, cost, performance, and schedule were missed. In the final operation, the new function was never used. In retrospect, when the implications of the additional requirement were first recognized, the requirement should have been reduced or deleted. Before long it was too late. Too many subsystems had been completed to go back and start over.

System architecting is a matter of balance. Extreme requirements work against that balance, creating unexpected misfits and deficient performance elsewhere. As Art Raymond expressed it, a good design is a compromise of the extremes. There are circumstances where extreme requirements can be justified—public safety or system survivability, for example—but the likely costs elsewhere in the system demand that

> **Extreme requirements should remain under challenge throughout system design, implementation, and operation.**

RECHARACTERIZING THE INTERFACE

In mathematics, there is a technique called change of variable for the solution of certain kinds of equations. Equations that looked unsolvable became recognizable as solvable in the new form with the new variable. Typical changes would be *from* or *to* sines, cosines, exponentials, or complex functions. An analogous technique can sometimes be used in systems architecture to change what seemed to be difficult interfaces to simpler or more malleable ones. Is the electrical interface best described in terms of current, voltage, or power? Is the communications interface an apparently random digital signal, the highly structured output of a multiplexer or an error-correcting coded bit stream? Is the mechanical interface rigid or flexible? Is there a simple conversion possible from one software language to another? Can the interface be linearized if better parameters are chosen? Can dimensionless parameters be chosen to minimize the effects of scale? In making cost comparisons, is it cost, cost effectiveness, or cash flow that is critical? In each of these questions, the choice directly affects the manageability of the interface, just as a change of variable solves some equations. Hence:

> **When confronted with a particularly difficult interface, try changing its characterization.**

Example:

A serious problem in the early days of guided missiles was control instability. Control was accomplished by moving control surfaces or swiveling engines, feedback coming back to the autopilot from the actuators of those devices. The feedback was a measurement of actuator position. But it was then realized that the critical parameter was not actuator position, which functionally was unrelated to the physics of the problem, but force. Force feedback was substituted and the problem cleared up.

Example:

For a spacecraft to fly by a planet on a precise trajectory, a highly accurate navigation system had to be in place ahead of time. But the locations of the planets, although determined from centuries of optical measurements, were uncertain to tens of thousands of miles. The velocity of light was uncertain to a part per million. Consequently, the predicted flyby distances were so uncertain as to make the missions questionable. The solution was to convert distances within the solar system to measurements of time intervals that were far more precise than any other measurements. The basic instrument was a precision radar/radio, which first bounced signals off Venus, communicating later on the same frequency with the outgoing spacecraft. By measuring the time intervals to Venus and the spacecraft in the same coordinate system, time, navigation precision of tens of miles were then achieved to distances of billions of miles. The subsequently invented technique of gravity assist was thus made practical, and, hence, the exploration of the outer planets.

Example:

A second problem for planetary exploration was communicating with rapidly moving distant spacecraft with limited power and antenna size. It was conventional at the time to use frequency modulation with bandwidths at least wide enough to accommodate the vehicle's Doppler frequency, a technique whose high noise level precluded accomplishing the mission. The solution was to think of the receiver as a tracking servomechanism. The parameter to be tracked was phase, not frequency. The resultant equivalent bandwidths were then a factor of 100 smaller than the Doppler shifts. As a further gain, synchronous communications and phase-locked clocks could then be used. The end result was small-antenna low-power communications to billions of miles.

Changing variables is not the only mathematical substitution technique with analogies in interface management. Fourier transforms, in the form of electrical, mechanical, and optical transfer functions, have dramatically changed the character and partitioning of signal- and image-processing systems. A good recent example is the use of optical elements to accomplish Fourier transformation, multiplication of variables, and massive parallel interconnection in neural networks.

APPLYING CONSTRAINTS

The heuristics up to this point could apply to almost any system. They are largely independent of context. But the range of potential system solutions might still be too great to explore completely. It is time to apply contextual sense.

Example:

In the previous spacecraft communication problem, it was evident that the spacecraft had to obey the laws of motion, that is, for most of its flight, its motion could be described in terms of position, velocity, and acceleration. To track the phase of its received signal without bias, therefore, required a receiver that, in addition to its noise-reducing transfer function, was constrained to track a term in phase that was quadratic in time. Mathematically, the result was achieved using conventional noise theory constrained by variational calculus. The result was a further narrowing of the required bandwidth and an increased communications range.

Example:

A widely used seismic exploration technique is to set off a sharp explosion at one point on the Earth's surface and listen for its acoustic signature at a number of other locations. The received signals are very complex, having been modified appreciably by subsurface conditions. But geologists know a great deal about what subsurface conditions are physically possible. Expressed in acoustic-signal terms, only certain transformations are possible. These transformations can be enhanced by matched-filter techniques.

An effective way of finding hidden constraints is to check for inconsistent assumptions, such as assuming that system parameters are independent when they are not. For example, it is most unlikely that system performance, cost, and schedule can be separately specified. If one or more are specified, the others are certainly constrained, if not predetermined. Hence,

> **Once the architecture begins to take shape, the sooner contextual constraints and sanity checks are made on assumptions and requirements, the better.**

And, in a particularly important form for advanced systems,

> **Build reality checks into model-driven development.** [Larry Dumas, 1989]

ON MAKING ARCHITECTURAL DECISIONS

The preceding sections of this chapter have posed the challenges and suggested some of the better approaches to system complexity and unboundedness. The approaches all involve decision making. The dilemma is that the critical decisions must be made early, when very little information is available. The criticality of these early decisions has been noted in many contexts. Two of the more succinctly stated descriptive heuristics are as follows:

> (Software version) **In architecting a new software program, all the serious mistakes are made in the first day.** (Spinrad, 1988)

Or

> (Aerospace version) **In architecting a new aerospace system, by the time of the first design review, performance, cost, and schedule have been predetermined. One might not know what they are yet,**

but to the first order all the critical assumptions and choices have been made that will determine those key parameters.

But how does one know that a serious error has been made?

When choices must be made with unavoidably inadequate information, *choose* the best available and then *watch* to see whether future solutions appear faster than future problems. If so, the choice was at least adequate. If not, go back and *choose* again.

In the vernacular, if a choice clears the air, good. If everything is going to hell, not good. Evident enough, but note that the heuristic has three parts. The first part, how to make the best apparent choice, is the subject of a large body of decision theory. The second part, watch for the ratio of future solutions to future problems, is equally if not more important because it evaluates the choice. Mathematicians would call it detecting the first derivative, or slope. Software architects would recognize it as the "hill-climbing" heuristic. Neural engineers would relate it to the "global stability" of neural networks.

The third part of the heuristic is often the hardest. It takes courage to reverse a decision, particularly if much time and energy has been expended or if group think has set in. Choose–watch–choose is one tough heuristic. On the other hand, it gives some encouragement to architects in the midst of ill-structured and wicked situations. If solutions appear faster than problems, prior decisions were *probably* good ones!

SUMMARY

The essence of systems is relationships, interfaces, form, fit, and function. The essence of architecting is structuring, simplification, compromise, and balance.

The challenge is the control, if not the reduction, of complexity and uncertainty. Architectural techniques useful in this control are as follows:

- Expansion or reduction of the architectural problem to a realistic, workable size
- Partitioning the overall architecture into implementable, reasonably autonomous, elements
- Identifying the likely misfits, fuzzy regions, and multiple interrelationships that can cause trouble—and architecting to minimize and/or manage them
- Watching and, as necessary, correcting the consequences of critical architectural decisions made with unavoidably incomplete information
- Keeping the system in balance

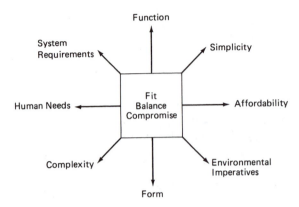

Figure 2-3. Some tensions in systems architecting.

Figure 2-3 diagrams some of tensions that must be resolved through fit, balance, and compromise. A later figure (Figure 7-1) expands this diagram significantly.

RECOMMENDED READING

ALEXANDER, CHRISTOPHER. (1964). *Notes on the Synthesis of Form.* Cambridge, MA: Harvard University Press. This book is a classic in the theory of architecting with focus on interface fits and partitioning. It has since been modified to include patterns of interfaces, but it is a good place to start.

BOEHM, B. W. (September 1976). "Software Engineering." *IEEE Transactions on Computers,* C-25, 12, 1226–41. This is a classic article on software-system architecture.

FLOOD, R. L., and E.R. CARSON. (1988). *Dealing with Complexity.* New York: Plenum. See especially Chapter Three for characterizing and partitioning systems (pp 35–61) and Chapter Six for a variation on rational theory and an attempt to establish structure for solving "soft" (nonrational) problems. The text concludes that the approaches to hard and soft systems have yet to be brought under a single rubric.

NADLER, G. (1981). *The Planning and Design Approach.* New York: Wiley. See especially Chapters 7–10. This is a detailed look at the axioms and propositions of system theory and the designer's time line. Emphasis is placed on repeatedly returning to the purpose (function) of the system as it is being designed and built, a key to retaining design integrity.

SAGE, A. P. (February 1981). "Systems Engineering: Fundamental Limits and Future Prospects." *Proceedings of the IEEE* 69, 2, 158–66. The book assesses the limitations of systems engineering (and architecture) in the unbounded ill-structured context within which complex systems exist. It is applied to energy policy analysis and technology forecasting.

TO BROWSE, DEPENDING ON INTERESTS

ASHLEY, HOLT. (August 1988). "Flutter Suppression Within Reach." *Aerospace America,* **26,** 8, 14–16.

COURTOIS, P. J. (June 1985). "On Time and Space Decomposition of Complex Structures." *Communications of the ACM* **28,** 6, 590–603. The article suggests a useful partitioning of hierarchical systems such that internal actions are fast and external ones are slow, a variation on the minimum communications heuristic.

IEEE. (May 1988). "Fuzzy Wuzzy (in Japan) is a Subway Motorman." *The Institute.* The article presents an evidently successful application of Fuzzy Set Theory to Japanese subway-system control.

KLIR, G. J. (1985). *Architecture of Systems Problem Solving.* New York: Plenum. This is a recent GSPS (general system problem solver) text. Insights into system characteristics and complexity are given. It is for the mathematically and operations research inclined.

LENAT, D. B. (September 1984). "Computer Software for Intelligent Systems." *Scientific American* **251,** 3, 204–13. This article applies human heuristic approaches to the computer solution of system problems. It is an overview of what this text would call architectural heuristics in a computer context.

MINUCHIN, SALVADOR. (1981). *Families & Family Therapy* (1974) and *Family Therapy Techniques* (1981) Cambridge, MA: Harvard University Press. The family as a system, with the therapist rearchitecting the relationships to restore functionality, is described.

POPOLI, R. F., and J.M. MENDEL. (1988). *Heuristically Constrained Estimation for Intelligent Signal Processing,* University of Southern California Signal and Image Processing Institute Report 122, Los Angeles. The report describes the incorporation of inexact knowledge to signal-estimation problems with seismic-signal application.

ROWE, ALAN. (1988). *The Meta Logic of Cognitively Based Heuristics.* Los Angeles: University of Southern California. The metalogic approach relies on a combination of inductive logic with intuitive reasoning and creativity to find solutions to complex problems. This is one of the finest short dissertations on the nature of heuristics to be found.

TAUSWORTHE, R. C. (March/April 1976). *Simple Intuitive Models of Programming,* JPL Deep Space Network Progress Report 42-33. Jet Propulsion Laboratory, Pasadena, CA. This report presents simplified intuitive models of software productivity. Examples of results: **Organize personnel tasks to minimize the time individuals spend interfacing. Try to determine which nodes are most error-prone.**

3

MODELING, SIMULATING, AND PROTOTYPING

The most important single element of success is to listen closely to what the customer perceives as his requirements and to have the will and ability to be responsive.— J. E. Steiner, architect of the Boeing 727

Success is defined by the beholder, not the architect.—Chapter 2

DECISION MAKING, VALUE JUDGMENTS, AND WORKING THE RIGHT PROBLEM

Two different kinds of decisions, both critical to success, are made in architecting—value judgments and technical choices. Clients and customers decide relative value. Architects and engineers decide technical feasibility. It is difficult to overemphasize the importance of each kind of decision being made, and only made, by the appropriate party. In this chapter, we deal with the earliest decisions in architecting, the value judgments of the client. In the next chapter, the primary role is the architect's.

A client—a sponsor of a major program—of course can preempt or overrule the architect, risking technical failure in the process. But it is an unprofessional architect who will preempt the client and make value judgments. As one architect put it, "No architect should decide questions of the client's life style. If asked, 'What would you do if you were me?' the architect must respond with questions which lead the client to answers based on the client's values—not those of the architect."

The two kinds of decisions are intertwined. And, therefore, the architect and the client, between them, have to decide what functions the system is intended to do, how, and why. For small systems, like consumer products, in which the customer is a diffuse marketplace, the two kinds of decisions seem independent. In practice, they come together in product evolution. Products that succeed have, in one way or another, received good customer input. Those that fail usually have not.

Articulating the intended functions in a well-understood and well-structured form is not easy. Required functions may not be affordable. Desired performance may not be physically possible. As requirements and engineering principles come into conflict, priorities may have to be rearranged.

In the beginning, neither the client nor the architect may know just what will be affordable, possible, or of most value in the long run. Attempting to lay out a complex system's objectives completely, consistently, and in priority order is seldom possible without some concept of what the final system might look like.

It takes diplomacy and patience, but the first thing the architect and the client need to determine is what is "the real problem." Unless this is clearly established, it is all too easy to make an error "of the third kind"—solving the *wrong* problem. Ideally, the real problem will surface early. But sometimes it takes some preliminary design to bring it out.

Example:

In the case of the DC-3, the client originally asked for a three-engine airplane. Discussion showed that the real problem was an airplane that could fly safely and profitably over known routes. The client, however, only provisionally accepted the two-engine design, pending flight demonstrations. The resultant DC-1 was at best marginally successful, but it helped establish the client's priorities and demonstrated the limitations of the DC-1 design. Following a short production run of the DC-2, the larger and greater-powered DC-3 aircraft satisfied the client's needs in full.

Example:

In the case of the Strategic Defense Initiative, the President asked for a way of making strategic nuclear weapons obsolete, presumably by building a near-perfect shield against them. A more realizable possibility might have been to decrease the likelihood of nuclear war by adding defensive shields to the offensive swords in the arsenals of the superpowers—a posture explicitly recognized in the ABM Treaty. If so, then the architectural problem would have been to conceive a valuable, affordable, feasible, but limited shield—rather than an impenetrable one.

Example:

In the case of the ARPANET, the sponsor originally called for a communications network that would interconnect widely dispersed computers, each possessing specialized capabilities, for the purpose of solving complex scientific problems. The real problem, as it turned out, was not to connect the computers, each of which was virtually self-sufficient, but to connect the researchers through E-mail, so that problem-solving *ideas* could be exchanged.

Hence,

Don't assume that the original statement of the problem is necessarily the best, or even the right, one.

This heuristic sometimes leads to a quick solution all by itself. The technique it suggests is to keep rethinking the problem until the solution is obvious (Nadler, 1981; Parsaye and Chignell, 1988). It works best when the problem and its solution are not too far apart, that is, when a few leaps of imagination may bring problem and solution together.

Other techniques useful in finding quick linkages when the gap is not too great between problem and solution are as follows:

- **Work forwards and backwards (forward and back chaining)**
- **Generalize or specialize (expand or partition)**
- **Explore multiple directions based on partial evidence (hill climbing)**
- **Form stable substructures (nearly autonomous subsystems)**
- **Use analogies and metaphors (and prescriptive heuristics)**
- **Follow your emotions (develop a "taste" for the best answers)**
  (Rubinstein, 1975, © 1975 Prentice-Hall, Inc. Englewood Cliffs, N.J. Adapted by permission of the publisher, 1990)

These techniques, where they apply, are particularly satisfying. They induce more *Eureka!* responses than most others. But, as with other prescriptive heuristics, they must be used with judgment. The risk in the *Eureka!* heuristics is that of enthusiastically jumping to the wrong conclusion and driving on to disaster. The safeguards are evident enough—to "sleep on it," or as bridge players do, to "review the bidding" before committing too much.

Another technique that sometimes leads to a quick solutions, especially to communications and sensor problems, is to structure the system so that it resembles the problem to be solved, that is

System structure should resemble functional structure.

Example:

There is considerable interest today in parallel computing as a way of achieving faster computing times than are achievable with conventional (serial) computers. For some problems, parallel computing does very well. For others, it evidently makes little difference. As expected, it does well with problems that are inherently parallel, for example, large-scale meteorological, electromagnetic, and plasma physics phenomena that can be modeled as many small interacting cells. Computational speedups of tens of times have been reported with the Navier–Stokes equations in aeronautics and Maxwell's equations in electromagnetics. On the other hand, parallel computing shows little advantage in problems that are inherently serial, for example, sequential logic and algebra. Software for general-purpose parallel computing has also proved to be much more difficult to build than anticipated. It perhaps is not surprising; the number of interrelations between parallel elements can be very large. Conclusion? Parallel computers will do well for parallel-structured problems, serial computers for their counterpart problems, and hybrids for theirs.

Example:

Multiple physically spaced receivers are a good match to multipath transmissions.

Example:

Until a decade or so ago, attempts to simulate the behavior of the human brain were largely unsuccessful. Computer simulations as a collection of simple input/output signaling devices did not even approximate the observed behavior of as simple an animal as a sea slug. At the same time, it was evident from biological studies that nerves are interconnected in almost unbelievably complex ways, each neuron making hundreds of connections with hundreds of others for no readily discernible reason. More recent measurements, however, indicate that memory is required at each connection point, that such memory is cumulative, and that the accumulated memory triggers or inhibits the response to signals from hundreds of other neurons. Technology has now made possible computer architectures that physically have structures similar to that of the nervous system; the result is similar behavior, albeit at a primitive level.

Example:

A number of pseudorandom codes, fractals, and models of chaos can be generated by recursive equations—equations that feed back on themselves to produce random-appearing results. Simulating these results on either a serial or parallel computer is generally slow. But binary recursive circuits (shift registers with multiple feedback), physically resembling the equations, do well.

Example:

Most local-area communications network architectures match the organization charts of the organization they support. Similarly, highway and street maps generally reflect traffic patterns.

One favored approach to architecting, then, is to structure, redefine, and even change the functions to be performed in such a way that subsequent architecting is simpler and satisfactory system performance is more readily apparent. Clearly, these steps must be taken by the architect and the client working together. The architect will be striving for a clear path for subsequent system design. The client will be looking for an early understanding of the benefits that the end system will produce. In civil architecture, this step is called "programming" (Peña, 1977). For reasonably structured situations, the outlook for acceptable solutions is good.

For more complex situations, a more powerful technique is needed. The previous examples have suggested it—the use of a conceptual model to put functional requirements into a possible system context.

CONSTRUCTING THE MODEL

It is often assumed that the starting point in the development of a complex system is a well-structured list of requirements, an assumption that poses an immediate dilemma. Until the client knows what system might be proposed, it is hard to be specific, or even consistent, about the relative importance of one requirement over another. Quite probably, some requirements will have been missed and some will be extraneous. Depending upon what is proposed, particular requirements might conflict with others, or even be impossible to meet. In a crunch, how important is cost compared to a particular feature or to schedule? What might have seemed a highly desirable requirement may prove to be too expensive in what otherwise was an acceptable proposal. That same requirement, in another proposal might be readily affordable.

In brief, a complete consistent a priori list of requirements for complex systems is virtually impossible to generate independent of some idea of what the end system might be.

Consequently, the de facto initial step in the development of complex systems is for the client and architect to take whatever requirements do exist and construct, through discussion, a rough model of a system that might satisfy most of them. In aerospace and electronics projects, this step is often called "Phase 0." In it, all decisions, whether by client, architect or builder, are necessarily provisional.

The rough model soon produces questions, some unique to that model, that call for client value judgments and architectural analyses. The model may have to be changed or discarded. But, in due course, the requirements and the model converge to produce prioritized requirements and a mutually understood model to satisfy them.

Models have long been a primary form of communication among clients, architects, engineers, and builders. Their importance in human communication is recognized in many fields:

(From psychology) **If the concepts in the mind of one person are very different from those in the mind of the other, there is no common model of the topic and no communication.** (Taylor, 1975)

Or

(From telecommunications) **The best receiver is one that contains within it a model of the transmitter and the transmission channel.** [Parks and Lehan, 1954]

Command and control engineers, in studying the process of issuing and executing orders, came to recognize that effective human communication takes four steps (Jacobs, 1964):

1. translating one's ideas into the other's understanding,
2. embedding those ideas within the other's model,
3. maintaining them with constant reinforcement, and, finally,
4. verifying their validity for further action.

These same steps are required when architect and client exchange their initial ideas of what the system might do and what it might look like. In the process, they build the conceptual model. The perception that the architect conceives a brilliant design independent of any client, sells it intact to a client, and then implements it to wide acclaim is fiction. When attempted, the result most often is either failure or major retrofit. It is equally erroneous to assume that a client—regardless of stature—can edict an immutable set of requirements with the architecting then "left to the students," so to speak. Architecting is an iterative process, of which architectures are a result.

This is not to say that the architect, the client, the builder, and the user will be perfectly satisfied. On the contrary,

No complex system can be optimum to all parties concerned nor all functions optimized.

Architecting is, and always has been, a matter of fit, balance, and compromise of many factors and many interests.

Models come in many forms—sketches, physical-scale models, program descriptions, network maps, computer simulations, sets of equations, spreadsheets, block diagrams, charts, and graphs.

Some models—scale models of buildings, for example—are easily built and understood. By implying a great deal of internal structure, they communicate a wealth of information in a simple aggregated form. A model of a house is quickly understood by all parties, not only in its external shape, but in its likely electrical, plumbing, and air conditioning systems, its living space, and its relationship to its surroundings. Causal models, those that tie causes to effects, like a standard X-Y graph or a 2×2 matrix, can be similarly communicative. [Rowe, 1988].

Other models have proven to be very difficult to build, prime examples being knowledge bases, expert systems, and various engineering processes (Finin, 1986; Parsay and Chignell, 1988); Complex system models can contain an almost overwhelming number of supporting documents, including statements of purpose, general descriptions, top-level specifications, estimates of costs and schedules, and implementation procedures. Generally, however, a kind of natural selection process occurs, and

> **Amid a wash of paper, a small number of documents become critical pivots around which every project's management revolves.**
> (Brooks, 1982)

This heuristic might be considered a kind of Pareto's law for documentation, that is, 20% of the documentation determines 80% of the system results, more or less. The trick is to choose the right 20%.

With all this sometimes conflicting information, how can an acceptable model be generated? In part, by quick brainstorming and using heuristics to discard improbable configurations, ones with just too many misfits. In part, by pursuing a few dissimilar models that will dramatize the effects of different trade-offs, forcing conscious value judgments by the client.

Each dissimilar model represents a different structuring. It explictly partitions the overall context into what is outside and what is inside the system. It specifies the context and structures the required knowledge base. It provides a specific architecture for risk analysis. It allows requirements to be (re)formulated in a practical context. And it helps keep the project's purpose and objectives in mind as the project proceeds.

We should not be surprised, then, that the original political and military needs for a strategic triad are reformulated into proposals for Peacekeepers, Tridents, and B-2 bombers, which thus determine what subset of the original needs will actually be satisfied. Nor, in another context, should we be surprised that needs for computer support in problem solving become reformulated in specialized software languages, themselves models, that determine what in fact will be provided—and what can *not*. It is important to remember the following:

> *In the model-building process, some of the original requirements are, or can be, lost or deferred. If unrecognized in the beginning, the losses can later be the cause of disappointment, frustration, and recovery costs .*

Approval of the model and approval of whatever preliminary design is necessary are key steps in project go-ahead. A specific partitioning into subsystems is implied if not specified. Potential misfits will have been identified if not resolved. Subsequent development will be channeled. *Structure and limits will have been imposed on the program.*

But, for all the attempts to create practical and realistic models:

A model is not reality.

At times, this can be difficult to remember. Mathematical models, so elegant and pristine, can be particularly deceptive. The ancient Greek philosophers believed more in "perfect circles and perfect spheres" than in the "imperfect" objects around them.

A model is an abstraction of what the participants think (and hope) the end system and its environment will look like. What actually results is almost always different.

Next to working on the wrong problem or using the wrong initial assumptions, having the wrong model of the environment is probably the worst initial error. Designers of spacecraft have surprisingly often made such an error by being too accustomed to everyday phenomena close to the surface of the Earth. We engineers are used to 1-g gravity and forget its role in maintaining flames, in providing orientation, in giving us a firm base on which to stand, in providing vertical stress in structures, in holding things together or in place, in making fluids flow, and the like. We are used to a surrounding atmosphere and forget its role in supporting aircraft, in assisting aircraft in maneuvering, in convecting heat to and from objects, in slowing motion, and so on. The *physics* in space and the *physics* on Earth are the same. It is the environment that is different.

It can be very frustrating when something unexpected happens in space (or deep in the ocean or at very high Mach numbers) that, after the event, is so easily explained.

In the early years of space, such experiences generated the notable heuristic:

Before the flight, it's opinion. After the flight, it's obvious.

Example:

Based on luminosities of the moon in its different phases, it was predicted that the surface of the moon would be meters-deep dust. It was not. Solar wind and lunar gravity made the difference.

Example:

Explorer 1 was supposed to be spin stabilized along its long axis for a protracted period. It went into a flat spin within a few revolutions. Drag losses and conservation of momentum had not been properly taken into account.

Example:

Spinning satellites went into apparently irretrievable tumble, something ruled out by rigid-body dynamics. The problem was finally traced to the motion of a small amount of fluids on board.

Example:

Lubricants, both solid and liquid, have behaved very differently from predictions based on ground-level testing. Reflective materials turn opaque. Insulators turn into conductors and vice versa. Some materials completely disintegrate. None of these were predicted, even from experiments in the best of thermal vacuum chambers on Earth.

Radiation, ionized atoms, and hypervelocity particles in the near vacuum of space are the probable causes.

Example:

Spacecraft operators became concerned that satellites drifting in near-synchronous orbit could collide. But even at drift rates as slow as two degrees per year, they will miss by 1000 ft.

Example:

In space, to catch up, slow down.

Example:

In or on any space object of significant size, there is no such thing as zero gravity. Self-gravity of a space station caused by its own mass exceeds a few micro-g's throughout the station except for a few cubic meters near the center of gravity of the station.

Example:

The human experience of flying around in the atmosphere can be misleading in considering the practicality of recovery and repair of satellites traveling in orbits differing in altitude and inclination from that of the repair vehicle.

Example:

Astronauts have had astonishing experiences in trying to reduce the tumble of Solar Max, to take a shower, or to identify "bright objects in formation" (accompanying debris).

One does not have to go into space to be in unexplored territory. The early days of aircraft, computers, handheld calculators, and PCs are rife with similar examples. Between new technologies and complexity, we can count on many more.

System models consequently have often been in serious error in the past. In man–machine systems, the model of the user has been wrong and the machine made unfriendly. In aerospace launch vehicles, the economics has been wrong, leading to unrealistic pricing, distorted user incentives, and flawed operations. In weapon systems, the combat model has been wrong, leading to unexpectedly simple countermeasures by the opponent. In defense communications, the command and control procedures have been wrong, leading to avoidable operational tragedies.

Even the simplest models can be wrong. A good example from signal processing is shown in Figure 3–1. (Kay and Marple, 1981)

The true spectrum of a received signal is shown in the upper left-hand corner. It consists of three sine waves and a humped continuous spectrum. All the other spectra on the figure are what different receiving systems *thought* the spectrum was, depending on the model (or algorithm) that the receiver used. For our purposes here, the specific algorithms are not of interest, just that they

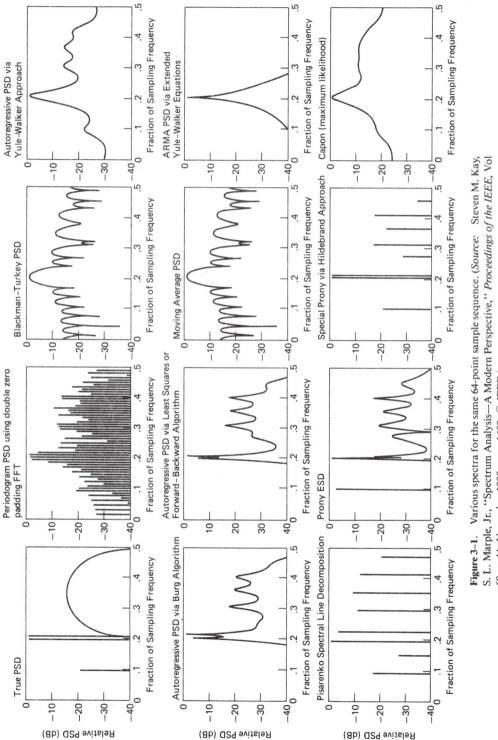

Figure 3-1. Various spectra for the same 64-point sample sequence. (*Source:* Steven M. Kay, S. L. Marple, Jr., "Spectrum Analysis—A Modern Perspective," *Proceedings of the IEEE,* Vol 69, p. 11, November 1989, page 1409. © IEEE.)

61

obviously did not reproduce by wide margins what was actually received. Their internal models clearly did not represent reality.

But the most dramatic disconnect of a model with reality might be called *the mission that never was.* Despite the best efforts of clients, architects, and builders, missions that were assumed to be the most important and valuable—and around which the system was designed and built—proved to be ephemeral. The systems that are most susceptible, obviously, are those entering new and unexplored markets and mission areas: satellites, personal computers, supersonic aircraft, information nets, high-tech defense systems, and smart systems. Each of these in recent times has missed the mark, which is dismaying, but not surprising.

And not always bad—because, at times, a quite different mission appears, for which, with a little luck, the new system proves to be a great success. Well, maybe not with just a little luck. Maybe also with systems whose underlying architecture was strong enough to carry the new load with a few modifications here and there. Among them: the Macintosh™, the Hewlett-Packard hand-held calculator, the ARPANET, the Delta launch vehicle, several military aircraft, air-dropped sensors, and the surgical applications of modest-powered lasers.

What is the lesson? New architectures for new missions will encounter new environments, new risks, and/or new threats. Architecting for new missions and markets, by definition, is exploring the unknown. But a few precautions can be taken.

In new missions and markets, expect the unexpected.

So, do not overrefine a new design for a new mission. Try to keep some options. In computer and software terminology, design an "open architecture," with key "hooks" that permit extensions with the minimum internal disruption. In commercial aircraft, make provisions ("scars") for stretching or shortening the fuselage, extending the wings, or replacing the engines. In launch vehicles, do not design out strap-ons or added stages. In networks, provide entry points and order wires. In built-in computers, make provisions for complete reprogramming. Provide for relatively easy replacement of any and all parts and elements. One never knows.

Civil architects sometimes put it this way:

Design the structure with good "bones."

which an anthropologist might illustrate by using the now erect, once horizontal, human skeleton.

And, whenever possible, explore the unknown by simulation and prototyping.

EXPLORING BY SIMULATION

Simulating is substituting for, or imitating, reality. If a system has been built, simulation provides it with an artificial environment for purposes of test and evaluation. If part of a system has been built, simulation acts like the missing parts to emulate overall system testing. If nothing has been built, simulation—usually on a computer—can describe major features of the system, for example, its performance in its environment, its costs, its operational characteristics, and the like.

Computer simulation, in effect, is a model of the system model, a model with its own idiosyncracies. The computer may have to operate much more slowly than real time, thereby distorting time-dependent effects and interactions. Or it may digitize waveforms, adding otherwise non-existent noise to the system. But these shortcomings notwithstanding, computer simulation is now widely used and often trusted more than the tried-and-true analog simulators, for example, wind tunnels, shake tables, and simulated field exercises. But the debate over which simulator—computer or physical test facility—most closely resembles reality is by no means over. The conservative architect usually uses some of both. Harry Hillaker, the architect of the F-16 fighter aircraft, preferred the use of wind tunnels, but used computer models to narrow down the number of expensive tests. Spacecraft engineers use models that certifiably mimic selected *parts* of reality, accounting for the rest by use of system hardware and software, physical laws, and the like.

The major advantage of computer simulation is low cost, which means that many more "what if" (sensitivity analysis) questions can be asked and answered than ever before. The chances of finding major design errors are increased accordingly, from the first conceptual design through the analysis of operational failures. A later section of the book focuses on testing, diagnostics, certification, and evaluation, but a few key points need to be made here.

The first point is the value of even partial simulation in verifying the accuracy of the system model, an importance driven home when unexpected system failures occur during test or operation. The first question usually asked is, what was the cause? A system malfunction? A failure of the model (on which the system was based) to predict the failure under the imposed stress? Or a stress exceeding the design limits? In other words, was it the system or the model that was at fault? Answering questions like these can be difficult and contentious. Few clients or managers will be satisfied until the failure can be exactly repeated or credibly simulated.

The second point has to do with the determination of the margin of safety for a system that cannot be fully tested before going into operation. The lack of testing can come about for many reasons. The system can be too valuable to test to the breaking point. Sufficiently large and instrumented facilities may not be available. Complete simultaneous simulation of all parts of the environment may not be possible, a situation common for space systems. In such cases, the recourse is to test within safe limits and then to use the model to extrapolate to the assumed system limits. Performance at the limits may be quite different from that in the normal range due to fatigue, yielding of materials, and other nonlinear phenomena. The design of partial simulation, and the conclusions drawn from it, must take such behavior into account.

Ideally, system-model verification should be accomplished *before* crises develop, that is, simulation testing should precede operational reality. Otherwise, the model will be of limited utility in system test, system certification, operations, failure analysis, and system recovery.

The third point is the essentiality of continuously verifying the design by analysis, simulation and testing to maintain control of the implementation of the system (Jacobs, 1964). The model, as we have seen, represents an agreement on system function and form. As soon as the system begins to deviate from the model, some form of action needs to be taken. If none is taken, the system design will drift, and before long, control of it will have been lost. Whether the model or the system is changed to bring model and system together is less important than that the action is clear and understood by all parties. The drift can be quite subtle. Hidden software routines, incompletely described internal interfaces, substitution of materials and processes, rewritten operational procedures, undocumented "hooks" and "scars," poor configuration control, and changes in critical personnel are common causes of trouble. Fairly regular simulations and tests are cost-effective—if sometimes tardy—methods of assuring discipline and design control.

In short, like many other things in systems architecting, modeling and simulation must fit each other. Otherwise, a system, particularly a new one, may be built with undetermined performance, cost, and schedule.

EXPLORING BY PROTOTYPING

> Levity should be a prime concern for aeronautical engineers.—Peter Lissaman as quoted by J. D. Burke (1980)

> Be quick, be quiet, be on time. If you can't do it with brainpower, you can't do it with manpower—overtime. (Johnson, 1985)

Prototyping is certainly one of the most popular ways of validating the feasibilty of a new concept. In its unadulterated form, prototyping focuses on a clearly stated unchanging goal and uses the simplest available means to achieve it (J. D. Burke, 1980, describing Paul MacCready's Gossamer Condor project). Its popularity among architects, engineers, and builders is understandable. Its "fly-before-buy" approach has been adopted by almost all government mission agencies—NACA, NASA, DARPA, the military services, and others—by the Congress, and by industry.

In a typical example of prototyping, the YF-16 predecessor to the General Dynamics F-16 fighter, there was only a minimal Request for a Proposal, no MILSPEC, no Statement of Work, no data requirement, no design reviews, and a hands-off nonadversarial "skunk works" management with full system program office authority [Hillaker, 1989]. Prototyping was the basis for the Lockheed U-2 and the Blackbird series of surveillance aircraft (Johnson, 1985), the NASA/JPL Goldstone 70-meter antenna, the Apple™ family of personal computers, the IBM 360 operating software, and the first Hughes synchronous satellites. Prototyping is the essence of the Defense Advance Research Projects Agency (DARPA) charter. Without exception, the architects not only are enthusiastic about, but they express great enjoyment and personal satisfaction in, working in this mode.

The basic justification for prototyping is risk reduction. A decision to prototype, therefore, is a decision that its benefits outweigh its costs.

Benefits	Costs
Risk reduction for new missions	Incomplete design
Risk reduction for new concepts	Increased early costs
Validity of assumptions and priorities	Delays full production
Confidence building	Nonstandard procurement
Demonstration to clients and markets	Delays full operation

A key question in designing a prototype is the nature of the risk itself. Is the risk one of technical feasibility? Of performance limits? Of production uncertainties? Of cost overruns? Of operational utility? Does the risk involve the whole system or only parts of it?

The right prototype clearly depends upon what the risks are. Prototypes aimed at technical risk may be as simple as electronic breadboards and computer simulations. Those aimed at operational uncertainties may be as complete as the final system. Either overbuilding or underbuilding can be expensive.

By definition, a prototype is an incomplete system, constrained by its very design. Thus, there is not only the question of what to build, but what will be left out. Though some problems can be put off to the future, ignoring others can be fatal. But if too many problems are addressed in the prototype, the resultant complexity may so delay obtaining results that the mission or market is missed—the competition or the opponent takes over.

Because formal controls are usually omitted in prototyping (see the previous F-16 example), unless care is taken along the way, the original objective—the building of an operational system—can be lost in the enthusiasm of building the prototype. Seemingly minor decisions, interface modifications, process innovations, and configuration changes can go undocumented with the consequences not felt until after full-scale production starts.

Prototype design, therefore, is a critical task of the systems architect.

But prototyping costs money and time. A balance is required. An important determinant in this balance is the ratio of the costs of the prototype to the anticipated costs of production and operation. If the ratio is small, as with consumer products or mass-produced aircraft, prototyping usually pays. As the costs become comparable, as with small-lot spacecraft, the net value of prototyping declines rapidly. The balance to be sought by the architect in the design of the prototype is the greatest risk reduction at the least cost in money and time. Given the performance and cost risks inherent in prototyping, achieving a satisfactory balance can be difficult. Horror studies abound of order-of-magnitude cost overruns, poorly engineered and unreliable prototypes, and prototypes that proved impossible to convert to producible systems.

The architect's interest in the prototype by no means ends with the design of the prototype itself. Maintaining the integrity of the original concept, understanding the later consequences of prototype lessons learned, and modifying the prototype as necessary are essential from the time the prototype is conceived until the end of its useful life.

The prototype's useful life is itself an important architectural decision. It is tempting, after a prototype's initial successes and after the expenditure of considerable time and money, to want to use the prototype for operational purposes. Unless architected and built with that in mind, deciding to do so late in the game incurs potentially dangerous risks. As mentioned before, a prototype is incomplete in many ways—technically, managerially, and in the process by which it was built and tested. Attempting to determine margins of safety, for example, may involve testing the prototype well beyond intended operational conditions. Repeated testing in an effort to find solutions to problems may literally have worn out some components. Worse yet, the testing may have been ad hoc and poorly documented. Completing the design in order to go operational can involve difficult and expensive retrofits.

To be useful operationally, the prototype must be an almost complete system. But, additionally, it must not have been subjected to excessive, uncontrolled, or undocumented conditions or tests. In a sense, an "operational prototype" is a contradiction in terms in that the freedom to experiment, characteristic of prototyping, must be sharply constrained.

But, when "prototypes" cost hundreds of millions of dollars, as is the case for some NASA and DOD satellites, it is hard to argue with the program directors who want at least "a residual operational capability" at the end of the prototyping phase. The dilemma, of course, is that such prototypes are almost as expensive as a full system, require the same kind of management, and go directly counter to the "low-cost free-and-easy skunk works" style of prototyping that is so appealing to its practitioners.

As a purely practical matter, near-operational prototypes are almost as difficult to sell and manage as an all-up system. Nonetheless, they are favored by NASA, whose operational experience shows them to be as successful as later fully operational systems when the proper precautions are taken. They have also proven useful in retaining client confidence during production startup and in providing credible demonstrations of system performance for prospective customers.

The usual approach, nonetheless, has been to restrict the use of heavily tested prototypes to simulation, failure analysis, and training.

STRATEGIC CHOICES BY THE CLIENT

Very early in the development of the model, the client and the architect are likely to be confronted with basic *strategic* architectural choices that only the client can, or should, make. Depending on the choices, the architecture can take very different forms. Some typical value-laden choices are

Should the system be single-purpose or multipurpose?

Should the system be expendable or reusable?

Should the system be manned or automated or some of both?

Single Purpose or Multipurpose

A single-purpose system can be more tailored and efficient for its specified purpose or mission. Right or wrong, the client often feels that a single-purpose system results in more control over the design and operation of the end system. But it can also be too expensive for only one purpose, which calls for cost sharing with other missions. Or by overspecialization, it can be too vulnerable, which calls for alternate or backup modes elsewhere. A multipurpose system usually costs more initially and less overall. It can have a larger total resource base and be more powerful, flexible, and resistant to stress. But it also has to satisfy more users; resolution of their conflicting needs can be difficult.

The choice, therefore, becomes a value judgment—the province of the client. Some of the choices that are particularly important in aerospace and electronics are shown in the following examples.

Example:

Between multimission upper stages and propulsion integral to each spacecraft. The choice has usually been for multimission stages if more than 20 total flights are anticipated of missions that have only a few flights each.

Example:

Between single-purpose and multipurpose spacecraft, aircraft, and ships. Few of these craft have been successful at accommodating more than two or three missions.

Example:

Between a single shared communications network and dedicated networks for each user group, for example, intelligence, command and control, logistics, etc. A useful solution here, where the users need full resources on demand but only sporadically, is a shared system, perhaps with special-purpose additions, which is so controlled that the demands of each user group are satisfied with minimal penalty. A typical penalty is a short delay, the acceptable length of which is a key parameter in system design.

Expendable or Reusable

Another value judgment is between expendable and reusable systems, for example, expendable or reusable launch vehicles, satellites, container systems and consumer products. The key technical parameter is usage. If system usage is low, as it has been in most space launch systems, expendables are less costly initially, in operation and in total. They pose the least cost risk since their nature is "pay as you go, order when needed." They are also more resilient to failure; the loss of one unit has less of an effect on the total operation than the loss of a reusable unit. But if system usage is high, as in most computer and communications systems, reusables are superior, though initial cost and the investment at risk during each use are high. Reusable systems, therefore, have to have more reliable components if total costs of losses are to be reasonable. Maintenance and refurbishment costs often dominate the budget. The key parameter for heavily used systems is, therefore, replacement rate, as illustrated in high-orbit service satellites. They are few in number, recovery is expensive, and they become obsolete, technically and economically, before they fail. Hence, they are replaced rather than refurbished at end of life. On the other hand, low-orbit astronomical research satellites, like their Earthbound counterparts, are intended for scheduled reinstrumentation and possible recovery. They more nearly resemble base facilities in their lifetimes, modification schedules, and customer base than they do expendable payloads.

The choice between expendable and reusable systems is relatively easy for very low and very high usage. The tough choices are for those of moderate use in an uncertain market, for example, heavy lift space launchers.

Manned or Automated

The choice between manned or automated systems can be difficult, contentious, and costly because of the inherent uncertainties in future technology and human acceptance.

Example:

What should be the degree of automation of a manufacturing line?

Example:

How much automation should there be in the cockpit of a passenger airliner?

Example:

Should outer space be explored by manned or automated spacecraft? How important is a permanent manned presence in space for purposes of national sovereignty, prestige, defense, science, and technology?

In principle, the answers should be based on the best features, and should minimize the worst, of both man and machine. From a technical point of view, the questions are not whether systems include people, but why, how, and where? Man is unquestionably exploring space, but most of the exploration is with instruments on the ground or sent into space. And people are engaged in manufacturing, but in partnership with increasingly sophisticated machines. As painful experience has shown, the answers are not simple. People and their emotions are involved. To complicate the issue, technology itself is advancing, continually changing the nature of the questions.

Clearly, a major factor in any decision concerning automation is sociopolitical, involving as it does not only people directly involved in building and operating the system, but also those who support it with resources, tax dollars, justifications, and enthusiasms and those that resist it with comparable vigor. It is an unfortunate fact that attempts to implement automation in manufacturing plants are unsuccessful 50% to 75% of the time. Parenthetically, of the failures, the great majority are traceable to human resource and management practices that focus on what is to be done but not how (Majchrzak, 1988).

In some cases, the choice is moot. The man or the machine is simply incapable of doing certain tasks. Human response times may be too short to be able to control certain events. Man operates best within a narrow work-load regime; too much or too little work degrades performance. Man's span of attention and ability to handle complexity are limited. Despite these known human limitations, the client may still demand "man in the loop." The choice is understandable. Machines, too, are limited. New machines can behave in unpredicted ways. And if the machines are complex enough, there is no known way to keep them operating except by manned intervention and repair; but how complex is "complex enough"?

All in all, the choice between manned and automated systems is one on which the client, architect, builder, and user have to reach agreement and understanding very early. Either approach can encounter potential obstacles. But only the client can judge which path, with which potential problems is acceptable.

Making the Strategic Choices

Looking back over these typical strategic choices, we can see that all have much in common.

First, none of the choices is an absolute. All are matters of degree. Fit, balance, and compromise can come into play. Provisions can be made to accommodate changes in applications, technology, economics, and human resource imperatives.

Second, the appropriate choices depend on more than facts and figures. They depend, too, on the client's preferences, past experience, and willingness to take risks. For example, a military client concerned about system control might prefer centralization. An optimistic client might overestimate system usage and prefer reusable systems. A client faced with potential labor unrest might hold back on the wholesale introduction of automation. Client judgments can—and should—push the answers to one side or the other of the "technical optimum."

Third, all these choices call for the use of common sense.

THREATS, NICHES, AND TRAPS

An important responsibility of the architect is to warn the client of potential threats to the system. One of the earliest pitfalls is a mission niche too easily closed by overlapping potentially competing systems.

This threat is most evident for families or product lines with capabilities "stepped" from smallest to greatest. In the computer business, such a family might span the range from consumer PCs to supercomputers, for example, the IBM family. In transportation, they are fleets of trucks, buses, airliners, and space launch vehicles. In the military services, they are naval fleets, combat aircraft, and armored units.

An *intermediate* system is one whose capabilities lie between, and may be overlapped by, two adjacent members of such families. If the overlaps are minor or if extending the overlaps is impractical, then a useful mission niche might exist.

On the other hand, if the adjacent systems' overlaps can be extended, or if a combination of the other systems can diminish the utility of their "missing" capabilities, the overlapped intermediate system will be suppressed. In marketing terms, the intermediate system lacks sufficient "differentiation" to be successful. In military terms, the intermediate system is likely to be defeated by a combination of enemy systems.

Example:

Navies of the world are well acquainted with failed intermediate ships. A recent example was the pocket battleship, a ship better armed than a cruiser and faster than a battleship. Unfortunately, it was also slower than a cruiser and lesser armed than a battleship. In battle, it lost to a combination of fast cruisers that could trap it until slower ships (aircraft carriers, battleships, and submarines) could overwhelm it.

Example:

Computers with combinations of processing power and memory that are readily achieved by networking larger computers with inexpensive smaller ones.

Example:

Ramjets caught between conventional jets and rockets that overlap ramjet performance at its lower and upper airspeed limits.

Example:

The Northrop F5-G (subsequently, the F-20) caught between the equivalent of an upgraded F-5 (the Mirage 2000) and a downrated F-16 whose purchase was encouraged by national policy.

The key architectural question is, how wide is the gap between adjacent systems and can it be closed easily by them? A narrow closable gap is a trap. A wide unfillable gap is a potentially valuable niche. Aerospace, computer, and communications experience would seem to indicate that if the performance ratio between adjacent systems is roughly an order of magnitude (a factor of 2 to 3), then any system in between is an intermediate one and a probable trap.

Example:

Trucks come in sizes of $\frac{1}{4}$, $\frac{1}{2}$, 1, 2.5, 5, 10, and 20 tons with few in between.

Example:

Communications baseband channels are $48/n$ kHz wide, where n is 1, 2, 3, 6, 10, 20, etc.

Example:

To be competitive and reasonably long-lived in the marketplace, a low-end personal computer should cost half as much for the same capability as its next higher competitor.

Example:

A larger space launch vehicle than the Shuttle should lift about twice the weight. A factor of somewhat over 2 would permit lifting twice as many of the same payloads as the Shuttle; a factor of 1.9 would not.

Example:

In parallel computing, the utility of progressively larger parallelism probably requires at least doubling if not quadrupling the previous structure.

Example:

Random-access memory comes in factors of 2 or greater.

If these examples are typical, and if the existing separation was a factor of 2, the conclusion might be that even being exactly in the middle (i.e., at the square root of 2, or at a 40% or less differentiation in capabilities) would be questionable. A 10% separation would be a clear trap, but a separation factor of 4 could open up a niche. So, as a warning:

Watch out for intermediate systems. They may lead to traps instead of useful mission niches.

SUMMARY

Modeling is a process of communication between client, architect, and builder. It gives initial form to the functions the system will be called upon to perform. The model itself is an essential tool of the architect. But the model is *not* reality. Reality must be explored and anticipated through simulation, testing, and prototyping, all of which are of vital interest to the architect. It is the architect's responsibility to point out the importance to system success of certain early choices (e.g., breadth of purpose, reusability, automation, and market niche size) in the interest of well-informed decisions by the client.

RECOMMENDED READING

BROOKS, F. P., JR. (April 1987). "No Silver Bullet, Essence and Accidents of Software Engineering." In *Computer* 20, 4, 10–19. This is a followup to Brooks' *Mythical Man-Month* referenced earlier. It states that the hard part of building software is the specification, design, and testing of the conceptual construct, that is, the concepts that underlie the chosen model or architecture. Problems are complexity, conformity, changeability, and invisibility. In other words, the difficult thing is deciding what one wants to say, not saying it. Expert systems, automatic programming, graphical programming, and program verification are discussed. It reiterates earlier themes that great designs come from great designers. It is generally not too optimistic (there are no silver bullets) about massive breakthroughs, but is great reading, nonetheless.

FININ, T. W. (1986). "Interactive Classification: A Technique for Acquiring and Maintaining Knowledge Bases." *Proceedings of the IEEE,* 74, 10, 1414–20. This is a good example of one of the most difficult of expert-system and software problems: the architecture, control, maintenance, and updating of knowledge bases. The core of the problem is how to model (partition, characterize, etc.) knowledge itself.

FLOOD, R. L., and E. R. CARSON. (1988). *Dealing with Complexity.* New York: Plenum. See Chapters Three and Nine. It gives examples of diagrammatic models of processes in various applications.

JACOBS, J. F. (1964). *Design Approach for Command and Control.* The MITRE Corporation SR-102. This is a classic in the theory of designing command and control systems. It broadens the concept of common models to embedding, maintaining, and verifying the transferred concepts. It discusses design chains and their level-to-level concept communications problems. It states an important heuristic: **Choosing the appropriate level of aggregation for dealing with the design of systems is critical in the design approach.** It observes that "computer-aided man is essentially different from man aided by other devices . . . not so much in the sorts of things he can do but in his capacity to do certain things more quickly." It gives a good discussion of the concept and orientation of the designer (architect) in a constantly modifying system.

JOHNSON, C. L., with Maggie Smith. (1985). *Kelly.* Washington, DC: Smithsonian Institution Press. This is the autobiography of "Kelly" Johnson, the architect and director of the Lockheed Blackbird aircraft program. See especially Chapter 16 and his 14 basic operating rules for successful "skunk works" projects.

PARSAYE, K., and MARK H. CHIGNELL. (1988). *Expert Systems for Experts.* New York: Wiley. See Chapters 4 and 5, pp. 119–210. A special problem for expert systems is how to model *knowledge,* that is, how to describe its elements, its organization, and input/output.

PEÑA, WILLIAM. (1977). *Problem Seeking, An Architectural Programming Primer.* New York: Cahners Books. The book addresses the principles and techniques of architecting that precede design (called "programming" by Peña), which is roughly equivalent to problem definition. It contains five steps: (1) establish goals, (2) collect and analyze facts, (3) uncover and test concepts, (4) determine needs, and (5) state the problem. And it concerns four major considerations: function, form, economy, and time. The book emphasizes client–architect relationship and the iterative nature of seeking the (real) problem for the designers to solve.

RUBINSTEIN, Moshe F. (1975). *Patterns of Problem Solving.* Englewood Cliffs, NJ: Prentice Hall. This is a very readable text from a well-known UCLA course on solving intellectual problems to aid the human brain (with its limitations and constraining learned material). It gives a good discussion on modeling, with particular emphasis that a model is not the real world. It notes the importance of changing problem perspective, symbols, etc., to reach a solution.

TAYLOR, R. W. (June 1975). "Relation of Interactive Computing to Computer Science." *IEEE Proceedings,* 63, 6, 843–46. Psychology of communications using models.

TO BROWSE, DEPENDING ON INTERESTS

KAY, STEVEN M., and S.L. MARPLE, JR. (November 1981). "Spectrum Analysis—A Modern Perspective." *Proceedings of the IEEE,* 69, 11, 1380–1418. The source for Figure 3-1, it is a summary of the modern techniques for spectrum analysis of discrete time series.

MAJCHRZAK, ANN. (1988). *The Human Side of Factory Automation.* San Francisco: Jossey-Bass. The book gives managerial and human resource strategies for making automation succeed.

TANIK, MURAT M., and R. T. YEH, (eds.). "Rapid Prototyping in Software Development." *Computer,* 22, 5, 9–10. (May 1989). This is a special issue on rapid prototyping in software development, software evolution, object-oriented data-base management, flight research, and programmable networks.

TAUSWORTHE, R. C. (1976). *Simple Intuitive Models of Programming,* JPL Deep Space Network Progress Report 42-33. This report presents a set of simplified intuitive and heuristic models of software-program productivity, for example, (1) organize personnel tasks to minimize the time individuals spend interfacing, (2) readability (use structured programming), and (3) development (try to determine which nodes are most error-prone). This is an interesting start on the use of heuristics to minimize the search for mathematical models of the process of programming.

WALLICH, P. (June 1984). "The engineer's job: It moves Toward Abstraction." *IEEE Spectrum* **21**, 6, 32–37. This is a commentary on the continuing trend of engineering to higher-level conceptual work, automated modeling, analysis, and knowledge-based systems, that is, architecting. It traces this trend to the 1920s and the subsequent development of computers. It notes the increasing use of engineering to develop tools and even tools to develop tools.

4
THE ARCHITECT'S KIT
OF TOOLS

Chapter 3 focused on the *what* of the model, its general form and functions. This chapter focuses on the *how*, its structuring by the architect. In the *what* phase, the need was for value judgments, so the client made the key decisions. In the *how* phase, the need is for professional expertise, for which the client turns to the architect. This chapter, therefore, gets down to the nuts and bolts of architecting, the architect's kit of tools for constructing a more detailed system model. It is the next step toward reality. Later chapters focus on the *how well*—the quality of its implementation.

But, first, it may be helpful to clarify some terms.

- The "system" is what is built.
- The "model" is a description of the system to be built.
- The "system architecture" is the structure of the system.
- The "overall architecture" includes the structure not only of the system, but of its functions, the environment within which it will live, and the process by which it will be built and operated.

The systems architect is concerned with the overall architecture, not just the system architecture, and not just the model.

The model is a tool, essential but not all inclusive.

Three different and complementary processes are involved in the construction of the model. The first is the aggregation of closely related functions.

The second is the partitioning, or reduction, of the model into its parts. These first processes are closely coupled during concept development. The third is the fitting, or integration, of components and subsystems together into a functioning system. All three make use of many of the same heuristics. Briefly, restating some of them from earlier chapters:

- Fit the form to the function.
- Aggregate functions into a few—but not too few—groups.
- Partition into autonomous—but not too autonomous—elements.
- Whenever possible, simplify.
- The name of the game is fit, balance, and compromise.

It is possible, of course, to begin with a collection of parts and fit them together to make a system—the "bottom-up approach." For a modest evolution from an existing system with an established architecture, the chances are good that a predicted system improvement can be realized. If any part is greatly different from its predecessor, however, a rearchitecting will probably be required for the system to succeed. Nuclear reactors are not simply substituted for diesel engines in a submarine, nor jet engines for propellor engines on an aircraft, nor satellites added to a communications network without major changes throughout the systems.

Indeed, if a new element is incorporated in an older system without considering the overall architecture, the results to the system as a whole can even be negative. In the jargon of the trade, "It was a great idea, but it didn't work out as a system." Any change in a system carries with it costs that must be counted against the benefits. Typical costs are those for integration, for modifications of other elements, diminution of other functional capabilities, and collateral effects on support systems such as manufacturing, logistics, and maintenance. These changes may, in turn, affect system reliability, survivability, and lifetime.

Therefore, for new or heavily modified systems, the preferred approach for complex systems has become "top-down,"—partitioning and refining until the elements and interfaces become clear. A frequent goal in this approach is elements sufficiently independent of each other that they can be designed and developed separately. They can be represented by blocks on a block diagram. They can be "modularized."

The top-down approach differs from pure partitioning, or reductionism, in an important respect. Pure partitioning to the lowest level followed by pure integration to the system level can result in omitting real-world linkages and interfaces—of which more later. The top-down approach integrates each level after each partitioning, level by level.

At each level, all interfaces must fit. Each level, as a whole and not as separate parts, drives the elements of the next lower level. And all levels work together to produce the completed model.

In theory, this is an orderly disciplined approach.

In practice, design problems arise that may require modifications of the model. "Design drivers" will appear that will force the design down particular paths with consequences elsewhere in the model. Hence, the architectural decision process will not be as orderly as a pure level-to-level approach would suggest. The skilled architect will anticipate the design drivers, will work to resolve their difficulties as early as possible, and will focus on the likely interface misfits that may result. In the meantime, other elements that may be impacted by the design drivers cannot be designed without the risk of major internal change.

This situation is common in systems constrained by power, size, and weight.

Example:

Such a system so constrained is a satellite whose computer elements are impacted by design drivers in other system elements. As other elements confront intractable hardware problems, the inclinations are to solve them within the computer's software. But the computers have had to be sized in memory, processor capability, size, and weight themselves. The results have often been not only major software redesign, but drastic changes in the computer hardware late in the program and a rearchitecting of the model as a whole.

Using the heuristic of relatively autonomous elements does create a special class of system problem—a potential lack of visibility into the interiors of the elements. The developers of each element, understandably, will endeavor to solve their own problems, even at the expense of internal complexity. Additional internal functions, routines, and attributes may be incorporated, which may be hidden from view at the interfaces and at the system level. Autonomy does involve risks. The top-level model might not reflect internal reality. System reliability, survivability, and performance limits may depart significantly from what might have been expected. Reducing these risks is a management problem. Management must assure sufficient visibility for the architect into all elements, sufficient understanding by all element developers of the overall system, and sufficiently detailed models to track the progress of design drivers in detail.

And this calls for refining an earlier heuristic:

The efficient architect, using contextual sense, continually looks for the likely misfits and redesigns the architecture so as to eliminate or minimize them.

The architect, it is apparent, is and must be continuously on the job. In the real world of architecting, the functions, the model, the system architecture, and the overall architecture all continue to change as the system develops.

CONSTRUCTING THE MODEL: THE BUILDING BLOCKS

Fortunately for the systems architect, most models do not have to be built from scratch. They can be built in large part using other existing models—subsystem models, software programs, expert systems, algorithms, laws, theorems, axioms, equations, figures of merit, graphs, correlations, and heuristics. All are useful. All are forms of prepackaged knowledge that the architect can fit together to form elements of the overall architecture.

An integrated body of prepackaged knowledge is of enormous value. Indeed, it is true wealth.

As Peter Drucker noted at the 1988 University of Southern California Lord Lecture:

Today, wealth is no longer best defined as ownership of land, goods, capital or labor. It is knowledge and knowing how to use it.

His most telling example is the history of technology transfer from the United States to Japan to Korea, the last having become far wealthier far sooner than any other wealth transfer could explain. This lesson has not been lost on the other developing (and developed) nations. Nor should the value of the architect's knowledge base be lost on the architect! So, build, maintain, and safeguard it!

A well-understood personalized collection of applicable models is vital in constructing the system model, in assessing project progress, designing test programs, certifying performance, and analyzing anomalies and failures. Nadler (1981) lists and categorizes literally hundreds of widely applicable design techniques and models.

The advent of easily used personal computers networked into institutional mainframes has resulted in a rapid development of customized and commercial models in many fields. System houses have begun constructing *supermodels* by tying together other models to solve large-scale multidisciplinary problems, for example, solid rocket internal dynamics. There clearly are many choices. Perhaps too many. It can be difficult to get started.

Fortunately, systems can be modeled in more than one way. A first approach may lead to an increasingly more complex model. But, with client concurrence, the starting point can be changed. Performance can be characterized in different terms. Assumptions can be restated. System performance under extreme conditions can be permitted which under normal conditions might be less than desired, for example, less precise, less convenient, or less cost-effective. But the result may be a much simplified model and system. As the KISS heuristic suggests, the simplest model that will do a satisfactory job is probably the best one.

The most familiar system model is probably the block diagram, which partitions the system and defines the principal interfaces. Block diagrams are so familiar to engineers and architects—so familiar that they are like graphical languages—that they need little discussion here. They work best for hierarchical (tree) and sequential (series of input–output) systems describable in two dimensions. They work less well if the relationships between the elements are multiple and complex.

A quite different system model is a spreadsheet, now made much more powerful by computers, but not yet too familiar to the architect. In essence, a spreadsheet is a two- or three-dimensional table with parameters listed down the vertical and across the horizontal axes. The influence of any parameter on another is specified (e.g., by equation, algorithm, correlation) and stored in the computer. Thus, when any one parameter is changed, all the interactions of it with others (and with still others in turn) are computed and the whole table changes. Spreadsheets with tens of parameters are not unusual. They have been used for economics and business administration for decades, though with calculations laboriously done by hand until recently. Their applicability to complex systems, particularly in modeling concurrent or parallel events, is just being recognized.

A third kind of system model is the rule-based model (e.g., a sequential set of "if . . . then" statements), particularly applicable for modeling hierarchical and branching processes. Logic trees, failure-mode-effects analyses, piecewise calculations, control-system design, and integrated-circuit certification are examples. Rule-based models are based on stimulus-response (input–output) relationships. They are inherently deterministic and are best suited to systems having complete well-specified sets of rules. As might be expected, they do less well in inherently ill-structured situations, a prime example being processes requiring human creativity and imagination.

Although a number of attempts have been made, success has been limited in applying deterministic models to human processes such as architecting, designing, and engineering. Some architects, like F. P. Brooks of software fame, have virtually given up on rule-based process models for software engineering. And, in truth, computers have not yet done too well in designing software. The incentive is certainly there—software design is still highly manpower-intensive and hence difficult to schedule or cost. Nor have rule-based (expert) systems done too well in emulating human experts except in very narrow domains (Parsay and Chignell, 1988). Rule-based models, in other words, have not done too well in helping us build other models. It is worth a short diversion to speculate why this might be so.

One of the distinguishing characteristics of architecting, designing, and engineering of complex systems is that given the same starting point, different professionals will come up with different system designs. Part of the reason is subjective judgments on risks, relative priorities, the criticality of certain assumptions, public acceptance, and market timing. Another part is differences in the *order* in which different architects introduce assumptions, impose constraints, and make design choices. (We are all familiar with the differences between buildings that are designed exterior first or interior first.) Rule-based models, on the other hand, given the same starting point, *must,* unless an error or failure occurred, come up with the same answers every time. Perhaps, then, creative human processes need to be partitioned such that some steps in the process are carried out by the experts and others by rule-based computer aids.

A fourth kind of system model is language. Linguists have long known that language is patterned after thought and that thought is dependent upon one's model of the world. Thus, languages are based on internal models. Different languages deal with different "worlds." We usually think of languages in the ethnic sense. But there are many others. It is a good guess that most professionals know at least a half dozen languages. There are mathematical languages of great power (algebra, calculus, binary logic, predicate calculus) and software languages (from FORTRAN to SMALLTALK) of great specificity. We are now seeing the proliferation of wordless graphical languages as well. Street signs are a common example, and computer icons are another. And, of course, there are the jargons of the trade—computerese, governmentese, and alphabet soup.

The choice of language, therefore, is a choice of a model, complete with its opportunities for creativity, its internal assumptions, and its constraints. Languages, among people who speak them, provide rapid transfer of knowledge, implied consent with the underlying connectives, and agreement on stated conclusions. Well, this is almost the case. Languages can also be ambiguous, and some are deliberately so. They can be misleading when taken out of context or are used outside of the field that produced them. They can be extraordinarily awkward if the subject of discussion is in a different world with different rules.

Efforts to impose a particular software language on a system with a different underlying model will generate the same kinds of difficulties as any other language misapplied. Some languages are error-prone, hardly the right languages for complex systems requiring high levels of certifiability. Some languages are precise and others fuzzy. Some are quantitative and others qualitative or heuristic. Some are well developed and others still in preliminary design. Some are widely used and others are just for experts.

Generally speaking, the language needs of architects are for the higher-order languages, providing they couple well with the lower-order languages on which they operate, and providing the model base of the lower-order languages is consistent with the architect's system model.

The future will show to what extent systems architects will generate their own system-level modeling languages. A beginning has already been made with linear programming, predicate calculus, process-oriented languages (SIMULA, SIMAN, SLAM II), artificial intelligence (LISP), and object-oriented programming (SMALLTALK).

As with any language, it takes time to develop the necessary vocabulary, knowledge representation, structures, rules, and general usage for new languages. For the present, suffice it to say that knowledge of applicable languages is becoming as important to systems architects as knowledge of the major ethnic languages is to an internationalist.

CONVENTIONAL CONSTRUCTS OF SYSTEMS AND THEIR MODELS

A construct is a structure built according to specific principles or using a particular set of construction units. House constructs, for example, include wood frames, concrete blocks, steel trusses, and geodesic domes. Computer constructs include serial, parallel, analog, and digital structures. The choices of constructs for the system and its model—they may be different—are critical early decisions, yet often made unthinkingly. But by choosing "the obvious," creative alternates may be missed and the model mismatched with system reality. As we shall see later, a special interface problem occurs in complex systems. Different elements often have different constructs, complicating the matching process.

Serial and *parallel* constructs differ in whether operations are carried out sequentially or all together. The operations are usually thought of as being in time order, but they could also be ordered in space (stacking, front to back, etc.), priority (filing, knowledge bases, message transmission), or by some other index (alphabetical, numerical, organizational). These constructs are seen prominently in information processing, launch-vehicle staging, networks (energy, communication, transportation, manufacturing), and system acquisition.

Linear and *nonlinear* constructs differ in whether or not the response of the system to two different inputs is the sum of the responses to each, that is, is the system response directly (linearly) proportional to the size of the input? Linear system models are very common in engineering for several reasons—partly because they are much easier to analyze, partly because their performance is more predictable, and partly because with a technique called *feedback* some otherwise nonlinear systems can be made to perform as if they were linear. In this technique, part of the output of the device is negatively fed back to the input (or control) such that the device need only operate on the difference between what is desired (the input signal) and what is produced (the controlled output). One might say that the effect is to control the device in the small instead of in the large.

The concept of feedback to reduce the effects of nonlinearities, bias, drift, aging, and instabilities was a major accomplishment of the 1940s. It is now widely used for precision control of high-power devices, for example, turbines, motors, generators, amplifiers, actuators, and industrial machinery. It is the essence of many tracking systems, for example, radars, phase-lock receivers, and servomechanisms.

There is an alternate to the use of feedback around a device, and that is to make the device itself better—more linear, more reliable, and with tighter tolerances. Feedback does add complexity and if it is disabled, the results can be catastrophic. A decision to use feedback, for all of its great advantages in achieving near-linear performance, should be taken advisedly.

Example:

A common technique to improve the performance of mechanical devices is to use electronic feedback. However, the latter is subject to its own set of failure mechanisms, for example, cosmic-ray upset of integrated circuits. Which failure is more likely? Which will cost less?

Example:

Electronic feedback around high-power systems, should it fail, could release catastrophic levels of uncontrolled energy, for example, sudden loss of control of rotating machinery. Precluding this loss requires still more complexity. Great improvements in materials and manufacturing processes have considerably improved the reliability and performance of moving parts over what had been assumed when the shift to electronic feedback occurred some years ago, for example, in compressors and turbines. Which approach will lead to a more reliable better-controlled system?

All that having been said, most real world systems, if pushed to extremes, will become nonlinear. They may hit limits, saturate, hang up, or break at large inputs. Or they may operate strangely due to stiction, overheating, or wearout. It is worth remembering, too, that nonlinear behavior is a *common* biological response to natural phenomena. To give an important example, the human senses are logarithmic, for example, the eyes and ears respond to contrast, not absolute levels of light and sound. Nonlinearity clearly is successful in solving survival problems in the fiercely competitive natural world. If nature is a guide, then avoiding nonlinearity could result in a noncompetitive man-made system.

The principal difficulty in modeling with nonlinear systems is that each kind of nonlinear system has to be analyzed differently, whereas the vast class of linear systems can be analyzed by the same powerful techniques (Fourier transforms, Laplace transforms, linear differential equations, etc.). Linear systems operating in a noise environment, for example, can now be treated relatively easily. The same cannot be said for nonlinear systems.

A special kind of nonlinearity is found in *saturated* systems, systems that refuse to respond proportionately beyond a certain limit. Typical of these are communications links of limited numbers of channels, computer memories, freeways, and the like. Demanding more and more performance from such systems produces no greater, and sometimes much less, performance, for example, gridlock, breakdown, and stall. For some saturated systems, a definite purpose is served. For most, however, saturation is a serious and unwanted condition.

There is very little theory for managing saturated systems. The Bell System gives up on automated control when all channels are saturated on Mother's Day and Christmas. To the extent that theory does exist, the key seems to be control of *access* to the system, for example, a busy phone signal or traffic control lights at freeway entrances. It is sometimes difficult for the public to understand that it is a waste of time and energy to try to force a system over its limit. "The freeways are moving right along, why do we have to wait so long at this #%&! signal light?" It is difficult for the individual user to understand that more access means less throughput once the maximum capacity is exceeded.

Why not add capacity? There might not be a choice—more capacity just may not be available at a reasonable cost. In this case, an architecture, including operations, may have to be used in which saturation is an acceptably controlled mode.

The saturation problem becomes much worse if the input energy cannot be controlled (wind shear, turbulence, jamming, blitzkrieg attack), in which case, it must be dissipated, or shunted away, or severe damage is likely. Then the system problem is damage control. Such situations are a way of life in defense contingency planning, shipboard damage control, safety systems, fire fighting, emergency relief, and medical triage. Some valuable heuristics have been developed as guidelines. For example:

Contain excess energy as close to the source as possible.

(The medical triage) **Let the dying die. Ignore those who will recover on their own. And treat only those who would die without help.**

Constant and *time-varying parameter* constructs differ in whether the system's internal parameters ("constants") remain the same or change with time. Strictly speaking, almost every system changes internally if one waits long enough. So a more useful distinction is whether the internal changes occur slowly or comparably to input rates. If the time rates of change are different enough, the variables can be separated and treated independently. If not, then analysis has to be on a case-by-case basis.

Given the choice, the architect would prefer a time-variant linear construct to any of the nonlinear ones. Hence, it is worthwhile to express an otherwise nonlinear system in time-variant linear terms if possible.

Example:

Aircraft and launch vehicle performance can change dramatically in a rapid climb from sea level (high humidity, low speed, ambient pressure, and temperature) to extreme altitude (extreme cold, low external pressure, and high speed). But providing the vehicles fly nominal trajectories, engine thrust, control-system dynamics, and aerodynamic performance can all be specified.

Example:

A space vehicle reentering the atmosphere from orbit passes through various flight regimes in rapid sequence. For a nominal trajectory and a nominal atmosphere, the control problem can be reasonably modeled. The danger, clearly, is for those nonnominal conditions (storms, wind shear, unexpected gravity waves, incorrect reentry angle) where the timing and location of the flight regimes cannot be specified to the control system ahead of time.

Continuously variable and *discrete* constructs are ways of modeling systems that change state in a continuous manner or in discrete steps, respectively. Most natural systems change state continuously. Describing their behavior has been a driving force in physics and mathematics for hundreds of years, resulting in the powerful tools of ordinary and partial differential equations, differential and integral calculus, linear transforms, and all their derivatives. In contrast, a number of man-made systems change state abruptly and discontinuously— bang-bang servomechanisms, power-switching relays, frequency-shift keyed (FSK) transmitters, pulse-code modulators, and digital computers are examples. If the shifts are small enough or occur infrequently enough, these systems can be modeled as if they were continuously variable or were "piecewise" linear. But if the changes are large, driven by randomly occurring discrete events, and/or are nonvariant between changes, few modeling tools exist. (See the January 1989 issue of the *Proceedings of the IEEE*).

Stationary and *nonstationary* constructs arose when it was realized that certain long-term properties of random phenomena could be described on average in the large that could not be described instantaneously in the small, that is, the phenomena were statistically "stationary." Some examples in the history of science are gas molecule dynamics, Gaussian noise, and turbulence. Their instantaneous values are indeterminate, but their average properties are very stable. Of great importance, many problems could be expressed in stationary terms and solved by linear systems, for example, determining the best ratio of signal to noise power that can be produced, on average, by a suitably equipped receiver. Mathematically optimum systems, considerably better than earlier systems designed by trial and error, were produced. Although the most success has been achieved for statistically stationary sources and linear systems, progress is being made for nonstationary time-variant and/or non-Gaussian sources and nonlinear systems. Examples are impulse noise, cochannel interference, television "ghosting," and multipath propagation.

The assumption of Gaussian stationary conditions, leading as it does to linear system designs, carries with it a key proviso: the architect must make sure the proposed system remains linear in the presence of a noise source. Unlike deterministic and predictable analytic sources, noise sources can exhibit sporadic bursts of considerable size. If the system does not respond proportionately, but instead limits, saturates, or otherwise goes nonlinear, system performance can deviate significantly from what the linear model would predict. The frequency spectrum of the noise can be changed, the signal and the noise inextricably intermixed, and the signal level drastically suppressed.

Example:

For reasons of efficient use of power in power-starved communication relay satellites, the transmitters are often operated at their amplitude limits. For relaying constant-magnitude frequency-modulated signals, this technique works very well. But if a much larger source of interference enters the receiver, it too will be relayed, taking its share of the transmitter power and diminishing the signal power below the receiving capability of receivers on the ground.

Example:

A similar phenomenon occurs in photography. The response to light of camera film is generally linear around an average light level controlled by the camera aperture, but only within a limited range of light intensities. Outside this range, the film is either underexposed or overexposed, effectively wiping out scenic details whose brightness is too far from the average. An extremely bright source, detected and acted upon by an automatic aperture, can wipe out the whole picture; the "dynamic range" of the film is too small.

Example:

A digital receiver sampling its input at too low a rate can convert or "alias" wide-band noise or edge-of-band signals into in-band interference directly overlaying the desired signal where little or no interference had existed before. The phenomenon is similar to that of strobe photography, which can make wheels appear to be counterrotating.

CONSTRUCTS STILL UNDER DEVELOPMENT

The effort to understand complex phenomena is receiving a major boost with new mathematical models of fractals, chaos, and noise. It is probably premature to add these constructs to the architect's kit of tools, but, in due course, they may be as influential in how one thinks of problems as are control theory, information theory, and statistical communications today. The new models change, once again, what we think is "noise" and what we think is "signal," or, in other terms, what we think is random (statistical) and what we think is structured (deterministic).

In effect, the new models indicate that there is more structure in apparently random phenomena than had been thought, which means that more events are predictable and, hence, potentially controllable than previously thought.

One can only speculate on the impact of these new models on vortex control, turbulence abatement, flutter suppression, improved fracture mechanics, pattern recognition, signal coding, and the reduction of $1/f$ noise in ultrastable clocks.

A comparable revolution in thinking came about in information theory some 50 years ago. Prior to that time, noise was regarded as interference and signal theory was largely a matter of comparing signal-modulation schemes, for example, debating AM versus FM. Then Claude Shannon showed not only that signal transmission was a function of both signal and noise, *but that the best signal form was noiselike!* It is true that his model applied only to signals and noise that were statistically describable and to distortionless channels. But the new insight led to an explosion of communication developments—pulse-code modulation, spread spectrum signals, pseudonoise modulation, optimum filters, and new code formulations. Most importantly, in connection with other theories being developed at the time by Norbert Wiener and others, it was shown not only that there were limits to how well one could communicate, but that there were communications systems that could reach such limits. There was at best, an optimum, against which all other systems of the same type could be compared.

The impact on communications systems design has been profound. How long did it take to become standard practice? Several decades. But that is the time span of many of today's complex systems and well within the career times of many readers.

Codes and *chaotics* can be viewed as intermediate between deterministic (exactly specified) and statistical (random). The mechanism that produces codes and chaotics is mathematically deterministic. That is, the mechanism can be described by equations, usually nonlinear and/or recursive. A random source is not needed to produce their apparently random outputs. Yet the resulting real-time continuing phenomena appear to be "random" if tested against the usual criteria for randomness. For example, codes and chaotics exhibit stable correlation functions and apparently continuous frequency spectra. Yet the apparently random output of a coding machine can be duplicated exactly, knowing only its initial state and its generating equation.

The same can be said for chaotic phenomena, although, in this case, the initial condition and the generating mechanism must be specified with extraordinary precision. Unlike codes, however, chaotic mechanisms apparently cannot be run in reverse. Curiously, once started, most chaotics do remain within certain bounds, seemingly held there by "strange attractors." They were first discovered when attempting to model peculiar biological phenomena such as seemingly erratic insect infestations. They have more recently been observed in networked computers and in oscillator phase noise. They are now understood to exist at many levels of complexity, that is, their descriptive equations can be of high order.

Being able to exactly replicate an apparently random phenomenon can be of significant value in validation and testing of systems that in operation will be confronted with random stimuli (inputs) but which fail during system test. Controlled "randomness" permits separation of the failure mechanism from the randomness mechanism. So far, codes but not chaotics have found use in repeatable test applications.

A more common application of codes and chaotics, however, is in systems that have to respond to coded and chaotic phenomena themselves. In principle, the systems should be able to respond better than if the stimuli were pure random because the underlying mechanism is deterministic. That is, there is structure in the stimulus and that should be exploitable. In the case of codes, the problem is to "crack" unfriendly codes and synchronize with friendly ones, a technique almost as ancient as generating the codes themselves.

A corresponding technique for "cracking" chaotics has not yet been developed, though a variety of techniques exist for generating and describing them. In a sense, codes are sequential and chaotics are interacting parallel, one chaotic stream mixed nonlinearly with another to produce the resultant output. If so, cracking chaotics may not be possible.

Another newcomer is the *fractal* construct. Fractals are patterns that are the same, regardless of the scale at which they are observed, generated by equations of noninteger (e.g., fractional) dimensionality. They, too, occur in nature and are seen in trees, clouds, beach sand, terrain, and ocean waves. They are so common in nature that realistic scenes of mountains and valleys can be generated by appropriate equations. Truly beautiful (which probably means naturelike) patterns have been generated and published as works of art. Of perhaps more practical interest, fractals have been used in image compression of natural scenes (Zorpette, 1989).

INTERFACING DIFFERENT CONSTRUCTS

As mentioned earlier, models can be combined to produce still larger models. Many of the elements will have constructs different from those of their neighbors. In an aerospace vehicle, the communications system may be designed along stationary, linear, and analog/digital lines; the control system along nonlinear time-variant lines; and the guidance computer using discrete-event techniques.

If the **minimum communications** heuristic is taken as a guiding principle, then the elements won't "know" much about each other. Yet their properties near their boundaries can be very different. Sharp structural discontinuities will then occur at the interfaces. Interfaces, instead of being simple boundaries between compatible elements, become complex elements themselves. Constrained by the demands of the adjacent elements, they can become major determinates of system performance.

Example:

Perhaps the most notorious example of interface discontinuity is the differences in the gauges of railroad tracks between nations and even districts all over the world. The original reasons for the differences were technical, but were reinforced by considerations of national defense and political autonomy. The present result is otherwise valueless transshipment costs and delays.

Example:

To provide secure voice communications between two widely separated locations often requires passage through several links and across national boundaries. For technical and political reasons, each link may have its own protective encryption system based on quite different constructs. Some encryption methods destroy the low frequencies, some diminish the high frequencies, and some are highly susceptible to external interference. If such encryption methods are in tandem, the result can be a severe loss of voice recognition and intelligibility.

Example:

Control of interfaces between related products can produce a formidable competitive advantage, as seen in computer, communications, and aerospace markets. The competition must either comply with the interface or provide special adapters if their products are to be a part of the same market. Standardized interfaces, on the other hand, open up the competition—the merits of which depend on one's point of view. As the news media make clear, interface standards are a major issue in today's global marketplace. They can be as effective as any trade agreement in restricting or opening up trade.

HIDDEN, FORGOTTEN, AND UNSUSPECTED REAL INTERFACES

It is sometimes forgotten that what might appear on some system diagrams as simple lines are instead major interface systems in their own right. For example, consider a diagram of a geographically dispersed manufacturing, distribution, and sales organization. The existence of a line on such a diagram implies more than a connection between the dispersed elements. It also implies that something *moves* along that line, either physical transportation or communication. The system effects of changing these movements can be pronounced. The effects on local American industry of changes in global transportation and communication have been to make local markets into global ones and to reduce the local manufacturers' assurance of their local markets. Global transportation and global communications have brought global competition into what had been captive markets. The lines between manufacturer, wholesaler, retailer, and customer have long been present on product-flow diagrams, but now rather abruptly they have become global systems instead of local services taken for granted.

One of the more potentially destructive interfaces is between high-energy elements and the control and instrumentation elements that work with them. Each can do severe damage to the other. The former can send bursts of energy into the latter, destroying them. Or the latter can command the former to take self-destructive action, for example, slamming into hard stops or overstressing structural elements. The architect's problem here is not so much the danger— that is usually understood—but its *dimensions*. Unless the interface is completely characterized and controlled, unsuspected linkages coupled with unconsidered scenarios can destroy the system.

Recognizing the damage that one element can do to another, Arthur Raymond [USC, (1988)] suggested another version of "the greatest leverage is at the interfaces" heuristic:

The greatest <u>dangers</u> are also at the interfaces.

In complete agreement with Raymond, Bernard Kuchta [General Dynamics, (1989)] suggested two antidotes:

Be sure to ask the question, "What is the worst thing that other elements could do to you across the interface?"

And, referring to the risks that incomplete interface specifications pose:

Unbounded limits on element behavior may be a trap in unexpected scenarios.

The specific problem in Kuchta's case was an unbounded upper frequency limit for an electrical connection that permitted a high-energy electrical impulse to reach and destroy a control element, a failure mode easily eliminated by a low-pass filter. But the heuristic applies equally well to mechanical, chemical, physiological, and other parameters whose levels, either too high and too low, can be harmful.

Another serious problem with interface elements is the time they take to operate. Involving as they do movement from one element to another, they generate unavoidable fixed delays. Some examples are the propagation time along wires in a computer, the transport time of fluids in launch-vehicle plumbing, the action time of mechanical relays in a regional electric power grid. These delays are notorious in producing system instability—the "Pogo effect" in launch vehicles, major outages in electric power grids, chattering relays, timing errors in synchronous computers, and oscillations in manufacturing plant deliveries.

A particularly troublesome hidden interface is what electrical engineers call "sneak circuits," unsuspected connections among elements. The more infamous sneaks such as ground loops, parasitic capacitances, and signal paths through power supplies are usually caught by design rules. But many are created by specific design configurations and have to be caught in system tests where they appear as instabilities, glitches, and occasionally severe damage.

The best antidotes to unsuspected interfaces seem to be experience, good partitioning, and simple interfaces. Overly complex integration increases the likelihood of trouble. And system tests should probably be progressive rather than "all up" at the first opportunity. Progressive testing is standard operating procedure for new aircraft to minimize catastrophe and to avoid confusion for new networks. But it can be difficult, if not impossible, for highly integrated spacecraft, where interactions are strong. Hence:

Be prepared for reality to surface a few interfaces of its own.

STRUCTURAL STABILITY

At this point, we need to add another factor, one certainly required for any structure, whether physical or conceptual—stability. Unless the architect creates *stable* structures for the system and its model, either or both may collapse. The need for structural stability is widely acknowledged in engineering, not only for civil structures, but for ships, aircraft, networks, computers, software, human organizations—almost any structure. Less well appreciated, perhaps, is the need for stability as the system is built and evolves. "Collapsed during construction" is an epitaph of more than buildings. It has applied to every kind of structure, whether physical or informational. "Wasn't viable in the new environment" has applied to everything from transportation to organizational structures. The underlying reasons are much the same:

- built on too narrow a base
- poor foundations, physical and logical
- structural inadequacy until fully assembled, that is, each level or element was not able to stand alone
- unstable when assembled, that is, coupling was wrong between elements.

The situation is the same in system models. System models are comprised of subsystem models, which, in turn, are comprised of subsubsystem models. These individual models may not stack up properly. Interconnected software may go unstable or crash. The right connection points may not exist. The internal data bases of the different models may not only be different, their data bases may contradict each other.

One way of ensuring some stability is to build models, like systems, only out of stable elements, working from the simplest configuration to the more complex, making sure each step works before proceeding (Brooks, 1986). It is an approach long used in civil works construction, where at each step in the construction, the structure must be stable and safe. It is a principle for the assembly in space of the U.S. Space Station Freedom that at the end of each assembly flight a completely functional spacecraft should remain.

All of which suggests a technique for building and evolving man-made models and systems. As stated by Simon (1981),

> Complex systems will evolve from simple systems much more rapidly if there are stable intermediate forms than if there are not.

It is an attractive idea but, if misapplied as a rationale for bottom–up evolution, it can have a serious drawback. It may not be clear ahead of time just where or to what it will lead. A different choice of the first aggregation or a different ordering of the design decisions, and a different system—not necessarily satisfactory—could result. As the expression goes, "If you don't know where you are going, you probably won't get there."

In biology, endless trial and error and survival of the fittest eventually led to stable surviving systems. But it is not an approach for systems architects aiming for a predetermined objective in a predictable time.

So it is necessary to put Simon's statement into the context within which he wrote it—a large architectural framework with top–down partitioning into stable elements. Thus, the original statement might be more completely stated as:

Complex systems will develop and evolve <u>within an overall architecture</u> much more rapidly if there are stable <u>intermediate forms</u> than if there are not.

In some sense, this heuristic is a cousin of the **minimum communications** heuristic with a substitution of stability for autonomy. It is not, however, a cousin to KISS in suggesting simple beginnings. On the contrary, the stable intermediate forms, as in biological ones, may be quite complex. Their crucial parameter is stability, not necessarily simplicity.

To appreciate the difference, consider designing a *family* of products from the simplest to the most capable [Spinrad, 1988.] One of the most important characteristics of a product family is compatibility, that is, each product does much the same thing in much the same way but to a different degree. The top architectures of each product in the line are basically the same. The customer can move up or down the product line depending on need.

But this means that the product at the bottom of the line must perform the same functions, albeit in a limited way, as the one at the top. The architecture of the simplest product, therefore, must make provision for—and certainly should not preclude—all the functions of the product family. Otherwise, product-line growth and evolution are blocked.

In short, the "simplest" or lowest-level, product is not necessarily *architecturally* simple. Putting it another way, one seldom can build on something that was not designed for it: ask anyone who has wanted to build a second story on a one-story house or to add a new feature to a closed-architecture computer.

EVOLUTIONS AND REVOLUTIONS

Despite the enthusiasm that greets new technologies, the system architect is inherently conservative in introducing them. There are good reasons for this conservatism. The touted benefits in one element may not be realizable at the system level without a complete rearchitecting. The new technology is almost certain to have quirks of its own. And, perhaps most importantly, the new technology may not transition successfully from the laboratory to the production plant. On the other hand, the architect is progressive in conceiving new systems out of new *combinations* of technologies.

A common fallacy is that major new systems arise soon after the appearance of a new technology in one of the elements. Although the technology may open up new options, experience has shown that improvement at the system level almost always requires comparable developments in other elements. History has certainly shown this to be true for such new technologies as jet engines, rocket engines, nuclear weapons, gyroscopes, lasers, computers, and integrated circuits. Before they could be exploited, major engineering developments were needed in other system elements—structures, materials, software, production methods, airports, launch pads, inertial platfoms, delivery systems and software architectures, to name a few.

Studies (Lautenschläger, 1984; Sherwin, 1967) over the years have confirmed the limited immediate importance to major systems of single "breakthrough" technologies. For the weapon systems and platforms studied, major operational advantages came not from single dramatic new technologies, but from comparably important engineering advances in many system elements. Basic research results seldom affected major operations for at least 20 years, but their results could be revolutionary over a span of 50 to 100 years. Strategic nuclear weapons delivered by inertially guided ballistic missiles are a case in point. Others include the following:

Example:

Aircraft structures can now stand 10-g or higher stresses but the pilot cannot. To create a higher man–machine performance will require more sophisticated control systems, new support devices for the human body, more responsive engines, and better programmed maneuvers.

Example:

Virtually indestructible automobiles can be built; unfortunately, like tanks against jeeps, they demolish most other automobiles in a crash. The indestructible automobile, therefore, may or may not reduce the casualties in the total transportation system.

Example:

Some computer elements can operate at extraordinarily high speeds, but their interaction times with other elements are limited by the speed of light across their interaction distance. To obtain an overall system improvement may require a repartitioning of the software.

Example:

Mines for naval warfare could be improved significantly. But delivering those mines, protecting them in place, and controlling their action still determines their system utility.

Example:

The exceptional communications, navigation, and surveillance performance of existing military space systems demonstrably could be improved still further. But to be militarily effective in wartime, they must be more survivable, a challenge demanding new developments in many fields.

Example:

Commercial communications satellites, which made dramatic changes in long-distance communications compared with earlier cable and microwave relays, are now being challenged by fiber-optic cables. The ''cycle time'' for such developments is 20 or 30 years, most of it spent in deployment and in establishing the necessary infrastructure.

Example:

The architects of the DC-3 and of the Concorde both have stated that the number of major innovative features on each aircraft was quite low. The revolutionary architectures, they said, were primarily an evolution by a process of steady development, hard work, and a deeper understanding of aerodynamics.

What kinds of new technologies might initiate the long and broad development of new systems and their associated elements? Sensors, propulsion, and electric power are the easy ones. More complex breakthroughs are the availability of materials; ''bridges'' from one discipline to another, for example, from signals to symbols to patterns; new information transformations, representations, and organization; and smart systems and new software architectures. To exploit these technologies fully, however, will require much more than their own development.

In short,

Evolution, much <u>less</u> *revolution, is complex in complex systems. Success is seldom the result of a single breakthrough.*

ON OPTIONS

The foregoing material illustrates, perhaps too well, the wide array of considerations and choices that can have major impacts on the system model and overall architecture. Although there might be several architectures that would perform the desired functions satisfactorily, there can also be a number that cannot. And which is which may not be obvious in the early phases of architecting.

What simple actions can be taken that will relieve the situation? Though it pulls against KISS to some extent:

Build in and maintain options as long as possible in the design and implementation of complex systems. You will need them.

And

Hang on to the agony of decision as long as possible. [Spinrad, 1988 at USC]

Why options? Barriers may appear for which an alternate path is the only solution. Or new opportunities may even come along for which there is no point in foreclosing. Most options at this stage are as inexpensive and simple as leaving hooks in software, attachment points in structures, accessible nodes in electronics, or procurement options in contracts. The options need not be full-scale backup developments.

ON TRANSITIONING TO IMPLEMENTATION

At some point in the continuing design process, the initial design must transition to implementation. The transition requires agreement not only by the client and the architect, but by the potential builder. The builder's perspective, from the far side of the transition, must now be added to those of the client and architect, whose primary attention to this point has been on functions, form, and conceptual design.

The builder, understandably, wants to build something that will be accepted and paid for by the client at a profit to the builder. To do this, the system design must seem—to all parties—to have a good chance of passing acceptance tests and of being constructed in an expeditious cost-effective manner.

Acceptance tests are an explicit confirmation that the system *functions* properly. The conceptual design, therefore, must make a clear connection between the functions to be performed and the tests that will confirm that performance. Maier (1988) expresses this, somewhat tongue in cheek, as

> **The ulcer heuristic: System performance is understood well enough when implementers of the system feel only moderately ill about accepting the performance estimates as acceptance requirements for the system they will be constructing.**

Expeditious cost-effective construction results from the choice of a practical system *form*. From the builder's perspective, this usually means that the design allows reasonably independent development and subsequent integration of the system elements. More generally,

> **Concept formulation is complete only when the builder thinks the system can be built to the client's satisfaction.**

For the client and architect to refine the design further, without the participation of the builder, is likely to be a mistake. Not only will a source of expertise be missing, but a sense of responsibility for the design may be lacking in the builder if detailed design is carried too far. The builder will have few options other than to "build to print."

ON COMPARING ALTERNATE ARCHITECTURES

In ill-structured situations where the functions to be performed are uncertain and the priorities fuzzy, it may prove worthwhile to develop several alternate architectures in some detail. But at some point before the stopping point, the choices have to be narrowed down to one or two.

The developed architectures clearly will have valued attributes or they would not have been developed as far as they were. But comparing valued attributes may be like comparing apples and oranges at this stage. A clearer choice may appear by comparing drawbacks:

The choice between architectures may well depend upon which set of drawbacks the client can handle best.

The drawback heuristic, when applied to a proposed new architecture to replace an older one, forces an explicit look at both the benefits *and the costs* of going to a new system. The decision may well be to proceed, but it will be made with eyes open. Cost mitigation will begin early. And it may avoid premature phaseout of an earlier system.

TO PAUSE AND REFLECT

Having reached the point where conceptual design may be near completion, we now take a page from behavioral science studies of top architects and designers:

Pause and reflect!

Stand back at this point and review the process to date. Prior decisions may have been made in the wrong order. Would changing the order make a difference? Look forward in time. Have there been decisions that you may have cause to regret? What can be done to reduce likely costs?

Of the prior options considered and rejected, were any of them close enough to the chosen one to keep parts of them under study?

What was the closest competing model? What happens if your opponent or competitor elects that model?

Use the **choose watch choose** heuristic. As the model has developed, have solutions appeared more often than problems?

How much did technology determine the chosen model? If strongly, keep a close watch on those technologies that might change the name of the game, for example, neural networks, object-oriented programming environments, expert-system heuristics, higher-capacity communications, more cost-effective transportation, drastic changes in the cost of energy, changes in the availability of materials, tailored materials, and new manufacturing processes.

Is the client enthusiastic? Worried? About what? Are "what if" questions still being asked? Have past decisions truly been accepted? In short, is the client "comfortable?"

SUMMARY

The architect's kit of tools is large, diverse, and steadily increasing in power and application. A personalized kit, used with skill, is invaluable. Prepackaged knowledge in the form of models, simulation methodology, lessons learned, and heuristics is available and needs only molding to the architect's own needs. Much of this knowledge was created within the last decade or so, a direct product of the new knowledge age.

The architect's leverage, authority, and unique value to the client lies in the system interrelationships. There also lie the greatest opportunities for success or failure.

RECOMMENDED READING

BROOKS, F. P., JR. (April 1987). "No Silver Bullet. Essence and Accidents of Software Engineering." *Computer* **20**, 4, 10–19. Or it is available from the University of North Carolina, Dept. of Computer Science, Chapel Hill, NC 27514. This is an excellent article by a master. He writes that "The hard thing about building software is deciding what one wants to say, not saying it. . . . The flowchart is a very poor abstraction of software structure. . . . The most radical possible solution for constructing software is not to construct it at all [but rather to buy it]. . . . The approach necessitates top–down design, for it is a top–down growing of the software [that leads to dramatic results]. . . . The most important single effort we can mount is to develop ways to grow great designers."

COOPER, N. G. (Fall 1983). "An Historical Perspective: From Turing and von Neumann to the Present." *Los Alamos Science* **9**, 22–27. This is an article on self-replicating systems, self-ordering systems (order from chaos), and their relationship to statistics and entropy. It is a history of one search for the fundamentals of complexity.

DECARLO, R. A., S. H. ZAK, and G. P. MATTHEWS. (March 1988). "Variable Structure Control of Nonlinear Multivariable Systems: A Tutorial." *Proceedings of the IEEE* **76**, 3, 212–32. This article addresses the difficult problem of controlling systems that are both nonlinear and time-variant. It presents an excellent bibliography on the subject.

EISNER, H. (1988). *Computer Aided Systems Engineering.* Englewood Cliffs, NJ: Prentice Hall. See especially Chapters 10, 12, and 13. It is a fine exposition on the analytic tools of systems engineers for evaluation of top-level alternative models in communications and transportation systems. Well referenced, it has many case studies.

HO, YU-CHI, (ed.). (January 1989). "Special Issue on Dynamics of Discrete Event Systems.'' *Proceedings of the IEEE* **77**, 1, 3-6. This is a special issue on the modeling and control of systems controlled by discrete events, for example, manufacturing lines, computer/communications networks, traffic systems, and military C^3I systems.

TAYLOR, THOMAS D. (April 1988). ''Fitting the Computer to the Job.'' *Aerospace America* **26**, 4, 34-36. It is a good commentary on the choices between general-purpose and special-purpose, serial and parallel, Nosenchuck's work with a systolic array for the Navier–Stokes equations, and the effects of advancing technology on the solution.

ZORPETTE, G. (October 1988). ''Fractals: Not Just Another Pretty Picture.'' *IEEE Spectrum* **25**, 4, 39–44.

TO BROWSE, DEPENDING ON INTEREST

ALEXANDER, C., HAJO NEIS, ARTEMIS ANNINOV, and INGRID KING. (1987). *A New Theory of Urban Design*. New York: Oxford University Press. This book presents the results of a simulation of urban design without a direct urban plan, external constraints, or implementation procedure. De facto substitutions proved necessary, including ''vision,'' an initial set of rules and subrules, and frequent interaction of all parties.

BUZBEE, B. L., X. METROPOLIS, and D. H. SHARP. (Fall 1983). ''Frontiers of Supercomputing.'' *Los Alamos Science* 62-71. The article describes the importance of supercomputers and the need for massively parallel computers to handle problems in magnetic fusion, plasma physics, and nuclear test analysis. It presents a short tutorial on the efficiency of parallel processing.

CHUA, LEON O., (ed.). (August 1987). *Special Issue on Chaotic Systems, Proceedings of the IEEE* **75**, 8. A tutorial.

Discover (February 1989). ''Terminal Chaos.'' (p. 12). This article describes the discovery of chaotic phenomena from astronomy to zoology, including in computer networks, at the XEROX Palo Alto Research Center.

LAUTENSCHLÄGER, D. (1984). *Technology and the Evolution of Naval Warfare 1851-2001*. Washington, DC: National Academy Press. It notes that single technologies have not produced operational breakthroughs, that cycle times are (at least) 10-15 years, and traces modern changes from inception through operations.

LINSAY, P. S. (November 1981). ''Period Doubling and Chaotic Behavior in a Driven Anharmonic Oscillator.'' *Physical Review Letters* **47**, 19, 1349-52. This article presents a description of one of the earliest recognized forms of chaotic behavior, with experimental results.

MAIER, MARK W. (1988). *A Comparison of Four Theories of Architectural Design* and *An Extension of Concepts and Heuristics in Modeling*. Unpublished graduate reports, University of Southern California, Los Angeles.

RAMADGE, PETER J. G., and W. M. WONHAM. (January 1989). ''The Control of Discrete Event Systems.'' *Proceedings of the IEEE* **77**, 1, 82-96. This is a tutorial on discrete-event systems and their control.

Sherwin, C. W. (June 23, 1967). "Project Hindsight, A Defense Department Study of the Utility of Research." *Science* **156**, 1571-77. This is a management study of research payoffs to DOD systems, controversial at the time, but consistent with the Lautenschläger (1984) study. The most controversial finding was "The popular concept that a marked increase in system performance generally results from new, key scientific ideas is without foundation."

5

INFORMATION SYSTEMS

Systems for communicating, calculating, and storing information have existed for thousands of years, from clay tablets and abacuses to global electronic networks and supercomputers. But within the last few decades, information systems have become so pervasive that it is no longer sensible or competitive to put them outside any system's boundary.

Example:

Scientific instruments not only make measurements, they do complete experiments—printing calculated results in any desired format, displaying relationships among variables, and documenting the exact procedures that were followed. They virtually write the final report.

Example:

Automobiles are now far smarter, safer, more reliable, more fuel efficient, and less expensive than their computerless predecessors.

Example:

Commercial buildings have become sophisticated machines. Private residences are following close behind. Concrete structures now have embedded within them fiber sensors to detect temperature, stresses, and cracks.

Example:

Most jet aircraft and most spacecraft could not perform their missions without onboard computers. Operating time constants are too short, and the interrelationships among variables too complex, for human intervention to be effective.

Example:

Personal computers now assist the user not only in making calculations, but in setting up those calculations, alerting the user to inadvertent errors, controlling format, storing and accessing files, obtaining assistance from remote assets, and sending results to other locations.

INTELLIGENT MACHINES AND THEIR MODELS

The strong upward trend in machine intelligence is apparent in the degree to which machines can use, modify, create, and exploit models in contributing to the systems of which they are a part.

The simplest level of contribution is responding, in a predetermined way, to step-by-step instructions from others, human or machine. Though the response might require millions of simple calculations, the intelligence level is low.

The second level is to use built-in models—equations, algorithms, sets of rules, and programs to solve known problem types. A simple example is a receiver that follows a signal of known form but of varying frequency, repetition rate, amplitude, and information content. A more complex machine at this level, a "shallow logic" expert system, mimics human experts in system diagnosis and control in accordance with predetermined rules and stored information.

A machine at the third level changes its internal models to improve its response to inputs, perhaps shifting from one course of action to another. It could "change its mind," so to speak. A third-level receiver could decide, based on its inputs, that its original model of the signal form was wrong, that the incoming noise was not Gaussian but impulse, or that an incoming signal was from an unfriendly transmitter and should be discarded. It would then, without external instruction, change to another internal model and modify its response.

At the fourth level, the machine, unsupervised and based upon its experience with otherwise unmodeled information, constructs and stores for future use wholly new models. Machines at this level become steadily smarter through learning. They can conclude that $E = mc^2$, the speed of light is a constant, that lasers should work before any had been built, and that errors exist in a train of logic (Lenat, 1984). Such conclusions, though derived earlier through human intelligence, were not self-evident to either humans or machines before the right model was conceived; indeed, prior models had indicated that such conclusions were impossible. Very few machines have reached this level and only in limited contexts. On the other hand, very few humans demonstrate this ability, either. A fourth-level battle-management machine would conclude that the enemy had adopted a completely unpredicted strategy, derive the basis for that strategy, and respond with a suggested counterstrategy.

A remote-sensing satellite would conclude that it was seeing a completely new object or phenomenon, characterize that new thing sufficiently to reject all known things as explanations, give it a new label, inform the operators and recognize it whenever it showed up again. Based on how it reoccurred, it would build a more complete model of it.

A decade ago, there were no such machines. It is a mark of the rate of progress in this field that they now exist, even if at a primitive level. They are seen in neural networks (multiply interconnected electronic elements that resemble the architecture of neurons in the brain) that learn to talk much as human children learn to talk. Humans, after only a remarkably short exposure to them, respond to such machines as if the machines were human—particularly if the computer responses are expressed in sympathetic user-friendly terms.

The fifth level might be called self-awareness. The machine would understand the importance of self-survival and act upon it. It would not commit suicide on command, at least not without considerable discussion! This response takes more than simple interlocks. It implies sensing damage, remembering and avoiding danger, and even evaluating the motives of its presumably friendly operators. It means searching for the simplest ways of accomplishing things, of avoiding frustration, of forgetting the useless. At this level, machines exhibit what we would call judgment and self-interest were it exhibited by a human being.

The highest level of machine intelligence might be called awareness of interdependence. At this level the machine knows it is a member of a team. It modifies its imperative for survival, depends upon other members, and adjusts to changes in the team's operations. It is trusted as a full partner, including its right to issue orders commensurate with its assigned area of responsibility. The most likely place to find such machines will be in environments that are dangerous, unexplored, and unfamiliar to humans, for example, the human exploration of the solar system. The reader might recognize one in ''Hal'' of the science fiction movie *2001*.

HOW SMART THE MACHINE?

The question of how smart a machine should be is not an idle one. A smarter machine may or may not be more valuable, depending on the overall system architecture. A machine can either be too smart or not smart enough. Two examples from space exploration illustrate the point— the division of the smarts between a spacecraft and its operators.

The designers of the Voyager interplanetary spacecraft, concerned that the spacecraft receivers might fail and hence not transfer commands from the Earth to the rest of the spacecraft, built in an instruction that if commands were not heard from the Earth for a week, the spacecraft should switch to a backup receiver. If commands still were not received, the instructions were to proceed on its own.

Unfortunately, due to other pressing business, flight controllers on the

Earth did not send any commands for a week, the spacecraft switched to the backup receiver, which indeed *was* faulty, and the spacecraft in effect disabled its receiving system. Had the receiving system remained disabled, the later, magnificent but as of then unplanned, achievements of Voyager at the outer planets would not have been possible. In a sense, the spacecraft had been made too smart for its own good.

The sequel was happier, though. Human ingenuity and a hair-raising set of command and control actions managed to restore Earth control, but not through prior contingency planning. This particular contingency had not been foreseen. Nor were the human corrective actions instantly apparent. It took a team of humans and machines quite some time to determine what to do, and to do so in a way that did not make the situation worse.

A less fortuitous example occurred with a Soviet spacecraft enroute to Phobos, a moon of Mars. An erroneous command was sent from Earth, aborting the mission, although the spacecraft was healthy. Neither the ground transmitter nor the spacecraft receiver was smart enough to question the command, a provision now found in more and more machines that must interact with fallible humans.

One could indeed argue that the foregoing problems were not the fault of the machines but of their human operators, that more smarts in the machines, anticipating human error, would have been better in both cases. Perhaps. But there is a trade-off. With smarts come complexity and still further failure modes.

CENTRALIZED VERSUS DISTRIBUTED SYSTEMS

Nowhere is the question of "how smart?" more important than in multielement systems. The core of that question is one of system *control*, because, in a practical sense, all systems are distributed to some degree. Products are marketed through distributed outlets. Communications systems allocate channels through distributed switches. Aircraft are flown using distributed control surfaces. Computer memories are built out of hundreds of thousands of distributed active elements. But none of these systems can operate properly without some form of control.

Hence, the critical features of centralized/distributed systems are not how many elements are located where, but how they are coordinated to perform as a system. The key questions are how much control—what, when, and to what purpose? Answering these questions means knowing how the elements operate, what their requirements and constraints are, and how they will respond to inputs and instructions.

Controlling complex systems takes intelligence, communications, and a mechanism for exercising authority. At the simplest level, it takes someone or something in charge, a "central." The more elements in the system, the more critical, complex, and potentially vulnerable the central becomes. At the most complex level, it takes a "command, control, communications, and intelligence" (C^3I) system with a carefully designed delegation of the central control authority. But how much authority should be distributed, where, and when? Too little distribution and the central is overwhelmed. Too much distribution and there can be conflict, confusion, and breakdown. More accurately, too much distribution of authority *without distributed intelligence* and there can be unresolvable conflict, confusion, and breakdown. The statement applies whether the distributed intelligence is human or machine.

In short, much of the solution to distributed authority is distributed intelligence. If the elements or nodes are smart enough, they can be made to work in concert, sending only necessary information and responding intelligently to it.

One could thus restate the centralized-versus-distributed question in system architectural terms as:

How smart is each element and node?

It is not an overstatement to say that until that question is answered for a proposed system, its architecture is not yet defined. To answer it means specifying all information flow, all control parameters, and all responses expected throughout the whole system. Few questions are as systemwide in their affect on system design.

Be that as it may, the question has been moot until relatively recently. Technology could not support the higher levels of machine intelligence. The architectural options were few. But recently, in a major technological revolution, computers have become so powerful at such low cost, size, and weight that deliberate overdesign of the nodes, coupled with central management of their smarts, may become a preferred architecture. It would answer the question of how smart the node needs to be with the answer, "As smart as need be at the time." It would postpone the decision from an immutable one during conceptual design to an operational one later, converting the static "how smart?" question to a dynamic one of real-time allocation of machine intelligence assets. The precursor strategy is already here—complete reprogramming of remote computers by a central authority. It was used, incidentally, on the Voyager spacecraft, whose story was told earlier.

NEW FAMILIES OF INTELLIGENT ARCHITECTURES

The distributed intelligence picture is beginning to change. New kinds of intelligent architectures are becoming feasible. The new architectures exhibit system properties quite different from those using conventional computer hardware and software. One property, particularly important for hostile environments, is a tolerance for partial failure. A network that *collectively* does many of its functions can be partially disabled and the remainder will compensate for the loss. Some systems already exhibit recognizable, higher-level, intelligent behavior. All show promise of faster progress than was expected only a few years ago.

It is already clear that practical, higher-level, machine intelligence will transform the future tool kit of systems architects. It already affects how we look at present architectures, for example, the existence of neural networks already affects how one views parallel computing. Neural networks are more than massively parallel "strings"; they are collectively interactive systemwide. They produce true <u>system</u> effects not readily apparent in the properties of the individual elements. They redefine the meaning of partitioning and boundaries.

COMMAND, CONTROL, COMMUNICATIONS, AND INTELLIGENCE SYSTEMS

Widespread command, control, and communications (C^3) systems comprise some of the most critical information systems in the world today. They present particularly difficult architectural challenges, not only to their own systems architects, but to other architects who must design systems to fit with them. Responding to the challenges is clearly a role for specialists, but understanding the C^3 challenges is important to all modern systems architects. Aircraft architects must understand the challenges in air traffic control; computer architects, the challenges in intercomputer communication networks; weapons systems architects, the challenges in military C^2 systems; and so on.

The first challenge is the difficulty of accomplishing change in established networks, even relatively small ones. In principle and starting "with a clean sheet of paper," a communications network could be cleanly partitioned into links, controls, protocols, and user nets—all parts of a top–down architecture. A few national networks (e.g., the Bell System) and special-purpose networks (e.g., the NASA/JPL Deep Space Network) approach this goal, but most communication networks are built by evolution and aggregation of smaller, and not always compatible, subnetworks.

Architectural decisions in such situations are almost always suboptimizations—by supplier, by subnetwork, by military service, or by country. At the time of the decision, of course, few of the decisions are perceived as suboptimizations. They only become that when the network being designed becomes a subnetwork in a still larger network, a continuing trend for all networks. The few changes that are then feasible can only be evolutionary and, for practical reasons, will have to be compatible with the earlier architecture. And one lives with even those changes for decades. Seldom, if ever, will a subnetwork be able to relieve its special problems through changes in the main network.

Example:

The Defense Communication System (DCS), in contrast with the Bell System, was built out of specialized subnetworks that for various reasons were neither designed nor intended to be interconnected. Improvement in any of the specialized networks is unlikely to make dramatic and sudden improvements in the overall command and control of the military forces. Indeed, Robert Everett (1981) has discounted top–down architecture as a practical development option for the DCS. Instead, the acquisition approach has been evolution by suboptimization at the Unified and Specified Command level.

Example:

Broadcast television, cable television, local-area networks, and communications satellites are built and operated to different standards in different parts of the world. Any change, such as the proposed introduction of high-definition television (HDTV), produces widespread trauma in suppliers and buyers alike.

At least, this is the picture in the short run. But it would be a serious mistake to discount top–down architecture for established networks just because of the difficulty of making changes in the short run. The problem of established systems inhibiting major change is not a new one. It arises in transportation, computer installations, test facilities, and in manufacturing plants. A major change in architecture generally must wait for a new technology that can greatly modify or add a system function. Automobiles for horses. Trucks for canal barges. Progressively higher radio frequencies for the overloaded lower ones. Satellite communications for high-frequency radio and television distribution. Jet aircraft for propellor aircraft.

But to accomplish a top--down architectural change requires recognizing the opportunity presented by a new technology at just the right time.

Too soon and the new architecture is rejected; the fragile new technology is forced to do the same tasks as the old one. Too late and the new architecture is faced with the de facto standards of the early developments.

Some examples of timely changes to new architectures are the progressive conversions of missile and space telemetry from analog high frequency to FM/FM ultrahigh frequency to coded S-band to secure K-band; the progressive conversions of telephone centrals from manual to cross-bar to electronic switches; the conversion of highway systems to interstate beltway and spoke configurations; and the conversion of land and undersea cable systems from copper wires to light fibers, radically changing the constraints imposed on them by limited bandwidth.

A second challenge is posed by the continuing growth of most communications networks. As the amount and nature of widespread communications increases, the problems of establishing connectivity among disparate users also increases. Saturation, interchannel interference, overly long delays and susceptibility to breakdown all increase.

At some point, it becomes neither practical nor cost effective simply to increase the number of links or the capacity of each link. The network must instead operate "smarter," which means that each communication "node" must be smarter—better able to route efficiently, to report status, to compensate for local or network anomalies, to establish special services (teleconferencing, supervised lines, priority communications), and to respond to centralized control (if any). The key problem, as anticipated from an earlier section, is how smart to make each node.

A present example of the smart node issue is seen in the architecture for commanding and controlling the Strategic Defense System (SDS) with its sensors and weapons distributed on the ground, in the air and in space. How smart should be each of the SDS sensor, weapon, and battle management elements? How will the distribution of smarts affect effectiveness, vulnerability, even feasibility? The answers fundamentally affect the design of every element.

The smart node question is evident enough for the architect specializing in C^3. Less evident is its importance to architects designing systems that connect with the C^3 network, that is, architects of computers, information management systems, public service systems, and the civil and military systems for national security, police and fire protection, disaster relief, antiterrorist operations, and international crisis management.

Real-time intelligence systems pose a special challenge: the need to respond promptly and reliably during crises—just when it is most difficult to do. Intelligence reports typically come from a number of sources, each report differing from the others in nature, reliability, and time late. All must be consolidated (fused) into assessments of direct value to a remote commander. Fusion requires real-time judgments of the validity of each report, of the immediate needs of the operational commander, who will be preoccupied and impatient, and of the information imperatives of the chain of command, which has its own responsibilities to fulfill.

A centralized fusion approach, like any centralized design, can be disabled if its inbound and outbound communications channels are saturated. But saturation is normal in a crisis. Crises affect many different authorities, each searching for critical information in order to act. Understandably, everyone demands—and needs—access to communications at the same time. The problem is endemic. The solution is control of access, gradually restricting it so that system degradation is slow. In the future, such systems may warn the users of impending degradation through progressively stronger alerts, encouraging and then forcing the users to modify their behavior.

A different approach to distributing intelligence information is a "data-driven" architecture. The basic premise of this architecture is that for some systems, it is easier to continually dispatch all incoming intelligence to where it might be useful rather than to fuse it in response to individual user questions. In this architecture, the data seek the user instead of the user seeking the data. But it does require continual screening, assessing, and filing by the user, who, as we said before, is already preoccupied. In effect, this architecture shifts the smarts from the fusion center to the commander or the intelligence-analysis staff, at the risk of saturating the commander's incoming communication channels and intelligence-assessment capabilities.

Unfortunately, this command, control, communications, and intelligence (C^3I) challenge is seldom met. Major disasters have resulted: Pearl Harbor, the *Liberty* and *Pueblo* surveillance ships, and, at least for the British, the surrender of General Cornwallis to a combined American land and French naval force equipped with a far better C^3I system. In periods of high tensions, like the Cuban missile crisis, deficient C^3I has been a major threat to world peace. The antagonists seldom understand each other, intelligence is limited, and key participants cannot be reached through saturated communications links.

A further challenge in both military and civilian C^3I systems is that critical interface between the system and the commanders, the command center. Unlike first come, first serve networks, a C^3I network must be a priority system, and priority is in the eyes of each user. Yes, rank can be confused with priority. Yes, logistics support can take priority over combat.

With many individuals calling for priority, someone has to keep order. Someone has to command and control the C^3I system. In crises, that most often is the commander. The command center is the mechanism. But not all military and executive officers come from the same mold. To compare just American examples, consider Generals Eisenhower and MacArthur, and Presidents Kennedy and Johnson. All were successful, but far from alike. Their individual ideas of how to command were sharply different. Some preferred to operate "out of their back pocket" and others demanded quite sophisticated support systems. And every one of them knew the adage, "Rank gives me the authority, but only with communications [and intelligence] can I command."

The C^3I systems architect is thus faced with a problem: whether to design the C^3I architecture to fit the commanders or to make the commanders fit the architecture. Clearly, a major C^3I system cannot be restructured for every commander, but command centers can. They certainly are easier to change than the ideas of a commander on how to command.

Command centers are fine examples of the heuristic:

The greatest leverage in system architecting is at the interface.

The commander and the C^3I system come together there. The architect can most easily make the system match the commander there. And the rest of the system knows what it must support.

But the architect should not be dismayed when the next commander comes on the scene and demands that everything be changed!

And, finally, a future challenge: the integration of real-time global surveillance with comparable command, control, communications, navigation, and weapon systems into a *tactical* superarchitecture, but with global reach. Each of these systems have now developed truly global capabilities, largely due to the rapid and effective development of space and missile assets. The military and political consequences of a combination of these systems into a complex "megasystem" are just being appreciated. The enabling development will be a survivable C^3I architecture.

What help can the architect expect in meeting the challenges from new technologies? Some technologies may indeed alleviate some of the C^3 and C^3I architects' problems, at least for a few years. Fiber-optic networks promise relatively unlimited bandwith for users at fixed locations whose needs for bandwith are very large but for only very short times—"bursty" communications. Satellite links can efficiently serve users who can tolerate delays of a few seconds—television broadcasts, facsimile transmissions, remote servicing of equipment, transfer of data bases, and the like.

SIGNAL- AND IMAGE-PROCESSING ARCHITECTURES

Signal- and image-processing systems, like C^3I systems, are of importance to more than the specialists. They are the face of the system to the user, converting and enhancing electromagnetic signals for suitable presentation to human users. Radar reflections become television descriptions of targets. Navigation signals become maps. Encrypted signals from satellites become recognized voices. They are the heart of command centers. Well designed, they maximize system utility. Poorly designed, they severely limit it. An automobile dashboard, an aircraft cockpit, an instrument front panel, a multicolor computer graphics display, a high-quality voice network, a user-friendly personal computer, a battle-zone surveillance display, an easily understood nuclear facility control console—all, to the user, *are* the system, regardless of how much is behind the front panel.

From the user's perspective, the top architecture is what's on the front panel. If it isn't there, it can't be important. Conversely, if it isn't important, it shouldn't be there.

Example:

American fighter/bomber aircraft engaged in the Vietnam War were equipped with devices that by flashing lights warned the pilots that surface-to-air missiles (SAMs) were targeting them. But the pilots were also busy fending off enemy aircraft, changing course and altitude, and avoiding collisions with other aircraft. The SAMs were only one of the threats, and the pilots thought little of them. In any case, the lights were distracting, so the pilots taped them over. So much for the warning system as part of the aircraft top architecture.

Example:

Modern fly-by-wire aircraft perform with just the right combination of yaw, pitch, roll, and thrust to achieve whatever maneuver the pilot might want, achieving peak performance with minimum stress on the pilot and the aircraft. If the pilot wants to turn sharp left and stay at altitude, the aircraft computer translates that command into programmed changes in engine thrusts and control-surface positions. Yaw, pitch, roll, and thrust no longer need concern the pilot; but the pilot who is used to "hands-on" control of each control surface and each engine speed has to learn to fly again. Meanwhile, how much information about those now hidden controls should be displayed? Should they be part of the top architecture, the "front panel?" If not, could other mechanizations work as well or better? Or must the older way of flying still be available as a backup along with all the older instrument dials?

Example:

Question: Would the reader like a fly-by-wire automobile with speed and direction being the only controls? Some automobiles already have cruise control as a fixed-speed substitute for the accelerator pedal. Most automobiles have automatic transmissions that do, indeed, eliminate the clutch pedal and improve fuel efficiency. So, what about a control system that combined the accelerator with separately controlled brakes, assuring the safest possible maneuvers within performance limits with good fuel efficiency and without hitting obstacles and other cars? Technologically straightforward. If you did not need to know about accelerators, clutches, side-view mirrors, and squealing tires and exceeding performance limits—the way you no longer know what goes on under the hood—would you be better off?

What features are both necessary and sufficient in the top architecture—in that symbolic "front panel?" How simple but complete can it be? As Einstein answered in another context, "As simple as possible but no simpler."

A major part of the answer depends on how smart the system is behind the front panel. A smart system need display only the essentials. A primitive system must display almost everything, leaving it to its operator to determine its significance.

In the early days of flying, the pilot's hands, feet, eyes, ears, seat of the pants, and face in the wind were all needed to control the flying machine. The pilot was deep into the machine and its environment, aware of even the slightest changes. Flying on instruments took great trust in what was displayed on a few dials—the processed signals from primitive barometers and gyroscopes behind the panels. Today, most flying is on automatic pilot, a necessary and sufficient top-architecture element to accomplish much of what the busy pilot used to do most of the time.

The same story holds true in many other systems. The front control panel—of whatever system—defines the top architecture to the user. Its signal and image processing determines its apparent complexity. The more advanced the processing, the simpler the front panel can be or, alternatively, the more capable the system behind it can be.

Signal and image processing have progressed far beyond extracting known patterns out of a background. Finding and tracking a sine wave in noise is no longer a mystery, nor is recognizing straight lines in a visual image. The challenges, now, are to do what humans do so naturally—rapid recognition of voices, faces, and moving objects almost regardless of background, orientation, intensity, or direction of motion—and to combine that with rapid access to knowledge about them. In seconds, we identify a bird on the wing, a familiar car on the road, a small object that does not belong on the living room rug, and a plane flying through the clouds.

Signal and image processing, recognition and understanding, is an extraordinarily sophisticated field. Yet its functions can be performed by any normal 3-year-old. But it is also a field aided by advances in other new fields: neuroscience, expert systems, neural networks, optical processing, VLSI technology, computer models, and cognitive psychology. The field is steadily producing new architectures—pyramidal (Ogden et al., 1985) and fractal-image reconstruction (Zorpette, 1988) being two of the more recent.

We return to image processing in Part Two, endeavoring by analogy with human sensing and processing systems to project a possible future for their machine equivalents.

INFORMATION AND CONTROL SYSTEMS FOR MANUFACTURING

Manufacturing systems, under heavy competitive pressure, are undergoing major change, forced by a number of key factors changing at the same time:

- The rate of change in products is increasing, each product now having a shorter economic lifetime.
- The demand for higher quality at lower cost is forcing a revamping of the manufacturing system from bottom to top, from the lowest-tier supplier to the finished-product assembler, and from designer to customer service.
- The utility of manufactured goods is increasing; goods are getting "smarter."
- Mechanical systems are being replaced whenever practical with electronic systems.

As a result, manufacturing strategy is changing its focus from end products to the process by which they are designed, manufactured, and sold. A major factor in the change is the architecture of manufacturing information and control systems. Total Quality Management Systems (TQMS), Just-in-Time (JIT) inventory control, and flexible manufacturing systems (FMS) are some of the better known methodologies.

A driving goal is a sharp reduction in the time taken from product conception to appearance on the market, demanding closer cooperation among what have been separate groups—designers, engineers, manufacturing, quality assurance, marketing, and sales. Efficiently achieving this cooperation demands an end-to-end architecture for the presently disparate computer aids developed by the separate groups. Eliminating unnecessary delays and errors just in transferring information from one group to another calls for end-to-end integration of computer-aided design, engineering, manufacturing, inventory control, diagnosis, repair, sales, and service. As of now, the situation is chaotic. Each group, driven hard by its own needs, has developed its own computer aids to improve its own operation, with little thought to the needs of other groups for information each group generates and uses. Only rarely does one find a "process architect" with concern and responsibility for the waterfall process from end to end.

In the long run, the increasing productivity of the manufacturing sector, even at a few percent per year, will in a few more decades produce a result comparable to that achieved by American agriculture—much increased sales of manufactured goods, but with steadily declining manufacturing employment to make them. There are already many products whose manufacturing labor costs are 10% or less of the sale price; arguments about the relative costs of domestic and foreign labor costs are almost irrelevant for these products. The costs, instead, are increasingly for materials handling, process control, record keeping, audit, and distribution—significant portions of which add little value for the customer, for example, work in progress, log-in times, screening for faulty supplies, waiting for tests and records, rework, and excess inventory.

It has been estimated by the DOD Defense Sciences Board that 20–30% of a weapons system cost is excess "paperwork," much of it generated by and for information and control purposes. Some paperwork clearly is essential. Equipment pedigrees are vital for very high-quality systems if causes for failures are to be substantiated, flawed components are to be purged, and/or fraud detected. Like financial audits, technical audits require massive paperwork, though most is never read except by the author—until there is trouble.

But other paperwork is clear waste. For example, if all supplies and systems were perfectly made, vast amounts of paperwork could be eliminated. Suppliers complain vigorously about the paperwork that they must supply; but few of these suppliers will decrease the paperwork they require from *their* suppliers. Paperwork, like screening and testing, is a function of the quality of all elements of the manufacturing system. Until that quality is upgraded and certified, no responsible official will unilaterally reduce the level of paperwork required to protect the quality of the end product. One way of determining whether quality-related paperwork is excessive is to compare its costs with the cost of a warranty. Both protect the user, but which costs the user less? That is, can warranties be used in lieu of quality-related paperwork? If a buyer can obtain a warranty for, say, 1% of the sale price, then paperwork intended to provide the same protection should not cost much more than that. Ten percent clearly would be excessive.

Another and probably more practical decrease in paperwork can be achieved by better information architectures. If most of the paperwork is never going to be read, why distribute it everywhere? Why not store it in readily accessible electronic data bases? Why not have it entered only once, preferably automatically at the "point of manufacture," much as many transactions are entered and completed at the point of sale?

Data entry and storage require only very low levels of intelligence. Why are they ever done by error-prone humans who take so much time to do it? Data query, on the other hand, requires high-level intelligence, so why not make it as efficient as possible by user-friendly displays and near instantaneous access?

Appreciating these points, manufacturers have now established a major productivity objective: the reduction of nonvalue-added operations, such as excess information generation and distribution, to a bare minimum. It is now not unusual to hear of 20–30% reductions in product cost and factors of 5–10 reductions in time to market as a result.

Accomplishing this objective requires changes across the board, that is, a rearchitecting of the manufacturing process for both enhanced efficiency and quality. Reducing only the paperwork without quality improvement, reducing inventory without reducing the need for spares, and reducing testing without demonstrating it is no longer needed are all prescriptions for disaster. We return to this subject with a still broader perspective in the next chapter.

EXPERT SYSTEMS

Expert systems are information architectures in which the knowledge of human experts is captured and, using a set of logic rules, used to answer questions from the user. They are most effective when the knowledge is explicit and easily represented and when precise and logical inferences can be made from it. Their early successes were in diagnostics, inferring causes of diseases from symptoms or failures from measureable effects. The responses of these expert systems to queries are now so perceptive that users establish an almost personal relationship with the machine, trusting it as they would a helpful human expert.

One of the reasons for such trust is that modern expert systems, when queried, indicate the reasoning behind their answers, progressively building human trust and confidentiality.

Example:

X-ray radiography and cardiography can now be accomplished with machines that provide a partial diagnosis as well. The diagnosis is at least as good as that of a general practitioner and almost as good as that of a specialist, given the same record. At the present time, the accuracy of any one diagnosis is at best 80%, whether by machine or expert. Greater accuracy requires more information as will be seen in the following.

Example:

Diagnosing anomalies and failures in satellites is the first step in restoring them to service. Continuous human monitoring of normally healthy satellites is tedious, especially to experts. Yet when an anomaly does occur, prompt expert action is needed to prevent permanent damage. Some failures exhibit subtle symptoms well in advance—progressive slowing of a bearing's rotation or increasing power consumption of a control system—observable only over long periods. Military satellite control adds another complication. For combat survivability reasons, dispersal of control to remote locations is highly desirable, but dispersing human experts is impractical—there are not enough of them. The evident solution is expert systems to assist trained troops. The expert machines can be located on site or in the satellite, with various degrees of damage-control authority at each location.

Designers of expert systems are encountering several limitations as they attempt to design for other applications. The first is a limitation in how knowledge can be represented and processed. Not all diagnostic knowledge is quantifiable. Nor are all situations alike.

Example:

In the early days of Apollo, the medical specialists concerned with the health of the astronauts were asked what instrumentation they would choose if there was only one channel available from the astronauts to them. The anticipated answer was heart beat or some other quantitative measurement. Their answer: "Show us the astronaut's face. That will tell us more than any other single thing." No wonder the family doctor "wants to see you"!

Medical practice then, and now, is a mix of quantitative, semiquantitative, and qualitative factors: patient medical history, present and past life style, diet, medication, heredity, psychological condition, statistically likely diseases for that particular patient (lung cancer, cirrhosis of the liver), and very importantly, the doctor's general impression of all these factors. Twenty years ago it was estimated that only 20% of a doctor's diagnosis depended on quantitative factors. That figure has now considerably increased due to a wide array of studies of many patients and many diseases over protracted periods. Risk factors are known with some confidence and doctors increasingly use them in diagnosing and caring of patients.

Designing expert systems to aid doctors is becoming easier as more quantitative knowledge is accumulated. Even so, the wide diversity of the human condition continues to make individual patient diagnoses difficult to trust to expert systems alone.

The same limitations exist in any expert-system application where data are either inexpressible or incomplete. It is a truism in geophysical exploration, for example, that "oil is where you find it" and often not where one's data analysis says it should be. Satellite failures are never the ones that were anticipated; if they were, they would have been eliminated by design. Teachers know that no two students are alike; teaching aids need personalization.

A second major limitation is the difficulty of structuring the expert's knowledge, a problem not only for the machine, but for the expert as well. In a very real sense, the expert is part of the problem. The more specific the problem domain and better organized the knowledge of it, the easier problem solving will be, both for the expert and the expert machine. Both do well given well-organized knowledge and specific rules tying cause to effect or actions to situations.

In practice, this limits present expert systems to narrow applications, highly context-dependent (Parsaye and Chignell, 1988). Not surprisingly, attempts to date to use either general systems problem solvers (GSPS) or heuristics in expert systems have failed. GSPS are too far from the context. Heuristics are too far from specific rules. Consequently, expert systems are not yet useful as conceptual design aids nor as architecting tools. They are much better at being problem solvers, valued decision aids in well-structured operational environments, tireless diagnosticians, and complementary partners to less informed error-prone humans. In the right circumstances, they cannot only diagnose, they can treat and control other machines and operations in a predictable and reliable way.

In these feasible applications, the knowledge-structuring limitation takes a more mechanical form. How should knowledge be organized so that it can be used to respond efficiently to a wide variety of questions? The familiar filing system is organized to handle a specific set of questions. If a different set of questions must be handled, even if the data is the same, a different filing system is needed, hence, cross-filing. Extend that cross-filing manyfold to serve many users and the filing problem can become acute. A new technique, HYPERCARD™, helps address that problem in a way that is much like using a thesaurus. Its problem is a human one. Like that of using a thesaurus, the risk is in becoming lost and disoriented in the labyrinth of possible directions to take in searching out key information. But it is much better than starting a new filing system for each new batch of questions.

A third difficulty is extracting *efficient* expertise from the experts. Experts, like everyone else, have their own models of their world. These models are strongly conditioned by the expert's whole career. Replicating the expert's complete model and experience is impractical—something like building a model of a computer complete to the part level without building an identical computer.

An expert can determine causes from effects by, if necessary, analyzing the complete model in its historical and environmental context. Engineers, given enough time, can construct a failure modes and effects analysis (FMEA) through understanding a complete system design, its physics, its manufacture, and its operation. Incorporating all that knowledge into a computer and keeping it up to date, the "deep approach" to expert system design, is expensive in time, money, and equipment.

So designers of expert systems usually opt for the "shallow approach," determining causes by using unique, measurable effects and bypassing the technical chain that connects effect to cause. Expert systems built this way imply a model, but do not contain it. They cannot be expected to dig deep for answers nor respond well to new situations. By their very construction, they cannot respond as human experts do in realistic, that is, new and confused, situations unless their knowledge and rule base are as complete as the expert's.

The degree to which expert systems can mimic the experts thus depends on the expert's judgment of which parts of the whole model are necessary and reasonably sufficient for an expert system to be effective. Extracting that crucial knowledge has proved to be very difficult in any short period of time, which brings us to the expert's own internal model. If the situation is well-structured and the model is sufficiently complete, the expert can diagnose disease or failure in a structured, analytic way. If the situation is ill-structured (having more than one failure at the same time, for example, or having incomplete information), the expert, like architects, will start using common sense in order to make some progress in treating the problem:

- **If it ain't broke, don't fix it.**
- **Let's wait and see if it goes away or happens again.**
- **It was just a random failure. One of those things.**
- **Just treat the symptom. Worry about the cause later.**
- **Fix everything that might have caused the problem.**
- **Your guess is as good as mine.**

This author has heard all these commonsense heuristics espoused in system-failure reviews where they were indeed *responsible* responses to reality. They were indeed expert opinion. They permitted decisions to be made with incomplete and ill-structured knowledge.

And for those reasons, there would seem to be no reason why a suitably constructed expert system could not make the same responses, adopting the expert's heuristics.

There is also no reason why experts should not keep adding to an expert system's knowledge and rule base as new insights come about. Expert systems could learn from mistakes and better recognize their own limitations. If direct and immediate causes are not determinable, the systems should be able to sharply narrow down the number of likely ones.

But before that can be done, we need to know more about the experts, themselves—how they think and how they act.

ACCESS, PRIVACY, AND SECURITY

One of the more complex problems in communications and knowledge bases is the trade-off between access, privacy, and security. The legitimate user wants ready access, good privacy, and affordable security. The unauthorized outsider strives for undetected access and unattributable interference, even a measure of control, and takes advantage of any weaknesses introduced by the user's trade-offs.

Parts of the user's problem can be handled technically. Information can be encoded. Electronic barriers can be established that, even if breached, will register attempts at interference. Physical and personnel security can be established. Passwords or other authenticators can be used so that only designated individuals can access the information base. For the highly structured case of dedicated, known opponents, the opposing parties' motivations are reasonably clear. The attack and defense possibilities are more or less determinable. Cost/benefit ratios can be estimated, along with the risks and costs of being, or not being, detected.

A more difficult architectural problem is the ill-structured one involving surreptitious opponents, unknown intruders, hackers, and disloyal insiders. It is the problem of computer crime. Curiously, curing this problem is difficult not because the cost of computer crime is high, but because it *is not,* that is, it is not worth the trouble and expense. Or at least that is the perception of the users.

The computer security profession recognizes four kinds of computer crime, each of which calls for a different approach to prevention:

1. The computer as an object of attack, for example, physical damage.
2. The computer as a repository of value, for example, data theft.
3. The computer as an instrument of attack, for example, embezzler's tool.
4. The computer as an image, for example, using "the computer made a mistake" as a coverup for deliberate criminal intent.

Encryption and access keys only partially address the problem. In any case, they can do little about misuse of data bases by authorized but criminal users. But even for protection against electronic embezzlement, the solutions may not be implemented. For example, some years ago, there was a push for greater security for financial transactions. More and more financial information was in computer form, accessible remotely. Computer hacks were demonstrating the ease of unintended access. So encryption using a National Bureau of Standards system was developed and placed on the market. There was essentially no interest from the banks. Why?

Because far more was lost to insider embezzlers (or so the data indicated) than to electronic thieves, and embezzlement insurance was a normal, affordable cost of doing business. The risks evidently were much higher in personnel than in the electronics. Furthermore, the systems were cumbersome to use. Encryption keys had to be protected and changed, a nuisance with no apparent benefit. So people stopped changing keys, which negated the protection. After a few trials, no banks purchased the systems, though some foreign parties did.

Electronic teller machines now use access codes, but their cost effectiveness is open to question. The principal value seems to be in public relations, the encouragement of customers to use the machines by building confidence in their apparent confidentiality. It appears that the social climate will have to change before much more is done.

A highly contentious architectural problem is the sociopolitical one of conflicting interests in access to information. In short, the right to privacy. As recent Supreme Court confirmation hearings before the Senate so dramatically illustrated, even experts in the Constitution of the United States cannot resolve the issues, which by no means makes the architectural problems go away. Should the overall architecture of an access system under any circumstance permit access by other than the owner of the protected information?

Example:

Should one branch of the government have access to the knowledge bases of another branch? Should the IRS, the FBI, or the Department of Defense have access to an individual's credit rating files or even police records?

Example:

Should the public or the media have access to private files in the interest of the public's "right to know"? Should the rules be different for people in the private and the public sectors or for different kinds of information (financial, medical, arrest, conviction, unsubstantiated allegations in security files, etc.)?

Example:

Should a credit rating organization have access to nonfinancial data bases in other organizations in the interest of determining trustworthiness?

Example:

If access in any of the previous cases is to be permitted, must notification of that access be provided to the original party? Before or after the access? Can the owner appeal the decision?

The answer to most of these questions is probably, "Well, it depends upon the situation. . . ." Is national security involved and who said so? Are criminal activities suspected and by whom? Is there reasonable cause for search and who decides? Will innocent people be hurt and what is their redress? A case-by-case resolution is hardly practical. So rules have to be established, rules that are an essential part of the architecture. And rules depend upon assumptions of who can and who cannot be trusted.

Access, privacy, and security problems are unlikely to be resolved to everyone's satisfaction. At best, it is a complex trade-off, a delicate balance of conflicting interests.

And, as security professionals will point out, the performance of security systems is inherently uncertain. One can only reduce the risks. It is a good field for security systems architects, but a potentially treacherous one for the amateur.

INFORMATION SYSTEMS AND SOCIAL INTERVENTION

Communication between individuals or organizations is inherently a social activity, whether for business or pleasure. What might be less apparent is that any change in communications means a change in that social activity. A new information system *intervenes* in the structure if it is at all effective. It may greatly facilitate a new activity. Or it may provoke vigorous resistance.

More commonly, it may produce different results in different situations or with different groups (Schwartz, 1975). The results may not be as predicted. And there may be ulterior motives and hidden agendas behind the stated requirements of the parties concerned.

Example:

An integrated information network was proposed for all law enforcement activities in a particular state. It was violently opposed politically and was not implemented.

Example:

A local-area computer network was installed in a company and worked well until it became known that higher management was monitoring computer usage, ostensibly to see who rated more computer capacity. But monitoring also revealed who was working how hard and on what. An uproar followed. The Big Brother Syndrome in the workplace.

Example:

An important form of communications is a road network, permitting people to interact with others more easily. In a Southeast Asia country interested in helping the populace market their goods efficiently, but plagued with insurgency and drug problems, the local roads were upgraded and paved. The principal beneficiaries turned out to be the insurgents and drug suppliers, who could move about more freely and control the roads at will.

Example:

Communications in the armed services have historically been funded and built by the services to requirements of the military chain of command. It is characteristic of any chain of command, military or civilian, that each individual in the chain wants limited communication from above and excellent command to subordinates; an architectural impossibility. Furthermore, each individual resists communications to subordinates coming from outside—whether from other commands or from someone further up the chain. The resultant military communications systems therefore often precluded direct electronic interorganizational communication, forcing all such communications to go through a few designated individuals, usually at command headquarters. The phenomenon is not unique to the military services. A similar arrangement is often enforced in business organizations for written correspondence. Attempts to implement interoperability of all military service communications have consequently been very difficult, even after military events showed the dangers incurred by not doing so.

Example:

The likely consequence of a company installing a computer network that technically could allow everyone to exchange technical or business information with everyone else is a proliferation of off-line "protected" data bases. The rationales are honest and real: protection from undocumented change or viruses, dangers of premature disclosure of unaudited or uncertified information, and privacy of personnel records. But the effect can be the opposite of what the proponents of open information exchange might have desired.

Example:

The telephone companies relatively recently initiated an Information Access Service (dial 976) for prerecorded messages. It is now being curtailed because the access it provided was one that parents did not want for their children.

A real-world architecture includes the resultant social change. Difficult as it may be for the architect to predict, introducing or modifying a complex information system intervenes in the social fabric. The system architecture, to succeed, must be able to adapt.

SOCIAL INTERVENTION BY MACHINE INTELLIGENCE

Earlier in this chapter, the question was raised in a technical context of how smart a machine should be. We raise it again here, but in a sociopolitical context. Machines can be made too smart for their own good if their presumed intelligence offends human sensibilities, prerogatives, beliefs, or feelings of self worth.

How is this rejection of high-level machine intelligence expressed? By maintaining that computers will only be "aids" to doctors, engineers, military commanders, national leaders, airline pilots, and other decision makers that make judgments that affect our lives. By insisting a priori that computers do not make decisions or judgments, even if they are faster, have better models, draw more informed conclusions, and exhibit a much lower error rate than people do.

No doubt such rejection will lessen with time. The younger generations are much more accepting of computer intervention in their lives. For example, if different age groups were asked the question, " Can computers think?" the oldest respondents would probably answer, "No." The middle ones would respond by asking, "What do you mean by 'think'?" And the youngest might respond, "Of course."

Human error rate is already recognized as unacceptable in certain critical situations; machine intelligence is accepted as preferable. This necessity has long been recognized in manned space flight systems. Psychologically, however, it may take some time or a serious change in circumstance before the general public will be willing to accept the machine as smarter and/or as having better judgment than humans.

Introducing machine intelligence, perhaps even more than introducing nuclear energy, will have to take human sensibilities into account or the introduction may be long delayed. There is, however, a heuristic well known to psychologists and experts in personnel relations:

> **In introducing technological and social change, *how* you do it is often more important than *what* you do.**

Or

> **If social cooperation is required, the way in which a system is implemented and introduced must be an integral part of its architecture.**

These heuristics apply to more than information systems, of course. They are introduced here because strong rejection to the introduction of machine intelligence may catch many systems architects unaware. The mitigations are known: (1) participation in the conceptual design phase by customers, workers, and the public; (2) an agreement on the management of the information system, that is, on its software and on the rights of human intervention; and (3) provisions for making changes when and where needed.

And hence:

Don't make an architecture too smart for its own good.

It should be noted, nonetheless, that there is risk in backing off too far. An institution—group, company, or country—that accepts intelligent machines in a man–machine partnership will have as great an advantage over a non-accepting competitor as one that uses superior mechanical machinery and sensing instruments now. Truly, wealth is knowledge and knowing how to use it [Peter Drucker in Lord Lecture, USC 1988]. Machine intelligence can greatly, perhaps by factors of thousands, increase access to and use of knowledge. But only if it is permitted to do so. Experience in the attempted introduction of nuclear power should have convinced us of that truth.

SUMMARY

It is a rare system architecture that does not contain an information-system element within it. Placing that element outside the system boundaries is no longer sensible. Key architectural parameters are the level of intelligence of the machine and its elements. The important parameter in distributed systems is the distribution of control authority, the success of which depends upon distributed intelligence.

The introduction of intelligent systems and of new top–down architectures requires careful timing and social cooperation. Machines can be made too smart for their own good. Nonetheless, with the advent of new technologies and architectures, major changes are foreseeable in C^3I, signal and image processing, manufacturing, and expert systems—with consequent changes in the many other systems that contain them as elements.

RECOMMENDED READING

DAVIS, R. (February 1986). "Knowledge-Based Systems." *Science* 231, 957–63. This is a short summary of the field and its principles. It presents architecture, models, spreadsheets, and examples of current systems in geology, electronic troubleshooting, aeronautics-astronautics, chemistry, medicine and mathematics. And it contains research issues.

EVERETT, ROBERT R. (Summer 1981). "Command, Control, and Communications." *The Bridge* National Academy of Engineering 11, 2, 17–26. This is a short history of military C^3, its current problems, and an approach to its improvement.

FROSCH, R. A. (1982). *Robots, People, and Navies,* the Charles H. Davis Lecture Series. Washington, DC: National Academy Press. This book focuses on the technology of remote operation using robots and its central problems—the need for very high reliability, the need for better consideration of economics, and the human and ethical problems of intelligent systems, for example, their control and their effects on people.

LENAT, D. B. (September 1984). "Computer Software for Intelligent Systems." *Scientific American* 251, 3, 204–13. This special issue on computer software shows the application of human heuristic approaches to the computer solution of system problems. It is an overview of what this text would call architectural heuristics in a computer context. See especially the description of the expert system EURISKO.

LERNER, E. J. (June 1988). "Computers That Learn." *Aerospace America* 26, 6, 32–34, 40. This is an update on the newest neural networks and their ability to learn, including work at Johns Hopkins, Hecht Nielsen NeuroComputer, Hughes Malibu, Cal Berkeley. It discusses NETtalk, MARK IV, and ADAPT. It focuses on pattern recognition and learning language.

PARSAY, K., and M. H. CHIGNELL. (1988). *Expert Systems for Experts.* New York: John Wiley. See especially Chapters 1, 2, 8, and 9.

SALTZER, J. H., and M. D. SCHROEDER. (September 1975). "The Protection of Information in Computer Systems." *Proceedings of the IEEE* 63, 9, 1278–1308. This presents the structures necessary to support information protection. It is one of the best papers for architects on the trade-offs and problems of security, privacy, and access.

Scientific American. (October 1988), 259, 4. The whole issue is on advanced computers, architectures, applications, networks, etc.

TO BROWSE, DEPENDING ON INTEREST

BOYES, J. L. (ed.). (1987). *Principles of Command and Control.* Washington, DC: AFCEA International Press. These are essays on command and control, principally but not exclusively naval, and its architecture.

BUSH, VANNEVAR. (July 1945). "As We May Think." *Atlantic Monthly* 101-8. This is a classic in the field of information capture, storage, and retrieval, both human and machine, predicting automatic cameras, HYPERCARD™, HYPERTEXT™, and point-of-sale developments even before WWII had ended.

BUZBEE, B. L., N. METROPOLIS, and D. H. SHARP. (Fall 1983). "Frontiers of Super-computing." *Los Alamos Science* **9**, 65-71. This examines the importance of super-computers and the need for massively parallel computers to handle problems in magnetic fusion, plasma physics, and nuclear test analysis. It is a short tutorial on the efficiency of parallel processing.

CONLEY, R. E. (January 1979). "Military Command and Control (C^2)." *Signal* **33**, 4, 14-17. Views C^2 as resource allocation. It introduces concepts of volumes of percep-tion, deception, and influence, and their dynamic changes during combat; nested C^2 systems; and dialogue versus orders.

GERSHWIN, STANLEY B. (January 1989). "Hierarchical Flow Control: A Framework for Scheduling and Planning Discrete Events in Manufacturing Systems." *Proceedings of the IEEE* **77**, 1, 195-207. This describes the synthesis of operating policies for manu-facturing systems, that is, the feedback laws that respond to potentially disruptive events and that are computationally tractable.

HAYES-ROTH, FREDERICK, D. A. WATERMAN, and D. B. LENAT. (1983). *Building Ex-pert Systems.* Reading, MA: Addison-Wesley. See especially Chapters 5 and 8, max-ims (heuristic guides) on constructing and evaluating expert systems.

NAGLER, G. R. (ed.). (1987). *Naval Tactical Command and Control.* Washington, DC: AFCEA International Press. With references, this book presents essays on command and control and its architecture.

OGDEN, J. M., E. H. ADELSON, J. R. BERGER, and P. J. BURT. (September/October 1985). "Pyramid-Based Computer Graphics." *RCA Engineer* 4-15. This is found in an issue on computer graphics. A novel "pyramidal" architecture presenting images on both large and small scales by representing the image mathematically on many dif-ferent spatial scales. Useful for image restoration purposes, creating shadows, shad-ing, and fractals.

PATT, YALE N. (ed.). (January 1989). "Real Machines, Design Choices/Engineering Trade-offs." *Computer* **22**, 1, 8-10. This describes the business of producing comput-ing machines and the choices to be made in succeeding in the marketplace. The stories of six real designs (Cydra 5, Convex C2, Cray X-MP, TI Advanced Scientific Com-puter, NS32532 microprocessor, and H-P Precision Architecture) are told in subse-quent articles. It gives retrospectives, reflections, lessons learned, and the group priorities.

RECHTIN, E. (Fall 1983). *The Technology of Command,* the Charles H. Davis Lecture Series. Washington, DC: National Academy Press. The book presents the opportuni-ties and risks of using technological systems in support of naval command and con-trol.

Schwartz, M. (ed.). (October 1975). "Special Issue on Social Implications of Telecommunications." *IEEE Transactions on Communications* **23**, 10, 1009–11.

Seering, W. P. (April 1985). "Who Said Robots Should Work Like People?" *Technology Review* **88**, 3, 59–67. This is a look at robots used in manufacturing and how they might best be designed, that is, let both humans and machines do what they do best in intelligent operations.

Snyder, F. M. (1989). *Command & Control: Readings & Commentary,* Program on Information Resources Policy, Harvard University, Cambridge, Massachusetts. It describes the command and control process in warfare.

Zorpette, Glenn. (October 1988). "Fractals: Not Just Another Pretty Picture." *IEEE Spectrum* **25**, 10, 29–31.

6

BUILDING THE
SYSTEM

The preceding chapters have focused on the architect's role in conceptualization—in deciding on the *what* and *why* of the system. This chapter focuses on implementation: *How well* can the system be built? Much of the answer, of course, depends on the adequacy of the conceptual model—no builder can remedy a fundamentally flawed concept. But, given a sound architectural foundation, success now depends on the skill of the builder, which is not to say that the architect is, or should be, uninvolved or unconcerned with system implementation.

Systems architects by their role and position are the participants who best appreciate the system's objectives and requirements in technical terms, who are specifically charged by clients to monitor and report on immediate or potential deviations from those objectives, who are routinely asked for advice on rectification of those deviations, and who are properly held accountable when difficulties in the later phases are traceable to conceptual flaws. Architects, in the interests of all the participants, provide a continuity from conception to final operation of the system. Of immediate interest, architects are more responsible than any other participants for the successful transition from conceptualization to implementation, that is, from systems architecting to systems engineering.

As should be expected of the keeper of system integrity, the architect's participation during system implementation peaks whenever deviations from the system objectives occur or seem likely. Ideally, participation is more by exception than by rule, more by monitoring than directing. One reason is purely practical—too much is going on for the architect to be everywhere. The other reason is the nature of system engineering.

THE ARCHITECT'S ROLE IN SYSTEMS ENGINEERING

By the end of concept development, there should be no disagreement between architect and client on the basic system concepts. If the system is a computer, the decision should have been made as to whether it is serial, parallel, or hybrid. If a launch vehicle, whether it is liquid or solid propelled. If an Apollo to the moon, whether the rendezvous is in Earth orbit or lunar orbit. The conceptual model, in other words, should be well structured.

The next phase is system engineering and design. In civil architecture, this transition is equivalent to going from architectural programming to architect-engineering. In defense systems, it is leaving phase 0 for phase 1.

If, as is often stated, the single mind is the essence of architectural integrity, then "the disciplined team" is the essence of engineering integrity. Tens and even hundreds of systems engineers must work to achieve carefully stated objectives, precise specifications, organized documentation, and tight configuration control, otherwise the system will disintegrate.

It therefore serves little purpose to debate here the jurisdictional question of just how much system engineering is done by the architect (not much because there are not that many architects) or how much system architecture is done by the typical systems engineer (not much—too many cooks spoil the soup). Overlap is essential—this interface looks fuzzy from either side. The serious mistake is to leave a gap.

The architect's task is by no means finished at the end of the conceptual phase. Progress must be monitored, not for supervisory reasons, but for checking the validity and consistency of the original system concepts and requirements. If things are going to go wrong later, the first symptoms will occur in systems engineering. Interfaces will act up. Designs will become overly complex. Estimated costs will be all over the map. The architect should then remember the **choose watch choose** heuristic and attempt to trace any problem back to the decision that might have been the source of it. It might well have been conceptual.

The systems architect today has a particularly strong professional interest in systems engineering because it, like architecture, is undergoing a revolution. Again, the agent is computer aids. The combination of system complexities and government regulations has led to a wealth of computer tools in analysis, engineering, programming languages, scheduling, costing, modeling, simulation, risk analysis, decision analysis, and for many of the "illities." Fortunately for the architect, these tools are teachable and are becoming available (Eisner, 1988).

Whether carrying out, participating in, or monitoring systems engineering, the architect must be abreast of these developments and speak the systems engineers' language.

DESIGN

The term "design," like "systems," means different things to different people. As used in this text, design is the next, more detailed phase after engineering. Like the systems to which it applies, design is relative. Just as a system to one individual can be a sub- or supersystem to another, what to one individual is a design may be an architecture to another. But, lacking a better term, design here means detailing within a broader, engineered architecture.

The architect encounters detail design by exception—generally because of a system failure caused by a misapplied bolt, a sneak circuit, a flaw in the thermal design of a rocket nozzle, or a misinstruction in a computer program.

Can the architect be held responsible in part for failures during systems engineering and design? Yes, if the cause of failure can be traced to the conceptual model, for example, system-level requirements and specifications. Were too many technologies stretched too far? Were the requirements inconsistent? Was the selected physical configuration such that unreliable parts could not be replaced without dismantling major elements of the system? Were contract provisions mismatched to the job, for example, were the contract provisions at variance with the client's priorities? If so, then the architect was in part at fault.

If systems engineering must be highly disciplined, system design must be even more so. Indeed, "careful design" is virtually synonymous with "design." And sloppy design leads to failure.

These truths are self-evident to designers. Complex systems, however, are putting new pressures on designs and designers. As noted earlier, and will be discussed further in Part Two, the demands imposed by complex systems for element quality and reliability are becoming so high that for all practical purposes the elements must be "perfect." The techniques used for "good enough" products will no longer be adequate. This fact is most apparent for complex systems that expanded from modest beginnings with little or no rearchitecting along the way.

Example:

When computers were first used, they operated independently, as "stand alones." To obtain still more computational power, computers were then interconnected through communications systems. But the users still expected the same system reliability even though more units, say five, were involved, each with a "good enough" reliability, say, 0.95. The resultant 0.76 reliability was virtually disabling. To retain the acceptable 0.95 for the system as a whole, each element had to be 0.99, that is, five times as reliable (one-fifth the failure rate). There is a prevalent misconception that "a bolt is a bolt is a bolt," regardless of the complexity of the system of which it is a part. *This example applies whether the element is a bolt, a fixture, a landing gear, a launch vehicle, a computer program, an organization, or a process for design, production or testing.*

Example:

Almost all space launch vehicles, including the solid rocket boosters for the Shuttle, trace their design to the early ICBMs. For early ICBMs, a failure rate of one in five flights, with quantities in the hundreds and with payloads worth a few million dollars each, was acceptable. They met the objective of being cost-effective deterrents to strategic war. They were logical candidates to launch the early satellites. With a great deal of effort, they were improved to an operational failure rate of less than 1 in 10, occasionally reaching 1 in 25, but by then the cost of the space payloads they were launching was hundreds of millions of dollars each, the payloads were few of a kind, and the financial risk per flight had reached a billion dollars. The demand, now, is for failure rates of less than 1 in 50.

Hence the lesson learned:

An element "good enough" in a small system is unlikely to be good enough in a more complex one.

This heuristic has serious implications in systems engineering and design. Unthinking acceptance of previously acceptable elements and processes can be a serious error. Spacecraft designers soon learned to subject off-the-shelf components and subsystems to the same evaluation rigor as new developments. Later on, it was realized that prior flight experience of itself did not qualify a component for future flights. It was not enough to say that because something had always worked before and had not failed yet that it would not fail on the next flight.

These experiences were quantified in a 1974 study by the Department of Defense on the reliability of aircraft avionics. In a large family of products, from the least expensive to the most complex and built in much the same way, as Figure 6–1 shows, it was found that:

Within the same class of products and processes, the failure rate of a product is linearly proportional to its cost.

The remarkably linear relationship of cost and failure rate may seem strange. Aren't more expensive things supposed to be better? Is the relationship anything more than a correlation, a coincidence? A likely physical explanation is that both factors depend upon parts count. The more parts, the higher the cost and the higher the failure rate. Similarly, a reduction in parts count by system simplification, consolidation, and tighter tolerances reduces not only parts cost and failure rate, but also the costs of system test, rework, maintenance, and warranty.

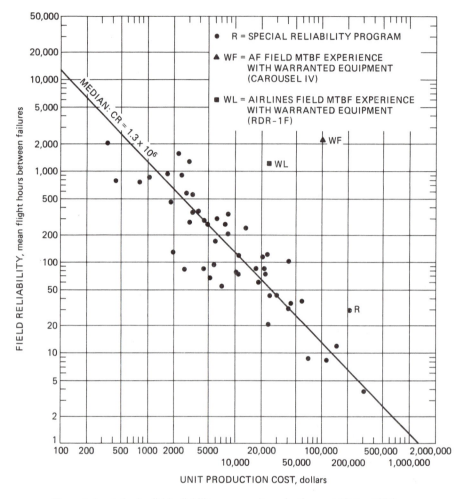

Figure 6-1. Avionics field reliability versus unit production cost (Gates, 1974).

In this 1974 study of 1970-vintage military aircraft avionics, the failures per hour equalled the cost in millions of 1974 dollars. (To account for inflation to 1990, divide the failure rate by about 3. To modify for commercial products in benign environments, further divide by about 10.)

Example:

If the DOD avionics relationship was applied to the NASA Shuttle avionics, comparable in vintage and operating environment and costing, say, $500 million in 1974 dollars, the failure rate would be 1 every 7 seconds, a clearly unacceptable result. Conversely, if the allowable failure rate were less than 1 for each 100-hour flight, Shuttle avionics would have to be at least 50,000 times better than military avionics.

How can such challenges be met? Historically, upgrading has been met by (1) trial, error, and redesign; (2) screening for defective parts; and (3) redundant elements and spare systems. These techniques work for systems that are simple and reliable enough that failures occur singly and independently, are correctable short of disaster, and represent only a small fraction of the total project cost. They are demonstrably inadequate for complex systems demanding upgrades by many orders of magnitude (e.g., the factor of 50,000 for the Shuttle).

Such challenges can be met only by changing the design and the process by which products are made. The challenge must be recognized for what it is—a challenge to the implementation process as a whole—and for what it is not—a mandate for more intensive trial, error, and correction procedures.

This leads to one of the better-known heuristics:

Quality can't be tested in, it has to be built in.

Or, perhaps more accurately,

High-quality reliable systems are produced by high-quality architecting, engineering, design, and manufacture, not by inspection, test, and rework.

Inspection and test are *certification* mechanisms, certifying that the concepts, design, and fabrication are satisfactory. Treating them as design aids in a trial-and-error approach is too late, too expensive, and may be hazardous to the system's continuing health—particularly if the trials to find the errors are passed to the users.

Stating that quality depends upon the complete implementation process implicitly acknowledges that all phases contribute to system failure. Conceptual design failures are catastrophic more often than not. If discovered late, recovery may be impossible and the system abruptly terminated. System engineering failures, for example, poorly engineered interfaces, can lead to unnecessary complexity, cost, and delay. But recovery is usually possible prior to system certification; if not, some loss of function and/or increase in cost is the usual consequence. Design errors, because so many piece parts and elements are involved, are the most common causes of system failures, particularly the early ones.

It is important to appreciate that the breadth and variety of design errors that occur even in the best of aerospace systems preclude a single easy solution. None of the real-world errors that follow was detected prior to failure under test.

- Improper ratings of component
- Inadequate design of power supplies, wiring harnesses, and connectors
- Stressing otherwise qualified components beyond their originally intended limits
- Lack of self-protection provisions against possible test goofs

- Inadequate venting of a spacecraft fairing
- Use of nonmetallic fairings on a launch vehicle, causing increased susceptibility to lightning
- Placing power circuits on slip rings adjacent to signal-circuit rings in the same assembly, risking catastrophic electrical short circuits
- Brackets and fittings that aggravate the effects of vibration through resonance enhancement
- Locating failure-prone elements where they cannot be replaced without system teardown
- Software coding errors

The architect can do very little about design errors like these prior to their discovery, other than to alert system engineers to potential errors that have occurred in other systems.

After discovery, recovery is primarily up to the designer, the system engineer, and the system architect in decreasing frequency, but with increasing consequences to the system as a whole.

The designer can change the component and its immediate surroundings. The system engineer can alter functional interfaces. The architect, with client concurrence, may have to change the system functions themselves. Fortunately, providing the cause of a failure is clearly identified, recovery by redesign and product change normally eliminate it as a source of future failures. Failures traceable to design, therefore, have a special characteristic—they steadily decrease as system development proceeds. Thus, one way of determining the real-world status of system implementation is the rate at which design errors are detected and corrected. If the rate is high, the system is still in development. If it has become very low, the system is close to operational.

It is naïve to declare that participants are responsible only for their own errors. In system implementation, all participants must be responsible for understanding the system consequences of all errors and taking appropriate action in the interests of the system as a whole.

Hayes et al. (1988, p. 224) make the point particularly well. Their particular context was manufacturing-process control. But the point applies equally well to the implementation process as a whole. Stated as an heuristic:

In correcting system deviations and failures it is important that all the participants know not only *what* happened and *how* it happened, but *why* as well.

The underlying cause of a component failure may be much deeper than a detailed design error. It could trace back to conceptual design or an assumption of components or materials that could not be made—the infamous "nonobtainium."

The other side of unexpected failure is unexpected success. As a matter of fact, if implementation from conceptual design to acceptance has been very well done, the chances of unexpected successes can approach those of unexpected failures.

A true story:

Some of the most astonishing unassisted recoveries from failure occurred in the early NASA/JPL spacecraft on their way to Venus and Mars. Potential disaster was replaced by remarkable success. The disbelieving engineers said it must be Just Plain Luck, only fitting for a laboratory with those initials. But Bob Parks, the flight project leader, had a better explanation: "If you have done everything that you can as well as you can, and then go back and check every step, then the breaks have to come your way as often as they go the other way!"

The chances of unexpected success or failure, of course, can depend upon how conservative the original assumptions were in conceptual and system design. If the assumptions of system performance turn out to be very conservative, the system may indeed perform better than was expected, although if too much better, the system will be criticized for being overdesigned. But if the unexpected success can be exploited—just as unexpected failures can be corrected—there is a clear gain. Again, the sooner a deviation is detected, the greater the chances of making a system gain at minimal cost in time and expense. Therefore:

> **Next to interfaces, the greatest leverage in architecting is in aiding the recovery from, or exploitation of, deviations in system performance, cost, or schedule.**

On closing this section on design, it is worth noting that many of the heuristics given in the earlier chapters on conceptual modeling apply to the system engineering and design phases as well, for example, those on interface discontinuities, interface characterization, problem expansion, challenging extreme requirements, sanity checks, expecting the unexpected, unbounded limits, and retaining options.

DEVELOPMENT

Very few modern systems are simply aggregations of existing elements. Even those constructed in new or expanded configurations may require upgrading of seemingly mature elements—as noted in the **not good enough** heuristic before. Most modern systems, and particularly those in the aerospace and information fields, are driven by attempts to exploit new technologies for new purposes or lower costs.

The result is a need for development, not only of novel elements, but of new interfaces, relationships, and system consequences generated by the new technologies. All these developments involve uncertainty and risk, many traceable to the assumptions made in the conceptual model, for example, just how much of the promise of a new technology can be realized in this particular system?

The purpose of development is to reduce those uncertainties and risks, the sooner the better. There is little disagreement on this point. The differences arise over individual judgments of the levels of uncertainty and risk involved. As might be expected, researchers underestimate the difficulty of development of their technology, developers underestimate the difficulty of incorporation of their developments into systems, and systems designers underestimate the difficulty of manufacturing a system demonstrated, at best, in prototype form.

And everyone underestimates the biggest cost increase—the cost of the "standing army," that is, all the people responsible for other subsystems and tasks that are held up waiting for the pacing element.

The architect's problem is not the developments as such. Those are for the specialists. It is with the system consequences of the developments, that is, the risks to system performance, schedule, and costs of immature technologies. Experience is slowly accumulating and being built into useful cost models for estimating the system consequences of introducing new technologies. Suffice it to say that the newer the technology, the greater by far have been the system consequences in cost, cost risk, and schedule delays.

This reality is not a call for conservatism—no risk, little gain. It is, instead, a call for better understanding, right from the beginning, of the level of system risk introduced by each new technology. It is a call for the architect to identify and estimate the risks and to indicate how they might be reduced.

The client, nonetheless, has the right and responsibility to decide on the level of risk—in effect, on how fast to proceed from concept into manufacturing. The architect's task is to help reduce the uncertainty in that decision to one of calculated risk as soon as possible. The costs of miscalculation can be very high once manufacturing has begun.

MANUFACTURING AND PRODUCTION

This book began with an expanded description of the conventional waterfall (Part One introduction), the process by which the system is built.

It is now time to add another dimension to that waterfall, one that stands behind all the blocks—the *resources* required to implement each phase of that waterfall. The resources, both human and physical plant, can be envisioned as a "template" on which the system is built. Thus:

> **Just as a piece and its template must match, so must a system and the resources that make, test, and operate it.**

Or

> **The product and the process must match.**

This heuristic is clearly evident in the field of robot design. Engineers engaged in the application of robotics to manufacturing have a special expression: "simultaneous engineering" for achieving the match. Robots have certain strengths: repeatability and precision, and weaknesses: tactile feedback and control. These characteristics are best used for products of particular shapes *different* from those best handled by humans. Simultaneous engineering designs the product and the robotic process together. Designing either independently has proven to be a costly error.

By looking at the acquisition waterfall as a whole, one sees that some of the largest and most important resources are those for manufacturing and production. Given sound engineering and design, manufacturing and production largely determine how well a system can be built.

To manufacture and produce a major complex system requires a comparably complex system—a production complex—of interconnected supply, manufacturing, assembly, test, and distribution facilities; information systems for monitoring and controlling the processes; and skilled operators and managers to assure its efficiency, quality, and responsiveness to the projects it supports.

A production complex is a true "complex system" with all that that implies—functions to be performed, a form to be architected, a system design, multiple interfaces, evolutionary if not revolutionary upgrades, sociopolitical issues, quality problems, and a real world to deal with. It presents the systems architect with both opportunities and constraints.

Fitting the product and process together is a matter of mutual accommodation. It is rare that the only adjustments are on the process side. Production complexes are so large, take so long to construct, and must be amortized over so many products and years that forcing them to fit a preordained product architecture is seldom practical. The consequence to the system architect is:

A system architecture cannot be considered complete lacking a suitable match with the process architecture.

This statement implies that the final system architecture will depend upon which contractor builds the system. Consequently, the contractor must participate in both product and process architecting at least to the point of assuring that the two match. The penalty for excluding the contractor is a lesser and more expensive product than necessary. Only a doctrinaire systems architect would refuse a contractor's suggestions for adjusting the product architecture for a better fit.

When all is said and done, the major factor in fitting the two architectures, product and process, together is better understanding by each participant of the needs and problems of the other.

One way for the product systems architect to understand manufacturing and production is to recognize it as the complex system that it is. Then consider the following architectural perspective on achieving manufacturing efficiency by Hayes et al. (1988):

> The equipment, or hardware, by itself is rarely the primary source of a factory's competitive advantage. What matters is how that hardware is used and how it is integrated with materials, people and information through software—the systems and procedures that direct and control the factory's activities.
>
> The architecture of a manufacturing system—which includes its hardware, its material and information flows, the rules and procedures used to coordinate them, and the managerial philosophy that underlies them all—largely determines the productivity of the people and assets in the factory, the quality of its products, and the responsiveness of the organization to customer needs. Indeed, two factories with almost identical hardware may perform very differently if they have different system architectures. (p. 185)
>
> Developing an architecture for manufacturing begins with an assessment of the basic tasks that the factory must perform.

The authors then analyze manufacturing operations and, in general agreement with other authors (Compton, 1987) draw some notable conclusions.

First, manufacturing consists of three basic tasks: (1) conversion from incoming materials to outgoing product, (2) material flows, and (3) information transfer. Only the first adds direct value to the customer. Therefore, to achieve manufacturing efficiency, design an architecture with the minimum required materials flow (and storage), and with the minimum required communication between manufacturing elements—certainly in agreement with the **minimal communications** heuristic.

Next, they see three causes of manufacturing difficulty: differences in departments (often cultural), complexities, and uncertainties. The cultural difficulty, from the experience of many organizations, is best treated by mutual personnel transfer. The authors would attack complexities through simplification (**KISS**) rather than through elaborate informational procedures. Uncertainties would be reduced through disciplined, dependable operations.

Process control, they believe, is best achieved by control over critical process parameters watched by everybody on the shop floor and by management—instead of controlling people and procedures, as is now common.

They also believe that a continuous refinement of the normal manufacturing process (a reportedly Japanese approach) is a better approach to process control than reacting to abnormalities (deviations). Architects focused on a single system might disagree with this approach, but architects of a family of products would probably support it.

And summing up the architectural perspective, Hayes et al. (1988) conclude that "The effective combination of product *and* process development increases the returns from each."

What does this mean to the systems architect? It gives hope that the same factory with the same hardware can be structured to some degree not only for its own greater efficiency, but for higher-quality products and responsiveness to the customer's needs.

Note, too, that one of the keys to a better fit between product and process is information flow, one of the most adaptable of subsystems for both products and processes. Hayes et al. simplify information flow by changing manufacturing control from procedures to parameters. The equivalent change for the systems architect would be to focus on what specific information should flow between waterfall steps rather than on integrating their internal data bases into a massive management information system.

Will such changes solve all the problems? No. But they might be traded for some that are more tractable. For example:

- Minimizing excess communication up the management chain is a trade-off with some loss of control of the manufacturing process.
- Continuous process improvement trades with process stability.
- Changing process architecture to better fit a product trades with a different architecture for every product—an impossibility if there are more than a handful of products on the manufacturing line.

What can be done to improve the process so that product reliability can be retained or improved as complexity increases? Three factors are usually called out. The first is simplicity, which sounds like a contradiction in terms unless it is achieved by better interfaces, fewer but more reliable elements for the same functions, and distributed smarts—in short, a better architecture. The second is process discipline. The third is understanding the process well, that is, process characterization.

Process discipline, more than anything else, is the avoidance of goofs. A goof is a straight out, unintended lapse of attention. Again using examples from the space business:

- Dropping satellites on the factory floor
- Putting fork lifts through a satellite
- Crushing and warping fairings
- Setting off overhead sprinklers above exposed satellites
- Interchanging identical type connectors and applying power
- Moving satellites into obstacles in high bay areas
- Leaving contaminants in propellant lines
- Putting a shorting plug into a charged battery
- Moving the launch stage into a highway overpass

- Leaving tools in the satellite when launched
- Dropping tools and safety rails onto a launch vehicle
- Launching with expended ignitor in a solid rocket motor
- Reversing of sensor inputs to the range safety plotting board
- Using a wrong size crimp tool on wire connections
- Cleaning "excess" adhesive off edges of solar cells; protection lost.

Embarrassing and expensive as these goofs were, these or similar human errors are endemic to human activities. Pilot error certifiably causes at least 20% of the aircraft crashes. But, without humans in the loop to <u>prevent</u> disasters, the record might have been worse.

The problem for the process systems architect, therefore, is to conceive processes that are less susceptible to human error, that warn the human of possible error, and/or that are more "forgiving" when human error does occur. The solutions may be as simple as a procedural change or a correction in a document, or as complex as a redundant interlock. Much can be done through education and training, explaining the peculiar needs of the product system, and emphasizing the importance of reporting even apparently inconsequential events or changes.

Architectures with these forgiving characteristics are found in a number of areas, notably, freeway design, aircraft controls, and friendly personal computers. Further application of error-tolerant process architectures would seem to be an early step in improving production discipline, making the process more forgiving of human limitations such as limited memory, logic, span of attention, and reaction time.

Another step is better planned and managed introduction of any change in existing processes. It is not always evident to all concerned that advanced manufacturing technology, for example, automation and computerized monitoring, is advantageous. Recent studies (Majchrzak, 1988) have found that the vast majority of new introductions of technology are unsuccessful. The principal reason? A failure to understand the impact on the human infrastructure. It is not uncommon for the advanced technology to make things worse, for example, if they result in information overload and added time delays in production. More straightforward human resource usage has often proved superior, for example, changes in assignments and responsibilities.

Process characterization is the third process change needed as systems become more complex. A surprising number of manufacturing and even computer program building processes are "black arts." As long as they are working, few people are concerned with them. When they stop working, few if any people know why. The semiconductor industry is notorious for a sudden loss of the production process, but so are specialty chemicals, speciality materials, precision machining ("only the master can make this part"), and others.

A case can be made for this state of affairs. Competition is keen, time is short, the technology is changing rapidly, the old process will become obsolete before it can be improved significantly, and "why fix something that ain't broke." Many researchers believe, with some justification, that they will do better to work on the next process than to try to understand the present one in detail. Most production managers, on the other hand, faced with a continuing series of immature processes and berated when they face shutdown of the production lines as a consequence, think otherwise. In any case, few would advocate depending on a manufacturing process that could not be trusted.

One way out of this dilemma, of requiring a trusted process but not having sufficient time to establish that trust, is:

1. Determine what *can* be trusted without question or test.
2. Determine what can be certified with minimum test.
3. Determine what remains that can be *eliminated* as a problem by product and process design, for example, superclean rooms to eliminate particle problems, tighter machining tolerances to avoid excessive tolerance buildup, supplier and operator certification, self-monitoring machinery, and well-maintained production areas.
4. Put what then remains on a "watch list" for close monitoring.

Although this approach might seem to be more expensive in the long run than understanding process limits in detail, it may be quicker and may reduce the risk of catastrophic loss of the process.

Make no mistake, increasing process discipline and characterization are not easy. It sometimes takes a disaster to force the changes. Some real-world examples that forced change during ongoing production are:

- Undocumented "improvements" in component manufacture
- Failure to test, but reporting that it had been done
- Refusal to supply composition information on "proprietary" adhesives, lubricants, solvents, and other chemicals
- Uncontrolled and undocumented storage conditions
- Uncharacterized processes leading to "time bombs" in operation
- Flawed histories of part manufacture, test, and storage
- Parts substitution without notice or engineering certification
- Contaminated work areas
- Hiding mistakes that later caused failure (a mistake is forgivable, but failure to report a mistake is not)

Unfortunately, many production failures, particularly in the early preproduction phase, are undocumented and "fixed on the spot." The same failure will predictably occur again—if not in that plant, then in another one unaware of the experience of the first.

ASSEMBLY

It is surprising how often systems are architected with little or no thought of the assembly process and even less of disassembly. Assembly, after all, is the time-sequential establishment of system interfaces and a critical part of the system architecture. But architects and designers concentrate so much on the fully assembled configuration that partially assembled configurations can be left vulnerable to electrical, mechanical, thermal, and procedural damage. Even when systems are well designed to be assembled, it may not be possible to disassemble them without serious damage. Some examples of assembly problems and challenges:

Example:

A major spacecraft was designed to be as efficient as possible in size, weight, and power. But its elements were so tightly bound together that any failure called for complete disassembly. But breaking and remaking any connection raised the risk of damage of a connector or part that previously had been tested and approved. Hence, repairing any failure during assembly and test raised the possibility of still more failures being created. There was a real risk that successful assembly could never be completed.

Example:

One of the difficult design problems of Space Station Freedom is to so configure its elements that as each element is launched and added to the partial station, the new configuration is a safe operational entity. More than a dozen launches will be required, mandating that more than a dozen different partial configurations be separately safe, stable, and capable of operating indefinitely. The design problem would be straightforward if each element were completely autonomous, but for many reasons, that is not practical. The station as a whole is a unified system, with many of its elements—electrical, thermal control, hydraulic, life support, attitude control, propulsion, etc.—spread in different ways through all of its major modules. A major challenge is to be sure that all partial configurations during assembly or emergency are operationally viable.

Production and assembly problems of this kind led to the common manufacturability question:

Sure it may work, but can you build it, assemble it and then disassemble it safely?

ON SCHEDULES

Not the least of the uncertainties in the implementation of a complex system is its schedule. The more complex the system, the more uncertainty there is in the time it will take to resolve interface problems, incorporate new technologies, and accommodate "unknown unknowns."

The schedule to produce a system is an essential element of the conceptual design, often being a design driver. In one form or another, the old rule stands:

Performance, cost, and schedule cannot be specified independently. At least one of the three must depend on the others.

In the normal course of building a system, performance and annual cash flow tend to be held constant; changing either is more difficult managerially than taking more time—the necessary time in man-hours—to get the job done. But if the schedule slips excessively, client needs may not be met, markets may be lost, and costs may rise. For some systems, and planetary exploration comes to mind, slippage past a fixed date is equivalent to program cancellation.

When slippages occur, efforts are made to catch up. If schedule recovery seems impractical, a day-for-day slip of the end date for every present day's slip is a common response. The implicit assumption is that the remaining part of the schedule will still go as planned.

The assumption is probably wrong. There are many reasons given for schedule changes, but two most common are "the job is more complex than we thought" and unpredictable funding. Both tend to be characteristic of a given program. Some programs are straightforward and routinely supported, others complex and controversial. If so, we should expect the *rate* of schedule slippage to be about the same throughout the program. This phenomenon leads to the **rubber schedule** heuristic:

Schedule stretch is a system constant.

Or

The time to complete is proportional to the time spent.

For example, if the research and development part of a project is taking 50% more time than estimated originally, then the expectation should be that production, assembly, and test will also take 50% longer. In other words, if you think R&D was complex, wait until you get into production. And what makes you think testing won't be comparably complex?

According to legend, the heuristic was first phrased by the Director of NASA's Johnson Space Center, Chris Kraft, a decade or so ago as:

In projects like ours (the manned flight series), take whatever the schedule is projected to be at the moment and multiply by 3/2.

Kraft is an outspoken realist. The "3/2 schedule" statement was a shocker, coming as it did while the Shuttle was in development. But his prediction held. It also held in complex systems outside NASA. "It's on a 3/2 schedule" proved a better characterization of program status than the short term "It's on a day-for-day slip schedule at the moment."

Not all programs are on a 3/2 schedule, of course. Some might be on a 1.1 or 0.9 track, as measured by prior adherence to schedule. Norm Augustine's Universal Fantasy Factor is 1.33, based on averaging the schedule slippate of 81 defense programs (Augustine, 1982). The heuristic, in addition, indicates that, barring major program changes, prior schedule adherence provides an indication of future adherence.

For the architect, schedule slippage is a likely indicator that complexity and perhaps quality are not what was originally estimated. If so, options should be explored to adjust the program accordingly, from objectives to system acceptance. If a schedule must be maintained regardless of other consequences, then options should be provided in the original program plan to make the adjustments possible. A similar heuristic may apply to cost, that past overruns indicate proportionally larger future ones, but the author has not yet seen a confirming study on that relationship. The underlying reasons—complexity and unpredictable funding—would seem to be the same.

SUMMARY

Although success in the building process is primarily the responsibility of the builder, the system architect has major roles to play in transitioning the conceptual model to systems engineering and aiding in the recovery from or exploitation of deviations in system performance, cost, or schedule—whatever the cause. The greatest system deviations, positive and negative, tend to be associated with the introduction of new technologies. The architect's task is to convert their uncertainties into calculated risks for use in client decision making.

The system architecture must match the architecture of the process by which the system is built, two key factors being process discipline and chararacterization.

Whereas the key questions in conceptualization are the function and form of the system, those in system building are how well can it be built, on what schedule, and for what cost?

RECOMMENDED READING

COMPTON, W. DALE (ed.), (1987). *Design and Analysis of Integrated Manufacturing Systems*. Washington, DC: National Academy Press. This is a collection of papers of a National Academy of Engineering conference that took place on February 25–27, 1987.

EISNER, H. (1988). *Computer-Aided Systems Engineering*. Englewood Cliffs, NJ: Prentice Hall. The systems engineering of large, complex systems and the use of modern tools to accomplish it are described.

HAYES, ROBERT H., STEVEN C. WHEELWRIGHT, and KIM B. CLARK. *Dynamic Manufacturing: Creating the Learning Organization*. New York: Free Press. See especially Chapter 7, 8, and 9. The book defines the architecture of a manufacturing system by its hardware, its material and information flows, the rules and procedures used to coordinate them, and the mangerial philosophy that underlies them all.

MAJCHRZAK, ANN. (1988) *The Human Side of Factory Automation*. San Francisco: Jossey-Bass Publishers. **1, 2,** p. 95–102. Lack of advanced human resource planning has been shown to be the reason that 50–75% of the attempts at introducing advanced manufacturing technology into U.S. factories are unsuccessful. Suggests organizational, training, and management strategies for overcoming the obstacles. Summarizes with a list of do's and don't's.

NADLER, G. (1981). *The Planning and Design Approach*. New York: John Wiley. "Design" in this text is used in its broadest sense, from initial purpose to final use. Particular emphasis is placed on focusing on the purpose of the system throughout the design process.

TO BROWSE, DEPENDING ON INTEREST

GATES, H. P., B. S. GOURARY, S. J. DEITCHMAN, T. C. ROWAR, and C. D. WEIMER. (1974). *Electronics-X: A Study of Military Electronics with Particular Reference to Cost and Reliability,* Report R-195, Vol. 2. See especially p. 59, Figure 11–5, avionics field reliability versus unit production cost, and Appendix E for source data. The report shows the linear relationship between price and failure rate.

LEVERTON, W. F., W. H., PICKERING, and J. F. KOUKOL. (1981). *Space and Missile Reliability and Safety Program,* prepared by Pickering Research Corporation as NSAC-31, Nuclear Safety Analysis Center, EPRI, Palo Alto, California. This report was prepared for NSAC on the special reliability and safety procedures followed by the space and missile programs.

NORMAN, D. A. (1988). *The Psychology of Everyday Things*. New York: Basic Books. Chapter 5, "To Err is Human," is a good catalog of the kinds of errors humans make, followed by Chapter 6, "The Design Challenge," giving the reasons for common design errors. See also Suggested Readings, p. 237f.

7

SYSTEM TEST, ACCEPTANCE, AND OPERATION

There is no activity, no step in the waterfall, no event in the system's life cycle more important—even traumatic—than a client's acceptance of a major system from a builder. Passing acceptance is akin to a final exam for the builder. Certifying to the client that the system will do what the conceptual model promised is the toughest professional judgment the architect will make.* Accepting, and completing payment for, the system is an irreversible decision for the client. System ownership, responsibility, and liability now shift from the builder to the client, or end user. If the user is the general public, the baton passes from manufacturing to marketing and sales. In the military field, the system transfers from a systems command to an operating command.

There is a natural conflict of interest in the acceptance procedure. Builders want to sell what they have built. The client wants a product that does everything the conceptual model promised. These wants are seldom identical. The common meeting ground is a mutually agreed upon set of acceptance criteria. Meeting those criteria, for example, passing acceptance tests, becomes the builder's goal and the client's assurance.

Regardless of what has gone before, the acceptance criteria determine what is actually built.

The builder has a strong incentive to meet the criteria, preferably with

---

*Certification is usually thought of as applied to hardware. It equally applies to software, security systems, documentation, training procedures, and the like.

flying colors, but not to go beyond that. Going beyond is a needless expense for the builder and comes straight out of profit. The client, on the other hand, wants nothing less than what the acceptance criteria call for and will hold up acceptance until that is accomplished. Thus:

> **For a system to meet its acceptance criteria to the satisfaction of all parties, it must be architected, designed, and built to do so — no more and no less.**

Unless they are well planned, acceptance proceedings can be contentious and frustrating. Mistakes, omissions, uncertifiable characteristics, or claims that "surely, it was obvious that . . ." will get little sympathy for the aggrieved party, whether builder or client. The inevitable response is, "it says here . . ." And no one is more responsible than the architect for "what it says here." Stretching out the process by issuing waivers just prolongs the agony.

The architect should make sure that the criteria are accurate, complete, and satisfactory to all parties *well before* acceptance, and, ideally, before the signing of the contract between client and builder. A convincing argument can be made that the acceptance criteria should be a part of the conceptual design; imperatives, options, and conflict-resolution procedures certainly should be part of the builder's contract.

An essential task of the architect, one that no one else can perform, therefore, is to assure throughout concept development that the client understands, and agrees with, the progressive conversion from ill-structured needs to function, then to form, and then to acceptance criteria. A client left behind during these early steps is almost certain to be dissatisfied if not litigious by project end.

The acceptance criteria's most important provisions are the qualification and acceptance tests.* Did the system pass the tests or not? It may seem obvious, but:

> **Qualification and acceptance tests must be both definitive *and* passable.**

Example:

The desired system was a large antenna that would continue to operate in 60-knot winds and during earthquake ground motions of 0.5 g laterally and vertically. But how could the builder demonstrate compliance with such specifications prior to acceptance or be liable after provisional acceptance for such system performance? The solution was a set

---

*Qualification test: How well will the system perform at its operating limits? It is normally performed after development and before production, for example, during prototyping.

Acceptance test: Will the system perform properly in the expected operating environment? It is normally performed just prior to system delivery.

of resonant-frequency tests of the structure and control subsystems that the architect certified would be acceptable surrogates for a real-world test.

Example:

It is technically impossible to test spacecraft on the ground in a way that will duplicate the operational environment of space, for example, prolonged free fall; a very tenuous but high-temperature atmosphere; full extension of booms, solar arrays, and antennas in a weightless vacuum; slow rotation about a precise absolute vector direction; thrust and maneuver actions, and so on. For this reason, tests in space are part of the acceptance process. Knowing that with few exceptions repairing or modifying a spacecraft in orbit is impractical, a crucial question is whether an incompletely tested spacecraft should be launched. Answering that question takes a carefully constructed series of ground tests, a validated system model, and closely watched design and manufacture.

Example:

The Department of Defense from time to time has wanted contractors to warranty their products during the product's military service, much as commercial products are warrantied in civilian service. The contractors object, saying that they are willing to accept the risks of not passing specified tests and of making corrections at their expense, but how can a contractor warranty a product for an unknown wartime environment? The issue remains unresolved.

The architect sees the criticality of well-defined tests in several quite different ways:

- As crucial in achieving client acceptance of the builder's product
- As a necessary element in system architecture
- As essential as part of the client's agreement with the promises of the conceptual model

All participants—clients, architects, and builders—need to understand that:

The realities at the end of the conceptual phase are not the models, but the acceptance criteria.

Thus,

Define how an acceptance criterion is to be certified at the same time the criterion is established.

A direct corollary of the foregoing heuristics is:

To be tested, a system must be designed to be tested.

For a number of practical reasons, it is also advisable to design the test to be repeatable. In software, because of its complexity, repeatability usually means automating the test.

Unfortunately, too many systems have been built that are very difficult to test. Test setups have been assembled with few system considerations in mind. The results have been costly in time and money. Estimates vary, but flawed setups at launch sites and other remote test sites have been responsible for tens of percent of the failures observed during test. Yet seldom is the test setup shown on the block diagram of the system to be tested. Few architectures specify the appropriate test setup, yet the latter is a major element and presents a critical interface to the system. In those cases where the final system test is intended to be at a general purpose test facility (e.g., the missile test ranges), it is not unusual for that setup to be different from that at the builder's factory; test results from one setup then do not match those from the other. Then, if something fails, did something happen to the system between the two test periods or was it the test setup? Should the system elements be sent back to the factory for retest? (They can pass at one and fail at the other.) The alternate approach, to duplicate a dedicated system test facility at all necessary locations, is usually judged as too expensive for the risks incurred.

Perhaps the most useful heuristic for the architect to recognize in such situations is that, whether so conceived or not,

The test setup for a system is itself a system

with all that that implies to the *overall* system architecture, interfaces, and interactions.

Complex systems pose a special problem. When fully connected, they exhibit characteristics in addition to, or different from, those of the elements separately. Thus, the system dynamic characteristics at the interfaces may be much different from the static ones when the elements stand alone.

In simple systems, architects and systems engineers can concentrate on designing the system to work when assembled and make provisions for testing later. But in complex systems, where multiple interactions determine complex performance, where breaking connections precludes that performance, where physical or electrical conditions prevent test access, where simulation is necessarily incomplete, the situation can be quite different. A good example is a high-gain negative-feedback system; testing it "open loop" is unrealistic and can be destructive. Further:

Example:

A proposed unidirectional transmission cable consists of a series of transmitters, links, and receivers, with each receiver restoring its received signal to produce a clean transmitted bit stream for the next link. If the system abruptly produces trash at the final output, which element in the chain was the cause?

Example:

A spacecraft was designed using heat pipes to conduct heat from one part of the space-craft to another. The heat pipe configuration, designed to work in the free fall of space, was three-dimensional. Unfortunately, vertical heat pipes do not work on the surface of the Earth—the force of gravity is greater than the thermal forces in the pipes. How, then, can the three-dimensional system be certified?

Example:

VLSI chips now contain far too many elements to be individually tested by external access. How can they be certified?

Example:

Some elements cannot be tested without destroying them. Pyrotechnic (explosive) elements, solid rocket motors, and other expendable items are of this type.

Example:

Some automatic redundant systems are designed to switch configurations on failure instantly and automatically with no perceptible effect on performance. How then can all redundant elements be certified externally as operational prior to use?

Example:

When a redundant system is operating properly, should redundant elements be checked out from time to time or should action be taken only when a failure occurs on the presently operating element? (Shifting from one element to another for a redundancy check risks failure, too.)

These examples pose a dilemma: how to apply the **testable systems** heuristic to complex systems, parts of which are untestable?

First, we must recognize that the dilemma comes about because of the structure—the architecture—of the complex systems themselves. In the digital communications system illustrated before, what is needed is a reverse channel to signal self-detected trouble. The heat-pipe system should be structured out of relatively autonomous, single-plane, subsystems or it will risk test failures and complexities unrelated to the eventual environment.

The VLSI example raises the general question of the level in a system at which testing is done, that is, its depth of penetration into the system. If the system were a simple resistor, we would not test every molecule, although we do test for total resistance, structural integrity of the resistive material and the wires, etc. The resistive material undoubtedly has imperfections in it, but unless they affect the total resistance appreciably, they are inconsequential at the system level. The question in the VLSI example, therefore, is whether it can be tested and accepted *solely at the system level*. If not, then redesign, with some inefficiencies, is the first recourse.

If redesign, in turn, is not practical, then the next step might be to expand the problem. The objective would be to be able to certify the system as operable even if the untestable elements fail. That is, enlarge the system architecture to one that can tolerate the failure. Alternatively, the effects of untestable failure modes might be limited by the addition of limit switches, bounded outputs, circuit breakers, defaults, and fail-safe modes. Elements that are destroyed by testing, such as fuses, pyrotechnics, and other one-shot devices, are commonly treated by networks of other elements in series and/or in parallel.

Testing redundant subsystems by switching back and forth between them during operation has long been a subject of controversy. On the one hand, there is the "If side A shows signs of failing, we must know whether the redundant side B will work before making the switch" school. On the other hand there is the "If side A is working, don't mess with it" school. Both schools make legitimate arguments, buttressed by examples. In more than three decades, this author has seen no clear resolution of the issue. But one thing is clear enough. It is dangerous to ignore the testability heuristic, that is, if it must be violated, it should be done so consciously and with an understanding of the risks involved.

The testability heuristic is not easy to satisfy for complex systems. The ideal approach would be to resolve the problem at the source through design rules such as the **minimum communications** heuristic, making the elements as autonomous and independently testable as possible. System test is then primarily concerned with certifying interface relationships, not parts reliability. Then, if the system as a whole works at all, its elements are probably working properly. Such designs, however, require a high level of design expertise and sophisticated analytic tools. Software architects have reached a similar conclusion. Because we do not yet know how to design error-free software for whole systems we limit the problems in certification by partitioning. One good piece of advice: the design rules may be as difficult to formulate as the software programs they are intended to support.

HOW MUCH TESTING?

One of the most perplexing questions in complex aerospace and electrical system programs is, "How much testing?" In the space business, where so much rides on every launch, testing is both elaborate and expensive. A reasonable question is whether total costs could be appreciably reduced, say, by as much as 20%, if much less testing were done? For example, could tests be combined and, if so, how?

There are good reasons for reducing testing beyond just reducing its cost. Testing imposes risks of its own. If the test setup is not well matched with the system, there are risks of unexpected delays and serious damage. Stress testing can wear out mechanical devices. Operating all elements just to test a few can risk collateral damage to all in the event of nonstandard behavior by the few.

The incentives to reduce testing certainly exist. But too little testing risks major failure and far higher costs than those for the tests themselves. Three recent reports give insights into the question.

The first report (Bollman and Blockinger, 1982) concluded that spacecraft lifetime in orbit would have been significantly reduced without the present (extensive) level of testing. The second (Hamberg and Tosney, 1989) quantified the value of testing, by type and number, on the expected rate of spacecraft failure in orbit. Present testing levels reduce the early (the first 45 days) failure rate to between 0 and 2, with none being catastrophic. Omission of even a few ground tests would more than double it. On the other hand, a few more months of testing might reduce that early failure rate by half. The third report (Musa, 1989) indicated a similar result for software, extending the idea to using the failure rate during development to predict how soon the software would reach its reliability requirements.

In the spacecraft examples, the amount of testing was consistent with the original system objectives, the available technology, and the present production processes. (Spacecraft are more nearly handcrafted than quantity produced.) But could the testing be further reduced?

It has been evident for many years that the earlier in the implementation process a failed element is detected and corrected, the less expensive it is. To a rough approximation:

> **The cost to find and fix a failed part increases by an order of magnitude as the part is successively incorporated into higher levels in the system.**

Likewise,

> **The least expensive and most effective place to find and fix a defective part supply problem is at its source.**

Example:

If a part costs $1.00, then to find and fix it at its arrival at customer receiving may be $5; at unit test, $25; at element test, $125; at system test, $625; and in operation, $3125—and it might well exceed $100,000.

Clearly,

> *The amount and cost of testing is a strong function of the expected failure rate of the system elements. To reduce the first requires reducing the second.*

The clear incentive is not only to find failures early, but to build things right in the first place. If everything were truly perfect, of course, there presumably would be no need to conduct tests to detect component failures. More realistically, if everything were perfect (zero defect) on delivery at every stage of manufacture, the subsequent testing should be much less.

The zero-defect approach is increasingly being adopted by competitive companies. Instead of the company simply rejecting a failed part or a questionable batch lot, the supplier is disqualified for further business pending requalification. Requalification is intensive and intrusive into the supplier's operations.

Testing for purposes of system certification is a different story. There is relatively little controversy over the justification or cost of system testing—it is the heart of system acceptance. The frustration is the high cost of tests aborted and rescheduled due to component failure during the tests, another reason why test costs depend upon component failure rate. Here the questions are less whether the elements work than whether they work together, whether the interfaces match, and whether the overall architecture performs as intended. The questions are most apparent in man-machine systems (aircraft, process control, C^3, and radar). Some analysts maintain that many catastrophic operational failures attributed to human error were, instead, system failures due to flawed assumptions, poorly designed interfaces, and inadequate system simulation and test (Perrow, 1984). In other words, the flaws are architectural *and the responsibility is the architect's.* To the extent that this is true, the amount of system testing will depend upon the architecture—its complexity, its testability, and its risks.

FLEXIBILITY IN THE ACCEPTANCE CRITERIA

Two important needs pull against each other in laying out the criteria for system acceptance:

- The need for system integrity
- The need for flexibility in response to unexpected change

The case for the first need has been made in the earlier sections. Carried to extremes, however, it can produce rigidity. In the systems business, absolute and unyielding criteria, specifications, requirements, and procedures can break a system. Costs can rise out of control. A budget change can lead to irrational production changes. A technology may prove too immature to be developed in time.

So, clearly, a good argument can be made for flexibility. A self-evident case is seen in consumer products: most customers do not appear until the product is for sale. The architect is faced with designing a product for hypothetical customers, making value judgments that a client or customer would otherwise make, including whether the product will be salable. Preestablished acceptance criteria may turn out to be irrelevant. Hewlett-Packard has an interesting technique for handling this situation—the next-bench syndrome. Hewlett-Packard engineers work at adjacent benches as they develop different instruments; so one way of getting a customer opinion is to ask the engineer at the next bench. Other engineers and architects rely on strongly held personal beliefs of what the customer will want. Steve Jobs, ex-chief of Apple Computer, Inc., believed he knew what the customers wanted in a Macintosh, a belief that needed revision and intensive reengineering once the product went on the market. Flexibility in adjusting the product to the real world of customer acceptance is a sine qua non in consumer products.

But flexibility can be carried to extremes, too. The results are loss of control of the product and process. The system "drifts"; system acceptance becomes ambiguous and confusing. Both client and builder suffer.

The balance between these conflicting needs is the use of retained options and planned, controlled flexibility. Aircraft companies call these measures "scars." Software designers call them open architectures, "hooks," and "patches." Military procurement professionals specify ranges of parameters within which the system is acceptable—minimums, goals, not-to-exceed prices, and sliding-scale cost incentives.

Flexibility does complicate the architecting, designing, building, and testing of a system. Not only must the nominal values of the system parameters be specified, but so must their acceptable limits. To complicate the problem further, the system must still be acceptable when any and all parameters are at the limits of those ranges simultaneously. Testing to such a criterion is impractical, so recourse must be made to key tests and to models that can extend the test results to the untested system limits.

Given all these complications, the architectural lesson learned is to incorporate options and flexibility very early in the conceptual phase, relinquishing them grudgingly and as late as possible—but also endeavoring not to add new options just because they become available.

DIAGNOSTICS

Diagonostics is used here in the medical sense, the diagnosis of ill health or failure of a system that previously appeared healthy. The emphasis is on difficulties that occur in operations after the system has been certified and accepted—rather than troubleshooting of systems under construction.

If the problem is relatively simple and there is sufficient time, then fault isolation by elimination (i.e., by first checking what seems to be working) is probably the easiest and least confusing approach. It is an approach that calls for a good but simple model of the system, preferably a model whose elements are relatively independent. It also calls for instrumentation designed to find the problem.

Failure modes and effects analysis (FMEA) is a powerful aid if its failure tree does not have too many branches. A tree with many branches, a model with many cross connections, or a failure with symptoms common to other failures can make for a tedious failure search.

If the fault has occurred before and the symptoms match almost identically, present expert systems can identify the situation rapidly and suggest preplanned corrective action. Expert systems have worked well for years for medical diagnosis and are now being used for spacecraft failures—wearout, electromagnetic interference, loss of synchronism or timing, and the like. They are also useful for solving problems in computer systems, knowledge-based systems, and robotics (Gerhardt, 1989; Smith, 1989; Wood et al., 1989).

Expert systems, in short, most easily handle common repeating failures, where direct ties between cause and effect can be established so that detailed models are unnecessary. These "modelless" diagnostic tools, with their limited knowledge-base architectures, can steadily improve themselves through discovering and learning these direct ties heuristically (Pazanni, 1987).

Major complex systems present a different picture. It is an interesting point of history that in almost all U.S. spacecraft programs to date, no catastrophic failure has yet occurred in orbit that was anticipated beforehand. In these necessarily well-engineered and tested complex systems, if a failure were anticipated, it would have been designed out or countered long before it occurred operationally. If the problem were unavoidable (e.g., wearout), it would have been monitored so that diagnosis and response could be prompt enough to avert catastrophe. The responsive architecture would be in place. Participation by the architect would not be required.

The architect is needed, instead, when failures occur that are uncommon, unanticipated, perhaps one of a kind, inadequately instrumented, and seriously disabling if not catastrophic. The architect is then almost always a member of the failure analysis and recovery team, as having a better understanding of the system model than others on the team.

A diagnostic question that arises early in any failure review is whether the model then in use can explain the failure or not, that is, how close is the best available model to describing reality?

Should the model be believed or not? Could the model itself be faulty and if so, where? Vehicle dynamics, orbital mechanics, thermal performance, and space radiation—all phenomena difficult to characterize completely—are invariably suspect. Were the observed failure modes predictable by the model but not noticed before they occurred during operations? Inquiries have ranged from structural dynamics, fracture mechanics, stress corrosion, and lubricants to integrated-circuit flaws in trying to solve the diagnostic puzzle.

Can the model's predictions of structural and electronic integrity be believed? If evidently not, is the discrepancy due to incorrect assumptions, to oversimplification, to errors in physics, or to mistakes in calculations? Is the discrepancy in the description of the system or of its environment? Was the system built according to the model or were substitutions and changes made during engineering and manufacturing? Was the problem in design or workmanship (the two most common causes) or in procedures?

The arguments can wax long and hard. Questions of liability intrude. Acts of God and small-number statistics are bandied about.

The urgent problem, however, is what to do next. And for answering that question, the architect is indispensable. The two available tools are the systems model and whatever factual data exist. The latter can be deceptive because:

The first "quick look" analyses are often wrong.

The likely reason for this heuristic is that people tend to look for the expected and obvious. But, for the most part, preventive measures have been taken against the expected and the obvious by design, by careful testing, and by mandated procedures. The expected, in other words, is unlikely. The real causes are more subtle. Early reports on airliner crashes are notorious for erroneous snap judgments. The *Challenger* accident was at first erroneously attributed to launching when it was too cold, the presumption being that launching when it was warmer would solve the problem. Explorer 1's violently changing signal strength was at first attributed to oscillator failure, when the real cause was conservation of momentum during energy loss. A Titan explosion was initially blamed on a flawed joint in the solid rocket motors; diagnostics showed it to be propellant breakaway from the casing.

Further, some of the most initially perplexing failures are the result of special circumstances that, together, create an unexpected total environment. Individually, none would cause the end result. It is a phenomenon that occurs in many fields—medical, environmental, electric power distribution, computers, manufacturing, and aerospace.

The *Challenger* failure mode was a combination of a misapplied O ring, a poorly designed joint, a joint leak (which, however resealed itself) pointed right at a critical support strut, a severe wind shear at the worst possible time, and aerodynamic pressure, which flexed the resealed joint just enough to reopen it while the solid rockets were still attached. Had one or more of these factors not existed, *Challenger* might have survived.

Intermittent failures of electronic equipment, loss of spacecraft in certain orbits during unusual solar activity, and the regretted reentry of *Skylab* similarly occurred due to unexpected coincidences.

Particularly disturbing are failures that the model predicts should not have happened. Contradictions between model and apparent reality can generate severe program-management crises. Management is confronted with conflicting but seemingly valid sets of information—some from the model, some from instrument readings, some from all-too-evident failures and anomalies—that lead to opposite conclusions on what to do next.

The conclusion: be skeptical and take your time. It is not unusual for the final conclusions of a failure review board to take many months. A primary reason for taking so long is

Recovery from failure cannot be considered complete until a specific failure mechanism *and no other* has been shown to be the cause.

The reason is evident. Unless this heuristic is satisfied, the wrong corrective action will be taken, undue expense will be incurred, and the failure will reoccur. It is not uncommon in diagnostics to be able to postulate several plausible causes early in the investigation, only to spend the rest of the investigation proving that all possibilities except the correct one could *not* have occurred.

Another heuristic worth remembering during diagnosis is one that originally came from aircraft flight test experience, some of it with fatal consequences. Aircraft are designed, whenever possible, to be fail-safe, that is, to be flyable under severely degraded conditions. Providing that the pilot or the aircraft can identify the conditions promptly enough to take appropriate action, recovery—a safe landing or bailout—is possible. Major failures have characteristic symptoms, corrective action for which can be almost reflexive. But when symptoms from several causes overlap, producing a "spectrum" of canceling, reinforcing, and interacting effects, time can run out for diagnosing and correcting the multiple causes.

Even if multiple causes could be identified in time, the actions taken in response to one cause may aggravate the effects of another. Meantime, the original failures can have created still further complications and recovery is unlikely.

Analogous situations exist in human illnesses, electric power distribution systems, computer networks, and transportation systems.

Less urgent but comparably frustrating circumstances arise in the after-event failure analysis. Most failures are traceable to a single cause and are correctable with some confidence. But, occasionally, a single cause cannot be found for all the symptoms, though one's intuition may say there *should* be one. The reluctant but necessary response is to treat all the symptoms, regardless of cause. The fixes may or may not correct the underlying problem. Only time, and more information, will tell.

As a rough estimate, these multiple-cause situations occur in perhaps 5% of the total failures in present-day launch vehicles and spacecraft. But the cases remain on the books as open issues—and open worries—until subsequent events clear them. The architect, meanwhile, is still on the hook. Thus the heuristic:

Chances for recovery from a single failure, even with complex consequences, are fairly good. Recovery from two or more independent failures is unlikely in real time and uncertain in any case.

OPERATIONS AND SAFETY

The reader will have concluded that many of the issues first raised in this last chapter of Part One are best resolved—or obviated—way back in the conceptual phase. The conclusion is true and intentional. It demonstrates once again that the perspective of the architect is a broad one, covering all system elements throughout their life cycles. Some issues must be resolved in the beginning, not because of their immediate consequences, but because of consequences far down the road.

Safety issues are a good example. Safety provisions clearly are important during development and construction. But over the lifetime of the system, safety is most important in operations where many people over many years are involved.

Even the best, most alert, and dedicated people can and do make mistakes. They fail to read or remember instructions and fail to follow procedures. They short-cut and are subject to opinions of the moment. They work best over a relatively narrow range of work load—neither too much nor too little. They are limited in attention span, vigilance, stamina, concentration, and tolerance of stress. For a variety of reasons, they may refuse to comply with system needs. In other words, they are human and not machines, for better and for worse. Most architects assume that the operators are at their best. The safety engineer cannot assume so. The machines that people control are enormously powerful and, inadequately controlled, can be dangerous.

Professional safety engineers attack the safety problem in several ways. Checklists help assure compliance with specific standards and regulations. Failure modes and effects analyses help evaluate the system, although they do not lead directly to hazard prediction. Diagnostics and fault trees help find the cause of failures. But, so far at least, safety heuristics for the architect are relatively few. Two of the most broadly applicable ones are

Place barriers in the paths between energy sources and the elements the energy can damage. (Kjos, 1988)

Knowing a failure has occurred is more important than the actual failure. (Kjos, 1988)

Safety engineers were among the first to endorse "forgiving" architectures. It is clear enough that systems must be tolerant of human failings if they are to work well. Safety adds the requirement to anticipate likely human *mis*use, intentional or not. Failure to do so, in addition to the likely damage and loss that may be suffered, may subject the company to tort liability for injury or death to the customer. For the architect, no failure can be worse nor longer remembered than one traceable to poor safety design. Safety, like quality, must be built in.

FINAL ASSESSMENT

No discussion of final assessments could be complete without an ironic heuristic that everyone suspects, but for which only anecdotes are offered in support. Its origin goes back at least 35 years, but its equivalent may some day be found in an Egyptian architect's tomb:

> **The probability of failure is proportional to the weight of brass in the immediate vicinity.**

Somehow, things that have worked satisfactorily during preparation fail to work when higher authorities, the brass, come to observe crucial tests.

On a still more serious note, an architecture is only as good as its many external judges—the client, the media, the courts, the government, the general public, historians, and the architect's peers—conclude it is. Because success or failure is in the eyes of the beholder, the final assessment may well be mixed. It is likely to be spread out in time. Some judgments, particularly for politically charged systems, may be quite subjective. Some of the most widely acknowledged successes began with a concept that was seriously flawed—but correctable.

Perceived success can be relative. If very little exists in a field, a factor of 10 to 100 improvement there is hailed, although its total impact may be much smaller than a lesser advance of a major system in another field.

Success is often a matter of timing. Some perceived successes became so only because of fortuitous changes in market conditions, public opinion, or government regulations, otherwise, they might have been ranked as failures. Or vice versa.

But when all is said and done, if the client accepts the system from the builder, the architect has achieved the primary objective, a satisfied client, a proud builder, and, in due course, an enthusiastic user as well.

SUMMARY

There is no event in the system's life cycle more important than the client's acceptance of the system from the builder. To achieve acceptance, the system must be architected, engineered, designed, built and tested to meet that objective—no more and no less.

Acceptance criteria and their corresponding qualification and acceptance tests determine the system that will be built. The architect should not confuse that reality with the abstraction of the conceptual model. Final assessments may vary considerably, but the architect will have succeeded if the client accepts the system from the builder.

A SHORT SUMMARY OF PART ONE, SYSTEMS ARCHITECTING, A COMPROMISE OF THE EXTREMES

Arthur Raymond, chief engineer of the DC-3, summed up architecting as a compromise of the extremes. Figure 7-1 expands that summation as pairs of competing factors pulling in opposite directions, held together by fit, balance, and compromise—the essence of systems architecting.

Figure 7-1. The tensions in architecting.

RECOMMENDED READING

BOLLMAN, V. S., and R. A. BLOCKINGER. (1982). *Spacecraft Redundancy and Environmental Tests, An Historic Evaluation,* Calabasas, CA: Lockheed Corp. This is a presentation made at the Satellite Services Workshop, NASA Johnson Space Center, giving results of Lockheed's extensive space vehicle experience during test and operations.

PERROW, C. (1984). *Normal Accidents.* New York: Basic Books. This book makes the case that dangerous accidents lie in the system, not the components.

TO BROWSE, DEPENDING ON INTEREST

GERHARDT, LESTER A., Chairman. (1989). *Advanced Robotics for Air Force Applications,* Washington, DC: National Academy Press. A good reference on the use of smart systems in logistics and combat support, esp. Chapter 2.

HAMBERG, OTTO, and W. TOSNEY. (January/February 1989). "The Effectiveness of Satellite Environmental Acceptance Tests." *Journal of Environmental Sciences,* **32,** 1, 20–26. This presents the results of analyses at the Aerospace Corporation.

KJOS, KATHRIN. (1988). *Development of Heuristics for System Safety.* Unpublished graduate report, University of Southern California, Los Angeles.

MUSA, JOHN D. (1989). "Tools for Measuring Software Reliability." *IEEE Spectrum,* **26,** 2, 39–42. The article shows that models can now predict, through a declining failure rate with development, how soon in the development cycle a software program may be expected to meet its reliability requirements.

PAZZANI, M. J. (1987). *Failure-driven Learning of Fault Diagnosis Heuristics,* El Segundo, CA: The Aerospace Corporation. An approach to learning efficient heuristics for the diagnosis of faults in systems. Focus on attitude control system of the DSCS-III satellite.

SMITH, DAVID M. (July, 1989). "Expert Systems' Role Broadens," *Aerospace America,* **26,** 7, 26–28. A recent summary of the status and issues in expert systems and a specific application to cockpit simulators.

WOOD, KEN, L. G. HANLEY, B. LAWSON, C. RANDALL, R. TURNER, and C. W. WANG. (July 1989). "Shuttle Failure Detection," *Aerospace America,* **27,** 7, 34–36. LATEST, a rule-based expert system in Ada, gives the reason for a hold or abort within three seconds of a Shuttle launch.

Note: The manager-reader will have noted certain similarities among systems architecting and concurrent engineering, continuous improvement, quality assurance and total quality management. All recognize that design and engineering should make provision for subsequent development, testing, certification, manufacturing and operations. All recognize or imply that product and process must match and that quality is cost effective. In addition, systems architecting makes the architect explicitly responsible for the conceptual design, for maintaining system integrity throughout the acquisition waterfall, and for certifying, prior to buyoff, that system objectives have been met. Further, the architect assesses the system-wide effects of proposed or actual changes and improvements in the system, process or context and makes recommendations accordingly.

part two

Challenges

INTRODUCTION

The central themes of Part One were (1) the nature of architecting and (2) the use of heuristics. Architecting of complex systems was described from several different perspectives—its origins, its models, its new tools, its new machine-intelligence options, and its role in system implementation. The heuristic approach to the nonanalytical and unbounded problems of complex system architectures was defined and a number of heuristics developed by example.

Part Two focuses on the special challenges faced by complex systems and the role of architects in responding to them.

The first challenge, addressed in Chapter 8, is that of ultraquality, a level of quality* so high that certification of it, in terms of statistical confidence, is impractical to demonstrate prior to acceptance or even before the end of design life. Nuclear power plants are required to be extraordinarily safe. Manned space systems are mandated to have failure rates of less than 1%. The challenge:

How can architects, engineers and builders design, build, and gain client acceptance for systems that cannot be certified by test and demonstration?

The second challenge is purposeful opposition. The architect faces an opposing architect. The proposed system faces a real or potential countersystem. Each may be imbedded in a still larger system. Chapter 9 discusses these "matched-pair" confrontations and the effects on the architectures of each. The challenge:

How can systems be designed and built that won't be made obsolete by a determined opponent?

The third challenge is the flow of time and and the system's place in that

---

*Quality, like architecting, has two facets, aesthetic and functional. The interest here is in the functional, that is, minimal functional deficiencies.

that flow. It deals with the effects of past architectural decisions and the potentials of present ones. The challenge is a serious one for very complex systems with decades-long development and operational lifetimes in a world of rapid change. The multidimensional complexity of modern systems makes them particularly vulnerable to disabling changes in any part of their environment. Not all architectures come to maturity in the form with which they began, nor is it always clear from looking at a final architecture just what originated it. Chapter 10 looks at forward and reverse architecting to help answer the question:

How can the architect maintain a sense of time and timing in designing and building long-term complex systems?

Chapter 11 addresses one of the most important developments in architecting—humanlike intelligent-machine behavior based on biological analogies. Philosophers may dispute whether machines can think, but there is little debate that anthropomorphic (humanlike) behavior is a consequence of special, and so far unique, human system architectures. The challenge:

How can human informational architectures be emulated so that problems so easily treated by humans can be handled or assisted by machines?

Of all the challenges, this one is the most dynamic. New architectures are appearing in the literature almost monthly—fighter aircraft cockpits that sense the pilot's intent and reconfigure themselves, insights into kinesthetic memory storage, new forms of content-addressable memory, and micromotors on a chip. It is truly difficult to keep up with the high rate of progress in biological and machine intelligence. Stay tuned.

Little recognized, until too late, is the profound effect economics and public policy can—or should—have on the architecture of complex systems. Yet these factors are difficult if not impossible to predict. Our understanding of them is best described as heuristic, and limited at that. The challenge for the architect, discussed in Chapter 12, is

How does the architect live with economics and public policy, knowing that one cannot live without them?

8

THE CHALLENGE: ULTRAQUALITY— EXCELLENCE BEYOND MEASURE

The greatest single challenge in architecting complex systems is ultraquality*—a level of excellence so high that measuring it with high confidence is close to impossible. Yet, measureable or not, it must be achieved or the system will be judged a failure.

As has been noted in Part One, there is a strong correspondence between a system's complexity and the quality demanded of its elements. As systems become more complex, their elements must be more reliable or survivable, as the case may be, or system performance will suffer. This relationship is the basis of the **not good enough** and **cost/failure rate** heuristics. For example, component failure rates of less than 0.001% may be necessary just to keep the failure rate of a 1000-part system in the range of 1-5%. But demonstrating 0.001% with reasonable confidence requires testing of 10,000 units, which may be greater than the total intended production. Without certification of the components, certification of the system as a whole will be open to question.

Ultraquality systems, containing millions of components, yet mandated to have failure rates well below 1%, raise the challenge almost beyond reach—

---

*Quality: a measure of excellence, that is, freedom from deficiencies. Ultra: beyond or greater than. Ultraquality: excellence beyond measure.

gaining client acceptance for systems that for all practical purposes cannot be certified by test and demonstration.

THE NEED FOR ULTRAQUALITY SYSTEMS

Half a dozen ultraquality cases come to mind, all subjects of direct concern to government, industry, and the general public. The fact that their requisite ultra-quality cannot be well certified is moot. Credible ultraquality must be produced nonetheless.

Case 1:

Unacceptable loss of life. It has been pointed out many times that 50,000 lives are lost on U.S. roads and highways each year. Not too much is done about that. But a very infrequent crash of a large passenger airliner with the loss of hundreds of lives causes great public concern and immediate investigation and correction. Nuclear power plants, demonstrably the safest of the major energy suppliers in casualties per year, are nonetheless perceived by many people as unsafe. The nation's manned space program, though no risk levels were stated publicly, evidently was expected to be ultraquality, that is, considerably better than a 1% system failure rate per mission. The lowest demonstrated launch failure rate prior to the Shuttle was about 4%, which makes the Shuttle, as of 1989, roughly comparable in quality to the lunar Apollo.

Case 2:

Leveraged dissatisfaction. Calling for a success rate of 99% would seem to be a call for high quality, yet a 1% failure rate, multiplied by the total number of customers, can lead to an uproar when the customers are in the millions and the products are worth a significant fraction of a customer's yearly income. Automobiles, computers, and consumer electronics are prime examples. Ten thousand dissatisfied customers, each expressing dissatisfaction to 10 friends, who pass it on, can damage a company's reputation for years. It is perhaps not surprising that the quality specifications on computer chips for automobiles are tougher than for most military procurements.

Case 3:

Small numbers. What is the meaning of specifying a 99.9% success rate, or 99.0% one for that matter, when the total number of units to be built ranges from 1 to 10? How can such a specification be demonstrated without testing far more units, or the same units for far longer times, than makes sense? Yet this situation is the normal one for space flight, for major ground installations, and for major naval combatants, carriers, cruisers, and submarines.

Case 4:

Smart systems. Modern smart systems, particularly those in the aerospace, energy, and manufacturing fields, control forces that could destroy the system itself. The calculations to do so are many and complex. Fly-by-wire aircraft (F-16, B-1, B-2), launch vehicles (Shuttle), and highly maneuverable spacecraft (Voyager and Solar Max) are well-known examples. A failure in these systems can wreak great damage in a very short time. A mission can be aborted when it should not be, or not aborted when it should. A spacecraft can lose all its control gas from a miscommand. A launch vehicle can be broken apart by commanding a too-violent maneuver or failing to accommodate a severe wind shear. In comparable business transaction systems, an irreplaceable data base can be lost or crucial deadlines missed.

Case 5:

Systems of extremely high value per unit. The cost of a single complex system now can be so high that a catastrophic failure, particularly one that could have been avoided, is worse than unacceptable; it is unthinkable. Its loss could bankrupt a major company, smash a program, generate virulent public criticism, ruin careers, and create widespread disruption in related areas. A nuclear plant costs billions. The Shuttle ready to launch costs $3 billion and its cargo may add another $1 billion. A Stealth aircraft costs $500 million; a B-1, $250 million; and a planetary spacecraft, hundreds of millions. Consequently, huge financial risks are taken with every operational decision. As one pilot put it, "How would you like to bail out of a $500 million aircraft when there was even the faintest chance that it might be saved?" Imagine, too, the pressures on the controller of a $700 million spacecraft in issuing a propulsion command that, if wrong or not communicated, could ruin the mission.

Case 6:

High-value systems under attack. What failure rate would be acceptable for the defense of a city under nuclear attack? For a critical satellite under antisatellite attack? For a strategic command and control system under jamming? For a critical data base against penetration?

In cases like these, any failure at all means that the objective cannot be met—and failure should be so rare that the system may well become obsolete before it fails. At the same time, lack of failure to date gives little confidence, statistically, that all is well.

THE BASIC RESPONSE: MURPHY'S LAW AND ZERO DEFECTS

Murphy's law and zero-defect implementation share in a notable and important omission—neither mentions statistics nor acceptable quality limits (AQL). If something can fail, it will. Perfection, not acceptable imperfection, is essential at every step.

No matter that perfection is an unreachable absolute. It remains the objective. Eliminate failure modes by design. Qualify every supplier. Stop the production line for every anomaly. Give incentive to every participant through pride, understanding, team spirit, peer pressure, and perhaps profit sharing and patriotism—whatever it takes. It worked for military systems in World War II. It worked when statistical analysis predicted that the Apollo mission could not succeed without the loss of 30 astronauts in flight to and from the Moon. And it is the foundation of most of the recent total quality managment systems

(TQMS). Although its focus is on the production floor, it applies equally well to designers in the loft and managers in the executive offices.

When fully implemented as a disciplined process system, it results in just-in-time (JIT) supply, minimum inventory, minimum rework and turnback, minimum accounting, and minimum cycle (throughput) time.

Its nemesis is acceptance of failure, that is, acceptable quality limits with statistical lot sampling and rejection used as postfacto control.

MANAGERIAL RESPONSE I: PROGRESSIVE REDESIGN*

There are three intertwined approaches to the ultraquality challenge—managerial, technical, and architectural. The architect must understand them all.

One of the oldest and most successful quality-assurance techniques is that of W. Edwards Deming and J. M. Juran made famous by its application by the Japanese in consumer, automotive, and electronic products:

- **Tally the defects**
- **Analyze them**
- **Trace them to the source**
- **Make corrections**
- **Keep a record of what happens afterwards**

To which should be added,

- **And keep repeating it.**

One Japanese expression for the technique (Hayes, 1981) is "The nail that sticks up gets hammered down." At the beginning of the process, the technique is managerial. As J. M. Juran expresses it, a company's "quality problems are planned that way." (Juran, 1988). At the end, as we shall see, it devolves to economics and science.

Example:
A major U.S. manufacturer of TV sets decided that the business was none too profitable and sold it to a Japanese firm. Prior to the sale, final inspection found 1.4 defects per set. Under Japanese management, although standards were set higher, that defect rate was cut by a factor of 100. To accomplish this near-zero defect rate, the product had to be perfect *at every step*, which meant that each step both inspected itself and demanded

*For an analytic treatment of this subject, see *Selected References on Reliability Growth.* Institute of Environmental Sciences, 1988.

perfection from those ahead of it. Inspection at the end of the production line was by the line supervisor, a matter of pride rather than control. The company is now profitable.

Progressive redesign takes numbers and time to succeed, but, by designing out each failure, a continuing improvement to an asymptotically high success rate is virtually assured. The technique works particularly well for components and systems with short turnover times, from integrated circuits to automobiles. To be effective, it requires a well-thought-out combination of careful design, minimal materials defects, replication by precision machinery, well-instrumented process control, tight tolerance design, and alert detection of product and process weaknesses.

Modified versions of the progressive redesign technique also can be seen at work in very large-scale systems—space launch vehicles, spacecraft, and software.

Example:

Current expendable launch vehicles, based on historical flight-failure data, have a present success rate of about 0.94 (Figure 8–1). This rate was achieved over a 30-year period of continued improvements. It was less, however, than 0.70 for the first 10 years. Studies show that the present figure could be improved by another 0.044 if all single-point failures were eliminated, 0.018 if workmanship and human errors were reduced by 50%, 0.014 with engine out capability, 0.01 with redundancy in avionics, and so on. At this

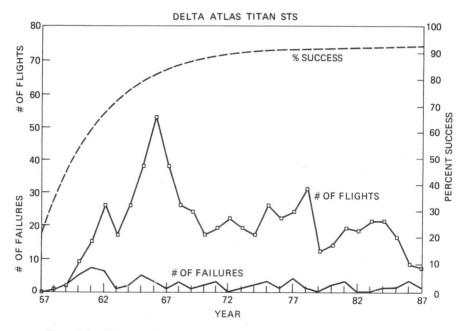

Figure 8-1.   U.S. space launches, 1957–1987. (Source: The Aerospace Corporation.)

advanced stage, still further improvement is neither easy nor cheap. The space shuttle development is following much the same redesign path, steady improvement based on lessons learned (Stever, 1988).

Example:

(Egan, 1987) Over the last 10 years, there have been 81 electronic part failures in a representative set of military spacecraft. Sixteen were traveling-wave-tube amplifier failures, 8 were gyros, 6 were tape recorders, 5 were transmitters, 3 were reaction wheels, 3 were receivers, 2 were power switching, and 38 were "other." The probable causes of failure were parts (55), design (45), quality (40), and environment (17). Software accounted for 4 failures. Attempts to improve the failing components have had only limited success— quantities are small, accommodations for the possible failures have been made in the designs, and the cost effectiveness of further improvement is marginal.

Example:

(Brooks, 1982, 1987; Musa, 1989) Software maintenance is primarily the continuing discovery and correction of software errors. The process results in a steadily declining occurrence of errors. Musa reports that by the use of models and by monitoring the error discovery rate, one can predict when requirements will finally be met. But there seems to be a limit. Brooks maintains that a point is reached where correcting errors generates still more errors and the error rate starts to climb again. He also concluded that rushing the discovery process by adding more software programmers may instead lengthen it.

It seems to be characteristic of the progressive redesign process that in the beginning, a few major problems dominate the development. Once they are solved, performance stabilizes at a treatable, if not yet satisfactory, level. To raise that level by reducing the failure rate requires solving a significantly larger number of smaller problems, and so on, level by level, that is,

The number of problems encountered in development is inversely related to their magnitudes.

If we assume that the difficulty of solving a problem is related to its magnitude, then it takes about the same amount of effort to reduce the failure rate by a given factor. Resource managers in the aircraft industry have expressed the result this way:

Reducing the failure rate by each factor of 2 takes as much effort as the original development.

Thus, if the original development cost X and resulted in a failure rate of 4%, then to reach 2% would require another X, to reach 1% still another X, etc. S. W. Golomb consequently suggests that quality levels might better be expressed as the logarithm of the failure rate than as the success percentages [Golomb 1990].

The same heuristic seems to apply to reliability, survivability, safety, software engineering, and electronic countermeasures.

Some of the highest-quality complex systems in the world are the space programs of NASA and the Department of Defense. Special procedures were developed for them (Leverton, 1981). The essential factors are strong discipline, accurate documentation, faithful reporting of any and all anomalies, independent reviews of all steps and decisions, and extraordinary attention to detail. Perhaps most important for future use by others, these techniques have proven to be cost-effective. Using the criterion of data produced per dollar spent, the high-performance, long-lived U.S. spacecraft have consistently outperformed their design goals.

Based in part on NASA and DOD efforts, the Department of Energy (DOE) and the nuclear power industry have further advanced the drive to ultraquality (Floyd Culler in discussion with the author, 1989).

The technique, design against maximum credible accident, begins with the failure modes and effects analyses (FMEAs) pioneered by the DOD. Each possible failure mode is identified and eliminated by design. A new system FMEA is then constructed, with further redesign, until a point is reached where issues of basic physics, chemistry, materials, and structural dynamics become the limit. Experiments are then devised and run until all concerned parties, including the Nuclear Regulatory Commission, are satisfied that a design is safe. One indication of a decade of progress is the reduction in unresolved issues from over 400 to less than 25, none of which would produce catastrophic failure. But as the DOE recognizes, even this is not enough. The public must still be convinced. To accomplish this means that: *"The engineering task is to design reactors whose safety is so transparent that the skeptical elite is convinced, and through them, the general public"* (A.M. Weinberg, 1989).

The Department of Energy design process is not inexpensive. It is not unusual for the cost of certification of a nuclear power plant design to be more than $100 million. (A typical nuclear power plant cost is in the billions.) And, for various reasons, there has been little opportunity to apply the new design techniques to new plants.

Designing against maximum credible accident is probably the ultimate in progressive redesign. It forces quality issues to the most basic level, the scientific unknowns, which are then pursued to a conclusion. Not every system needs to dig that deep on every issue. But one that does call for more fundamental effort across the board is the value of accelerated testing and burn in of ultraquality components and systems. Accelerated testing is a widely used method of attempting to certify, in a short time, a part or element intended for many years of operation. It has three important applications. The first is in early development, when go/no-go decisions have to be made on the use of new technologies. The second is in manufacture, when product lots are screened prior to incorporation into systems. The third is in system test.

In accelerated testing, the device is subjected to environmental stresses—usually temperature and vibration—far greater than expected in operation, but for a correspondingly shorter time. But the technique is controversial. It can harm otherwise good components and its results can be deceptive in predicting—or not predicting—future failures. It has been implicated in damaging high-quality semiconductors, although it can find mechanical flaws like poor bearings, loose parts, and poor connectors. The technique only emulates accurately those failure mechanisms for which high stress over a short period produces effects similar to those of low stress over a long term. Mechanisms that take time alone, like electrochemical corrosion, molecular changes in plastics, or exposure to radiation in space, may not surface. The architect and client may conclude that the system is better than it is.

The key, as with any test, is to understand which failure mechanisms are being induced in each test, which ones might be inadvertently activated, and which ones are not tested at all. That understanding comes from research, especially for ultraquality systems:

Testing, without understanding the multiple failure mechanisms to which a system is susceptible, can be both deceptive and harmful.

As a consequence: *untested or untestable mechanisms should be specified and accounted for in the design and in the acceptance criteria.*

Progressive redesign runs into another limit, profitability to the manufacturers. Once it becomes evident that necessary further investments can never be recouped, the projected losses will almost always force the maker to stop improving the product. Major system builders, needing the components, consequently risk the initial lack or loss of suppliers for whom participation would be unprofitable. The result is a limit to the *practical* quality that a given supplier can produce at a reasonable price and profit. A client needing small numbers of still better components may have to make them in house, that is, vertical corporate integration of the complete production process may be the only management solution. Vertical integration changes the economics of the component. Although the cost of making the component may be much greater than its general market would bear, its contribution to a particular system may more than justify limited production by the system builder.

TECHNICAL RESPONSE I: TECHNOLOGICAL SUBSTITUTION

One of the most dramatic improvements in component quality has been the integration of many circuits onto a single microelectronic chip, replacing thousands of individual electronic and mechanical components. It is the only technique in recent memory that has reduced failure rates by factors of thousands. It is a peculiar characteristic of chip manufacture that the rate of chip failure has remained about the same regardless of how many components are placed on it. Thus, the reliability *per component* is increasing at an almost exponential rate. The performance-to-cost ratio is likewise increasing, which means that far better quality can be achieved at the same or lesser cost. This last effect is important—it helps assure that ultraquality devices will be produced at a profit.

Microprocessors, by making systems smarter and more precise, have also enhanced product quality and performance. One of the greatest fuel-conservation and emission-control measures in recent times was the substitution of electronic fuel injection for the mechanical carburetor.

Lasers have greatly changed product and process quality through far better machining, instrumentation, and information handling.

Solid-state electronic devices, with their inherent high tolerance for vibration and shock, are increasingly being substituted for electromechanical devices—traveling-wave tubes, control switches, circuit breakers, radio receivers, compact-disk memories, etc.

MANAGERIAL RESPONSE II: TYING QUALITY TO COST

One of the most important effects of greatly increased global competition has been the simultaneous increase in quality and decrease in cost of commercially available products. Accomplishing both together was not coincidence. It was built into the methods used. Although based originally on American ideas (Deming and Juran), the close integration of several cost and quality methods evidently has been Japanese. *Reducing* cost thus became a *driver* for quality instead of a reason to slash quality-assurance programs. Value-added process-conversion operations were made more efficient while processes of little value to the customer—inventory, work in process, monitoring, and rework—were reduced.

In an effort to attract more customers, quality parameters of importance to the customer were selected, product factors that affected these parameters were determined by controlled experiment, and the product and process were designed to yield those factors in the most cost-effective manner—the Taguchi Method (Corcoran, 1989). Depending on the product, the result frequently was that higher overall quality was achieved at less cost. The apparent reason for this result was that although increases in aesthetic quality (appearance and styling) generally increase cost, increases in functional quality (reliability) decrease it.

The importance of the new approach, if widely adopted by industry, is that all systems could rise on the tide of increasing quality. Referring back to the

failure rate and cost heuristic, the constant multiplier will decrease. No longer need it be one failure per hour per million dollars, even for military avionics. For some systems, the improvement might be an order of magnitude reduction in system failure rate, a major step to ultraquality.

ARCHITECTURAL RESPONSE I: ULTRAQUALITY WATERFALLS

Process architecture is usually thought of in the context of a manufacturing system—machines, layout, procedures, product mix, flexibility, and the like. But, like any system, manufacturing is a part of a still larger system, the waterfall. If an ultraquality product is to be produced, not only the manufacturing step but the waterfall as a whole must be of ultraquality, excellent beyond measure.

A study of present-day waterfalls would soon reveal each element being carried out by a different group within its own culture striving for individualized objectives. Each group would have its own perception of the waterfall and its position in it. Each would have its own language and its own computer aids (computer-aided design, computer-aided manufacturing, etc.). Computer communications between groups would be rare and inefficient.

If ultraquality is taken to mean a near-zero error rate, most waterfalls could not qualify. There are too many possibilities for error.

The first step to ultraquality waterfalls is the same as the one already given for manufacturing—perfection at every step. The client and architect must be sure that there are no misunderstandings of system objectives nor of the rationale for trade-offs already made. Research and development must search out possible failure modes through careful experiment and analysis. Engineering should progressively redesign the product and process, designing out single-point failure modes, simplifying the product for excellent manufacture. Each element in the waterfall must pass along as perfect a product—as complete and free of discrepancies and potential failures—as possible.

Example:

In several major government agencies, systems are conceived and justified at a very high level. Analyses are done that compare alternate approaches, some of which are relatively close to each other in benefits and costs. A high-level consensus is reached and, in due course, the system is approved, perhaps with modification. Instructions are then sent to subordinate levels, but without including the prior analyses or the reasoning behind the modifications and trade-offs. The subordinate organization reinterprets the instructions to its subordinates in its own "language," again without explanation. Requests for proposals are sent to contractors, stating but not prioritizing the specifications. Contractors respond within the specifications, no doubt wondering why, given the realities of the manufacturing world, a somewhat different approach was not requested. The process is vulnerable to conflicting objectives, easy misunderstanding, stifled feedback, and ill-founded trade-offs.

Example:

Prototyping, as discussed earlier, is usually carried out under relaxed rules, as it should be. Unfortunately, the transitions to production and later operation are notorious for cost and schedule overrun. The developers too often assume their responsibilities end with successful demonstrations. Going back, reviewing, and documenting the appropriate difficulties and solutions so that others further down the waterfall are as informed as possible—much less suggesting how a redesign should be done—is rare.

Example:

One of the most common failings of research and development is the passing along of immature technology to manufacturing. It is the greatest single cause of overruns in space systems, integrated circuits, and other high-tech products.

Example:

A new rocket engine was needed in order to launch larger, and much more expensive, payloads to orbit. Reliability requirements were correspondingly much higher than for earlier engines. The contract was undertaken by a firm that had built successful engines for earlier, less demanding, missions. But the development phase was not upgraded accordingly. Funding was short and false confidence in earlier successes was high. A major developmental omission, therefore, was a test program to determine the thermal characteristics of the new engine. The design instead was certified "by similarity" with other designs. When an engine later failed during flight, the cause was inexplicable. 18 months of investigation followed in an effort to find the true cause, excluding all others. The cause was a flawed thermal-barrier design unique to that engine. Had the engine been thermally characterized in the beginning, the problem would have been identified and solved, and an 18-month delay of, and risk to, several hundred million dollars of spacecraft could have been avoided. The high-quality objective of the system had not been matched by high-quality development.

The second step, an architect's speciality, is to improve the interfaces between the elements. System-critical changes in one element need to be communicated quickly and accurately to all other elements so that the consequences throughout the system can be determined and accommodated or debated in a timely fashion.

One of the promising approaches to interface improvement is to integrate the computer aids that each waterfall group has developed. At present, the separate computer aids are generally incompatible. There are few common data bases. Software and hardware are different. Entry, control, and updating are major problems. One possibility, involving internal changes in the elements, is to integrate all the aids to a single master aid. But success in this direction has proven to be difficult. Everyone in each field would have to be reeducated to a new language; configuration control would be very difficult. Another possibility is to use computer aids specifically designed to bridge between the separate aids—a transfer model or an interpreter analogous to instant language interpretation in a multilingual conference.

Attempts have been along these lines. Progress has been slow and frustrating. *But the cause is not the lack of separate computer aids. It is the present lack of integration of the waterfall steps into end-to-end process architectures.* Computer integration requires mutually agreed upon answers to questions that had been treated separately in the different groups. The waterfall itself may have to be redesigned several times over in an effort to eliminate intergroup errors. For example:

- What documents and data that flow between groups are most beneficial to the parties concerned? What information is critical? What information adds value to the product and which does not? How are differences resolved and documented?
- Who should be responsible for keeping the waterfall up to date? Is information entered and displayed at the right locations? Does the same information have to be entered more than once? Is information entry a bottleneck on the production line?
- What is the most efficient top-level computer language for the whole waterfall?

The principal benefits of a computer-integrated waterfall may be as much in the integration process as with the end result.

MANAGERIAL RESPONSE III: WELL-ARCHITECTED DOCUMENTATION

Demanding ultraquality in a system is something like demanding a perfect budget proposal. There are so many things to be accounted for that it seems as if getting everything right is hopeless. There are always changes at the last minute, and always issues that cannot be resolved.

Comptrollers, however, have learned that it is a hopeless and unnecessary objective to have budgets and accounts be "right." It is only necessary that they be complete, internally consistent, precise, traceable, and authoritative. Assumptions may or may not be correct, but they can be clearly and explicitly stated. Only then can budgets and accounts provide solid baselines from which disciplined changes can be made. Only then can they be trusted to be as remarkably error-free as they are.

Much the same applies to ultraquality systems. Unless the system's documentation is solid and disciplined, widely distributed and understood, it cannot be free of error. The reason is easy enough. People must not only be informed, they must be completely, consistently, precisely, etc., informed, because:

Unless everyone who needs to know <u>does</u> know, somebody somewhere will foul up.

The foul-ups are almost always inadvertent. Many are the result of well-intended "improvements." Some are errors of commission; many are errors of omission. Lacking authoritative information on how things should be done, people will do the best that they know how. And it may be quite wrong. It can be as simple as cleaning a part with the wrong solvent or using an unauthorized symbol in a line of computer code.

Documents—policies, procedures, reports, memoranda, equipment pedigrees, military specifications (MILSPECS), electronic data bases, drawings, software programs, and the like—are the memory and lifeblood of a complex system. Handshakes, verbal agreements, and private understandings are its nemesis.

Well-architected documents do the following:

- Directly benefit the writers just in the process of writing them
- Define requirements, design characteristics, critical parameters, interfaces, tests, acceptance criteria, schedules and operational responsibilities
- Establish critical "paper trails" of component histories, FMEAs, prior performance, past anomalies, process changes, and decisions
- Control both the build process and the configuration of the system
- Establish well-reasoned operational procedures
- Form the foundation for future, more complex systems.

In the simplest of systems, a few individuals, writing "on the back of envelopes" and running the project "out of their hip pockets," could achieve success. In complex systems—those worth more than a few hundred thousand dollars each—there are too many variables, too many interrelationships, too much embedded corporate memory, and too high a demand for quality to take the risks of human fallibility. A manufacturer ignores or discards system documentation at considerable risk. An operator modifies them only for good and sufficient reason.

Example:

In the early 1970s, the Air Force did an interesting experiment. It sent out a Request for Proposal for a prototype of a new combat aircraft with the explicit provision that the bidders need not use MILSPECs and other similar documents; good "industry practice" would suffice. The bidders, however, would have to say what practice they would use. All bidders, without exception, elected to use government documentation. There was no substitute for what that documentation performed. Indeed, there was no "industry practice" sufficiently documented to be usable.

Example:

It is not unusual in doing final testing to come across an anomaly. When that happens under pressure to meet a deadline, the temptation can be strong to deviate from established test procedures. There are reasons for those procedures, and for not doing others, that are too easily forgotten. The risks are considerable that more harm will be done than good.

Few would argue with the principle that good documentation is essential for complex systems. The argument is over what kind and how much is required for ultraquality systems. Ideally, it should be complete without being voluminous, as error-free and fault-tolerant as the system it supports, easily modified but under tight configuration control, inexpensive, up to date, and readily accessed. This is a tall order.

The present situation is far from ideal. Few if any of the ideal characteristics exist today, much less exist as an integrated set. The rationale for many decision documents is seldom part of the document; so documents stay in effect after the conditions that established them have changed—making the document obsolete, but providing no procedural way of justifying a change. Documents refer to supporting documents to the point where hundreds of documents may have to be reviewed in order to change any one of them. "Tailoring," or the modification of specifications to better suit a particular system, is encouraged but seldom proposed, because the confidence in predicting the technical and financial effects of the changes is so low.

It is fair to say that documentation is expensive, time consuming, inefficient, far from error-free, distrusted, and generally unpopular. A common plea is to get rid of as much of it as possible.

The solution is not to call for its reduction, but to improve its quality. That means the right choice of events and parameters to document. It means improved methods of data-base management for document entry, control, and access. It means timely document review and maintenance. It means that the architect must recognize and act on the fact that

> **Ultraquality systems and processes demand ultraquality documentation—complete but concise and error-free.**

The challenge of ultraquality documentation is as difficult to meet as that of any element of the system. It is already confounding software developers, integrated-circuit manufacturers, manned flight system architects, and government procurement officials.

MANAGERIAL RESPONSE IV: INDEPENDENT REVIEWS

Without question, there are no people more interested in system success and quality than the system's architects, engineers, builders, and sponsoring clients.

If there are difficulties with the system, they want to find and correct them first, before anyone else. Their commitment to the system is, and must be, complete. As a matter of personal and group pride, they want the system to work magnificently, as error- and failure-free as it is possible to make it. Their internal progress reviews are as thorough and self-critical as they can make them.

They are not, however, the only people deeply concerned with the system and the process by which it is built. Two other groups, the end users and upper managment, have a considerable interest in how things are going. These groups feel the need for independent reviews, not to critique the work of the systems people, but for needs of their own gained from experience over the years.

End users found that systems were being presented to them, often after a decade of development and production, that did not fit their present needs. Much of the problem was the long development time. Conditions, needs, and people change. Part of the problem was lack of user contacts during conceptual design—or contacts with wrong or nonusers. Whatever the problem, organizationally independent operational test and evaluation (OT&E) was instituted toward the end of development, prior to full-scale production, to make sure that the end product would be useful and cost effective. Although the most formal version of OT&E is governmental, private industry does something similar during its product development—testing the market from time to time using representative potential customers.

Management found itself making critical resource-allocation decisions for which all sources of information were inherently biased. At the same time, management wanted to be sure that enough resources were made available at the right time and place to keep things on track. To do that required knowing—and judging for itself—the levels of risk being incurred in the project.

Independent reviews by independent expert teams, by surfacing the major problem areas and prior decisions (most of them resolved and validated, respectively), give top management a feeling for the risk level of the decisions they are called upon to make. They are a safeguard against the normal human tendency to solve all problems at as low a level as possible without "bothering" the higher levels—why report "solved problems?" But many problems are not solved; they are resolved at some risk level, for example, "we decided the risks were low and the costs were too high, so we decided not to take corrective action on this one." Fair enough, but how many such "low-risk" problems were there? And does the problem appear as "low risk" to others? Top management, by hearing a review of what has gone on before, from an independent group's perspective, is given a good opportunity to evaluate total risk, even if all prior actions are affirmed.

Putting it mildly, when independent reviews were initiated, they were barely tolerated by the systems people as a necessary evil imposed from above. They did take valuable time of key people. But with well-understood procedures, participants, and purposes, these reviews have unquestionably helped maintain discipline, encouraged good documentation, ensured accountability for decisions, and reduced operational failures. They have become an essential part of ultraquality processes.

Part of the benefit is direct. New ideas for improvement are indeed brought forward. Most of the benefit is indirect. The process of getting ready for an independent review, in the minds of many systems people, has been much more valuable than the review itself. Decisions are rethought. Problems are discovered that are easily and quickly fixed. Internal criticism is looked on favorably—what if the same criticism first surfaced in the independent review?!

At the same time, the user and management groups gain an appreciation of what are the problems and risks, what might be done to fix them, and how to deal with them if they do occur in operation. Independent reviews aid the system-acceptance process yet to come, relieving to some degree the client/user's trauma in accepting uncertifiable ultraquality systems. They keep raising the explicit question: *Do we, collectively, accept the risks—small, we hope—of the system not meeting its ultraquality objectives?*

The question focuses on the consequences of system performance—good and bad—instead of on the details of system implementation. In so focusing, client/users look for ways to minimize their maximum risks, technical, financial, and social. Objectives can be changed. The definition of success can be refined to make it better fit reality. The public can be better informed. Additional resources can be provided. Mitigation measures can be instituted to minimize potential damage. Backups can be acquired. If worst comes to worst, the system can be terminated or scaled back pending further technological developments.

In management terms, independent reviews allow the client/users to make provisional acceptance decisions well before the formal acceptance procedure. Actions can be taken that will yield a better system, better understood, at less cost and risk.

TECHNICAL RESPONSE II: ESTABLISHING RELATIVE RISKS

Specifying absolute risk levels for ultraquality systems ahead of time is, of course, just as impractical as certifying ultraquality for acceptance later on. In neither case, can the data be obtained by test or measurement. The specification becomes meaningless. Reliance, instead, defaults to counting on the presumed excellence of the systems team to deliver. Experience shows that approach to be dangerous. All problems, discrepancies, and anomalies will tend to be treated alike. Great effort may be expended where it is not needed. Too little effort will go to where the risks are the highest. The result in more than one major program was a thousand—all presumably low—possibilities for catastrophic failure. When the system proved to be less than ultraquality, it was hard to know where to start fixing it.

But if absolute risks cannot be estimated, it nonetheless may be possible to estimate *relative* ones. Is this element more or less likely to fail or succeed than another one, for example, does it have more parts or require tighter tolerances?

One of the techniques for answering such questions is failure modes and effects analysis (FMEA). The proposed architecture is laid out and the following question is asked about each component: What can fail, under what circumstances, with what relative risk, and with what consequences? FMEA is a tedious process. But it asks the right questions and forces consideration of every answer. It highlights single-point failures, those single failures that mean catastrophe. Ideally, all single-point failures would be eliminated by design. If not, the designer must be prepared to show why not. If accepted, some assessment of relative risk must be made, as defined by Figure 8–2.

Risk diagrams of this sort are clearly judgmental, but they accomplish the important purpose of distinguishing the critical from the merely important. If a failure mode is in the upper left box, it better be eliminated entirely. If in the lower right box, there are straightforward, less consequential choices to be made—fix now, fix later, accept the risk, etc. The difficult decisions are in the *medium*-risk boxes, and involve judgments of practicality of any fix, costs in money and time, and the likely consequences of the specific action being contemplated.

The test of a good architect, or of a good project manager, is the ability to put components and elements into the right risk boxes, after which the available resources can be most effectively allocated.

Presentations of risk assessments are a regular agenda item in launch-readiness reviews of Air Force space systems. Typically, there are no high-risk items, that is, items likely to occur that would fail the mission. The review would not be held until they were eliminated. But there are often a handful of medium risks and tens to hundreds of low risks. The low risks are usually accepted if both the systems people and the independent reviewers agree with the low-risk designation. The decision process for the medium-risk items can take weeks of presentations, discussions, experiments, and analyses. The review is risk management of the highest order. It is easy enough to decide no when everyone else so recommends. It is much harder to decide yes when everyone else says no. Yet, under national priorities to put critical space systems into immediate operation, the stakes are too high to take the easy way out. Such was the

		Mission Consequences	
	Risk	Failed	Degraded
Probability of Occurrence	Likely	*High*	*Medium*
	Rarely	*Medium*	*Low*

Figure 8–2.   Relative risk diagram.

case for the developmental U.S. ASAT (air-launched antisatellite) missile on September 13, 1985. It was a 50:50 risk, but the outcome was favorable. But for an equally urgent Titan 34-D, for which the consensus and decision was yes, a previously undetected manufacturing-process flaw resulted in an explosion just after launch.

Example:

An urgent launch was required of a critical satellite because an in-orbit satellite was degrading rapidly at the end of life. A medium-risk failure mode (a component of the type used in the satellite had failed in another application) was reported at the mission-readiness review. Launch was postponed until the applicability of the failure to the satellite could be determined.

Example:

Just before launch, a spacecraft experienced a component failure. The system architecture was such that the component was redundant and that work-arounds could be accomplished should its replacement fail (possibly due to the same as yet unknown cause). The spacecraft was launched and operated successfully.

Therefore,

If being absolute is impossible in estimating system risks, then be relative.

ARCHITECTURAL RESPONSE II: REDUNDANCY, FAULT TOLERANCE, AND FAULT AVOIDANCE

One of the oldest responses to equipment failure is the provision of a redundant or spare unit. Its algebra is deceptively simple. If the probability that one unit will fail is x and of another unit is y, then the probability that both will fail is the product, xy, *provided that* the failures are independent.

Thus, given two similar units that can fail randomly and independently, each with a failure probability of 0.01, then the probability that *both* will fail is $0.01 \times 0.01 = 0.0001$. If only one unit is needed for a mission, then by having two available, in this example, the failure probability has been reduced by a factor of 100.

Redundancy, as should be expected, is a favorite technique for raising system quality above that of the individual elements. It has been a mainstay of communications network, aircraft, and spacecraft design for many years.

In practice, the use of redundancy is more complex than it appears. The first complication comes with another bit of algebra. The probability of failure that *either* will fail is $x + y - xy$, or about 0.02 in the example just given. If both are needed, therefore, the mission failure rate is roughly twice as high as the failure rate of one unit. This algebra comes to the fore when a third element is added, the device that decides which element is working and which is not. Unless that device is at least as reliable as the redundant pair, that is, 0.0001, then its failure rate determines the mission failure rate. For example, if its failure rate were the same as either unit, 0.01, then the mission failure rate would be worse than having no redundancy at all.

The second complication comes from the causes of the failures. If both units fail for the same reason at the same time, there is no true redundancy. Or, if mission failure is due to a different cause than assumed, then the redundancy may have been applied to the wrong units, may have not applied where needed, or may not have been cost effective when viewed from a total system perspective. The launch-vehicle example given earlier in this chapter shows why redundant guidance systems have been debated for many years; their contribution to the failure rate is just at the borderline of cost effectiveness for 0.94-success-rate vehicles.

The architectural question to be answered is, therefore: *What is the purpose of the proposed redundant architecture and what failure mechanism is being countered?*

Is it early failure (usually workmanship), long-term random environmental response, wearout, or occasional overload? The architectures and operating modes are different for the different cases.

Example:

If the failure mechanism of concern is early failure, then close monitoring and quick, permanent switchover from a failed unit to an operating redundant one is the preferred procedure. The latter unit, having not experienced an early failure, is likely to last its full design lifetime. This technique has been one of the most useful ways of achieving the design lifetime of complex spacecraft.

Example

If the failure mechanism is long-term or wearout, then trend monitoring of a weakening operating unit should indicate when a redundant, previously unpowered unit should take over. But the switch from the weakened unit should be reversible. The redundant unit may fail early or emergency conditions may call for extending the device lifetime far beyond the intended period.

Example:

If the failure mechanism is the occasional overload of any one of a number of units, then the technique is usually a shared spare, available on demand, but unlikely to be called simultaneously by more than one overloaded element. The technique is common in communications networks, where spare channels and alternate routing are notably cost-effective. A single spare channel can often serve a dozen or more other channels on a given relay link.

Example:

If a failure mechanism is common to a whole class of units, then dissimilar redundancy may be called for, for example, the use of several, quite different, ways of achieving the same mission results. Navigation, for example, might be accomplished using either inertial, radio, stellar, or a combination of all. Command might be achieved using either radio or optical frequencies. Order wires for communications control might be either within or external to the main communications band. Different portions of a computer might be used to accomplish the same function. As they teach military officers at the Naval Post Graduate School, the more things you can do more than one way, the greater are the chances of survival.

Redundant design becomes much more complex if multiple redundancy is needed. Consider the "cross-strapped" configuration of Figure 8-3, a simplified version of a launch-vehicle control system. The purpose of the configuration is to accomplish four different sequential functions, any of which could fail.

The two parallel strings, 1–4 and 1'–4', provide redundancy, but only if the correct connections are made at the right time. Making each connection depends upon knowledge of the status of all elements and connections, a complex machine-intelligence problem.

The configuration was implemented successfully, but the redundancy-management element (not shown) turned out to be far more complex, more costly, and more demanding of computer capacity than anticipated. Certifying its operation was difficult. However, it did save a mission worth hundreds of millions of dollars. The cause of failure of the main unit was attributed to a computer upset triggered by a cosmic ray. The question remained, nonetheless, whether the same amount of time, effort, and expense spent making a single unit more radiation resistant might have been a better investment. The answer, as in most cases, depended on many factors: the other possible failure mechanisms, cost-effective measures that might be taken to prevent their occurrence, the criticality of the mission, and the client's tolerance for risk. In the end, it is a judgment call.

A more sophisticated approach than redundancy is fault tolerance—the capability to maintain control of the system, bound the effects of failures, and counter them so that system integrity is maintained.

Fault-tolerant design takes the approach that unit failure need not and

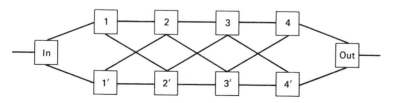

Figure 8-3.   Cross-strapped redundancy.

should not result in complete mission failure. If the system can be kept under control, the effect of the unit failure on the mission can be limited.

Hydraulic-brake failure on an automobile can be partly compensated by use of an emergency hand brake. The loss of an attitude-control sensor on a spacecraft can be detected quickly enough so that the spacecraft can be placed in a safe condition with its solar panels facing the sun to keep it from losing electrical power. Software bugs can be countered by stopping calculations when results go out of bounds.

Fault tolerance, like redundancy, requires control mechanisms—instruments to detect system status, decision devices, switches, multiple modes, and interconnections. Its use against unspecified faults is a poor strategy at best. It works best in systems that are inherently reliable, that is, the failure rate of the system to be protected must already be low or the protective elements will be so complex that they become a major cause of failure themselves.

A prerequisite of fault tolerance is, therefore, fault avoidance. If a fault, error, or failure mechanism can be avoided, it should be designed out first before fault tolerance techniques are considered. Avoiding faults through better components is certainly a preferred approach.

To sum up, fault-tolerant designs are indeed powerful approaches to very high-quality architectures. However, the basic reasons that they are used are deficiencies in system design or component quality. Unless the deficiencies are well understood and unavoidable,

**Fault avoidance is preferable to fault tolerance in system design.
Fault tolerance, when used, should be specific to fault type.**

ARCHITECTURAL RESPONSE III: CONTINUING REASSESSMENT

One of the distinguishing traits of a good architect, as noted in Part One, is to pause and reflect as the conceptual phase comes to a close, reassessing the proposed system model before advising the client that it is acceptable to move ahead. It is a trait that can be well used in striving for ultraquality systems. In the same way that builders improve a system by progressive redesign, the architect can improve it by continuing reassessment as the project proceeds.

Despite the best efforts to produce an ultraquality conceptual model, obstacles will arise later that will seem to thwart reaching the goal. A route will have to be found that avoids, goes around, or surmounts each obstacle. Like a pilot bringing a major ship into port, the architect must keep assessing the situation and be able to recommend a change of course to reach the desired destination—a credible ultraquality system.

Can we still make it? Is the planned route still the right one? Are we run-

ning into more and more serious trouble going this way? Is there an alternate destination that is still satisfactory?

And, underlying all of these, the continuing question:

Is the system inherently capable of ultraquality?

Problem 1: The Unrecognized Architectural Flaw

Of the many obstacles to reaching ultraquality, the most serious is an unrecognized architectural flaw—a system structure that will fail even if all the elements perform as assumed, yet not detected until late in development. The only preventive is repeated and, if necessary, independent critiques.

Example:

For multiengine aircraft and launch vehicles, can the mission be accomplished if an engine fails? *Any* engine? If not, then the architecture may be less reliable than one using a single engine.

Example:

Launching a payload into orbit with rocket engines is a matter of imparting sufficient kinetic energy to stay in orbit. That energy, to a first approximation, can be delivered either somewhat faster or slower than it is delivered on the nominal launch trajectory. Thus, if the launch-vehicle engines underdeliver in thrust due to a somewhat lower than normal rate of consumption of propellants, orbit may still be achieved, though at a later time. A recent launch vehicle contained a propellant-shutoff timer whose purpose was to preclude an uncontrolled thrust termination in case the guidance system failed to act. The timer was set for a few seconds after the nominal time. Unfortunately, the vehicle produced significantly less thrust than normal, the timer shut down the engines, and the vehicle failed to reach orbit. To preclude a relatively minor occurrence, a major failure was made possible.

Example:

One of the critical elements of an aerospace vehicle is the computerized attitude-control system. In a proposed design, three identical computers were to be used in parallel, with a majority vote used to choose the presumably correct output. But there was a concern that the identical software of all the units might contain errors. Therefore, another computer was employed using different and simpler software to run in parallel with the first three as a check on their majority-vote output. Question for the reader: Is the design robust? Hint: What happens when the fourth computer output differs from that of the other three?

Example:

A well-established communications security technique is to encrypt transmissions with a bit-stream code known to both sending and receiving parties. However, the codes must be changed from time to time, leading to a code-distribution problem. One proposal was to send two simultaneous transmissions on different channels. One transmission was the encrypted signal and the other the bit-stream code alone. For all practical purposes, each transmission was unbreakable. Comparing the two transmissions would then yield the original signal. Question for the reader: Why is the <u>system</u> not secure although the individual transmissions were?

Example:

Passenger and freight carriers seldom use fleets of a single vehicle. Manufacturers of fleet vehicles seldom make only one size or type of vehicle. Most fleets have vehicles with a geometric (multiplicative) relationship in sizes and weights. The same construct is found in telecommunications common carriers in multiplexed channels, alternate routes, and different communications media. An FMEA of the fleet would show the reason: a single vehicle type is a single-point failure of the fleet.

Problem 2: Excessive Internal Complexity

One of the most powerful techniques for reaching ultraquality is to keep attacking the quality–complexity relationship at its source—complexity. As Art Raymond puts it in a variation on **KISS,** "Simplify. Simplify. Simplify." Architects and clients alike would agree. It is just common sense to keep the conceptual model as simple as possible while still satisfying the client's needs.

But a too-simple conceptual model can hide underlying complexity that can put system quality at risk. Complexity is a breeding ground for errors. But it grows in a quite understandable way. One of the best partitioning heuristics, **minimum communications,** by calling for minimal external complexity for each element, can drive complexity inward into the elements. As each element is further partitioned, the system can become still more complex—and less likely to reach ultraquality. The question needs to be continually raised: *Is the system becoming increasingly complex as we move into design, manufacture, and operations?*

Are we fighting component deficiencies with complex fault-tolerant designs? Are we forcing software down to the assembly-language level? Are we demanding extraordinary precision or unprecedented cleanliness in manufacturing? Is documentation being burdensome?

A stubborn tendency for internal complexity to grow, in fact, may be traceable to a prior system decision, modification of which could reverse the trend. The **choose watch choose** heuristic provides a useful strategy here. If complexity keeps rising faster than simplification can reduce it, backtrack to the cause and eliminate it.

Problem 3: The Formulation of Ultraquality Objectives

The way in which ultraquality is expressed, the parameters that are chosen for ultraquality performance, will determine not only the development route to be followed, but also the obstacles that will be encountered. Some objectives may be virtually impossible to reach, whereas others, only slightly different, may be eminently practical. Some may be practical enough, but in achieving them, undesirable side effects may become apparent. A proper question to ask when ultraquality seems beyond reach is: *Are the stated quality objectives still the right ones?*

One might think that a requirement for high reliability, for example, would be easy to specify. But consider some of the ways communications reliability might be defined. A 0.01% failure rate could mean one 1 hour outage per year, or 10 seconds once a day, or a barely audible burst of static of one-tenth millisecond every second. Depending upon the particular communications service being provided—voice, electronic funds transfer, facsimile, etc.—the most important factor might be the mean time to recover (MTTR), the mean time between failures (MTBF), or even the time of day when ultraquality was essential.

To satisfy different statements of ultraquality, some architectures require ultraquality components, whereas others can use easy maintainability and repair. If cost were crucial, some architectures might aim for a minimum spares inventory, centrally located; others might opt for a distributed inventory of selected parts.

Example:

There is a U.S. national policy calling for assured access to space. On closer inspection, assurance depends upon the launch rate per year, vehicle failure rate, stand-down time after failure, probability of no failures while flying off the backlog, and the peak-to-average launch rate. It is not only the failure rate that counts, it is also what happens after a failure. Can the space transportation system recover well or will it collapse? In brief, assured access for fleet-design purposes is best stated as resiliency to failure, a complex parameter combining all of the ones before. The trade-offs among them are shown in Figure 8–4 (Bernstein 1987).

The resiliency to failure graph is a good example of a trade-off among a combination of subordinate objectives that retains the same overall objective. In it, resiliency can be maintained by different combinations of system reliability, stand-down time, and surge rate. If the former is less than expected, then stand-down time needs to be less and surge rate greater, with different combinations yielding different costs. By analyzing them, one could determine the cost effectiveness of greater reliability or the cost risks of not meeting specifications.

The usual presumption is that objectives are formulated and prioritized during concept development, reassessed at the end of it, and passed as firm requirements to system engineering. Having constant objectives and firm requirements are certainly ways of maintaining system integrity. But there is an architectural tension here, particularly for ultraquality systems. The fact that the conceptual model appears to be ultraquality is no guarantee that the system, once built, will be. Unexpected technical, budgetary, and financial crises will

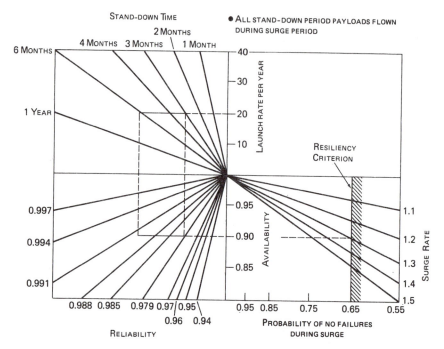

Figure 8-4. Resiliency to failure. (Source: Abbott and Bernstein, "Space Transportation Architecture Resiliency," The Aerospace Corporation 1987.)

occur. The objectives as originally formulated may no longer be achievable. The constant objectives and firm requirements may have to be revised.

The architect, once again, will be at the center, trying to achieve a compromise of the extremes and a balance of the tensions, trying to maintain system integrity during potentially chaotic change.

Ultraquality imperatives make the architect's problem particularly difficult—there is almost no margin for error. Reformulating objectives can be mandatory on the one hand and deadly on the other. There is nothing fundamentally wrong with revising objectives, even very late in the project, in the interest of reaching a practical, but still satisfactory, solution. Objectives are revised remarkably often in operational military systems once tested in combat; a practical answer may come from new tactics or use against different targets or counterweapons. A commercial manufacturer, highly responsive to market demands, may redesign and remarket a product in the middle of a production run.

Even so, unless well-understood options have been provided for the system itself to change, changing objectives may not help. Given the difficulty of achieving ultraquality in any case, retaining options as long as possible can be particularly important for ultraquality systems.

Problem 4: Reinforcement

There remains one more important reason for continuing reassessment of ultraquality objectives—making certain that they are repeatedly reinforced. Initial objectives can be easily forgotten. Other worthwhile but lesser objectives will intrude from time to time. Minor obstacles must not be overcome by major changes in objectives, otherwise, the fine edge that it takes to achieve ultraquality may be lost. It only takes one error to do it. It may seem tedious and repetitious for the architect to keep readdressing it, but the question should never go away:

Are we still meeting our system objective of ultraquality?

If not, the game may be over.

SCIENTIFIC RESPONSE: BETTER MEASUREMENT TECHNIQUES

A common occurrence in failure investigations is a demand for new diagnostic methods to determine the underlying physical causes of failures not yet explained. The need is to convert so-called random failures into well-determined controllable events. Such has been the case for the treatment of diseases, for Titan rocket motor failures, spacecraft electrical discharge short circuits, radiation-damaged integrated circuits, faulty circuit boards, and the collapse of structures.

In contrast with redundancy and other problem-expansion approaches to increased quality, this one attempts to reduce large-scale failures to smaller, even subatomic, phenomena that can be eliminated by design or process control. The resulting instrumentation now ranges over almost all the electromagnetic and sonic spectrums, heavily supported by data processing, simulation, models, and expert systems.

Better measurement capability is valuable in other important ways. It pushes still higher the level of ultraquality than can be achieved with some confidence. It extends further the point where ultraquality's "beyond measure" begins. And it relieves to some extent the need to carry out all the other responses to this challenge.

SUMMARY

The challenge of ultraquality is how to design, build, and gain client acceptance for systems that are of such high quality that they are impractical to certify by demonstration and test. The responses to the challenge are managerial, technical, and architectural. All are aimed at reducing or eliminating error, designing out failure modes, establishing acceptable risk levels, and continually reassessing system status.

RECOMMENDED READING

BERNSTEIN, H. (1987). *Space Launch Systems Resiliency.* El Segundo, CA: The Aerospace Corporation. This report presents a model of the operational dynamics of space launch systems operating as a complex transportation fleet.

CHRISTIANSEN, D. (ed.). (October 1981). "A special issue on Reliability." *IEEE Spectrum* **18**, 10, 34–35. It includes sections on how parts fail, how computers fail, the mission profile, reliable systems (design and tests), lessons from the military, lessons from NASA, overlooking the obvious, and quality control.

DEUTSCH, M. S., and R. R. WILLIS. (1988). *Software Quality Engineering.* Englewood Cliffs, NJ: Prentice Hall. The book presents broadly applicable techniques for achieving software quality: engineering it into the software, reviewing for defects, and testing for errors. It is the source of the heuristic: **You can't achieve quality . . . unless you specify it!**

EISNER, HOWARD. (1988). *Computer Aided Systems Engineering.* Englewood Cliffs, NJ: Prentice Hall. This is a text on system engineering as a whole as well as on CASE. See especially Section 15.3, Quality Assurance (pp. 413–420), for a discussion of MILSTD 21618 for evaluating the quality of software for mission-critical computer systems, of software quality factors and criteria, and of various metrics.

Institute of Environmental Sciences. (1988). *Selected References on Reliability Growth.* Mount Prospect, IL: Institute of Environmental Sciences. This has the best of the IES symposium papers over the last decade, MIL-HDBK-189, and portions of MIL-STD-781D and MIL-HDBK-781.

IEEE Spectrum. (June 1989). "Special Issue on Risk." *IEEE Spectrum,* **26,** 6. It presents performance risks and their management with examples in aircraft, telephony, nuclear plants, the Space Shuttle, and Bhopal. Lessons learned: importance of high-level management commitment, of risk estimation, and of high-quality design.

JURAN, JOSEPH M. (1988). *Juran on Planning for Quality.* New York: The Free Press, A Division of Macmillan, Inc. Especially worthwhile reading for all systems architects and engineers, whether primarily involved in quality assurance or not. Text follows waterfall from planning perspective, with many parallels to architecting. Based on the insight that a company's "quality problems are planned that way." From a master of the field.

STEVER, H. GUYFORD, Chair, NRC Panel on Redesign of Space Shuttle Solid Rocket Booster. *Letter to James C. Fletcher,* December 21, 1988, National Research Council. It gives the lessons learned in redesign: use of an inherently tolerant design, understanding how the design works, a full spectrum of tests, criteria for success and pretest predictions, validation of analytical computations, control of processes and materials, documentation of lessons learned, and risk reduction through product improvement.

WEINBERG, ALVIN M. (1990). "Engineering in an Age of Anxiety: The Search for Inherent Safety." *Engineering and Human Welfare NAE 25, Proceedings of the 25th Annual Meeting.* Washington, DC: National Academy of Engineering.

TO BROWSE, DEPENDING ON INTEREST

CORCORAN, ELIZABETH. (July 1989). "Quality Conscious." *Scientific American,* **261**, 1, pp. 75–76. This is an article on the Genichi Taguchi method for quality improvement—having cost drive higher quality through analysis of critical product factors and least-cost methods of assuring their achievement.

LEVERTON, W. F., J. F. KOUKOL, E. E. LAPIN, and W. H. PICKERING. (January 1981). *Space Programs Failure Reporting Systems.* Pasadena, CA: Pickering Research Corp. This report for the Aerospace Corporation details discrepancy/failure reporting systems used in NASA and DOD space projects. See especially Section 7, "Conclusions," p. 7-1, with its bibliography and references.

LEVERTON, W. F., W. H. PICKERING, and J. F. KOUKOL. (February 1981). *Space and Missile Reliability and Safety Programs Final Report,* Nuclear Safety Analysis Center, Palo Alto, California. This report was prepared for the Electric Power Research Institute. See especially Section 6, "Summary of Lessons Learned."

NORMAN, D. A. (1988). *The Psychology of Everyday Things.* New York: Basic Books. See especially Chapter 5, "To Err is Human," a catalog of the kinds of errors humans make, and Chapter 6, "The Design Challenge," which gives the reasons for common design errors. See also Suggested Readings, pp. 237–240.

ROSS, PHILLIP J. (1988). *Taguchi Techniques for Quality Engineering, Loss Function, Orthogonal Experiments, Parameter and Tolerance Design.* New York: McGraw-Hill. This book emphasizes system analysis applied to test design to minimize losses to the producer and customer.

9

THE CHALLENGE: PURPOSEFUL OPPOSITION

To this point, the challenges and responses have been technical and managerial. The waterfall, if followed carefully, led to success. The competition, if any, was presumably following a similar course. The winner would be the one who was more skilled at satisfying customer needs. Even in highly competitive businesses, there were rules against unfair competition, deceptive advertising, monopolistic pricing, and unethical business practices.

In this chapter all that changes. The opposition is dedicated to system defeat or destruction at any stage, at any system level, and by whatever means available. It is fully aware that complex systems are vulnerable on many fronts. Military combat systems are obvious examples, their opposition expressed in the form of countersystems and tactics. Both system and countersystem are, in turn, embedded in still larger logistic, strategic, and geopolitical environments, reaching the level of world war or superpower deterrence.

At the back of each system may be a chief architect and a client, each team bent on the defeating the other's system. Each will be probing the other's assumptions, constraints, weaknesses, errors, and mistakes. Each will be exploring new options, new applications, new upgrades, and new operating modes to gain an advantage over the other.

Success here is victory. In the usual case, the other side loses, although as we see it, it may be important that it does not. And the other side in part determines the nature of the victory.

DEFINING VICTORY AND SUCCESS

Nowhere is the explicit definition of success more important than in a competition, military or civilian. What is the victory that is sought—the other's destruction, a commanding position, deterrence, resources, reputation, power? What is its scale—less than defeat? What are the rules, if any? Who makes them? Are they fair or even supposed to be?

Before answering these questions too quickly, remember also that circumstances will change and with them the chances for success. An old football story illustrates it well. The local team was behind by four points after a long and bruising battle. There was only a short time left. The team was on its own 10-yard line. Its star quarterback had just broken his leg.

The coach, seeing defeat and wanting to get it over with no further injuries, turned to a rookie and said sternly, "Just do as I say. Go in there, run three plays up the middle, then punt. Do not come back to the bench. We are out of times-out. Just follow orders."

The rookie called the first play and the fullback ran 20 yards up the field. The team huddled, ran the second play, and this time the halfback went for 40 yards. The third time, on a quarterback sneak up the middle, the rookie went to within a yard of the goal. The crowd was delirious. The coach was speechless. On the next play, the rookie, as ordered, punted. The final gun sounded and the game ended with the score unchanged.

For the rookie, successful performance had been dictated—four well-executed plays in a row in his first time on the field. For the coach, the assumption that the rookie would violate orders in order to win was self-evident—and wrong. And, in fact, the coach's objective of no further injuries was achieved. For the team and the town, the plays spelled victory lost.

It was not the first time that a battle was won but the war was lost. Nor was it the first time that achieving a stated subobjective precluded reaching a larger one when conditions changed.

COUNTERING THE OPPOSITION

Most efforts to build and operate complex systems face some form of opposition. The intention of building any system is to change things. Change is seldom to everyone's advantage. The level of the opposition can vary from inconsequential to virulent. It may or may not prove effective. But it is a good working heuristic to assume for design purposes that

For every system, there will be at least one countersystem.

The countersystem may or may not be of the same type. A military hardware system may be countered by a sociopolitical system, for example.

The **system-countersystem** heuristic has a peculiar twist to it:

A system optimized for a particular confrontation is unlikely to encounter it.

The reason? The opposition will refuse to engage in a clearly losing situation, having done a similar analysis and knowing the likely consequences. Instead,

- The opponent may develop and produce a radically different countersystem, one that changes the name of the game.
- The opponent may move the conflict from one arena to another; for example, from technical to sociopolitical.
- The system may act as a deterrent to other conflict, for example, strategic missiles that deter operations against third parties.
- The system may prove to be false security, for example, the Maginot Line.

And consequently,

- The system may be forced to operate "off optimum", for example, strategic bombers in low-level conflict; or
- The system may need to be redesigned to provide broader capability off optimum at a cost in narrower optimum performance, for example, conversion of a fighter to a multimission aircraft.

The simplest confrontation is bounded and symmetric, like football or chess. Except for their uniforms, so to speak, the two sides are more or less alike. Their assets and options are essentially the same. The objective is to gain limited objectives within established constraints. It is the subject of a large body of game theory. Truly serious conflict, however, is unbounded, multidimensional, and asymmetric. The complex systems that are part of it reflect that complexity. We will take up the simpler symmetric case first, recognizing that a model is not reality.

MODELING SYMMETRIC CONFLICT

The simplest conflict model, illustrated in Figure 9–1, contains two opponents with similar purposes and commanding similar system assets. The systems meet in a confrontation region—a playing field, a race track, a marketplace, or a battlefield—limited in scope by circumstance or rules.

Figure 9-1. Symmetric Conflict.

The architect's first problem is to model the confrontation as part of the overall architecture. It is a crucial step. Clearly, the overall conceptual model can be no better than the model it contains of the confrontation region. For example, Dockery and Santoro, (1988) in a revision of F. W. Lanchester's (1914) model of warfare, considerably change the outcome by changing the confrontation model.

Realistic modeling is difficult enough, as seen in earlier chapters. But purposeful opposition makes it still more difficult. One of the actions the opponent can take is to change the nature of the confrontation, even in the middle of the game. Another is to deny the architect critical information—an action the architect no doubt will reciprocate. The architect's measures will be responded to by the opponent whose countermeasures the architect must countercountermeasure in the system design. An example of a more complex confrontation model, including both weapon and surveillance systems, is shown in Figure 9-2.

The cycle may begin at any point. To illustrate, start with a deployed system, say, the red one, under surveillance by blue, which develops, produces, and deploys a blue system to counter the red one. But then red observes, develops, and produces a new countering system, to which blue responds, ad continuum. An escalating "race" may or may not develop, depending on political tension, available resources, technological options, and on perceptions of the opponents' intentions based in part on surveillance.

Closed loops like that of Figure 9-2 have an inherent "time constant"—the time it takes to go once around—which can be years for major systems. Because of it, each side must project years into the future. If tensions are high, the incentive is to speed up. The loop can oscillate as one side, and then the other, starts a new cycle. But there can be stabilizing forces as well. One, shown in Figure 9-3, is earlier surveillance, which shortens the time around the loop.

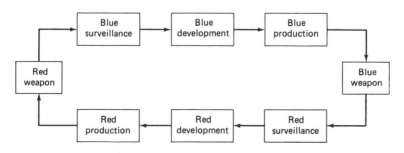

Figure 9-2. An action-reaction model.

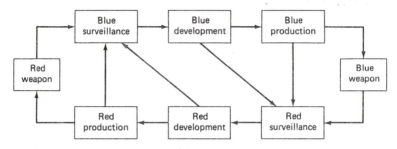

Figure 9-3. An action-reaction model.

As might be expected, the better the surveillance, the better and sooner the counter to it can be designed. The best countersystem, in fact, may not be one with the most capability. In national defense systems, for example, the result of better surveillance has been countersystems designed with *less* performance than might have been the case otherwise. With good information on an opponent's system, the countersystem need not be designed for the worst case, that is, the architect can avoid the "ten-foot tall" assumption about the opponent's presumed capabilities. Thus, the better the surveillance, the less the countersystem cost even to the point of standing pat with the present one, and the more stable the cycle. Every U.S. President since 1960 has commended this result.

Three of the better known action-reaction cases are as follows.

Example:

Electronic countermeasures. The systems in opposition are receiving systems on the one side and transmitting (jamming) systems on the other, attempting to deny the receivers the reception of desired signals. The receivers' antijamming countermeasures include special antenna designs, special knowledge of the desired signals, error-detecting and -correcting codes, denial to the opposing transmitter of knowledge of its effectiveness, and so on. The countercountermeasure by the jammers is transmission of interfering signals resembling the desired ones (spoofing), overpowering the receivers' detector with random noise, and detecting its own effectiveness through changed operations in other parts of the system of which the receiver is a part. Both parties attempt to use sporadic or unexpected operating times and locations to create uncertainty in the opposition. The measure–countermeasure cycle can be very rapid because the characteristics of an opponent's receivers or transmitters may not be known until they are used in combat. Quick-reaction programs are thus the norm.

Example:

Low observability (low probability of interception of signals, low detectability of air- craft, etc.). The opposing systems are systems that must *hide* and those that must *find* in order to survive. The confrontation can occur across many frequency bands, that is, it does little good to be almost undetectable at one frequency, but very visible at another. Technically speaking, hiding means showing low contrast against a particular background. Finding means detecting contrast against that background, then tracking, identifying, and predicting the future position of the target. Countercounter measures against finding include creating an artificial background in which to blend, mimicking other targets, and deceptive motion. Countercounters against hiding include multiple detection methods, multiple sensor locations, wide-spectrum utilization, accurate target characterization, image and pattern recognition, and the like. These techniques, although their electronic forms can be very complex, are as old as life on Earth. As natural (biological) history has shown over the millenia, in the "end game," both hiders and finders continue to exist, though usually in new forms.

Example:

Computers and computer crime. We earlier identified four elements of computer crime, viz., the computer as an object of physical attack, as a target of theft, as an instrument of attack, and as a camouflage for other crime. Computers are involved on both sides, offensive and defensive. The attacker uses computers to destroy or steal data in other computers. The defender uses computers to deny and record attempts at unauthorized access and to trace all inquiries to their source. As with other electronic confrontations, computer confrontations change very quickly.

Response time—timely surveillance results, rapid communications, expeditious decision making, responsive action—is clearly critical in confrontations such as these. Centuries ago when transportation, logistics and communications were much slower, response times of days to weeks might have sufficed. But in the age of global weapons, communications, and surveillance, responses in minutes have proved essential. Strategies for achieving such short times range from the Marines' "Action is preferable to inaction" to use of massive electronic data bases and decision aids.

But short is not necessarily best. At times, it is better to strategize first. The skillful use of military intelligence is a case in point.

Example:

During the Vietnam War, a group of scientists proposed distributing radio transmitting sensors around outposts that needed to be defended. The idea as originally formulated was that when the sensors were activated by enemy movement, artillery fire could quickly be brought to bear. It did not work. The enemy soon learned to spread out so that there were few soldiers near any one sensor. A countertactic was needed: whenever a sensor was activated, the fact was indicated on a map at the outpost. By watching the activity of all the sensors over time, it became apparent, in consort with other collateral intelligence, when and from where an attack was planned. Artillery fire was withheld until the enemy was set to the attack, and then used massively and effectively.

Military intelligence can illustrate another important point. In an electronic-information war, unique knowledge is wealth—not only knowing something, but knowing it without the opponent knowing that you do. To extend Drucker's definition of economic wealth to a confrontational setting:

Wealth is knowledge and knowing how, *where, when,* **and** *why* **to use it.**

The most dramatic demonstration of this principle was the history of code breaking in World War II (Lewin, 1978). Not only was the knowledge crucial during the conflict itself, it continued to be so valuable that the methods by which it was obtained and the way in which it was used were held in highest security for more than 30 years thereafter.

ASYMMETRIC CONFLICT

Except for on the playing field or the game tables, where great efforts are made to make it so, symmetric conflict is the exception. Asymmetric conflict is the norm, with each side having different objectives, resources, rules, definitions of success, tactics, and strategy.

Example:

Insurgent warfare has a long history. Victory has gone sometimes to the government and sometimes to the insurgents. An insightful model of this conflict is shown in Leites and Wolf (1970). As long as the conflict remains asymmetric, that is, a low-level insurgency, it can go on for long periods or until one side or the other is exhausted, discredited, or deprived of external support. But otherwise, if the rebellion is to win militarily, the war must escalate to full-scale conventional (symmetric) combat on the battlefield, where victory may or may not occur.

Example:

The earlier example of electronic countermeasures was symmetric in the sense of electronics fighting electronics with similar techniques. But the best way to get rid of jamming is for the opponent to decide not to jam—the jamming-to-signal ratio is then zero! Under the right circumstances, a number of techniques can accomplish this objective:

- Attack and destroy his jamming equipment
- Negate the command and control of the jamming station
- Deny the opponent any measure of jamming effectiveness
- Use the opponent's frequencies and relays from time to time
- Convince the opponent that there is always another way to achieve one's own objective in any confrontation
- Regularly demonstrate that successful operations are possible even with severe degradation of the system
- Keep introducing new and different systems
- Use an overall architecture of many interconnected units, well controlled and orchestrated, that is, expand the problem

Expanding the problem to one's advantage is a very old tactic, and a natural one in asymmetric conflict. Changing the name of the game by introducing new factors, changing or creating an advantageous asymmetry, is expected here in contrast to symmetric conflict, where tipping the level playing field is considered somehow unfair.

It can be self-deceiving and dangerous to be concerned only with direct combat systems, forgetting about other elements "outside" these systems. Yet, one of the more effective attacks, particularly against complex systems, is to attack the support systems they invariably require—a logistics train, communications, staff support, intelligence, public information, and the like. Support is all too often regarded as being outside the system, not the concern of the systems architect, not the province of war gamers or battle managers. This is believed despite evidence that such lack of concern has lost wars, denied otherwise rare opportunities, and given the initiative to the opponent.

The architect need not be particularly demonic in thinking of nasty measures and countermeasures. Architecturally, attacking the infrastructure can be viewed as just another way of exploiting the inherent unboundedness of complex systems. It suggests the prescriptive heuristic:

Sometimes the best way to defeat a system is to do so "out of bounds." It may also be the best way to preserve it.

Exploiting the unboundedness property of systems enforces the need to see the system architecture always in the context of the *overall* architecture—the bigger picture, the still larger "macrosystem." The higher levels, as well as the lower ones, may be where the keys to victory or defeat are to be found.

SOCIETY, THE SELF-ADAPTING MACROSYSTEM

There is a special type of purposeful opposition, that of a society as a whole to any change. Societal purposes may be complex and conflicting, but societies do share one common goal—self-preservation.

Opposition forms when a new or modified system, designed to change things to the advantage of a particular client, comes into the society. Any change is likely to affect other parties. Their natural reactions are to act to minimize effects disadvantageous to them and/or to take advantage of the change to their own gain. The result is not only direct opposition or support, but also conflicts among other parties. The internal forces within the society need to be rebalanced. The architect may well see a perplexing mixture of support and opposition for reasons that seem directly contradictory. Liberals and conservatives may support weapons-system research and development, but for quite different, even opposite, reasons. The supporters may at the same time differ vehemently on weapons production and/or deployment.

However contradictory the purposes, the general societal response will be to minimize or exploit change, to retain the status quo, and to maintain stability (Hughes, 1988). It will act accordingly, though the internal conflicts of interest within the society may make the final outcome unpredictable.

The architect that assumes that the "outside" world will not change due to the entry into it of a proposed new system is out of touch with reality.

Example:

The client may assume continued availability of resources (land, locations, work force, foreign government support, finances) presently provided to an existing system that may be denied to the new system by a rebalancing of societal priorities. Countries may abruptly deny base rights to new nuclear or surveillance systems.

Example:

Any change in a societal macrosystem may reopen issues that are presently quiescent, as past self-assessed "losers" try again to achieve their goals. A change in administrations may produce an agonizing reappraisal or a zero-based budgeting of systems that previously were well established as multinational cooperative ventures.

But the results do not always have to be zero sum. The macrosystem could experience a net gain, preferably with all parties benefiting to some degree . A societal system is not necessarily hostile, only adaptive.

The architect's task is to work with the client to benefit both the system and the society of which it is a part. To accomplish this may take energy, resources, public relations, and persuasion. It may well take more time than to implement the system itself. It is a lesson learned long ago by professional real estate developers, politicians, and diplomats:

Do not get in a zero-sum game with the outside world.

Or as another famous heuristic states, **"You can't beat City Hall."** Instead, design the system so that almost everyone gains; design for a positive sum.

ARCHITECTURAL RESPONSE I: ARCHITECT THE COUNTERSYSTEM

Purposeful opposition forces the architect to include the opponent and the opponent's system in the overall architectural scheme of things, taking into account the opponent's potential responses by the time the architect's system is deployed. To do that requires a peculiar thought process—simultaneously handling two conflicting concepts and constructing conceptual models of both the red and blue systems without bias or advocacy. It is easier said than done. There may be many forms the opposition could take and many scenarios that could be generated. Some would claim that for any system, there is always a scenario that results in its defeat. "What if?" questions can be asked interminably. "Paralysis by analysis" can set in.

But with skill and objectivity, credible system and countersystem models can be created. An "end game" results—a new balance between system and countersystem. Some of the key factors that determine that balance are as follows:

- The objectives or missions of each party. In some ways, offense is an easier mission than defense. It is easier to deny sea control than to sustain it. It is easier to attack computers than to defend them. It is easier to jam receivers than to protect them. The side with the easier mission may have an unbeatable advantage.
- The state of technology at the time. A given state of technology will make certain options possible for the system and its counter. A new technology may offer new options, preferentially favorable to one side.
- The amount of information available to each side. It can be of considerable advantage to know more about the opposition than it knows about you.
- The ability to exploit technology and knowledge. Neither is worth much unless used well and unless their products are available in sufficient quantity.

These factors act in combination. Thus, an advance in technology, though available to both sides at about the same time, may benefit one side more than the other, depending on the mission of each. Better surveillance may preferentially benefit the side best able to exploit it. One side may not be able to exploit certain technologies due to lack of a manufacturing infrastructure, raw materials, or of other technologies needed to build a complete system. Thus, an important fact, often forgotten in the debates over quality versus quantity: *better system technology and knowledge, while they may be necessary, are not sufficient for victory*. Missions count. Numbers count. Conversion of technology to practice counts.

To these four factors must be added one more, the achievable quality of the systems, themselves.

Example:

Antijam provisions. One of the better antijam techniques is an antenna with very low sidelobes, that is, one that collects very little radiofrequency energy outside its main beam. Undesireably high sidelobes are usually caused by irregularities on the antenna surface and nonlinear electrical contacts on the antenna surface or feed. Both are difficult to control, particularly on antennas subject to bad weather conditions and corrosion. A conventional antenna is able to reject signals entering the sidelobes by a factor of

100 to 1000. But to reject signals by a factor of 100,000 to a million requires precision and quality 100 to 1000 times better than that of a conventional antenna.

Example:

Low observability. Radars are sensitive not to the optical image of a target, but to "glints" from small mirrorlike surfaces on the target. Eliminating the few large corner reflectors, which direct incoming energy directly back to the sender, greatly reduces the radar signal return. But that having been done, there then remain many smaller glinting surfaces, joints, and openings that must be eliminated if further improvement is to be made. Leaving even a few of them changes the observability considerably from the level otherwise achievable. And so it goes. The lower the desired observability, the more precisely and carefully the low-observability system must be made, a relationship similar to that in progressive redesign to increase system quality.

Example:

Air-to-air combat. Generally speaking, the aircraft wins that shoots accurately at the greater range. But the ability to do so depends on the sensitivity and jamming resistance of the sensors and the precision with which the missiles can be controlled. Higher quality in these parameters translates into a greater range at which firing can commence, and hence success against an opponent with poorer equipment.

ARCHITECTURAL RESPONSE II: REDUNDANCY, FAULT TOLERANCE, AND FAULT AVOIDANCE

There are still other useful similarities between the responses to the challenges of ultraquality and purposeful opposition. Both endeavor to avoid failure. Both aim for zero defects. In both cases, key information is impossible to obtain. And so, with only minor modification, similar questions arise:

Are the system and support architectures inherently robust against attack?

Are the constructs inherently flexible, adaptive, fail-safe, and/or fail-soft in accomplishing the system mission? Systems can be "brittle" under attack unless specifically designed to be otherwise. By brittle is meant a shattering collapse if a particular element or more is damaged or disabled. Examples of the latter:

Example:

Single-string communications between two otherwise strong elements.

Example:

"Soft" command and control networks among major commanders.

Example:

Centralized authority exercised by unique individuals at a single location.

Is the system unnecessarily complex?

The more complex a system, the more difficult it may be to understand. Hence, it may have unexpected weaknesses. Complexity produced by attempting to satisfy too many requirements or added during the implementation phase in order to correct an engineering problem may in the process produce exploitable weaknesses.

Is the right set of confrontation problems being solved?

Was the original purpose well thought out; in particular, were various forms of opposition considered and their probabilities assessed?

Example:

Cryptographic systems. Was capture of the equipment considered? Can keys be distributed if normal communication is denied? Is the system vulnerable to procedural errors?

Example:

Fighter aircraft. Is positive identification of other aircraft mandatory before taking action? If so, long-range weapon use may be precluded. Is the opponent so constrained?

Example:

Information networks. Is overload of the circuits from a single station an option for a hacker?

Is there more than one way to accomplish the mission?

One of the best deterrents to an attack is the availability of mission alternatives, that is, dissimilar redundancy. In contrast to the use of redundancy to counter statistically unavoidable failures, its use here reduces the incentive to attack.

Example:

The strategic triad of submarines, aircraft, and ICBMs diminishes the incentives to attack any one element because unacceptable damage can still be produced by either of the others.

Example:

Multiple communications options, coupled with encrypted signals, can deny the opposition certainty of breaking communications linkages between specified parties, and hence deters attempting to do so.

ARCHITECTURAL RESPONSE III: ESTABLISH A RED TEAM

A red team is a group specifically tasked to analyze and counter the proposed system. Its function is analogous to the independent review and FMEA responses to ultraquality. It has similar advantages and handicaps. It finds weaknesses and works out ways to exploit them, often with a vengeance. It provides management and prospective users with an independent view of the effects of purposeful opposition.

A special difficulty is establishing the rules for the red team. Just how much information should be available to the team—is it far more than the actual opposition would possess? How much knowledge of what the red team is doing should be available to the project ("blue") team? How much intelligence knowledge of the actual opponent should be made available to the red team? Can the blue team keep fixing the system's vulnerabilities, never really committing to a firm design that the red team can assess with any certainty?

There are also psychological problems to be worked out. No blue team likes to be continually attacked and frustration can lead to personality clashes very easily. But being on a red team, thwarting the objectives of one's parent organization, can risk one's career.

Lack of an unconstrained, dedicated red team can be dangerous, leading the client to a sense of false security, to unpleasant operational surprises, to performance far below that promised, and to defeat.

> **What independent reviews are to quality, red teams are to survival, only more so.**

One reason is that purposeful opposition, being focused and selective, can be more effective than random failure in disabling a system. Another is that the responses to failure in an opposed system are more limited; the opponent is unlikely to permit a shutdown, a truce, or a time out while the system is fixed. A third is that the opposition is human, quite possibly fighting for its life, with few compunctions about changing the rules when survival is at stake.

Consequently, if the red team technique is to be effective, *the red team must be allowed to play as if its survival was at stake. The real-world opponent certainly will.*

SUMMARY

Systems facing purposeful opposition confront the architect with increased uncertainty and risk of serious failure or defeat. Opposing systems will exist or come into being. Modeling the confrontation well will be critical for a valid conceptual model of the system. Faced with societal opposition, whenever possible, avoid the zero-sum game. Try to design an overall architecture in which no one must lose, only gain less.

Especially for military systems, design, or at least sketch, the potential countersystem, use techniques analogous to those used in response to ultraquality, and establish an effective and unfettered red team.

RECOMMENDED READING

DOCKERY, JOHN T., and ROBERT T. SANTORO (July 1988). " Lanchester Revisited: Progress in Modeling C^2 in Combat." *Signal,* **42,** 11, 41–48. This makes the point that the validity of the models of the opposing systems can only be as good as the model of the combat in which they are engaged. It upgrades F. W. Lanchester's equations by adding randomness, fuzzy set variables, space (as well as time), and nonhomogeneous forces.

HUGHES, T. P. (Winter 1988). "The Industrial Revolution That Never Came." *Invention and Technology* **3**, 3, 59–64. Social oracles once believed that the coming of electricity and automobiles would make dirty crowded cities a thing of the past. Instead, the existing social structure bent these technologies to its own purposes.

LEITES, NATHAN, and CHARLES WOLF, Jr. (1970). *Rebellion and Authority, An Analytic Essay on Insurgent Conflicts.* Chicago: Markham. This is a classic book viewing rebellion and authority as a system. It views the system nonjudgmentally, indicating the strengths and weaknesses of both opponents. In a marked contrast with the "hearts and minds" theory of insurgent conflict, this essay supports the view that the population reacts instead to costs and opportunities.

LEWIN, RONALD. (1978). *ULTRA Goes to War.* New York: McGraw-Hill. One of the best, if not the best, books analyzing the techniques and results of the breaking of the German Enigma code during World War II. It rewrites the history of the war by documenting who knew what when and what was then done. Not all the results were positive—the commanders either did not, could not, or would not use the code breakers' product. The interceptions were only partial, and sometimes erroneous, indications of enemy intent and action. But, on balance, ULTRA was a critical factor in Allied success in the Atlantic, European, and African campaigns.

RECHTIN, E. (1983). *The Technology of Command,* the Charles H. Davis Lecture Series. Washington, DC: National Academy Press. It presents the architecture, design, and risks inherent in modern C^3 systems; countertechnologies and defending against them; the commander, and strategy considerations.

TO BROWSE, DEPENDING ON INTEREST

ADAM, J. A. (April 1988). "How to Design an 'Invisible' Aircraft." *IEEE Spectrum* **25,** 4, 26–31. This is a qualitative description of the basic physics of low-observability aircraft and of the countermeasures to them.

HANSEN, R. E. (1977). "Freedom of Passage on the High Seas of Space." *Strategic Review* **V**, 4. This is a forecast of confrontations in space by analogy to confrontations at sea from a military point of view. Reprinted for *Astronautics & Aeronautics,* February 1978, **16,** 2, 76–83.

LANCHESTER, F. W. (1914). *Engineering* **98,** 422. The classic analysis of the ratio of offensive and defensive forces likely to win or lose a battle. Indicates that the defensive forces must be larger because they must defend all areas whereas the offense only has to attack one.

MCDONALD, JOHN C. (1989). *Growing Vulnerability of the Public Switched Networks: Implications for National Security Emergency Preparedness.* Washington, DC: National Academy Press. This National Research Council report states that with economics now being the driver of U.S. telecommunications and with the proliferation of public switched networks, the nation's telecommunications and information networks are becoming more vulnerable to serious interruptions of service from natural, accidental and hostile agents.

10

THE CHALLENGE: A SENSE OF TIME AND TIMING

Great uncertainty always exists—of what has happened, is happening, and will happen. (G. M. Weinberg, 1988)

In introducing change, timing is vital. [Spinrad, 1988]

Those who would forget the past . . . should know better.

All architecture is in three parts: function, form and time.

Few qualities in an architect are more important than a sense of time—past, present, and future. Fitting its many "lines" together, and there are at least a half dozen of them, is a major challenge for which the architect bears heavy responsibility. Success is a well-timed product. Failure is a product ahead of its time or obsolete on arrival.

One time line is clock time—chronological, continuous, infinite, its intervals as unchanging as human ingenuity can make them. It is measured in familiar units of years and picoseconds, driven in today's world by the precise motions of atoms. It is the reference for our other time lines.

A second line is project time along the waterfall. It has an assumed beginning and end, but its intervals are determined by complexity and availability of resources, not atomic motion. Its points in time are milestones, achievements, and reports. When a project is planned, a schedule is established related to clock time. But "real-world" project time has "stretch" and **rubber schedule** dynamics. Forcing project time to meet clock time stresses other project dimensions—

quality, performance, cost, and management focus. In that sense, time can mean money, although the relationship is not a simple one.

A third line is budget time—the fiscal-year cycle, governmental approval cycles of 3–4 years, and annual decision windows. There is no value in being early or late in this time line, only in being *on* time. It is characterized by deadlines and driven by laws, regulations, and policies.

A fourth line is sociopolitical—elections, changes in administrations, national security cycles, major incidents, and conflicts. It is marked by discontinuities, epochs, and interacting social trends. Occasionally, it seems to be going backward. Its apparent speed ranges from long-term paralysis to cataclysmic.

A fifth is economic time—the so-called business, recession, and depression cycles, driven by the many factors that make them and the investment market so erratic.

By no means the least of these lines are the technological and process trend lines—the introduction, mastering, producing, and amortizing of technologies and processes. These time lines may branch, accelerate, and fade. Being behind in an accelerating trend means being further and further behind until the trend slows at maturity. Missing a trend can mean bankruptcy.

The time lines sometimes go their own way, becoming way out of step with the rest. Or they may intersect, producing either rare opportunities or catastrophes. What might have appeared as a fine technical system at its initiation may on its completion arrive at the wrong budget, sociopolitical, or economic time. The project time line may stretch to a point where it is out of phase with technological advances, new process developments, or budget cycles.

The challenge of rapidly changing time lines is a serious one for complex systems having decades-long development and operational times. Their multidimensional complexity makes them particularly susceptible to the vagaries of multiple time lines. The challenge, then, is

How can the architect maintain a sense of time and timing in designing and building long-term complex systems?

The time of greatest responsibility comes near the end of concept development—the pause and reflect time—when a sense of time and a longer view are most needed. It is a time of questioning. It is a time when the architect needs to be both an historian and a scout.

The short-term questions are those of the immediate future of the project. Has anything been left out? Are there possible "showstoppers"? Does it appear that there are more solutions than problems ahead? Does the project look promising as of now?

But there are other questions, questions over the longer time span, forward and back in time, that are comparably important to success.

THE RESPONSES

The responses to the challenge are as follows:

- Looking ahead, to make better present decisions and reduce risk
- Looking back, to exploit lessons learned
- Looking to the side, at concurrent time lines and applications

RESPONSE I: FORWARD ARCHITECTING

The most serious questions in the forward direction are those of technological and sociopolitical changes that could jeopardize system success. If there are such potential changes, can the architecture accommodate them? In today's computer parlance, is the architecture sufficiently "open"?

On the technological front, it can be argued that predicting future breakthroughs is difficult, if not impossible. Unpredicted technological revolutions abound—nuclear energy, nuclear weapons, solid-state electronics, powerful personal computers, television—the list goes on and on. If even tomorrow cannot be predicted, why waste time worrying about the next decade? Fortunately, the impact of a new technology on major complex systems is far from instantaneous. It typically takes 20–30 years from the first laboratory demonstration to widespread use. And the most effective use may be quite different from what was anticipated.

In practice, and for most complex architectures, a 10-year projection of trends, properly accounted for, is sufficient to avoid premature obsolescence.

Ten-year trends that can affect major systems are generally apparent. At the present time, for example, they point to a "knowledge age" accompanied by a ."materials age." Great improvements in information processing and distribution. Smart system elements. Advanced sensors. Replacement of mechanical components with electronics. New electronics/acoustics/photonics materials. Composite structural materials, perhaps even tailored electromechanical materials. Flexible and more productive manufacturing, perhaps true process architectures. Improved interactions between humans and intelligent machines, perhaps man–machine teaming. Further out: neural networks, electric propulsion, superconductivity, widespread use of low observables, counterlow observables, new software languages, and so on.

Fortunately, the architect need not forecast the details, only the general trends. Can the proposed architecture take advantage of them? Or will the system have to be cast aside? Is the present architecture aimed in the same direction as the trends of its technological base?

These general-trend questions are more important than they might seem when a project is starting. The conceptual model presumably contains the best technology available at the time. But modern complex systems may take several years to conceive and approve, take a decade to implement, and spend several decades in service. During this long period, the once new technology may have turned over many times.

One hears of systems, based on and heavily constrained by 15- or 20-year-old technologies, being virtually obsolete shortly after arrival. But this failing is not inherent in complex systems. The fault, if any, is in the way they were architected and produced. It is a fault that can be avoided.

Example:

The United States, admittedly at some risk, produced smaller but equally effective ICBMs and SLBMs 5 to 10 years sooner than conventional procurement methods would have produced by forecasting developments in nuclear weapons and rocket engines and incorporating them in the initial design.

Example:

The NASA/JPL Deep Space communications and navigation systems were designed to exploit technological trends for at least 25 years. The major elements were advanced together, producing a steady factor-of-2 gain in performance every 2 years for an improvement in 30 years of 70,000. It achieved progressively more difficult objectives of effective communication and navigation to the Moon, to the planets, and finally to the edge of the solar system.

Example:

Both Douglas and Boeing commercial aircraft series employ architectures that have accommodated technological changes for more than 50 years, advancing system capacity, speed, safety, and efficiency every year.

Example:

Open architectures are increasingly common in information systems, computers, software, communications protocols, networks, manufacturing plants, and even computer chips. The result is extended service, rapid response to change, and competitiveness in world markets.

Example:

As seen earlier, architects of opposed systems must project forward in time, architecting potential countersystems to account for future actions by their opponents.

In short, it is possible and practical to design major systems to accommodate technological change over several decades. Longer than that probably calls for planned obsolescence, more limited application, or outright elimination.

Sociopolitical, economic, and market projections are much less predictable than technological ones. Wars, sharp economic downturns, and disastrous governmental policies come about with little warning, caused as they are by unfortunate combinations of factors that alone would be more benign. Nonetheless, reasonable *ranges* of conditions can be considered and the system's resiliency to those conditions estimated.

For example, what would be the effects of a major change in customer support, or in the system capacity needed, or in the cost of critical materials? Would the effects be catastrophic or could they be alleviated by options built into the design? Could system implementation and/or operation be placed "on hold" for significant periods? Is the system highly sensitive to a volatile factor (e.g., cost of fuel for commercial airliners, availability of toxic materials for a manufacturing process, availability of parts from a foreign supplier, and availability of launch vehicles for a contracted satellite service)?

A primary responsibility of the architect, therefore, is to make sure that potential future changes, technological and otherwise, are raised for consideration during concept development. Not to do so is to incur considerable risks for the client, who should at least have the opportunity to assess them and to decide on appropriate action.

Predicting the future may be impossible, but ignoring it is irresponsible.

In a sense, ignoring the future while optimizing for the present is a form of overly narrow optimization. It is an error comparable to overoptimizing an opposed system for a particular scenario. Paraphrasing an earlier heuristic, a **system optimized** for the present is **unlikely to encounter** it in the future. The competition will see to that.

PROGRESSIVE RISK REDUCTION

An important form of forward achitecting is the design of progressive risk-reduction programs for high-risk systems. The more radical or advanced the system, the more important the progressive reduction of its risks.

An initial step, as in ultraquality programs, is an assessment of *relative* risks. Ideally, the greatest risks are attacked first and the lesser ones left until later. The greatest mistake is to begin with the easiest and most straightforward tasks, giving the illusion of progress. If the greatest risk cannot be overcome, the wastage can be costly indeed.

The greatest risks having been identified, the next step is to build confidence that they can be significantly reduced. One technique is to plan a series of progressively more difficult tests for progressively more complex "protosystems." Climbing this success ladder indicates real progress. (It may also indicate the probable stretch factor in a rubber schedule if success comes hard.)

It may turn out that the top of the ladder cannot be reached, at least with the proposed architecture and technologies. The client then has choices, some of which should have been foreseen by the architect before the risk-reduction effort began. The wastage, if any, should be as little as possible, considering the known risk. Some of the choices are as follows:

- Return the project to the research stage
- Change the system objectives and architecture
- Cancel the project

A series of successful tests, on the other hand, has another advantage—it helps assure continuing support, essential for complex systems taking years to implement. But, clearly, unless the successes clearly address the greatest risks, they can be misleading.

A critical risk is that the system, even if built as planned, may not be successful *operationally*. This risk is inherent whenever the client—the one that pays the costs of building the system—is not the end user. This situation is particularly evident in the Department of Defense, where the military services handle procurement, but the unified and specified commands (e.g., the Strategic Air Command and CINCLANT) are the users. Risk reduction in this case requires prototypes specifically aimed at early determination of operational utility. The first prototypes necessarily should be as simple as possible and aimed at the main operational uncertainties. Well-understood capabilities can be added later.

Because future acceptance and operational evaluation will be by the user, the more participation in the design and test of the operational prototypes by the user, the better. It is more than just good customer relations. It keeps the priorities straight. It reduces the risks associated with changing user needs.

A special form of early prototyping, system simulation, is required when the greatest risks are not in the elements of the system, but in whether they will work together as a *system*. The elements may indeed be quite conventional. It may seem that all that needs to be done is to assemble them together. But without system simulation, difficulties in system integration and testing will not be discovered until late in the waterfall. To anticipate them, some elements may be simulated, most need not be up to final specifications (e.g., weight, power, size, capacity, documentation), and few may be in production. But each must be the functional equivalent of the production element. The design of the early system prototype is of particular interest to the system architect. In simulating system performance, it helps assure the architectural integrity of the system as a whole, acts as an important diagnostic tool in the case of trouble, and provides a test bed into which production elements can be placed to determine their performance in the system as a whole.

RESPONSE II: REVERSE ARCHITECTING

Things are the way they are because they got that way. (Boulding, 1961)

By reverse architecting is meant looking back in time to when existing or prior systems were being architected. It is all too easy to discount the past, to judge prior systems by today's standards and needs. But it is a reasonable presumption that the previous clients and architects knew what they were doing *in the context of their time and circumstances.* Their systems deserve respect and study. Their successes and failures are demonstrations of life in the real world.

The extreme case of reverse architecting is archeology. Given only a few clay fragments, what was the system? Why was it built the way it was? Why was it not built differently? A closer look can reveal a complex interplay of available technology, sociopolitical and economic conditions, and human ingenuity. Some structures and systems we still do not comprehend either in purpose or in construction method. In others, we are discovering the clues to far more widespread trade, transportation, communication, manufacturing, and military complexes than had been imagined. Complexity certainly is not a new phenomenon.

Of more immediate benefit, perhaps, is reviewing one's immediate predecessor systems for which much more information is available. Statements of requirements, project descriptions, system models, preliminary designs, and interface specifications can be good sources. All too often, however, missing are records of the architecting process, how clients and architects (if even identified) determined system configuration, how requirements priorities were decided, and why certain trade-offs were made. These processes must be deduced through reverse architecting and engineering, through working backwards from final form to intended function.

Reverse architecting serves a number of purposes. It helps understand earlier systems and their trade-offs. It helps capitalize on past successes and avoid past mistakes. It provides reference architectures during concept development. Perhaps most important, it helps the architect maintain a long-term perspective.

Every architecture has both good features and inherent drawbacks. It is easy to criticize a previous architecture, whether of a system or an organization, and to propose a new system that eliminates the evident drawbacks. It takes more effort and objectivity to identify drawbacks inherent or introduced in the new architecture. The new, previously absent, drawbacks may not be recognized and dealt with. If not considered in the beginning, they can appear as unpleasant surprises later on. If considered and retained, their consequences need to be understood and accepted. The same can be said for positive, all too familiar, features of the older architecture that are missing in the proposed one.

Example:

In the mid-1970s it was decided to build an inertial upper stage (IUS) for injecting heavy payloads into precision high-altitude orbits from either expendable vehicles or the Shuttle. For reasons of Shuttle safety, solid propellants, rather than high-performance liquids, were chosen for the IUS. But a combination of low flight rates, the needs for more weight-lifting capacity to geosynchronous and planetary trajectories, and reduced interest in precision injection into orbit resulted in a decision to put high-performance Centaurs in the Shuttle bay, reversing the earlier safety decision. The IUS was criticized severely on grounds of cost and lower performance; further production was stopped;

safety considerations were forgotten. After the *Challenger* disaster, however, the safety requirement was recalled, the Centaur was dropped, and the IUS retained for Shuttle use as originally intended. Pending development of other upper stages, the IUS is now the only choice for many Shuttle-launched missions to geosynchronous orbit and deep space.

Example:

Communications system development is one of the most rapidly advancing fields in the world today: satellites, undersea cables, fiber optics, and lasers. And yet, most earlier communications systems continue to exist: land lines, high-frequency groundwave, ionospheric, and shortwave radio; ground microwave links; tropospheric scatter; and meteor-burst communications. Each still represents a special set of trade-offs still applicable in the niche that each system occupies.

Example:

For short-haul, short-runway, dependable, low-cost air transportation, the 50-year-old DC-3 is still an aircraft of choice. Its architectural reasoning is still valid.

Example:

Software, built at considerable cost in time and money, is often a major asset in a system and very difficult to replace or convert. A supplier's decision to introduce a new, but incompatible,software package thus can be a major risk to both supplier and customer. The advantages of the new software, therefore, must be almost overwhelming to justify a change.

Example:

Because of the inherent vulnerability of existing satellite and strategic missile fleets consisting of small numbers of large vehicles, it has been proposed to replace them with fleets of large numbers of smaller vehicles. But to change the vulnerability appreciably, the ratio of replacement to original numbers should probably be at least 10. But economy of scale and simplicity of operation so strongly favors larger vehicles that to accomplish the same mission will greatly increase the costs. Decisions are yet to be made, with the conclusion heavily dependent upon perceptions of international tensions.

The previous systems were, or still are, satisfactory in their own time and place. Others were terminated well before any operational use, raising the question of why they were started—as well as why they were stopped. They, too, need to be understood to provide perspective for new proposals.

Example:

The B-70 was an early 1960s aircraft intended for supersonic strategic bombing, a design requiring flight at relatively high altitude to conserve fuel. The first planes were just flying when it became apparent that Soviet surface-to-air missiles would make high-altitude flight too dangerous. Low-altitude subsonic flight was the only feasible regime. The B-70 program was cancelled. Its lessons are being applied in the B-1 and Stealth programs.

Example:

The Manned Orbiting Laboratory was a late 1960s proposal for a small military space station for remote-sensing purposes. It was cancelled for several reasons, an important one being a requirement that the onboard equipment should be able to operate without human intervention. But, if that requirement was met, why was an in-orbit human presence needed, that is, why not send the instruments aloft in expendable spacecraft controlled from the ground? The trade-off between the advantages of human judgment and flexibility in orbit and the costs associated with human transportation and life support proved unfavorable for human presence in orbit. That trade-off continues to be a controversial one for all space stations.

A special case of reverse architecting is found in technical intelligence analysis. Given limited information about an opponent's system, what might have been its design objectives and what are its operational capabilities? Answering these questions is made as difficult as possible by the opponent's denying access to critical information. Information is fragmentary, of different degrees of validity, and scattered among the system elements. It is common wisdom in the intelligence business that one seldom sees more than 20% of the jigsaw puzzle, although from time to time that 20% is enough to complete it. The rest of the picture is sketched by technical intelligence—reverse architecting.

THE LIMITED FUTURE OF BACKUPS

A common way of reducing the risks of introduction of a new system is to retain an existing system as a backup. Although worthwhile in the short run, history shows that backup systems seldom continue in that role in the long run. They either fade away or find a smaller niche.

As noted earlier, new systems have to have considerable advantages over their predecessors in order to be built. An earlier chapter suggests at least a factor-of-2 improvement is necessary in key parameters. Once the system is built, its advantages are quickly exploited and it becomes much preferred over the earlier one. But unless a system is used routinely, its performance suffers. For example, if launch vehicles are not launched, launch operations become rusty. If communications systems are not used, operator proficiency drops. Decreased performance further discourages use, increasing the cost per operation, and the backup is either discarded as too costly for what it provides or scaled back into a unique niche.

Example:

The history of telecommunications, as noted earlier, is a long series of new developments. Each has gone through the cycle of research, prototyping, introduction into limited service, expansion into a primary service, relegation into a backup status for a new development, and possible retention in a niche. High-frequency radio at one time was the primary medium for transoceanic and naval communication traffic. Undersea cables and satellites now fill that role. But a few high-frequency radio stations still exist, unable to handle the immense traffic carried by the other media, but useful in special circumstances. Communication satellites are now undergoing a similar transformation with the advent of optical-fiber cables.

This is not to say that backups are a mistake. Rather, it is a call for a backup strategy as an element of any new architecture. One such strategy is preplanned reductions over time in the capabilities demanded of the earlier system. Initially, the backup helps guarantee continuity of service, reducing the risks of using the new system, with all its growing pains and technological glitches. Few user organizations are willing to make an abrupt switch from a tried and true system to a new and untried one—not if the systems are critical for national defense, air safety, preservation of life, or even customer acceptance.

Then, as the new system proves out, the earlier one either needs to be assigned a subset of its original mission or be phased out. Phase out of any major system is traumatic, particularly for the people involved, but the trauma can be greatly reduced by planning. Even so, its termination is likely to "avalanche" as key people, usually the most mobile and most in demand elsewhere, leave. With these skills lost, performance in the final phase can be unreliable, unsafe, and expensive. As a problem, termination needs to be considered well in advance.

RESPONSE III: SIDEWAYS ARCHITECTING

We have seen the importance to new architectures of looking both forward and backward in time. Another perspective can be worthwhile—looking sideways.

One sideways look we have already noted—observing and interacting with the other time lines. Another is looking sideways in technology to generate new systems and applications from new combinations of present technologies. Some sideways systems have been quite unconventional, but filled a special niche. In the jargon of the trade, they are "silver bullets," critical for certain purposes (killing bad guys) but little else. Others uniquely solve special problems in fields far removed from the originating one, for example, laser surgery. Still others revisit earlier trade-offs and generate new opportunities.

Example:

The Pregnant Guppy: an almost whalelike cargo airplane designed to carry very bulky cargo, but at modest speeds.

Example:

The U-2: an airplane with very long gliderlike wings powered by a jet engine designed to fly very fast at very high altitudes.

Example:

The earth-circling Voyager aircraft: a novel aircraft configuration designed for extreme range and long duration but at very low speed.

Example:

A "limp blimp" (low-pressurization gas bag) designed for long duration and stability.

Example:

The Soviet Shuttle: a winged orbiter resembling the U.S. Shuttle, but without the main engines on board (they are on the booster). The Soviet Shuttle, using smaller jet engines, is then capable of near-normal atmospheric flight.

Example:

The quiet helicopter: a helicopter so quiet that it can pass by at 100 feet at 50 mph and not be heard against the rustle of tree leaves. The penalty is a reduced cargo-carrying capacity.

Example:

Lightweight satellites: originally a response to reducing the vulnerability of satellite configurations by fractionating the functions performed into smaller, more numerous units. More likely, the lightweight satellites will find special niches to fill.

A NOTE ON PROCESS ARCHITECTURES

The previous discussion and examples have concentrated on primary systems, but the principles apply equally well to the process systems necessary to build them. Process architectures, too, have trade-offs, are affected by concurrent time lines, and can benefit from forward, reverse, and sideways architecting.

SUMMARY

No system and no waterfall exists just by itself in its own time and place. Just as systems are part of other systems, project time is a part of a larger time, not only past and future, but with other time lines running concurrently. Project time must fit into this larger time environment. Assuring the fit is a prime responsibility of the system architect. The tools are forward, reverse, and sideways architecting.

RECOMMENDED READING

Boorstin, Daniel J. (1985). *The Discoverers.* New York: Vintage Books. See particularly Book I: Time, a history of how time has been perceived and measured and how its perception has affected human history.

Cooper, N. G. (Fall 1983). "An Historical Perspective: From Turing and von Neumann to the Present." *Los Alamos Science* 9, 22–27. This is an article on self-replicating systems, self-ordering systems (order from chaos), and their relationships to statistics and entropy. It is a history of one search for the fundamentals of complexity.

TO BROWSE, DEPENDING ON INTEREST

BOULDING, KENNETH. (1961). *The Image: Knowledge in Life and Society.* Ann Arbor: Ann Arbor Paperbacks.

COATES, JOHN F. (April 1989). "The Trireme Sails Again." *Scientific American,* **260,** 4, 96–103. The sea trials of reconstructed Greek warship confirm speed records in ancient writings.

DEMEIS, R. (November 1987). "Blimps Are Back on Board." *Aerospace America* **25,** 11, 34–37. This is a review of the latest Naval Air Systems Command program to determine utility of blimps as long-duration surveillance and communications platforms.

DERTOUZOS, M. L. (1984). "Software and Unorthodox Architectures: Where Are We Headed?" In *Cutting Edge Technologies.* Washington, DC: National Academy Press. This is a forecast of myria-processor systems containing hundreds to thousands of processors, of tightly coupled multiprocessors for sensory and intelligent computing, and of a diminished importance of programming.

GOODSTEIN, DAVID L. (Winter 1989). "High Temperature Superconductivity." *Engineering & Science* **52,** 2, 3–15. This is a system look at applications for high-temperature superconductivity—with the conclusion that all the acclaimed possibilities do not amount to much.

HAUCK, GEORGE F. W. (March 1989). "The Roman Aqueduct of Nîmes." *Scientific American* **266,** 3, 98–104. Reverse architecting using principles of fluid flow in channels, aerodynamics, and structural mechanics demonstrates that Roman engineers were remarkably sophisticated in their calculations and design, using techniques believed unknown until the nineteenth century.

LEKSON, S. H., T. C. WINDES, J. R. STEIN, and W. J. JUDGE. (July 1988). "The Chaco Canyon Community." *Scientific American* **259,** 1, 100–109. This describes the reverse architect-engineering of a 1000-year-old set of dwellings and roads in New Mexico. Why were they built and who lived in them?

KOWINSKI, WILLIAM S. (February 1988). "There's Still Time to Hop a Trolley—Vintage or Modern." *Smithsonian* **18,** 11, 128–36. This is about the resurrection of the street car as the light rail system in major cities beset by freeway gridlock.

LERNER, E. J. (October 1988). "Computing with Photons." *Aerospace America* **26,** 10, 28–38. This presents the "immense" technical and architectural problems of using photonics, noting the Japanese lead in this technology.

LEY, WILLY, and W. VON BRAUN. (1956). *The Exploration of Mars.* New York: American Book—Stratford Press. Considering the technology then available, this is a remarkable book by two of the pioneer aerospace architects.

MCCANN, A. M. (March 1986). "The Roman Port of Cosa." *Scientific American* **258,** 3, 102–9. This shows the use of reverse architect-engineering, combined physical archeology with clues on social structure and commerce to define a major center for international trade.

ORTLOFF, CHARLES R. (December 1988). "Canal Builders of Pre-Inca Peru." *Scientific American* **259**, 6, 100–107. The Peruvian equivalent of Egyptian canals, constructed about A.D. 1000 is described. It shows the interaction of needs, engineering, and geology.

STEINER, J. E. (1984). "Air Technology: The Transport Vehicle and Its Development Environment." In *Cutting Edge Technologies*. Washington, DC: National Academy Press. This is an architectural look at the air transport 2000 system, with its "enormous" integrative challenges. "The sum of twenty-first-century potentials will be derived from integrations of the air system, the air vehicle, and the airport environment (access and egress)."

VOELCKER, JOHN. (May 1987). "Learning from Earlier Systems." *IEEE Spectrum* **24**, 5, 67–72. This is an essay on redesigning and the need to plan for it. Quotes a circuit board designer, **"You can't avoid redesign. It's a natural part of design."**

VOELCKER, JOHN. (August 1988). "The iffy 'Orient Express'" *IEEE Spectrum* **25**, 8, 31–33. This is an assessment of the problems of hypersonic orbital transport.

11

THE CHALLENGE: BIOLOGICAL ARCHITECTURES AND INTELLIGENT BEHAVIOR

One of the most challenging puzzles in complex system architectures today is the ability of animals to perform certain intelligent functions with apparent ease that machines perform only with great difficulty, if at all—and vice versa.

Sea slugs can learn. Frogs can distinguish prey from predator. Pigeons can remember human faces. Hawks and bats can detect their small prey against a complex background from great distances, plan their attack, and carry out that attack with precision. Insects move, climb, avoid obstacles, fly, hide, find mates, and defend themselves. Human infants learn and construct languages, make associations of disparate ideas, recall past events with clarity, and reorganize their memory banks at extraordinary speed. Regardless of their speed, resolution, or size, present-day machines are incapable of performing these functions with any facility, if at all.

On the other hand, machines perform feats of logic, precision, consistency, and endurance that quickly exhaust even human capacities. They operate well in environments hopelessly hostile to living systems. They enable us to live better, longer, and far more effectively and efficiently than we could on our own.

This puzzle has occupied the best minds in the world for more than half a century. But it has been only in the past several decades that real progress has been made in building machines that emulate, albeit at a primitive level, intelligent animal behavior. Two facts stand out:

- Animals and machines are different in behavior.
- Animals and present-day machines are built differently, that is, they have different architectures.

One of the steps in solving the puzzle thus may be the insight that

Different architectures can generate different behavior.

The relationship between architecture and behavior has been, and is, a powerful tool in understanding and emulating human intelligence. Architecture both enables and constrains behavior. And behavior suggests architecture. Studying one gives clues to the other.

There are, therefore, at least three good reasons why modern systems architects need to understand biological architectures and intelligent behavior.

The most apparent reason is the puzzle we have just addressed. Humans and even small animals easily perform certain intelligent functions that our best machines cannot, for example, rapid feature recognition, classification, and association. The challenge is for our machines to do likewise. At long last, there is now real hope. Research in the neurosciences, physiology, behavioral sciences, psychology, cognitive (knowledge) sciences, and machine intelligence is now *collectively* beginning to describe in some detail architectures that make intelligent-machine behavior possible. As our understanding increases, so does our ability to construct systems that can sense, think, communicate, and act far better than ever before.

The second reason for understanding biological intelligence: even simplified, incomplete models of biological systems suggest practical ways of accomplishing new machine functions. Indeed, two of the most encouraging aspects of biologically inspired neural networks are the proliferation of new architectures for them and the new functions they perform.

But before becoming too enthusiastic about employing biological architectures in machines, we should note that the closer we get to emulating human intelligence in machines, the closer we get to its particular weaknesses as well as its strengths. Human intelligence is subject to exhaustion, to false and partial memory and associations, to leaping to the wrong conclusions, and to giving different answers to the same problem at different times. To err is human, and woe be to the architect that forgets it (Norman, 1988).

To be fair to the biological architectures, computers are not error-free, either. Virtually none have error-free software; most experts assert that they never will. They can crash. A wrong instruction can destroy all memory. And they can be catastrophically vulnerable to hardware failure—a characteristic much less prevalent in biological architectures.

The third reason for understanding biological systems is the most immediately useful. Machine systems are run by humans, the most advanced of all biological systems. Unless human and machine architectures fit together properly, performance will suffer. A clear course of improvement is to understand the biological side of the interface better; a good machine architecture requires a good understanding of human architecture and its behavior.

Today's systems architects are in a fortunate position. Our understanding of human sensing and thinking systems is increasing at an extraordinary rate. New insights and techniques are announced so often that publications more than a few years old are almost obsolete. Advances in computer technology are making possible modeling and emulation of human system architectures at higher and higher levels of sophistication and intelligence.

Meanwhile, there is a great deal that the systems architect can do with the knowledge at hand.

Let us begin with an architectural overview of intelligent systems that exhibit intelligent behavior. If the level of detail at times seems daunting, persevere. There is a method here: to appreciate the architectural consequences to machine intelligence of recent research in biological architectures and their intelligent behavior.

INTELLIGENT BIOLOGICAL ARCHITECTURES

Biological architectures, in general, are extraordinarily complex and multidimensional. Describing them in even countable dimensions is a formidable task. Probably the best description so far, from an architect's point of view, is given by James G. Miller (1978), a systems and behavioral scientist.

Miller begins with a discussion of systems in general and then narrows it to those systems that live as relatively autonomous entities. (No living system is independent of its environment.) To exist, a living system must perform certain critical functions—eating, moving, reproducing, self-defense, etc.—that Miller partitions into 19 "subsystems." These are reproducer, boundary, ingestor, distributor, converter, producer, matter–energy storage, extruder, motor, supporter, input transducer, internal transducer, channel and network, decoder, associator, memory, decider, encoder, and output transducer.

About half of these functions are directly associated with intelligent behavior.

Miller then identifies seven discrete levels of living systems: cell, organ, organism, group, organization, society, and supranational systems. Then, and most remarkably, he shows that with very few exceptions, *each level* has all 19 subsystems, including those that produce intelligent behavior. Therefore, *intelligent behavior is not limited to the highest-level species, nor need it be limited in capability in otherwise primitive living systems.* Each level is shown to have both structure (form) and process (function). Interrelationships between the subsystems are then developed and the whole system is functionally described with more than 150 hypotheses.

Yet, even the resultant thousands of combinations are insufficient to provide a complete picture. If, for example, one wished to consider the rise and fall of species, then time, circumstance, and, now, the effects of machines would have to be considered as added dimensions. Truly, living systems are unbounded. But they can be reasonably aggregated by function, for example, those of intelligent behavior shown in Figure 11-1.

There is a strong presumption in Miller's architecture that each level, from cell to supranational system, can be considered more or less on its own. That is, each level can operate with little knowledge or concern about other levels. Human beings, for example, operate without much conscious thought about what is happening at the organ level (until a pain signal is sent from it), and without *any* thought about the cellular level.

Exactly how this hierarchical architecture evolved is uncertain, but its survival supports its validity. As we saw in Part One, an architecture of homeostatic quasi-independent levels and functions seems to be characteristic of systems that evolve from simple beginnings into highly complex forms. It appears in the cell-to-supranational structure laid out by Miller. It appears between animal species exhibiting step increases in intelligent behavior compared with others. It appears in machine computers that have evolved both upward to higher-level languages and downward to data storage at the submicron level.

Architecturally speaking, this split into levels would seem sensible—a partitioning with minimal communications between them. It promotes internal development, stability, and flexibility in meeting both internal and external needs. Depending upon the development status of each subsystem at each level and how each is combined with others, a wide diversity of different biological systems and behaviors can be produced within the same architectural matrix—ev-

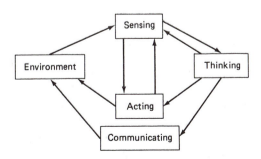

Figure 11-1. Intelligent behavior system.

erything from sea slugs, insects, and pigeons to humans. Consider, for example, the interrelationships between sensing, motion, and intelligence.

Example:

When extremely rapid reaction to a sensed danger is required, the sensed signal is processed at (or in) the sensor and transmitted directly to the action effectuators (muscles) without action required by a central intelligence (brain). Thus, birds, gazelles and other prey that survive through speed, although their eyesight otherwise is relatively poor, have retinal processors that directly activate a flight-from-danger response. The response (speed and direction) is far faster than that of the visually superior, thinking-and-planning predators.

Example:

Reflex action by animal limbs to impact and heat is a very fast, localized muscular response to signals from nearby sensors. Other examples of local, involuntary, and homeostatic processing are pupil dilation to accommodate changing average light levels and eyeball motion to bring peripherally sensed moving objects into the high-resolution portion of the retina. (Arbib, 1987)

Example:

One of the more challenging robotics problems is to make a machine walk as animals do. The conventional architectural approach to this problem is based on the position and orientation of the segments of the limbs, a multiple-coupled six-degrees-of-freedom problem of considerable computational complexity. Researchers at MIT recently took a quite different approach, that of force feedback and very simple algorithmic rules for limb response. They have built a very small, six-legged, light-sensing robot that walks, climbs, and responds to attackers. It effectively mimics crawling bugs, certainly not known for their intelligence but remarkable for their ability to survive (Brooks and Flynn, 1989). Architecturally, this system distributes intelligence to the point of requiring no central control at all. Extreme examples of this architecture are found in schools of small fish, swarms of bees, and colonies of ants, which collectively sense, find food, defend the community, and survive. (For a metaphorical view of this phenomenon, see Hofstadter, 1980.)

Miller's hypothesis that all functions must be performed at all levels if each level is to survive, while probably true for the chosen functions and subsystems, is arguable for biological functions in general. Looking upward in level, characteristic of all systems, *new* functions appear that are not present at the next level down.

More surprising, looking downward, the system as a whole might not perform—in point of fact might not be *capable* of performing—some of the functions of its subsystems (Bellman and Walter, 1984). It could be said that higher levels in biological architectures have "abandoned" capabilities retained by the lower levels. The human body as a whole cannot replace itself, although most cells and some organs can. Some of the lower levels can be considerably more complex than the levels above. In biological systems, unlike in machine systems, reduction is not simplification (Bellman and Walter, 1984). Nor is it necessary that each level contain the same kinds of components nor that they be connected using the same rules. It is certainly an oversimplification to model biological systems as simply the assembly, even if massively parallel, of simple identical elements at the next level down, or to assume that the architectures at all levels are conceptually similar.

We might expect, instead, that highly intelligent architectures will be combinations of constructs—analog and digital, linear and nonlinear, distributed and centralized, hardware and software—used as appropriate in each function and level. In machines, lower levels might be digital, mathematically correct, and virtually error-free. At higher levels, they might be analog, heuristic, and even error-prone in some circumstances—abandoning the precision and perfect memory of the lower levels in the interests of speed, response, rapid learning, association, and resiliency.

Neural networks that incorporate even a few biologically inspired architectural features, even if built of relatively few, simple, electronic elements, have exhibited remarkable feats of unsupervised learning, of almost instantaneous recognition of objects, of faces in quite different orientations, and of extremely rapid detection and analysis of moving objects anywhere in a field of view. These results are encouraging, not only in producing new behavior, but in indicating a course for future work. In particular, reaching higher machine intelligence will require more complex nodes, factors of hundreds in numbers of interconnections, multispeed networks, layered processing, and massively parallel constructs.

John J. Hopfield [Hopfield 1990] gives a telling example of the collective importance of these factors. As we know, image recognition is easy for animals and difficult for machines. One way of modeling image recognition is based on a raster scan—making a TV picture of the feature with many pixels and lines. Humans, even pigeons, far exceed present machines in recognizing images on that TV screen. But scramble the lines—put them in arbitrary order—and recognition evaporates. But with just a few software additions, the machine will do just as well as before. As Hopfield notes, the computational complexity of TV image recognition with the true and the scrambled pictures is the same—enormous—*if we assume the same sensing and processing constructs,* that is, a raster scan.

But the constructs are not the same. Just how different they are will be seen shortly. In any case, it is apparent that the human brain does not and cannot operate like present computers—it is far too slow, too error-prone, and is "wired" too differently to have the same architecture as computers and yet do all the marvelous things it does.

THE ARCHITECTURE OF THE BRAIN

In truth, we do not understand the brain very well. We cannot predict its behavior except at the lowest levels. Indeed, it is difficult to describe its behavior even in carefully prescribed situations. Reverse architecting to determine the underlying purposes, functions, and architecture, therefore, must be largely speculative.

However, progress is being made (Restak, 1984; Aoki and Siekevitz, 1988; Gerstein et al., 1988; Alkon, 1989). It would be hard to find a subject in which our understanding had changed more in the last few decades than in the nature of the brain.

New experimental techniques have made possible detailed mapping of the brain's activity when perceiving, analyzing, remembering, issuing orders, and even dreaming. Previously little understood diseases can now be seen as specific anomalies, injuries, and malformations. Ingenious tests of human sensory perceptions are yielding clues to the architectural construction of the brain and its extension, the retinas of the eyes.

From the behavioral and physiological sciences, we know with some precision many of the brain's system parameters—20–40 billion cells organized in 12 processing layers in the human cerebral cortex, 10^8 optical receptors, 10^6 nerve fibers to the brain, $1/30$ second for channel transmission, 18 thoughts per second, 7 items held in short-term memory at a time, 2 seconds to find an item in long-term memory with between 5 to 30 seconds to enter an item in it, about 20 minutes to firmly fixate memories of traumatic events that cannot be erased by a resultant coma, a storage capacity of about 10^{10} bits in a 50-year period, and so on (Miller, 1956; Stroud, 1960; Chase and Simon, 1974; Arbib, 1987; Gerstein et al., 1988).

We know from physiology that modeling the nerves as physically connected wires is a mistake. Rather, the nerves are more like membraneous conducting tubes. The outer sheath conducts high-speed electrical signals. The inner volume contains organic molecules and ionized atoms that slowly move into, out of, and along it. The ends and outer walls are specialized, electrically sensitive, membranes that either pass or block the movement of ionized atoms and molecules through them. The end membranes come close to, but do not touch, corresponding end membranes of other nerves and sensors.

Between the ends of the separate nerves are very thin boundary layers (synapses) containing molecules that, depending on their numbers and locations, determine whether signals will be transmitted or inhibited. The conductivity and even the existence of synapses are determined by past and present excitation.

Although the brain's "neural network" is just beginning to be emulated with computer components, it is clear that what had been modeled as simple connections in the brain are better modeled as nonlinear data-driven nodes driven by the memory of the magnitude and polarity of the signal traffic that has gone through them.

Furthermore, the brain not only stores and modifies signals in single neurons and nodes, it does so in patterns over major regions of its neural network. These patterns can overlay one another, that is, the same neurons and portions of regions can be involved in more than one pattern or activity. As is the case with individual nerves, new incoming information, if it generates a pattern similar to existing ones, will be reinforced. If not, it may have to be repeated many times to overcome the existing "bias."

Behavioral studies, confirmed by physiological evidence, show that the nervous system, utilizing different mechanisms, operates simultaneously in at least four different speed regimes. It operates electrically for fast responses, electrochemically for slow ones, and biomechanically for permanent structure and change. For sensor systems that must handle truly huge data rates—the skin as a whole, the ears, and the eyes—thousands of individual sensors and processors are used, each acting at a modest speed, but collectively processing the high incoming data rate. The ultrafast sensor architectures are massively parallel and multiply interconnected.

Nerves connect with each other in almost incomprehensible complexity, with local activity at each synaptic interface. Most remarkably, new connections are being established all the time, even into old age, while others are being dropped. The brain is thus not only engaged in electrical and chemical pattern activity, it is also physically reconfiguring itself. How (or if) the brain does this without distortion or disruption of prior memories and functions is not known.

Although the basic architecture of the brain does not appear to change after birth, structural details and even functions remain subject to experience for some time, particularly in the cerebral cortex. The effects of experience depend on when the experience occurs, whether the necessary sensory trigger is present during a specific interval of time (e.g., whether the brain is deprived of the trigger such as visual input), and to some extent on the duration of the input (some changes continue after deprivation is resumed) (Aoki and Siekevitz, 1988).

At a higher operational level of the brain, we are able to distinguish different ways that it "thinks" and, to a limited degree, just where in the brain the thought processes occur. One of the earlier ideas was that for right-handed people, the right brain was visual, perceptual, artistic, emotional, and nonanalytic, whereas the left brain was logical, language-oriented, and analytic. It is known with more certainty that the two halves of the brain, if surgically separated, will function separately, but that the brain then cannot accomplish functions requiring coordination between them. The left brain–right brain idea has been considerably modified in recent years. But what is clear is that there are certain regions in the brain that specialize in analytic functions and others that specialize in nonanalytic. For example, the human ability to recognize faces makes use of certain neural circuits in the right posterior cerebral hemisphere (Gerstein et al., 1988). The analytic regions "think" in symbols, in languages (of all sorts), and rationally. They allow us to read, hear, calculate, and reason. The nonanalytic regions "think" in emotions, perceptions, visual and auditory images, smells, and kinesthetic feelings ("gut," "in my heart," "in my bones," and the sense of space). The communication between the regions is limited, which helps explain why emotions, images, and kinesthetic feelings are so difficult to describe in any language. It may also explain why logical (mental) control of emotions is neither instantaneous nor very effective, particularly under stress.

Recognizing these different modes of thinking can be of practical importance in the design of man–machine interfaces. The more of the brain's modes that can be used, the better the bidirectional communication.

The Macintosh personal computer is a good example of exploiting the multimodal property of the brain. Its screen uses visuals as well as words, it emits sounds to attract attention, and its mouse provides kinesthetic sensations and matching actions. It is one of the easiest computers to learn to use. The instruction manual (words and symbols) is seldom required and long periods can occur between uses without losing facility in operation. Actions "come naturally," like riding a bicycle. These characteristics, derived from behavioral science research in the 1960s and 1970s, were explicitly incorporated in the original design.

Although there is a great deal still to be learned, it is becoming clear that the brain is not just an analytic rule-based symbol processor. Part of it certainly is, but not all. Models that assume that the analytic part can operate independently of the nonanalytic part, even on "pure" analytic tasks, are probably deficient to some degree. How much of a deficiency depends upon the relationships between the parts.

Judging from the behavior of simpler species than man, the nonanalytic part developed first, which would seem to say that the emotional, visual, and kinesthetic parts are fundamentally more important for survival. It would be surprising if they did not constrain and even partly control the operation of the analytic symbol-using part. What clues do we have that the nonanalytic part affects the logical processes of the analytic part? One is that when we are emotionally overwrought, we cannot think "logically." Another clue is partial and selective memory, the suppression or enhancement of past events. It is well established that concurrent emotional traumas imprint memory much more intensely than otherwise. At the same time, mental health seems to require forgetting or deep suppression of some events; the inability to forget can cause deep depression and confusion. Another clue might be the recognition of patterns (a nonanalytic process) in people's statements (symbols). Perhaps the (language) expression, "There is a *pattern* to all this data" is more indicative of communication between the different parts than we might have thought. It might signify the direct participation of the visual imaging-understanding region in an otherwise logic-only process.

Still another behavioral clue might be the "pause-and-reflect" phenomenon. Is it a call by the visual/kinesthetic (gut feeling) part for a quick review before undertaking a potentially risky action?

The idea of directly reaching and "hearing from" nonanalytic regions is not new. Media professionals communicate with them routinely to sell goods, color emotions, elect officials, send subliminal messages, and provide language-independent entertainment. Psychologists observe these regions by watching physical behavior—body English, facial expressions, involuntary vocalizations, laughter, even perspiration. These signals appear to be universal throughout the human race, independent of language or culture.

We should not be surprised that increasing machine communications with the nonanalytic portions of the brain generates social reaction, for example, the controversy over the use of polygraphs. The controversy has two parts.

The first part has to do with the credibility of the results of the polygraph process, a process requiring both a machine and a human operator. With research, that controversy might be diminished.

The second part is a perception of invasion of privacy in bypassing the defensive controls of the analytic (language) region. This part of the controversy is unlikely to change. The vulnerability is inherent in the structure of the brain.

THE MIND

The mind is defined as the conscious and subconscious *behavior* of the brain in thought, memory, perception, feeling, will, and imagination. Philosophically, if not physiologically, the mind has been characterized as the next highest homeostatic level above that of the physical brain (Hofstadter, 1980). In that sense, it does seem to be a separate and distinct entity from the level below it.

The separation of brain and mind cannot be complete, of course. The construction of the brain imposes constraints on what the mind can do. The brain is not an infinite resource. Its parameters limit the mind's operation. But its plasticity—its continual physical reconstruction and modification—is also known to be affected by the activity of the mind.

Architecturally, the brain and the mind together are a system with function, form, and characteristic behavior. Just how the two should be partitioned, if at all, is not clear.

The conscious functions of the mind are generally stated to be as follows:

- Sensing, particularly visual
- Memory
- Language
- Rational symbol processing (logic and analysis)
- Visualization (of images, principles, concepts, and space)
- Perception (evaluating, explaining, and understanding)
- Directing action

We will take them up in turn, focusing on what might be their underlying architectures. To do so requires some speculative reverse architecting at this stage of our knowledge.

THE ARCHITECTURE OF THE RETINA AND BRAIN
IN VISUAL PROCESSING

Research is clearly showing that the brain is physically configured not only by genetically determined hardware and firmware, but also by its sensory input. If certain inputs are not provided at certain times, the brain apparently abandons processing that class of inputs. If inputs are repeatedly or traumatically provided that are worth remembering, the brain evidently initiates new synaptic connections in response.

Of all the sensors, the eye is the most important for understanding the brain. Physiologically and by evolution, it is an extension of the brain. And because the eye provides by far the most sensory information to the human brain, it is probably the sensor with the most impact on its continuing reconfiguration.

Therefore, the way in which the eye and brain work together is critical in understanding intelligent behavior and deriving its underlying architecture. As will be seen later, it can also be important in designing man-made surveillance systems.

Like most biological structures, the eye–brain subsystem evolved. The functions most important to survival were developed first, as evidenced in the most primitive animals. Movement, depth, and then stereovision perception came early. Color came later. This evolution is still with us. Even in humans, movement, depth, and stereovision are still in black and white (Livingstone, 1988).

Roughly speaking, visual perception—our comprehension of what we see—increases in complexity as one follows the progression of an image from the retina through the optic nerve, the optical chiasm, the lateral geniculate nuclei, and the cerebral cortex (Granath, 1981). The signals leaving the retina are already differentiated by function (motion, color, etc.) and are highly encoded. Each function is sent to a different part of the brain for processing. It is not until a special section of the cerebral cortex is reached that perception and understanding of the whole picture is produced.

Attempts to model human visual perception that do not account for this functional structure, beginning with that for motion detection, will be deficient. And so will be the machines based on that model.

What might have driven this architecture? What were the key functions and their priority? One reasonable hypothesis begins with the imperative of survival. To survive, prey had to hide and predators had to find. Moving objects, within certain size and angular velocity ranges, were of high importance to prey and predator. Specialized processors were developed to detect them. The retina of the eye, in conformance with danger most often coming from the side, has the most motion sensors at its periphery—sensors that trigger responses and alert the brain well before the object is identified. Local, inward, spatial, and time differentiation are the observed elements of the motion-detection subsystem.

Danger from straight ahead presents a different problem. The processing for it is correspondingly different. One alert of impending danger is an object that expands in the field of view. The required processing is radially outward with spatial and time differentiation. Given two eyes, stereovision can provide further alerts by depth perception within threatening ranges. But two-dimensional sensors cannot create a three-dimensional world without ambiguity. Depth-perception processing is, therefore, an approximation, easily confused, but only in relatively unimportant situations.

Evidence is strong that each of these sensor-processing operations is carried out in distinct regions of the brain, parts of which are in the retina of the eye itself.

We also observe that the retina of the eye, like the brain of which it is a part, consists of multiple-connected neurons, some of which are connected to specialized sensors (rods and cones) that individually detect light and that collectively detect motion, determine size, and discriminate color. The retina generates the logarithm of the incoming light intensity, keeps the resultant signals within detection range, normalizes locally, and takes time derivatives before sampling in time (Mead, 1987; Micheli-Tzanakou, 1988).

One result is the remarkable phenomenon of color constancy—the perception that objects retain their color even if the illumination changes drastically in intensity and color. The phenomenon is created by a contrast measurement between neighboring sensor elements sensitive to the different colors. Light detected by the retina comes primarily from reflections from illuminated objects. The intensity and color of that reflected light depends upon the characteristics both of the illumination and of the reflected object. The latter is far more important for the animal to perceive than the former. Reflections from the objects permit their identification, classification, and indications for action.

For natural situations, illumination is generally constant and spectrally broad over the scene—sunlight, for example—whereas reflectance differs for every surface. The retina exploits this difference. As noted earlier, its processing is logarithmic-spatial, resulting in subtracting the illumination function but retaining the reflectance.

Local logarithmic processing, as contrasted with the linear processing characteristic of cameras, drastically reduces the dynamic range of the signals to be processed. Human sensors differentiate intensity levels that differ by a factor of about 2. Thus, if the brightness levels are from 1 to 1 million, the number of doubling steps is only 20. A valuable result of such processing is that objects almost never appear under- or overexposed, regardless of the average light level from near-dark to extreme sunlight. The exceptions are sudden and extreme changes in illumination and gazing fixedly at an illumination source—both of which can cause temporary disorientation and confusion.

The various signal- and image-processing centers send their results to several other locations for further processing or action. The quickest results go to the motor centers for reflex action. Others go to visual perception centers, where these and other results need to be combined into an overall picture. But combining them is complex. The inputs are ambiguous and ill-structured. Structure needs to be imposed by use of learned and preprogrammed "tricks" or heuristics. One such is assuming that objects are solid and move as units, not a bad approximation to the physical world. Another important mechanism is control and feedback from higher-level processors, for example, the perception center, to lower-level ones, for example, the retina. In other words, there is a two-way flow of signals in the retina–brain system.

All the processors are critical for survival, but they differ in sophistication, depending upon the needs of the animal, its evolutionary natural history, and its environmental niche. Although the distinction is not absolute, most prey have eyes with a wide field of view and with especially numerous and effective retinal motion detectors to trigger flight response. Otherwise, their eyesight is relatively poor, usually lacking both stereovision and color. Predators must sense small, barely moving, prey against a large and complex background. Predators' eyesight tends to be better than that of the prey, with good stereovision, higher resolution, wide dynamic range, and some degree of color discrimination. For whatever evolutionary reason, resolution in animals and man is far better in black and white than in color—something exploited by artists and regretted by photo interpreters. Functionally, these visual characteristics make sense—the predator looks for contrast and the prey attempts to minimize it. Demonstrably,

The name of the game in efficient sensing is contrast.

It is *not* system sensitivity, target cross section, static resolution, or color reflectance. These are subordinate factors, important primarily to the extent that they enhance or diminish contrast. High local contrast enhancement is worth more to the predator than the ambiguities and illusions that result from making it the first priority in image processing and perception.

The prey's first line of defense is camouflage—blending into the background as much as possible. When that is not possible, the prey must resort to speed, numbers, armor, and close-in weapons and tactics. But it is better not to be detected in the first place.

It is worthwhile emphasizing, in discussing the prey's perspective, that low contrast is not the same thing as minimum reflectance. At optical frequencies, minimum reflectance is seen as the color black, a good color only if the background is comparably of low reflectance (black). But minimum reflectance can be a mistake if the background is otherwise, for example, of high reflectance (white).

Also, the more colors the predator can see, that is, the more multispectral the detector, the greater the opportunity to observe contrasts and the more difficult it is for the prey to hide. But the image-processing task is also greater with more colors, a difference reflected in the greater size of the visual portions of predators' brains.

Thus, the predators' counter to low contrast is greater contrast enhancement to which the prey evolves still lower contrast. From evolutionary survival considerations, therefore, color discrimination should be, and evidently is, a relatively late development, motion detection and stereovision being developed much earlier. This conclusion is consistent with the physiological fact mentioned earlier, that the latter two are color blind. Considering the problems each sensing system is intended to solve, it is not surprising that the spatial resolution is high for motion detection and stereovision, but relatively low for color discrimination.

And the evolution continues. Humans have accelerated their own evolution in a special way—by machines. Human contrast discrimination is now enhanced by electronic image processing and the use of "false color." Machines allow us to heighten both brightness and color contrast throughout the visible range. We also "see" beyond visible wavelengths and can visualize other, quite different, parameters (heights, structural stress, molecular structure, etc.) as high-contrast patterns in color and space.

MEMORY

Human memory is much more complex, physiologically and psychologically, than the hierarchical storage and recall characteristic of computers. It not only operates quite differently as a whole, but it is disassociated into processes or systems that are fundamentally different (Gerstein et al., 1988). Human memory stores events and images only partially, reconstructing the whole on demand. It operates by association, a parallel process, and not by address, a serial process. And it makes characteristic kinds of errors.

Tests indicate that there are different kinds of memory located in different regions of the brain. One type is genetically "hardwired" in the most primitive parts of the brain. Another type is quite transient (a few seconds), whereas another is remarkably long-term (a lifetime) and yet still produces vivid, if imperfect, recollections. Some memory is kinesthetic, some visual, some auditory, and some in symbol form.

Experimental evidence shows that storage occurs as patterns in regions rather than element by element in point locations. One of the consequences is that major parts of the adult brain can be destroyed and yet memory can be retained or even restored. Yet, if other parts of the brain are destroyed or diseased, certain kinds of memory can vanish. Short-term memory, for example, is destroyed in Alzheimer's disease by strangulation death of specific parts of the brain.

The physiology of the brain gives some clues to the mechanization of memory in it. Its numerous interconnected neurons make chemical and electrical contact with each other through the synapses. These contacts continue to be made and unmade, even in old age. Recent experiments have shown that vigorous mental activity increases their rate of formation. Making and breaking contact take time (seconds to minutes), a process consistent with the time it takes to store events in long-term memory. Electrical monitoring shows unambiguously that short-term memory involves patterns of electrical activity across much of the surface of the brain (the cerebral cortex), a process that can be very rapid, but is difficult to maintain.

At the risk of oversimplification, one might theorize that memory in the brain is based on regionwide electrochemical and electrical patterns, that memory initiation consists of establishing such patterns, and that memory retrieval consists of electrical inquiry, recognition, and activation.

Such an architecture, when simulated in a machine, exhibits a number of characteristics of human memory that other machine architectures do not. It is fault-tolerant. It seems to be able to learn by itself. It makes mistakes similar to those of human memory. It remains to be seen whether, like human memory, such an architecture can generate missing ingredients of an event or "complete" visual and auditory images in order to make an apparently consistent whole.

From the architect's point of view, a memory architecture employing regionwide patterns is interesting precisely because of the functions it performs so naturally. Whether the brain actually works exactly that way or not is of less immediate importance. The biologically inspired machine architectures may, of themselves, provide ways of solving data-base management problems much more efficiently than can other architectures. Indeed, the Connection Machine reportedly already has done so.

Delving further into evidence now available, one of the well-documented characteristics of human memory is association, the relating or connecting together of different events, facts, memories, or ideas. Many creative concepts have arisen through the associative process—as well as outrageous assertions, hypotheses, and conclusions. And yet, despite the enormous number of memories that reside in the brain, these associations appear to be made near-instantaneously, as if similar parts of different brain patterns could activate the rest of each one.

The association mechanism may well be responsible for intuitive leaps from one idea (pattern?) to another, the recognition of the similarity *but not identity* of one pattern to another. This property has not yet been demonstrated in man-made data-base management structures. It is a good guess that, with the right architecture and devices, it can be. To date, the closest machine equivalents are nonrelational (i.e., nonhierarchical) memory structures, of which HYPERCARD™ is an example.

Whatever the architecture of the human memory system is determined to be, experimenting with biologically inspired machine architectures should give us a better understanding of why human memory behaves as it does. We know that "memory is not perfect" and before long, we may better appreciate why, a justifiable concern to any architect of man–machine systems. For example, how can a machine "correct" human memory without an antagonistic psychological response from the human? Should the machine treat observed discrepancies in human memory as indications of underlying human thought processes that need to be taken into account?

With these perplexing questions, we now leave the perspectives of biology, physiology, and psychology and follow another line of inquiry into intelligent behavior, that of the cognitive and information sciences.

THE ARCHITECTURE OF LANGUAGE AND SYMBOL PROCESSING

In contrast to the biological approach to human intelligence, which constructs it from the bottom up from the physiology and related behavior of the underlying levels of animal systems, the information-sciences approach is to study it from the top down from the highest level of human intelligence—the use of languages to express abstract thought, communicate, plan, and solve problems.

The information-sciences approach, variously called cybernetics and artificial intelligence, is closely related to systems theory and computer science. It attacks machine intelligence and human intelligence jointly, modeling each with the other. It is largely based on the Physical Symbol System Hypothesis that "A physical symbol system has the necessary and sufficient means for general intelligent action."* If the hypothesis is correct, then it follows both that computers can be programmed to think and that humans think in symbols.

For reasons evident earlier in the chapter, the hypothesis is arguable if applied to *all* human thought and intelligent action. It has a firmer base if applied to the more limited processes of logic and language, highly advanced processes that occur in definable portions of the brain as virtually autonomous cognitive subsystems.

The information-sciences approach, based on mathematics and analogies with digital computers, contains within it an implicit assumption—that of perfect, complete, and consistent operation, barring hardware failure or erroneous software. In such processes, logical operations can be extended indefinitely, step after step, to a clear and defendable answer.

---

*"The necessary and sufficient condition for any system, biological or mechanical, to be capable of thought and intelligence is that the system be a physical symbol system: that is, that it be able to input (read) symbols, output (write) symbols, create structures of symbols related in various ways, store symbols and symbol structures in a memory, compare symbol structures for identity or difference, and branch (adapt its behavior) on the basis of the outcomes of such comparisons." (Reprinted from H. A. Simon, *Artificial Intelligence, Current Status and Future Potential,* 1985, with permission from the National Academy Press, Washington, DC.)

Human thought processes demonstrably do not—indeed, can not—operate that way, although we might wish at times that they could. The reason is structural. Human memory is partial. There is no guarantee that the reconstruction rules for human memory are internally consistent, much less mathematically and logically correct. At the cellular level, it certainly is not error-free.

The computer-inspired theories of language and symbol processing are admittedly idealizations and abstractions. But like the mathematics on which they are based, they have materially aided our understanding of language, logical thought processes, and of their machine embodiments. Within that context, the theories clarify how symbol-processing architectures think, that is, in logical steps with defined rules. Language to a great degree is such a process.

Language is defined as words and their combination to express thought—a definition remarkably close to the definition of systems as different elements combined for larger purposes. A language is in fact a system with purpose and structure. Like other systems, languages

- Have different forms for different functions
- Are usually unbounded
- Are structured according to rules
- Contain models or perceptions of the world around them
- Are adapted, advanced, or removed, as circumstances dictate

By that definition, architects and engineers understand and use many languages—their own "natural" language, algebra, Boolean algebra, calculus, vector calculus, predicate calculus, FORTRAN, COBOL, LISP, C, ADA, Sign, aerospace jargon, governmentese, and so on.

There is no universal language any more than there is a universal expert or a universal system, and for the same reason—the functions to be performed and the problems to be solved are too diverse. A remarkable thing about languages in the human brain is that the brain is able to think using words and symbols of very different forms. In the auditory form—the usual conception of "words" because we speak them—it thinks in processed sound patterns. A few of these sounds are genetically programmed, but tens of thousands are learned. The brains of people born deaf and dumb necessarily think in visuals and hand, face, and body signals (e.g., American Sign language). Those born deaf, dumb, and blind think in touch and vibration patterns. Those that use algebra think in visual symbols ($x, y, z, a, b, c, +, =, >, <,$) or their vocalized equivalents.

The brain easily combines symbols to create new ones. Using genetic and learned rules, it forms meaningful sentences and patterns out of learned words. As might be expected, it makes mistakes and forms illusions when the patterns are too close to be differentiated. Did you say "fif*teen*" or "fif*ty*?" Is that a "1" (one) or an "l" (lowercase L)? Is that a drawing of a glass cube or a glass box? Machines built with the same capabilities exhibit similar behavior, including learning, when given similar inputs.

It is thus one of the great puzzles in artificial intelligence that the human mind has so much trouble with logical reasoning—a function that is so easy for computers, can be based on very simple devices and rules, and would seem to be so easy to implement biologically all the way down to the molecular level. Yet—or perhaps *instead*—it easily handles much more difficult situations—ill-structured, nonrational, recursive (self-referential), and approximate. One might say that the human mind operates heuristically more easily than rationally, that is, its architecture is more nearly data-driven than rule-driven.

Why should the mind operate as it does? Any answer at this stage of our knowledge is speculative. A not unreasonable answer is that the mind is built to handle the kinds of situations that confront it. In particular, the mind must still function in situations where the available information is known to be incomplete, overwhelming with irrelevancies, inconsistent, and contradictory. Reality and seeming logic must occasionally be set aside if progress is to be made. Were strict rationality imposed, the mind, like present computers, might stop functioning, unable to resolve the contradictions it faced. It would hang up. So a different design no doubt is mandated.

In brief, architectures based solely on rules seem to have run into an impasse in emulating human intelligence in all its modes. Meanwhile, what we are learning about logical thought processes and learning does provide new insights for designing intelligent machines.

The first insight comes from the development of natural languages. Languages are developed in the brain progressively; certain developmental steps must be taken at certain times. If the windows of opportunity are not taken, they are lost. The brain begins to specialize, using regions not occupied otherwise. Physiologically, critical connections were not made between the appropriate neurons. Other connections were made instead. History counts (Bellman and Walter, 1984). Yet, at each step, the system as a whole is functional. In brief, natural language systems grow. This growing process has been strongly advocated for the development of software (Brooks, 1987), but with an important provision—it must grow according to a top–down plan and to an understood end purpose. In biological systems, that is done genetically, not only for the system itself, but for the process that builds it.

A second insight is the nature of the language by which man and machine communicate with each other. Clearly, the internal languages of man and machine must be fitted together if the man–machine interface is to work properly. But this requirement is not necessarily a demand for machines to understand spoken or even written natural languages. It could turn out that the best man–machine communication is a bridging language that both humans and machines can learn, understand, and use with the least total difficulty.

If so, then the development of a man–machine language will follow the historical precedent of Creole languages. It will utilize the construction and words that least stress the participants while progressively increasing the communications between them. It will be a blend and a bridge between the original languages.

From the perspective of the machine, natural languages suffer from a too-complex syntax (structure) and are inherently if not deliberately ambiguous—characteristics that are costly in machine processing. A more specialized formal language—somewhat more logical, succinct, easily accessed, and processed—would stress the machine less without too much penalty to the human user. Several languages have been developed to the point of instruction, test, and use: predicate calculus (Genesereth and Nilsson, 1987) and structured English (De-Marco, 1979). The former is closer to computer language and the latter to natural language.

From the perspective of the human, the typewriter keyboard is too slow, too awkward, and too likely to cause human error. The human voice, augmented by visual signals, is the normal mode of transmission. Equally important, the normal mode of reception is stereophonic, background-rejecting, error-tolerant, and interpretive. It extracts meaning, not individual words, and depends heavily on a model of the context of the communication—as all good receivers should. On the other hand, if asked to play back verbatim, it either fails or slows to a crawl. Its memory subsystem and its interpretive subsystem are essential parts of its architecture. As with the visual system, the aural system easily accomplishes rapid classification, recognition, and association. Its sensors discriminate intensity, frequency, phase, direction, and motion. Its processors are logarithmic, spatial, massively parallel, and functionally distinct. It creates illusions and is fault-tolerant. Its architecture, in other words, resembles that of the eye–brain system in many ways.

Thus, if we are to create a spoken bridging language between man and machine, we will have to incorporate major elements of the human aural receiving system into the machine. To be facile, we will need to study aural machine languages, learning to speak them instead of typing them. We may have to begin them in elementary school or with people who already have developed multilingual architectures in the brain. To gain a lot, we may have to work a little ourselves.

PERCEPTION AND EVALUATION

Philosophers and artists for thousands of years have understood that perception is an individualized phenomenon. What we perceive individually is not identical with the reality of the external world. Information theorists can demonstrate that complete recording of all that impinges on the human senses would quickly fill the brain's limited memory bank. And so, for physical reasons alone, the human brain must enormously compress, discard, encode, and process the impinging information if it is to function effectively. Human memory not only is partial, it must be. The different intelligence functions are separable because efficient architecture and evolutionary growth demand it. The sensors are massively parallel because they must be.

But these imperatives mandate the inclusion of yet another functional subsystem into the architecture of intelligent systems, perception. The role of this subsystem (or more likely a set of sub-subsystems) is to bring together into a consistent model of external reality all the processed sensations—motion, size, shape, distance, color differences, light contrast, sound intensity and frequency, verticality, touch, pressure, temperature, and time. It must determine which past memories to reconstruct and which associations to use to create and modify the model.

Compared with our knowledge of memory and of the sensors themselves, our knowledge of the perceptual subsystem is limited indeed. It is believed that perception is responsible for dreams, phenomena that occur only when the input from the sensors is turned off. Because it must recreate memory from partial storage and internal rules, it is probably responsible for false memories, false associations, hallucinations, and illusions. Yet these perceptions are so complete and vivid that we think we are seeing reality itself.

The perceptions that are formed are then evaluated and actions taken. The perceptions can be incorporated into the knowledge base (cognition), often restructuring the knowledge base in the process. ("That new input completely changed my mind.") Instant action or planning for action can be initiated. [Action: the use of knowledge to create change (Gerstein et al., 1988).] This combination of knowledge organization and action control is the foundation of learning. Amazingly, this extraordinary perceptual-evaluative function can be found in many species, although at different levels of development. But we have almost no idea about its architecture. No doubt we must first solve the mysteries of sensing and memory.

REASONING

The most developed form of perception, perhaps a level unto itself, is reasoning. Reasoning requires restructuring knowledge, the generation and use of general principles and logical rules, and the creation of new understandings of the perceived world and self. Its principles are not understood. Intuitive reasoning—the qualitative reasoning about quantitative and other abstract concepts— is particularly difficult to understand (Gerstein et al., 1988). Reasoning is what many people consider "thinking," which raises the question: *Can machines think?*

CAN MACHINES THINK?

Yes and no. If by thinking is meant perceiving, learning, and acting sensibly in their environment, then machines can think as well as many animal species. If by thinking is meant intuitive reasoning, then the answer is a qualified no. As for emotions, self-awareness, and the like, we would have to admit that we have not yet built machine subsystems that correspond to the nonanalytical portions of the human brain and mind. And when we do build them, communicating with them may be as difficult as it is with our own "right brains."

Almost 50 years ago, Alan Turing, a British mathematician and World War II code breaker, hypothesized that a universal (Turing) machine could some day answer all "sensible questions" posed to the human mind.

The test was to be teletyped questions addressed by a human to a screen, behind which could be either humans or machines. The hypothesis was that, in due time, the questioner would not be able to tell the difference in the responses. In one sense, the Turing hypothesis is self-evident. If we keep modifying intelligent-machine architectures to more closely resemble their human counterparts, their behaviors should converge. In another sense, the hypothesis is arguable. It may not be possible to simply *modify* the architectures on which Turing based his hypothesis in order to achieve convergence. We may need architectures of quite different types.

The Turing-machine hypothesis grew out of the ability of a programmed machine architecture to handle very complex data (encrypted signals), given only enough time and processing. Even from the short description of the architecture of the brain given before, it is apparent that the brain's architecture is not fixed and preprogrammed. The brain's development is characterized by episodic change (opportunities), its connections are changed by events, its processing is approximate, and its nonanalytic elements probably affect many analytic processes.

Unless a Turing machine, by definition, can do anything that a human mind can do—which makes the hypothesis meaningless—it is difficult to imagine its presumably nonevolving, preprogrammed, precise, hardwire connected, perfect memory, serial architecture as exhibiting the same behavior as the a-logical human mind. If we are to emulate human behavior, we must emulate human architecture in more ways than we have to date.

A COMPARISON OF SELECTED HUMAN AND MACHINE INTELLIGENT SYSTEMS

For the present, it is not necessary to duplicate the human architecture to considerably advance the state of intelligent behavior in machines. Understanding just a few of its elements helps.

- Better man–machine interfaces can be produced.
- The interfaces can be moved in the machine direction more easily.
- Existing machines can be made more efficient by analogy.

Example:

For years, there has been a standing argument among those concerned with surveillance whether scanners (like TV cameras) or starers (like phased arrays) were better. A few years ago, an interesting experiment was done. The human eye was presented with an image that was always exactly in front of the eye, regardless of where the eye moved. In effect, the eye was immobilized with respect to the image. Within a very short time, the individual saw virtually nothing! (Not stated, but probably true, is that even slight changes in parts of the picture would have been detected and seen momentarily.) To see an image, the human eye must scan. It does this by keeping in constant motion, a phenomenon that as "rapid eye movement" (REM) occurs during dreaming as well. The eye combines array sensing with motional scanning! The processing required is not that much greater in a scanning eye than in a nonscanning one—the motion and position of the human head must be taken into account, in any case. Scanning also assists in fault tolerance, sensor refreshing, local time/space differentiation, and resistance to light saturation from point sources. It may also increase spatial resolution and minimize the effects of gaps between the individual sensors in the fovea (high-resolution region).

Example:

Cameras expose film whose sensitivity across the field of view is constant and whose exposure is proportional to light intensity on the film. The average intensity is determined by optics (as it is in the eye), but great deviations from the average result in local under- or overexposure. The logarithmic proportionality of the eye's sensors essentially eliminates these deficiencies. By not underexposing parts of the scene, the human eye is able to detect and characterize static and moving objects of very low reflectance in an otherwise bright scene, a particularly difficult problem for conventional surveillance equipment.

Example:

Surveillance camera–processor systems, to detect local motion in a scene, take a series of frames, process them as full high-resolution pictures, attempt to match observed features point for point, and look for small differences through the sequence. The last step is to highlight—with special colors or intensity—the moving object at full resolution. The human eye does the matching and differencing at each sensor in the retina *first,* determines where the change is occurring, and rapidly concentrates attention on that area. Only after that is accomplished does it generate a picture, and that picture has high resolution only in the center of the field of view. In addition, the eye and brain, by the tricks mentioned earlier, process areas, not points, for detecting motion, assuming that moving objects are solid, unitary objects. The result is far less processing than full frame by full frame. The machine no doubt is doing processing operations the hard way and probably in the wrong order.

Example:

In the pyramidal vision architecture, an unusual image-restoration architecture reconstructs damaged photographs by rephotographing them at different spatial wavelengths from very small compared to the damaged spots to several times their widths. Each rephotograph then is extended into the damaged spots separately, the longer wavelengths extending further into it. The extended rephotographs are then recombined with remarkable results. The eye does something similar in that many adjacent sensors see the same reflecting point on an object. Their results are combined in many ways, with decreasing weight put on outputs from more remote sensors. Locally damaged areas of the retina, therefore, have less effect on the perception of the whole picture than otherwise. Similar biological processing allows the conscious mind to ignore "floaters"—bits of debris in the aqueous fluid in the eyeball.

Example:

There is an unending technological battle between weapon systems platforms (aircraft, ships, and submarines) and the sensor systems that detect, identify, and track them (radars, radio receivers, infrared detectors, etc.). It is a battle analogous to that of prey and predator described earlier. As in that battle, the critical factor is contrast with a background, not simply quieting or low reflectance. Submarines that appear quiet in the very noisy Mediterranean will sound like beacons in the ultraquiet of the Southern Pacific. Platforms with distinctive emitter or reflectance "signatures" can be found even in high-noise backgrounds. Targets of very low reflectance can be detected if they obscure a bright source behind them—a technique used by astronomers to find and characterize planets as they move in front of distant stars. Although there is no such thing as an object invisible at all wavelengths, there are some whose probability of detection against known backgrounds by passive sensors can be very low. The biological and machine countermeasure is active (radiating) sensors. These sensors have some control over the appearance of the background, an appearance their target may have trouble matching. And so the battle continues, both in nature and in machines. The techniques and the outcomes are remarkably alike.

Example:

Distributed intelligence—data bases, processors, etc.—is a subject of considerable interest today. But it is an old subject in nature. Hofstadter (1980) spins a metaphorical tale about the distributed intelligence of a colony of ants. Researchers now can describe in some detail the collective intelligence of a hive of bees, complete with a daily refresher of the neuronal memory of the individual bee (roughly 100 kbits of volatile memory replenished daily) and the transmission of new information to the hive by the bee "dancing" on return from a flight. Flocks of birds fly and shoals of fish swim in complex formations, constantly changing their group appearance to a predator. And group behavior of large mammals is an effective means of defending the weaker members. The interesting aspect of this is not how much communication occurs among the members, but how little.

FITTING HUMAN AND MACHINE ARCHITECTURES

The importance of the interface between man and machine is widely recognized. It has received increasing attention and been greatly improved over the last several decades. It is an interface of especially great leverage for the systems architect.

This chapter has concentrated on a particular aspect of the man–machine interface, namely, the need for a fit of the *architectures* of man and machine if we are to produce the best in intelligent behavior.

It should be self-evident that different architectures will produce different behavior. This is not to say that the two architectures must be alike in order to be fit together. Indeed, for some situations, it may be better that they be different and that they be complementary. Perhaps strengths in one should complement weaknesses in the other.

Better human-machine communication might result from an architecture that mimics that of the brain in its partitioning of different thinking capabilities to different regions. If that were done, machine subroutines might become the equivalent of extended regions to be used by the brain (or vice versa). If so, then we will have to understand better how the brain's regions communicate with each other so that the machine's interfaces with the brain are more "natural." To some extent, such extensions are already happening. Hand-held computers have taken over tasks difficult for the corresponding parts of the human brain, like logical reasoning and remembering long lists. Conversely, human-controlled computer "agents," associatively activated through visual symbols, will soon do computer file search, a notably difficult problem in computerized data management.

As a general heuristic we should perhaps say,

For the best in intelligent behavior, the intelligence architectures of human and machine should be a matched pair.

Example:

In the Three Mile Island nuclear plant incident, the operators overrode one after another of the safeguards against severe damage, distrusting instrument readings and failing to diagnose multiple failures. These are typical human failings under stress. Yet subsequent investigation, without the pressures of stress, diagnosed the errors and listed the actions needed to correct them. Could an expert system have done so as the events occurred? Should the machine have automatically warned others elsewhere as to what was happening—as home security systems do? Should it have had a "self-awareness" of its own impending disaster?

Example:

A serious obstacle to building expert machines is extracting expertise from the expert that a rule-based computer can use. But experts are quick to point out that they use more than rules. They use common sense, a product in part of the heuristic, nonanalytic, qualitative regions of the brain essential for perception and understanding. Perhaps the next qualitative step in expert systems must await "right-brain" equipped computers.

Example:

"We speak (and hear) . . . and for 5000 years have preserved our words. But we cannot share vision. To this oversight of evolution we owe the retardation of visual communication compared to language. Visualization by shared communication would be much eas-

tion compared to language. Visualization by shared communication would be much easier if each of us had a CRT (cathode-ray tube) in the forehead." (B. H. McCormick, 1987)

The last example is more than speculation. We are compensating in part for our lack of forehead CRTs by communicating with each other through machines that *do* have CRTs in their foreheads. Display systems have now advanced to the point where a "super reality" can be presented, a kinesthetic and visual feeling that the observer is actually immersed in an active scene. If that scene were manipulated by more than one observer, an almost direct form of visual communication would exist, courtesy of the machine.

SUMMARY

Humans exhibit intelligent behavior that is very difficult for machines and vice versa. Recent research in several fields also shows that the architectures and elements of their intelligence systems are quite different. The challenge to the architect is to understand and perhaps emulate the biological architectures in the interests of increasing machine intelligence; efficiently performing surveillance, data-base management, and control functions; and improving the communications between man and machine.

Our understanding of the brain, the mind, visual processing, memory, language, perception, and reasoning has advanced more in the last decade than in the hundreds of years before. We are at the threshold of truly intelligent machines that will qualitatively change all major complex systems.

RECOMMENDED READING

ARBIB, MICHAEL A. (1987). *Brains, Machines, and Mathematics,* 2nd Ed. New York: Springer-Verlag. See especially Chapter 1, "A Historical Perspective"; Chapter 2, "Neural Nets and Finite Automata"; Chapter 4, "Pattern Recognition Networks"; Chapter 5, "Learning Networks"; and Chapter 6, "Turing Machines and Effective Computations."

BELLMAN, K. L., and D. O. WALTER. (1984). "Biological Processing." *American Journal of Physiology* **246**, R860–R867. Four major differences between biological processes and machine processes are given: (1) reduction is not simplification; (2) biological systems are typically specialized at many levels, both in the subsystems and in the interconnections; (3) biological systems never develop alone or de novo; and (4) biological minds are less constrained than formal machine logics.

BICKERTON, D. (1983). "Creole Languages." *Scientific American* **249**, 1, 116–22. This article suggests that children learn a language by first constructing an abstract form of creole, a hybrid language between previously uncommunicating individuals.

BROOKS, FREDERICK P., JR. (1987). "No Silver Bullet, Essence and Accidents of Software Engineering." *Computer* **20**, 4, 10–19.

BROOKS, RODNEY A., and ANITA M. FLYNN. (1989). "Rover on a Chip." *Aerospace America* **27**, 4, 22–26. This gives a description of very small, six-legged, roving, and attacking robots using distributed machine intelligence for walking and sensing with a minimum of central control.

DEMARCO, TOM (1979). *Structured Analysis and System Specification.* Englewood Cliffs, NJ: Prentice Hall. See especially Chapter 16, "Structured English," an example of a combined human/machine language using the vocabulary of the former and the rules (syntax, programming) of the latter to avoid ambiguities in instructions and actions.

GERSTEIN, D. R., R. D. LUCE, N. J. SMELSER, and S. SPERLICH. (Eds.). *The Behavioral and Social Sciences, Achievements and Opportunities.* Washington, DC: National Academy Press. See especially Chaper 1, "Behavior, Mind and Brain," a review of present (1988) knowledge of human seeing, hearing, and language; and of research opportunities and needs.

GRANRATH, DOUGLAS J. (May 1981). "The Role of Human Visual Models in Image Processing." *Proceedings of the IEEE* **69**, 5, 552–61. This article provides descriptions of retinal image formation, neural image sensing, and neural encoding based on experimental results.

HOFSTADTER, D. R. (1980). *Gödel, Escher, Bach: An Eternal Golden Braid.* New York: Vintage Books.

LERNER, E. J. (June 1988). "Computers that learn." *Aerospace America* **26**, 6, 32–40. This is an update on the newest neural networks and their ability to learn, including work at Johns Hopkins, Hecht Nielsen NeuroComputer, Hughes Malibu, and Cal Berkeley. It discusses NETtalk, MARK IV ADAPT. It focuses on pattern recognition and learning language.

LIVINGSTONE, M. S. (January 1988). "Art, Illusion and the Visual System." *Scientific American* **258**, 1, 78–85. Form, color, and spatial information (movement, location, and spatial organization) are processed along three independent pathways in the brain, as suggested by anatomical and physiological data. Speculation is given on the application to surveillance systems, robotics, and automatic navigation.

MEAD, CARVER A. (June 1987). "Neural Hardware for Vision." *Engineering & Science* **L**, 5, 2–7. This is an easily understood article on the differences between how the eye-brain system differs from a TV system, and why the former is vastly more efficient.

NIELSON, G. M., ed. (August 1989). "Visualization in Scientific Computing." *IEEE Computer Special Edition* **22**, 8. This is a report of a National Science Foundation study with remarkable graphic displays.

MICHELI-TZANAKOU, E. (September 1988). "Neural Aspects of Vision and Related Technological Advances." *Proceedings of the IEEE* **76**, 9, 1130–42. This is a recent report of results of physiological and psychological research on the eye, retina, and visual cortex of the brain leading to their mathematical and digital modeling.

MILLER, J. G. (1978). *Living Systems.* New York: McGraw-Hill. This is a morphological approach to the theory of living systems.

MINSKY, M. (1986). *The Society of Mind.* New York: Simon and Schuster. The book

RESTAK, RICHARD. (1984). *The Brain.* New York: Bantam Books. Cambridge, MA: See especially Chapters 5 and 6.

SIMON, HERBERT A. (1981). *Sciences of the Artificial.* Cambridge, MA: The MIT Press. This is one of the most widely quoted pioneering works in understanding complexity and the use of intelligence, human and artificial.

SIMON, HERBERT A. (1985). *Artificial Intelligence: Current Status and Future Potential,* the Charles H. Davis Lecture Series. Washington, DC: National Academy Press. This is one of the best short statements on the subject. It describes artificial-intelligence research and the Physical Symbol System Hypothesis.

TO BROWSE, DEPENDING ON INTEREST

ALKON, DANIEL L. (July 1989). "Memory Storage and Neural Systems." *Scientific American* **261**, 1, 42–50. Learning is accompanied by changes in the electrical and molecular properties of nerve cells. These changes suggest specific principles of design for neural networks, as demonstrated in the author's DYSTAL computer program.

AOKI, CHIYE, and P. SIEKEVITZ P. (December 1988). "Plasticity in Brain Development." *Scientific American* **259**, 6, 59–64. This article presents neurobiological and chemical evidence of the changes in the details of the brain's structure and function due to experience, particularly during the early months of life.

ARBIB, M. A. (1989). *The Metaphysical Brain 2, Neural Networks and Beyond,* A John Wiley Interscience Publication, John Wiley & Sons. Highlights parallels between observed behavior (function) and physiology (form) in the central nervous system. Develops the concepts of action-oriented perception and cooperative computation as schema (constructs).

CHISVIN, LAWRENCE, and R. JAMES DUCKWORTH. (July 1989). "Content-Addressable and Associative Memory." *Computer* **22**, 7, 51–64. This article describes the principles, obstacles, and applications of two new forms of parallel computer memory.

COMPUTER. (August 1989). "Scientific Visualization Issue." *Computer* **28**, 8. This special issue features articles with multicolored reproductions of CRT visualizations of fluid flow, turbulent flow, flames, medical, earth sciences, quantum electronic transport, and other scientific and engineering phenomena.

PERRY, TEKLA S., and JOHN VOELCKER. (September 1989). "Of Mice and Menus: Designing the User-Friendly Interface." *IEEE Spectrum* **26**, 9, 46–51. It describes the evolution of the personal computer mouse, icons, menus, and windows to make human interaction with computers simpler, and easier to learn and operate.

TREISMAN, A. (April 1988). "Features and Objects in Visual Processing." *Scientific American* **258**, 4, 113–125. The article describes the brain's use of specialized analyzers to decompose stimuli into parts and properties. It follows the quest for search "primitives"—basic elements in the language of early vision—with predictions and experiments, and from them develops a hypothetical model of the early stages in visual perception.

12

THE CHALLENGE: THE COMPLEX WORLD OF ECONOMICS AND PUBLIC POLICY

"What was the achievement? It was to build the first airplane that let the airlines make a profit."—Arthur Raymond, chief engineer of the DC-3, at the University of Southern California, 1988

"I therefore ask the Congress . . . to provide the funds which are needed to meet the following national goals: I. I believe that this nation should commit itself to achieving the goal, before the decade is out, of landing a man on the moon and returning him safely to the earth."—President John F. Kennedy, at a special session of Congress, May 25, 1961

"The three dimensions of technology, economics, and policy cannot be separated. Technology is necessary, but not sufficient. This harsh reality is the primary reason that the road to communications satellites has been so rocky."—Albert D. Wheelon (1986)

"Even though the primary justification for the Space Shuttle is not economics, for mission models at current budget levels and similar to those now in effect the Shuttle investment will be returned with billions to spare."—"Space Shuttle," a NASA proposal to Congress, October 1972

"The most apparent fact about economics is its complexity." (Bach, 1974)

THE MARKET IMPERATIVE

For a system to be useful, it must satisfy a real need. The system must have a market. The more specific the need and the more focused the market, the more straightforward is the architect's task.

The need for a new passenger airliner was clear to a financially struggling TWA. The engineers at Douglas Aircraft refined that need, envisioned the use of still-evolving technologies to satisfy it, and created the DC-3.

American national pride set an objective of landing on the Moon ahead of the Soviet Union; a unique architecture resulted and the project succeeded brilliantly.

The need for communication satellites was less clear, surprising as that might seem. It was vigorously pointed out by telephone companies in the early 1960s that the half-second time delays introduced by the transmission distance to and from synchronous satellites would sound like hesitant conversation, an annoyance to customers. But a prototype system using lower-altitude satellites proved cumbersome and expensive.Governments elected to step in, underwriting the risks, chartering new common carriers, and establishing international communication service. That service rapidly proved successful, transoceanic communications expanded rapidly, costs came down dramatically, and the world abruptly became smaller and more interdependent.

Satellite services for national security purposes—communication, navigation, environmental, surveillance, and intelligence—were soon established, although proving them cost effective and unique took some years of operational use. Their contributions to world peace are now widely acknowledged and their market is firmly established.

But other civil satellite services fared less well (Wheelon, 1986). Even had public policy been more supportive than it was, it was debatable whether an economic market existed or exists for them. Even though their technological feasibility was demonstrated early, operational service, if any, has been limited.

Example:

Public service satellite systems (two-way television for remote hospitals and schools, networks for law enforcement, warning systems for disaster relief, etc.) cost more than the beneficiaries could afford on their own. But the general public seems unwilling to subsidize them and very few exist today.

Example:

A wide-area remote sensing satellite such as LANDSAT, valuable as it might be for discovery and monitoring of Earth resources, is of varying value to different users at different times. Billing the customers for service is therefore very difficult. But a government decision to turn LANDSAT over to private interests has not been notably successful. A close cousin, the weather satellite service, is successfully operated by the government and funded from the general revenues.

Example:

Domestic satellite communication service was viewed as a potentially profitable market to the point where the government opened that service to all comers. It was quickly over-built. Markets were assumed that, for various reasons, did not materialize. Direct broadcast became just another cost element in the entertainment industry, constrained by programming and advertising realities.

Example:

Advocates of point-to-point networking (the Satellite Business System) assumed that companies would be transmitting large quantities of digital traffic between computer mainframes located in major divisions. In reality, conventional voice traffic was the only significant need and it is well served by conventional common carriers. The business is unprofitable to date.

Example:

Satellite communications and navigation service for mobile users (aircraft, automotive, ships, pleasure craft, submarines, tanks, soldiers, etc.) faced a different problem. Unless the costs of the satellite portion could be spread among many users, and unless the cost of the user's own equipment could be brought down through mass production, the benefit-to-cost ratio for civil users would be too low. Yet a very large investment in space assets was required before the service could be provided at all. Civil use was thus inhibited—the business risks were too high. In contrast, military combat utility was demonstrated within a few years. An operational service was funded and established for military use and made available for civilian purposes at marginal cost, that is, for only the cost of relatively inexpensive commercial receivers.

The Shuttle provides a special, but by no means unique, example of misestimation of market size. Similar cases can be found in projects as diverse as city bus lines, commercial aircraft, manufacturing plants, computers, and communications services. But because the Shuttle is a NASA program, its full story is more readily available.

For better or worse, the Shuttle, in addition to its other objectives, was intended to pay for itself. No allocation was made for costs, arguably half the total, that might have been charged to the essentially political objective of putting man in space.

The Shuttle's proposed economic rationale was originally based on 50 to 60 flights per year by a fleet of five or so Shuttles, each lofting on the order of about 65,000 pounds to low Earth orbit.

One fact should have provided an early alert of economic trouble: a Shuttle payload market did not exist for the 50 times 65,000 (or 3.25 million) pounds the fleet would loft each year. At the then costs of payloads, $6000/lb, the annual cost of the payloads alone would have been almost $20 billion a year, or five to seven times the 1972 market. (Today's costs of payloads are above $50,000/lb for an equivalent, but equally nonexistent, $160 billion/year payload market.)

This concern, when expressed, was countered by asserting that the market would consist of numerous inexpensive satellites that would require many in-orbit revisits for adjustments, changeouts, and repair.

Instead, payload cost effectiveness and advancing technology kept the total market demand for weight in orbit to somewhat less than a million pounds a year, the equivalent of only 12 to 16 Shuttle flights. Further, satellite reliability advanced to the point where repair in orbit was too small a market to be economically worthwhile. To reach even a million pounds per year, all payloads would have to be Shuttle-launched, an assumption, later a directive, that seriously damaged the space program as a whole.

The bottom line was that the market was misjudged by a factor of about 3. No transportation system—whether Shuttle, airline, trucking, city buses, or ship fleets—can be economically sound with a 33% usage factor.

In the end, operational problems and costs reduced the attainable flight rate of the Shuttle fleet to less than 12–16 flights/year. The reduced flight rate, coupled with serious underestimates of operating costs, belated recognition of wearout and loss costs, and of high fixed overhead costs, led to costs per launch five to ten times more than the original estimates.

Meanwhile, there is still no plan for replacement of Orbiters should they wear out or be lost to service. The chances of that occurrence are on the order of two to three per hundred flights or about one every four to six years.

The Shuttle case is by no means unique. In all fairness, its justification never should have been based, even in part, on economic grounds. But explorers of new frontiers, from at least Columbus on to modern researchers in many fields, seem to have used, or been forced to use, return on investment to obtain funding for their efforts.

Clearly, not all markets are economic ones in the sense of providing readily measurable benefits—even if their costs are clear enough. To pursue the market for exploration efforts further, if we put the "return-on-investment" justification aside, exploration has been, and still is, justified by institutions and countries on a number of grounds. In rough order of funding priority, these have been

- Survival against threats, constraints, or competition
- Sovereignty, the planting of the flag to claim territory or resources
- A demonstration of spirit, adventure, and pride
- The pursuit of science, the discovery of new knowledge
- The useful employment of institutions otherwise on standby for other purposes, for example, the armed forces and defense industries

Economics does, however, provide an *indirect* way of measuring the benefits received in these markets through asking the question: What are you prepared to give up to attain these benefits? Queen Isabella was reputed to have given up her jewels—although she may have hoped to get them back some day. Countries may have to give up part of their standard of living through increased taxes. A company may have to give up an investment in some other area, perhaps in new manufacturing equipment, to support its research.

The value or size of the market, however measured, is a primary factor in the design of a system and in the allocation of resources to produce it. Consider the following upcoming cases:

Example:

The choice of expendable or reusable launch vehicles is a strong function of the launch rate of the vehicle, of operating costs per launch, of fixed costs per year, and of vehicle life. Expendables are favored for the lower launch rates and when modest failure rates— a few percent—are acceptable to the customers (Ruppe, 1987). Reusables are favored for high launch rates, but demand very low failure rates if their initially high cost of introduction is to be amortized over a large number of flights and/or if risk to human life is to be very low. But what is the launch rate above which one crosses over from expendables to reusables? If the actual flight rate is misestimated, on which side of the crossover rate is it better to be?

Example:

Supersonic and hypersonic aircraft, with the technologies available today, are necessarily small and expensive per passenger mile. Their market is limited by the number of people who have to travel very long distances in a short portal-to-portal time. But because **ground transport**ation and logistic times are significant, there is a limit to how short that time can be, making it less worthwhile as the speed is increased, further limiting the market. These economic factors, more than concern over their potential environmental effects, negated the U.S. Supersonic Transport (SST) some years ago. For all practical purposes, the economics have not changed since. But suppose the cost could be sharply reduced with new technology, as has been the case with other aircraft to date. How much of a change in the aircraft design is necessary? How much of a change, also, is needed in the ground environment?

Example:

In economic terms, the Space Station is a remote base with its attendant cost structure, that is, there is a high fixed cost just to keep the base operating, including Shuttle visits for crew rotation and logistics. Unless these costs are allocated for "maintaining a presence in space" (i.e., unless users are only charged marginal costs), the costs to potential users will far exceed those of doing other worthwhile programs on Earth, that is, there is no economic market for the Space Station at full cost to users.

Example:

Commercial launch vehicles, unless a government contracts heavily for their use in launching its satellites, will depend upon the limited numbers of commercial communications satellites for their market. Two trends work against that market in the long term. The first is economy of scale in satellites, which drives to fewer, longer-lived, more capable satellites and hence still fewer launches. The second is competition from very high-capacity optical-fiber cable for trunk traffic between large centers, the principal communications market today. Optical-fiber cables, furthermore, avoid the "hesitant conversation" problem mentioned earlier, giving them an edge in customer preference.

It might seem that today's market for advanced aerospace vehicles is uncertain at best. But advocates argue that aerospace vehicles today should be compared with aircraft prior to the DC-3. Early aircraft, they point out, were also uneconomic, needed government subsidization, and had almost no commercial market. If this argument is true, then the question is the classic one of timing, choosing a time for entering a market in which technical, economic, and policy factors will come together.

It is not enough that the technology looks promising. It is not enough that government policy is now encouraging. It is not enough that times are good. The product's epitaph will read, "It was a great product, but its timing was off." Conversely, if the timing is right, the product or system may lead in the market for decades. Such has been the case in aircraft, computers, consumer electronics, public services, defense systems, and space systems for more than half a century. As many observers have remarked, estimating market size and timing are the name of the game. To which might be added: it's almost as important to know when conditions are *not* right.

Another market parameter of import is unit sizing—the size or capacity of individual units when multiple units are needed. Should the need be met with a few large systems or a larger number of smaller systems? Ellis (1975) discusses this question in some detail for communications system design. ICBM and "Lightsat" studies show similar results, that is, fewer large systems are less costly per total mission to be accomplished. There is "an economy of scale" that works to the advantage of larger units. The underlying reason is that the support structure of a system often grows more slowly than the system as the system capacity increases.

But this generalization can break down in several ways. Capacity seldom can be varied in a simple monotonic way; discontinuities occur because capacity comes in discrete chunks, for example, at standardized multiplexing levels in communications and at maximum weight-carrying capacity in launch vehicles.

A discrete upward jump in capacity also may not be matched with a corresponding customer demand, resulting in excess, expensive overcapacity. When this occurs, the supplier often searches for new customers to add, for example, more missions or applications to be accomplished on the same launch vehicle, spacecraft, communications network, or mainframe computer.

But more missions means more complication. Manifesting of several missions on the same system adds scheduling complexity, concerns over replacement if one mission's equipment fails, and unexpected interactions among the mission equipment. Experience shows that the number of critical missions on the same vehicle or communication system should probably be no more than 2 or 3.

Survivability considerations may also play a part. "Fractionating" a function, such as warhead weight by the use of multiple reentry vehicles or communications capacity by using multiple satellites, can make destruction of the system more difficult. But increased survivability generally means increased costs. For example, fractionating each 10-warhead MX Peacekeeper ICBM into 10 Midgetman ICBMs roughly doubles the total cost of that portion of the ballistic missile fleet.

From an economics perspective, three questions must be satisfactorily answered if a system is to have a sound market:

Who benefits? Who pays? Who supplies?

People who benefit but do not pay for it are receiving what economists call a "free good." They are likely to demand more and more of it. They are a false market unless someone else subsidizes it. In that case, the subsidizer is the true customer, whose needs and constraints may differ in important ways from those of the beneficiaries. The relationships will always be contentious. Public services find themselves in this situation from time to time.

People who benefit and pay directly will do so in accordance with perceived value. If the value per individual is small and occasional, individual payments will be small; however, if enough individuals are involved, the aggregate can be large. Good examples are the weather service paid for out of a small portion of everyone's taxes and the telephone system paid for by billing individual customers for their calls. In both cases, everyone pays and everyone benefits.

Public utilities, supplying telephone, water, gas, and electricity service, present special problems, both to the suppliers and the users. The supplier needs to make a profit to survive, yet the customer demands uninterrupted service. The conflicting interests are usually resolved through governmental operation, governmental regulation of a public utility, and/or partial regulation of open competition. The method used, however, can have a pronounced effect on system design and operation.

Example:

For decades, the Bell System was a system operated as a regulated public service monopoly, supplying most of the nation's telephone and associated services. The primary motivation of its people was service to the public. For a variety of hotly debated reasons, the system was dismantled and replaced by a partly regulated open competition, a change both in who supplies and who benefits. In so doing, it also changed who provides research and development and for what purpose. It changed the relationship between the supplier(s) and governmental users, particularly the Defense Department. It is too early to tell how the experiment will come out. (Brooks, 1988)

Example:

The primary beneficiaries of LANDSAT are the researchers, developers, and managers of natural resources. The values of the benefits are hard to quantify, many of them being in the speculative future. Pricing of the services is therefore difficult. To date, the costs to the direct beneficiaries have been minimal—virtually a free good. The paying customer, therefore, is the government, directly or through subsidy. Yet the supplier is a profit-making firm. The relationships among the participants are strained.

Example:

Cleaning up the environment has evolved from a social concern to an economic puzzle in which the questions of who benefits, who pays, and who does the work are central. Acid rain is produced by one group at one time and place; its elimination would benefit other groups later and often elsewhere. If ordered, the cleanup would be done by the first group, which would attempt to pass the costs to another group, its customers. But the customers might instead buy less expensive products from still another group, perhaps putting the first group out of business. To prevent a social calamity, still another group—local, state, or federal taxpayers—might be taxed. Further, groups that neither produce nor suffer from the pollutants, either by circumstance or through their own safeguards, may object to paying for the deleterious actions of others.

To sum up, the hard-learned lesson for the architect is not to proceed very far into concept development without satisfactory answers to four questions:

- Is there a viable market?
- Who benefits?
- Who pays?
- Who supplies?

Without satisfactory answers, a system is likely to be misarchitected and economically unstable throughout a difficult life.

A closing comment on the market imperative: "market" should not be taken as a factor of importance only to commercial businesses. As the examples have illustrated, "market" applies equally to major govermental programs and nonprofit services. Every product must be paid for, directly or indirectly. Every product or service must have customers willing to pay the bill, whether they are individuals, groups, companies, governments, or the general public.

THE PROFIT IMPERATIVE

"Profit" to most people means the difference between the price to the customer and the cost to the supplier, all of it going to the owners to do with as they please. At best, this perception is misleading. At worst, it can destroy the supplier. It also masks the fact that, legally speaking, nonprofits and governments also must make a profit—but the law mandates that the profit be returned to the business.

Why should this be important to the architect? It is important because the way that profit is defined has a direct bearing on system design.

Definition 1:

Let us begin with the commonly perceived definition that profit is the difference between price and cost and is distributed to the owners. The incentive to the owners, in this definition, is to charge what the market will bear and to cut costs. The primary criterion for success is a maximum "bottom line." Without making any value judgments, it is apparent that quality is a dependent variable—it is whatever is needed, but no more, to maximize profit. The more future-looking the organization, the more quality is seen as a possible factor in customer satisfaction and future purchases, but only if it can be shown to increase profits. But other factors with greater returns may be more important: styling and power for automobiles; features and speed for computers; early market introduction in high-tech consumer products; and quick profits for speculative businesses on the stock market. The architect in this business strives for his client's success in the short run.

Definition 2:

In this definition, profit is a *cost*—the present cost of being in business in the future. Using this definition, profit should go not only to investors (who might lose confidence and demand immediate repayment), but even more importantly to research, development, high-quality staffing, specialized facilities, and to assuring long-term customer loyalty.

Definition 2 applies particularly well to the nonprofits for which it provides a guideline for expenditure of what they call a "fee." But it also applies to companies whose own financial strategy is to grow through, and only through, their profits. The short-term effect is to keep annual growth to the same percentage as annual profits are to sales. The long-term effect is relative independence of outside financial control and of financial crises. Because it is future-oriented, this definition tends to put a premium on quality—the early customers have to remain in order that the total customer base can increase. The greatest assets are customer trust and a skilled and dedicated staff. In the era of increasing costs of capital, land, and buildings, continuing debt-free facility construction is a practical investment in the future.

Definition 3:

Profit, in this definition, is the difference between customer-perceived *value* and supplier cost. It is a premium, a sharing with the supplier of value added to the customer's system. It can come in various forms. In one form, the premium is a gratuity, a "tip," given voluntarily. In another form, it may be an agreement to fund a specific activity important to the supplier's future, for example, research and development, future planning, educational grants, capital equipment, buildings, and low-cost loans.

Customer-perceived value also comes in many forms, many of them unquantifiable. FleetSatCom provides a multiocean command and control capability that has assured U.S. primacy in several Mediterranean and Near East crises. Apollo delivered national pride and adventure. Interplanetary spacecraft give us unprecedented scientific results and high drama. Strategic weapons have been a major contributor to the deterrence of World War III. Commercial communications satellites, originally developed with government funding, returned their investment in drastically reduced telephone charges to people the world over. A continuing payment of premiums is a major asset. Indeed, it sometimes appears on the supplier's balance sheet as "good will," convertible to cash if the business is sold. It is also a mark of superior performance and quality.

Definition 3 is particularly applicable to governmental and educational institutions. It is no coincidence that when these institutions do well in their main missions, their future needs continue to be respected and funded. The customer (the U.S. Congress, for example) wants these organizations to continue to do well in the future and knows what it will take to make that possible. But when they do poorly, funding is critically reviewed, failures are long remembered, and the climb back into good grace can be long and hard. Good will is hard-earned and quickly lost.

But definition 3 does require that the premium be collected at or before the time of system acceptance, given the voluntary and arbitrary nature of premiums. One cannot collect a tip once the customer has left the premises, so to speak. If research and development for the next program is not done during the present one, if facilities are not acquired now for the future, and so on, the organization cannot be ready for the future when it comes. The need for future-oriented costs to be paid before the future arrives often has to be negotiated—perhaps quite informally, but understood and paid for—while customer satisfaction with the present program is high. It is foolhardy to approach the customer later; the natural response is, "But what have you done for me lately?" By then it is too late.

Example:

When NASA and JPL began the Deep Space Network (DSN) in 1960, it was informally agreed that a steady, approximately 10%, investment in research and development would be both needed and funded in order that the DSN could satisfy steadily increasing, albeit unspecified, flight-program needs. It was clear that this agreement held as long as the network performed well. The result has been a 70-thousandfold increase in performance over 30 years.

Example:

On the other hand, although one of the finest achievements of the twentieth century was NASA's Apollo program, no premium was paid during that program that, for example, might have been used to develop the Shuttle engines, upgrade the Titan for further manned flight, or to assure the operation of a modest space station. There was not even an agreement negotiated that manned flight would continue to be a national commitment.

Example:

In commercial companies, the rough equivalent of a premium is called "paying for the brand name." One pays more for a product from a well-known trusted company that delivers quality and performance. Customers go to a local merchant, whose products are somewhat more expensive, for the same reasons. The customer wants those companies to continue in business in the future. The premium is paid at the time of sale based on perceived future value.

The definition of profit used by the architect's client is a good indication of how the architect's client views the future. That view unquestionably affects the client's value judgments and project decisions. The architect is well advised to pay heed.

The definition 1 client is unlikely to want to pay for arguable system features that will not pay off in the immediate future.

The definition 2 client is unlikely to risk an established reputation on a high-risk venture that might destroy it. That client would give up profit first, that is, would invest in risk-reduction measures prior and during the program.

The definition 3 client will want evidence of continued success, either to pay a premium or collect it, depending on whether the architect's client is a customer or a supplier.

Even for the definition 1 "price-minus-cost" client, profit is future-oriented, albeit short-term. By representing an investment in the future, its value to that future depends on the present cost of capital. For example, if the profit is used to pay interest on a loan, the size of the loan depends on the interest rate; the higher the rate, the smaller the loan for a fixed cash profit. Alternatively, the higher the rate, the shorter time the loan can be afforded and the sooner it must be repaid from early profits. High cost of capital, therefore, leads to a short-term outlook. On the positive side, it also increases the incentive to reduce the time it takes to bring a product to market—or, conceivably, a weapons system to operation.

The cost of capital is a key consideration in systems design and manufacture, particularly for large complex systems with life cycles measured in decades. If initially underestimated, it can destroy a system before it can be built, wiping out the value of the anticipated profit. If a high cost of capital is anticipated, the pressure will be to design conservatively, using well-understood processes. If the outlook for the cost of capital is uncertain, the design should provide future options, fallbacks and/or quick advances in response to change.

The effects of cost of capital on short- and long-term outlooks are most apparent when different countries experience different costs. For at least a decade, for example, the cost of capital in the United States has been considerably greater than that of Japan. Consistent with this difference, the long-term outlook of U.S. businesses is generally much shorter, measured in years instead of decades.

COST IS NOT AN ABSOLUTE

There is an old saying that says that a good accountant can make a business look good or bad, profitable or unprofitable, depending on the definition of cost. As with the definitions of profit given before, the architect needs to understand the cost basis of the system to be built.

On the one hand, no one wants to pay an unwarranted cost, no matter how defined. On the other hand, not all costs are equally burdensome. Present costs seem more important than future ones. Consider the government's Five-Year Development Plan (FYDP) budgets. "Only the next year's figures mean anything," is the usual view. Or look at the tight restrictions on R&D funding, even when it is acknowledged that early money pays for itself many times over in reducing later overruns. For many reasons, annual costs are of greater concern than life-cycle costs, making the former real and the latter almost imaginary.

It can be said with considerable truth that governments really operate on a *cash-flow* basis, not a total-cost basis. One illustration can suffice. Few complex systems are built without running into unforeseen technical difficulties that will cost money to fix. That means asking the government for more money and/or permission to change performance or schedule. No manager likes to do this, but good management and government regulations require timely notification of the difficulties faced. The resulting inquiry is never pleasant, not because the government client lacks understanding, but because the necessary funds have to come from somewhere else. And no one else is volunteering. And so possible changes in performance are discussed, with little willingness to change them much—any change in performance in either direction will cost money, too, and immediately.

But the atmosphere changes quickly if the manager can say with assurance that no additional funds will be required either for this fiscal year or the one presently in front of the Congress. The schedule will need to be stretched out, of course, and the cost to complete will be higher, but no one is asking for cash now. Reluctant but relieved approval is usually granted. Hence, the de facto cost basis is cash flow, much as in individual personal finances.

The architect's challenge in cash-flow situations is to design sufficient flexibility into the program's implementation that unforeseen costs can be accommodated, usually by schedule slips, with no immediate cash-flow consequences. The challenge is a difficult one, particularly for complex programs having many suppliers on fixed-price contracts and working to fixed, and presumably cost-effective, schedules.

The impact of costs also depends on their allocation. Most readers are familiar with the question of whether a particular cost should be a direct cost (applicable to a specific product only) or an overhead cost (spread over all the company's products). The choice can strongly affect the apparent cost, profitability, and competitiveness of any single product.

Another way of allocating costs is by mission. The allocation of costs in the Shuttle program was mentioned earlier, for example, should the cost of maintaining a manned space program be an explicit allocated cost? A major effect of the breakup of the Bell System and of the "unbundling" of computer hardware and software was the immediate reallocation of costs, with different users now assuming different burdens. A longer-term effect was the restructuring of the systems involved to accommodate new cost imperatives, for example, a significantly changed billing system.

A long-standing cost-allocation controversy for facilities like wind tunnels, test facilities, launch bases, space stations, tracking networks, and university research centers is the one between annual institutional funding and user-reimbursed "industrial" funding. The former encourages a longer-term view and results in a more stable and experienced staff; it carries with it the risk of being unresponsive. The latter ensures responsiveness to customer needs; the larger the customer, the greater the response. Its risk is collapse when a large customer leaves, often for reasons unrelated to facility performance.

It is not in the scope of this text to discuss the pros and cons of each cost-allocation method in any detail. Suffice it to say, they can have profound effects on system architecture. What is "affordable" to a user under one cost-allocation method may be exhorbitant under another.

Without question, then, different cost parameters, like different definitions of profit, can force different architectural choices. Consider:

Example:

Which cost should be used in evaluating launch vehicles—cost per pound on orbit, total cost of the launch, or marginal cost of the launch? Should development costs be included? Facility costs? Insurance (loss) costs? What insurance—just for the loss of the launch vehicle or for the loss of the payload as well? The first costing option could call for the largest vehicles available. The second would call for the smallest vehicles available that can do the job, even in parts. The third would favor existing, already developed vehicles. The fourth would favor government facilities. And so on.

Example:

Cost perception is relative in time and circumstance. The U.S. federal deficit during World War II was a far higher percentage of the Gross National Product than it is today, yet it was not judged to be of much concern. Our freedom and that of our allies was valued even more. The deficit was judged to be worth it under those conditions. Whatever might win the war was accepted. In the late 1950s following the Soviet Sputnik, whatever would beat the Russians in space, including a NASA budget several times the present one, was deemed affordable. Apollo was widely supported; today's less costly space station is not.

Hence:

Profit is a matter of definition and cost is not an absolute.

The slogan, "The best product at the least cost" is, therefore, a poor criterion for a good architecture, because neither "best" nor "cost" is defined, the beholder is not specified (is it the customer or the supplier?), and the time scale is unmentioned (present or continuing?). To be useful in architecting, the slogan's terms and conditions must be more explicit.

DIRECT COMPETITION

Few today would debate the advantages of a global economy or question the interdependence of nations and markets that it requires. People the world over have a wider choice of better products because of it. But a global economy also means global competition in the local markets, especially the American, the largest single market in the world. And that means increased competition for regional producers. The basis of the competition, according to a number of high-level U.S. government studies is

- Rapid transfer of technology to design and manufacture
- Superior designs of marketable products
- Superior product quality

Conspicuously missing in this short list of competitive factors are greater investments in basic research and the technological base—the "know what" part of knowledge. Indeed, although U.S. investment in technology is greater, in many fields the United States is less competitive. But with everyone benefiting from American technology, the competitive advantage for the United States is relatively small.

The competitive battle, therefore, is being won primarily through expeditious technology transfer, superior design, and quality—"know-how." The winners are well-designed, well-made, well-timed products based on understood technologies. In short,

Competitiveness is more a matter of know-how than know-what.

Other government studies show that know-how is also much more difficult to transfer than know-what. Single scientific ideas diffuse very rapidly through the international science community. But design and production ideas depend primarily on the transfer of individuals, who bring with them a wide-ranging knowledge of how to do things, that is, of all the complexities of a process system. The most dramatic examples of this phenomenon are the extraordinarily effective transfers of Japanese managers to U.S. factories and the earlier transfers of American experts to the Soviet Union in the 1920s and to Japan in the 1950s.

A short list of highly competitive product/process architectures demonstrates the competitive importance of process know-how over technology know-what:

Example: DC-3 series of Douglas Aircraft Company airliners

Example: 707 series of Boeing airliners

Example: Apple/Macintosh personal computers

Example: Cray series of supercomputers

Example: Hewlett-Packard instrument series

Example: Japanese consumer product lines, from TV to autos

Example: French Arianne launch vehicle

Almost without exception, the technology with which each series began had been developed under other auspices—in the government (e.g., NACA, NASA, DARPA, ONR, and NBS); in supplier organizations (e.g., Texas Instrument silicon transistors, INTEL microprocessors, P&W and GE aircraft engines); in virtually autonomous industry/university laboratories (Bell Laboratories, Xerox Palo Alto Research Center); and more recently, in transnational company laboratories.

Conversely, success seems to elude companies that generate technology but seem unable to exploit it. The result is a curious economic phenomenon:

- Small startup companies seem best at expeditious exploitation of available technology through good design and quality.
- But small companies seldom have the resources to develop new technologies, only at best to evolve the technology they inherited from others.
- If the small companies do produce a continuing product line through steady evolution of a given technology, they may grow to a size sufficient to fund and develop new technology. At that stage, they almost uniformly believe that developing new technology is essential to their future and proceed to do so.
- But having developed new technologies, the now larger companies seem unable to exploit them as expeditiously as new spinoff companies can. Seeing their technology results helping others but apparently not themselves, the established companies limit their further development and decide against their exploitation. Meanwhile, other companies enter the established companies' hitherto profitable market.

- As profits decline, interest in cost reduction increases and development of new technologies suffers. Key contributors leave and start a new company, and the cycle continues.

This cycle is so pervasive that very few major companies are able to make a transition from an older, but still profitable, product line to a newer one *even in the same kind of business.* Barge builders did not expand into railroads. Railroads did not expand into aircraft. Vacuum-tube manufacturers did not take the lead in solid-state devices.

Where successful transition was accomplished in a mature company, it often was through the establishment of the equivalent of a "new company" as a speculative separable venture within the parent organization. Relatively unrestricted, the new venture then had the opportunity to establish the modus operandi needed for rapid conversion of technology to a new product line. In due course, the new venture matured as the new product line prospered; radical (or competitive) innovations were spun off and the cycle repeated.

A similar cycle can be observed in organizations that build large-scale complex systems. Ironically, it affects the most successful organizations the most. Having conceived, developed, and built a highly successful system architecture for the first of a new series of aerospace, computer, or electronic systems, the organization fails to win the competition for the next-generation system.

A plausible scenario for the loss might be the following. When it comes time for the customer to seek an upgrade for a successful but aging system, requests for proposals are sent to likely bidders. The builder of the present system, knowing more about it and how to improve it efficiently with a minimum need for additional resources, bids on a straightforward upgrade of the present system. The other bidders, realizing that they are most unlikely to win by making a similar bid, rethink the functions the client desires, study the new options made possible by changing times and technologies, and conceive new architectures. The new architectures generate new possibilities in performance, cost, and schedule unavailable in the conventional upgrade. Providing that at least one of the new architectures does not add unacceptable risks, the customer awards the contract to a new builder.

The reader has already surmised that architects as well as organizations can be caught up in this cycle. The original architect may be too enamored with the clearly successful first architecture to be willing to consider innovative changes or outright replacement. Or an architect in the original organization may find radical new system architectures, with all their consequences to engineering, development, and manufacture, are unwelcome and be forced to choose between acquiescence and leaving—often to an appreciative competitor.

MISSION COMPETITION AND TECHNOLOGICAL SUBSTITUTION

The preceding section dealt with direct competition between similar products and organizations. This section expands the competition to different products within a broader mission, for example, transportation, information processing, manufacturing, and message transmission. In this competition, one technology overtakes, or substitutes for, an earlier one with consequent improvements in performance and cost. Airlines replace buses, which replaced railroads, which replaced canals. Other sequences:

- Hand-held computers for minicomputers for work stations for a central mainframe
- Robots for computer-controlled machines for manually operated machines for handcrafting
- Observation helicopters for fixed-wing aircraft for balloons
- Optical cables for satellites for microwave stations for copper cables for high-frequency radio for couriers
- Xerography for mimeograph for carbon paper for hand copying

The system architect's responsibility in such situations is to forewarn the client of an upcoming substitution and, as appropriate, to suggest how to accommodate to it. As John Pierce, then of Bell Laboratories, said on the advent of satellite communication in 1960, "As a communications company, AT&T must be in the satellite communication business. We dare not be the American Association of Railroads in the era of airlines."

Although most substitutions take many years to complete, they can well occur within the anticipated lifetime of major companies, product lines, and military systems. The critical question, as it is with the introduction of a new product, is one of timing. But in outright substitution, a drastic restructuring of the organization may be necessary. The systems it builds, and the way in which they are built, may have to be rearchitected. Research and engineering will have to change. The clients and customers and their needs will change.

The architect better not be asleep at the switch.

PUBLIC POLICY, REGULATIONS, AND SYSTEMS ARCHITECTING

A completely free unconstrained market does not—and probably could not—exist in the real world. Instead, modern economies are instead a complex mix of regulated and unregulated, taxed and untaxed, highly interdependent enterprises. The kind and degree of regulation and taxation are determined by public policy, that is, by governmental value judgments. And interdependency is being rapidly increased by today's global markets.

Virtually all large complex systems and the organizations that build and operate them are regulated.* Indeed, some degree of regulation is desirable for them. A well-crafted regulation reduces uncertainty, provides standards, and protects suppliers and consumers against rapacious competitors. Poorly crafted regulation can do severe damage, overburdening and disrupting parts of the economic system.

To the systems architect, regulations are perhaps best thought of as part of the system's control software, with the regulators being the controllers. Regulators define and control markets, costs, and profits in accordance with public policy. In a sense, regulators are a special set of system operators with needs comparable to those of the more evident operators—the managers and employees of the system's organization. The architect is ill-advised to treat regulations and regulators as "outside" the system.

Regulations affect elements in the architect's system in many ways:

- They represent the imperatives of public interest.
- They provide some structure to the external economy, a structure that the architect's system must fit.
- From building codes to data-base privacy laws, they play a sometimes decisive role in system conception, construction, and operation. As noted before, they are part of the system's control software.
- Regulations are subject to public policy, which means that they are likely to change as public values change.

The implications of the first factors are clear enough. If a system is not in the public interest or does not fit the economy, it will not fill a real need. A building, aircraft, or computer must comply with regulations or it will be denied entry into the marketplace.

The last factor is of special concern here. Changes in public policy can dramatically restructure whole enterprises and the systems that support them.

The case of converting the public telephone enterprise from a regulated monopoly to a partly regulated competition has been described before (Brooks, 1988). The recent conversion of U.S. commercial air travel from a regulated competition to a largely unregulated one is another case. An important third was the conversion of the public mail system (U.S. Postal Service) from a gov-

---

*Regulation: A principle, rule, or law designed for controlling or governing behavior. A governmental order with the force of law. It is used here to include laws, orders, directives, tax codes, etc.

ernment service to a mixed private/government business. The most immediate effects have been:

- A shift in cost from one group to another
- A shift in cost from one set of services to another
- A shift in the system purposes and markets, for example, shifts between public service and profit-making enterprises
- A shift in the distribution of profits (see the previous definitions)
- A change in who controls the business
- A change in the motivations of employees and managers

These shifts, in turn, produced system changes, some of which are

- A change in the billing system, with consequent rearchitecting of the monitoring, controlling, and computing elements
- A change in the system configuration to better match the system purposes and markets, for example, changes in routes and locations
- A shift in the investment strategy, for example, R&D, financing methods, and time scale
- A reallocation of plant, facility, and human resources
- Changes in marketing, sales, and consumer relations
- Changes in government relations and operations

In short, changes in regulations can produce widespread behavioral and architectural changes. They can change a whole culture. It is probably true to say that many regulation changes were not anticipated and that not all of them were beneficial. But that conclusion was foregone, based on the complexity of major systems, economics, and societal behavior.

The architect may be confronted with culture change in a personal way—by changing clients from governmental to private or vice versa. Their regulatory environments are so different and so important that an inexperienced systems architect can easily make errors in assumptions, constraints, and priorities.

The architect also needs to be sensitive to the fact that not only do regulations affect the system, the system can affect regulations. A regulatory response can be triggered by the societal changes introduced by the system. We saw this earlier, in Chapter 9, in the response of a societal macrosystem to a system that created societal change. The response was to restabilize. The mechanism by which this normally is accomplished is by changes in regulations.

Concerns over public safety have produced a plethora of new restrictive regulations, from the days of the early automobile to nuclear power plants. As safety concerns abate, the regulations usually diminish.

Changes in public policy also affect the rights and accountability of system ownership, subjects of considerable concern to the system's owners. Owners' rights include control over access, use, and benefits. Owners' responsibilities include conformity with regulations and concern over product safety and the interests of others.

Example:

Who owns a spacecraft in orbit? A company? A nation? Who is responsible for dead spacecraft and depleted launch-vehicle components? Does the owner have the right to protect and defend them, both active and dead? If salvaged, must they be returned to the original owner? Is space debris the responsibility of those that deposited it? Should they be compelled to remove it if it can cause damage to other space objects? Can private interests establish space colonies? (Glazer, 1978)

Example:

Who owns information in a data bank? For example, who owns medical records, credit ratings, and law-enforcement records? The individual? The owner of the repository? The state? The nation? Who then can control entry, removal, and usage of the information? How can the rights of citizens be maintained? (Ware, 1973) How can "viruses" and other damaging activity be thwarted and punished?

Example:

Who owns the data collected by a remote satellite sensor? The experimenter? The spacecraft owner? Does national security override any owner's rights?

Example:

Who is responsible for the safe disposal of toxic wastes?

Public policy, by codifying governmental value judgments and promulgating regulations, provides the answers. But for the answers to be meaningful, they must be implemented by a system that provides protection, accountability, and enforcement of the rights of the owner and the public.

In particular, system provisions must be made for the following:

Protection of ownership rights: Real and intellectual property rights must be clearly defined. To be protected, a system must be protect*able*. Inherent vulnerabilities need to be minimized. Alerts must warn of possible attack. Records must document damage and its source. Countermeasures, both passive and active, should be in place.

Ownership accountability: To be held accountable, an accounting mechanism must exist. The cause, or lack thereof, of a problem must be identifiable. The effects must be tied to the presumed cause and to no other. Compensation, penalties, and corrective actions should be established prior to potentially damaging activity.

Intervention rights: If the rights of an owner are to be overridden in the public interest, there must be an understood mechanism or procedure by which this is done. For example, if national security can override an experimenter's rights to publish data, a mechanism for accomplishing that override must exist. The intervention rights and ownership compensation should have been established prior to intervention.

Enforcement of rights: Rights are only meaningful if they are enforceable. Unless an enforcement mechanism—physical, electronic, legal, or otherwise— exists, the rights of ownership, accountability, and intervention have no meaning.

Making provision for protection, accountability, and enforcement mechanisms in accordance with, and in the spirit of, regulations and public interest is a proper responsibility of the system architect. Failure to do so puts all parties— the client, the supplier, the owner, the user, and the public—in positions of otherwise avoidable risk.

RISK TAKING AND SHARING

We live in a real world of uncertainty, complexity, and risk. Further, we live in individual worlds of *perceived* uncertainty, complexity, and risk that, from the individuals' perspectives, are equally real. The latter can have equal or greater impact than the former on system design, construction, and operation. They appear at their most frustrating when demands are made that certain risks be made vanishingly small—that nuclear plants never experience an accident, that carcinogenic materials be banished, that security codes be unbreakable, or that ultraquality be guaranteed.

The challenge of proving that something can never happen can be endless. If no harm is shown at a lowest measureable level X and it then becomes possible to measure levels of $0.1X$, the question of proof simply gets asked again at the new lowest level. Where is the point where "we know enough to stop worrying" (Morgan et al., 1985)? Complex systems are faced with a special problem in achieving a no-risk posture, their inherent unboundedness. Almost by definition, and given the limitless nature of perceived risk, unbounded systems can have unbounded risks unless protected by law, for example, the liability protection provided to the Department of Defense and its suppliers. Even so, the legal boundaries are challenged from time to time.

Experience has shown the average nonscientific observer that risk estimation is chancy, value-laden, and of questionable validity. Murphy's law seems to occur all too often. For reasons unknown, perceptions of risk differ widely even from clearly provable risks, for example, the perceived risks of death due to accidents, smoking, cancer, street violence, and war are consistently ranked in the wrong order compared to actual measurable risks. Behavioral scientists have convincingly demonstrated that human intuition about risk, more often than not, is just plain wrong.

Yet it is the perceptions of risk that determine human behavior. Perceptions determine whether individuals will support or oppose a system. Thus, if social cooperation is to be secured, the *perceived* risks must be accommodated in the system design. They cannot be pushed to one side for long, particularly if the risks will be borne by people "outside" of the system.

Clearly, all risks must be taken by someone sometime. One way of sharpening the perceptual issues involved is by asking:

Who or what generates the risk? Who estimates it? Who bears it? Who benefits from it?

The answers seldom yield the same individual, the same organization, or the same system. The one who generates the risks may be outside the control of any of them. The estimator can be an advocate and/or an opponent. The one who bears the consequences may be neither. And the beneficiary may be a speculator. Each party involved will have a self-interest and a bias that will affect how any given risk is perceived. The architect is well advised to remember in complex system architecting that

Risk is defined by the beholder, not the architect.

Example:

The risks associated with electric power plants and transmission systems are perceived very differently by the utilities, the engineers, the regulatory agencies, and the local populace.

Example:

The claimed risks may be only a surrogate or cover for a deeper issue, for example, opposition to nuclear war, to encroaching development, to new technology, or to unpopular causes or authorities.

One way out of this contentious situation is to *share* the risks, both benefits and burdens, *as perceived* by all parties concerned. Whether this is practical or not is partly a question of price, partly one of perceptions of fair treatment, and partly one of assuring social cooperation.

The method for doing so is called risk mitigation and compensation, taking measures to reduce the burden and to distribute the benefits. Typical measures are system redesign, financial compensation, support for other programs of importance to those bearing the risks, employment opportunities, and so on. Without question, these measures should be planned well before public debate begins, which makes them elements in the conceptual design.

Failure to balance risks and benefits in a timely mutually agreed way can bring down almost any system sooner or later. Purely pragmatically, the sooner the question of risk is addressed, the better the chances for its resolution. If it is unresolvable, more drastic action may be necessary, from legal proceedings in one direction to outright cancellation in the other. But not getting in a **zero-sum game** is certainly the preferable direction to take.

SUMMARY

System economics is an essential element in any complex system architecture. The architect must help assure a timely identification of markets and competitors, a clear understanding of the meaning to the client of profit and cost, and an equitable treatment of uncertainty and risk. Virtually all complex systems are matters of public interest that through regulation directly affect the systems' architecture and economics.

RECOMMENDED READING

BACH, GEORGE L. (1974). *Economics, An Introduction to Analysis and Policy,* 8th Ed. Englewood Cliffs, NJ: Prentice Hall. This is a basic textbook on the subject.

BROOKS, HARVEY. (1988). "Reflections on the Telecommunications Infrastructure." In Ausubel, J. and R. Herman, eds. *Cities and Their Vital Systems, Infrastructure Past, Present and Future.* Washington, DC: National Academy Press. It discusses the effects of the breakup of the Bell System, that is, the shift from a regulated monopoly for the public interest to a market-driven competition driven by the requirements of a few of the largest users.

COMPTON, W. DALE, and G. E. SOLOMON. (1988). *The Technological Dimensions of International Competitiveness.* Washington, DC: National Academy of Engineering. This book gives a quantative description of the competitive posture of the United States with recommendations to industry, government, and the education system.

HUGHES, T. P. (Winter 1988). "The Industrial Revolution That Never Came." *Invention and Technology* **3**, 3, 59–64. Social oracles once believed that the coming of electricity and automobiles would make dirty, crowded cities a thing of the past. Instead, the existing social structure bent these technologies to its own purposes.

ROSENBURG, NATHAN, RALPH E. GOMORY, RICHARD J. MAHONEY, and ERICH BLOCH. (1988). *Industrial R&D and U.S. Technological Leadership.* Washington, DC: National Academy Press. The book makes the point that development and reduction to practice, and not scientific research, results in competitive advantage. Development, in turn, is inhibited in the United States by the high cost of capital, forcing the industry to make short-term decisions to avoid those costs.

ROWE, A. J., and I. SOMERS. (1983) "Methods to Predict Performance in Major Program Acquisition." *Omega, the International Journal of Management* **11**, 2, 155–173. It identifies four primary variables that contribute to cost growth: environmental uncertainty, technological uncertainty, customer urgency, and organizational slack. It presents a causal-integrative model to show the relationships among the variables and 26 contributing factors.

WHEELON, A. D. (January 1986). *The Rocky Road to Communication Satellites,* AIAA von Karman Lecture, Reno, Nevada. Various applications of communications satellites are examined in the three dimensions of technology, economics, and policy. It concludes that the three cannot be separated, and that if any is deficient, the program fails.

TO BROWSE, DEPENDING UPON INTEREST

ELLIS, L. W. (1975). "The Law of the Economies of Scale Applied to Telecommunications System Design." *Electrical Communication* **50**, 1, 4–19. This is a detailed look at the elements of telecommunication systems and the applicability of Grosch's law that system cost is roughly proportional to the square root of system size.

GLAZER, HENRY J. (1978). "Domicile and Industry in Outer Space." *Columbia Journal of Transnational Law* **17**, 1, 67–117. This is an article on the problems and options of space law on questions of ownership, resource extraction (e.g., mining), control, sovereignty, and language.

MORGAN, M. G., H. K. FLORIG, I. NAIR, and D. LINCOLN. (February 1985). "Power-line Fields and Human Health" *IEEE Spectrum* **22**, 2, 62–88. This illustrates the virtual impossibility of proving a negative, that is, that no risk exists—a problem common to electrical power transmission, drug certification, encryption certification, disease prevention, and carcinogens.

NAKICENOVIC, N. (1988). " Dynamics and Replacement of U.S. Transport." In Ausubel, J. H. and R. Herman, eds. *Cities and Their Vital Systems, Infrastructure Past, Present and Future.* Washington, DC: National Academy Press. It shows the times required to build and replace old transport (aircraft, auto, railroads, canals) infrastructures and energy transport systems.

RUPPE, H. O. (August 1987). "Launch Vehicles to Low-Earth Orbit." *Space Policy* 175–78. The article concludes that the choice between partly expendable (first-stage reusable) and fully expendable launch vehicles depends on the loss rate.

WARE, WILLIS W. (1973). "Records, Computers and the Rights of Citizens." In *Report of the Secretary's Advisory Committee on Automated Personal Data Systems.* Washington, DC: U.S. Department of Health, Education, and Welfare.

part three

Architecting and Management

INTRODUCTION

Successful architecting requires the architect to understand corporate management and corporate management to understand architecting. The purpose of Part Three is to help each understand the world of the other.

For architects, perhaps the most useful realization is that an organization is a system. Its organization chart outlines its structure. Its architecture strongly determines its behavior. A system perspective makes it easier to identify its imperatives and to avoid personalizing its structurally imposed tensions and limitations.

For those architects who become managers later on, it is worth remembering that architectural heuristics apply to the structuring and restructuring of organization. Indeed, it is a recognized principle of management that the chief executive officer of a company must also be its chief organizational architect, responding to the needs of its customers and employees, defining its organizational purposes and structure, and resolving the tensions created by the environment within which it lives.

For the manager first learning about—and wanting to do something about—architecting, a legendary story from World War II may well ring true. The Chief of Naval Operations at that time was the brilliant but crusty Fleet Admiral Ernest J. King, who in the long tradition of the Navy believed that the only important part of the navy was its fleets. Support functions ashore were far down his priority list until it became all too apparent that victory in the distant South Pacific would be critically dependent upon well-organized logistic support. After a short briefing on the subject—all briefings to the admiral were short—he thundered, "I don't know what this 'logistics' is, but I want more of it!" The manager may feel the same about architecting by this point, but before taking action no doubt would want a few key management questions answered first:

- How do I recognize a good architect when I see one?
- How do I tell a good architecture from a poor one?
- How do I manage and utilize the architecting function?

In what areas might it be useful? Product design? Process design? Organizational design?

How do I tell when it is going well?

Where does it belong in the organization?

How can it be developed?

Is research in architecting methods useful for this organization?

- What future projects are likely to require major efforts in systems architecting?

Part Three is intended to suggest some of the answers.

13

ON ORGANIZATIONS AND ARCHITECTURES

If systems architecting can be viewed as a part of the engineering function, it can similarly be viewed as a part of managing. Both architect and manager live in ill-structured unbounded worlds where analytic rationality is insufficient and optimum solutions are rare. Both have perspectives that are strategic and top-down. Top managers, like chief architects, must architect strategies that will handle the unforeseeable, avoid disaster, and produce results satisfactory to multiple clients—to boards of directors, customers, employees and the general public. Their common modus operandi is one of fit, balance, and compromise in the overall interest of the system and its purposes.

It therefore should not be surprising that of the 100 or so heuristics given in the first two parts of this book that several dozen are just as applicable to the architecting part of managing as they are to that of engineering. Here is a short sampling of previously stated heuristics adapted for organizing (or reorganizing) a management structure:

- No complex organization can be optimum to all parties concerned, nor all functions optimized.
- In partitioning an organization, choose a configuration with minimal communications required between its elements.
- Choosing the appropriate level of aggregation of functions is critical in the design of organizations.
- The choice between organizational structures may well depend upon which set of drawbacks the management can handle best.

- When choices must be made with unavoidably inadequate information, choose the best available and then watch to see whether future solutions appear faster than future problems. If so, the choice is at least adequate. If not, go back and choose again.
- In introducing change, how you do something is often more important than what you do.
- Predicting the future may be impossible, but ignoring it is irresponsible.

In fact, a number of these heuristics originated in the management context and were transferred intact to architecting technical systems. And some of the most perceptive writings on heuristics are by authors specializing in management (e.g., Rowe, 1988).

It is also true that when all is said and done, the reason technical systems exist is to serve people—individuals, groups, companies and governments. The more complex the human organization, the more complex the system tends to be that serves it; in turn, the more complex are the organizations needed to build and operate the system. Organizations and their systems are symbiotic—each needs and must fit the other.

The symbiosis is strongest between the system and the five organizations most concerned with it: the client's, the user's, the builder's, the affected governments', and, of course, the architect's. But each of these differs from the others in purpose, structure, behavior, and in the nature of its interests in the system. Inherent strains and misfits exist between them and between them and the system. The challenge to both architect and the manager is to alleviate those misfits by skillful system design, acquisition, and operation. It is a challenge regularly seen in communications networks, interlinked computers, spacecraft, aircraft, administrative, and security systems.

The purpose of this chapter is to highlight the close correspondence of organizations and systems. For our purposes here, an important simplification will be made: we focus on the structural rather than on the social and psychological aspects of organizations. Human behavior, in other words, will be assumed to be rational within each individual's context.

We begin with organizational purposes from which flow both structure and behavior.

ORGANIZATIONS AS PURPOSEFUL SYSTEMS

Three types of organizations, categorized by their primary objectives, are considered here: bottom line (profit seeking), bureaucratic* (rule following), and

---

*Defined functionally, not pejoratively. It is unfortunate that the term "bureaucracy" also has a connotation as an impedance to effective action, unfairly and indiscriminately denigrating the public services and most administrative functions.

cultural (team compatibility). All three are commonly involved in the acquisition and operation of a complex system.

The primary objectives of bottom-line organizations are quantitative and measurable, for example, profit margin, return on investment, or share of the market. These quantitative objectives provide a clear basis for measuring efficiency and productivity. The organization's products, typically, are expressible in quantitative terms—so many units of specified price, performance, quality, and rate. Bottom-line organizations are structured to do quantifiable things well. They work especially well for discrete tasks of specified size, cost, and schedule. Builders' organizations usually are of this type.

Bureaucracies originally were, and still are, established to provide a division of labor for long-term public-service missions—national security, social welfare, justice, education, and international relations. Bureaucracies also see extensive use in the service side of bottom-line and cultural organizations, where they administer personnel, security, accounting, finance, legal affairs, audit, and facility maintenance. Not only are their mission objectives imprecisely defined, as goals they are inherently unreachable. The Defense Department can never achieve perfect national security, national health can always be improved, and personnel problems will never go away. Efforts to quantify bureaucratic objectives in the interests of efficiency and effectiveness are therefore difficult at best. Management and assessment of bureaucracies are instead based on their performance in following and/or administering established rules, that is, regulations, laws, policies, and procedures. Although bureaucratic insistence on following the rules can at times be annoying, a little thought will show that this is exactly what we want and demand of these institutions. We punish the violators, particularly those at high level, severely.

Bureaucracies are best able to handle complex, large-scale, structured, stable, and rational situations. They are least able to handle novel, small-scale, unstructured, dynamic, and irrational situations for which the rules have not yet been written. For what they do best, they are unexcelled.

Cultural organizations have quite different objectives and specialties. These organizations aim for teamwork, for fraternization, for informal creativity, and for easy interpersonal relationships. Cultural organizations are usually small or, if large, are split into relatively autonomous small units. Operations are egalitarian and collegial. Volunteer groups, athletic teams, universities, and professional partnerships of architects, lawyers, and doctors are culture-based as are small research, development, and prototyping teams. Nothing is worse for a cultural organization or for one of its members than a loss of a hard-earned reputation for professionalism, skill, and compatibility.

The motivations, needs, and behavior of individuals in these organizations are determined to a large extent by what it takes to succeed in each:

Bottom line, in which you succeed if you produce a profit.

Bureaucratic, in which you succeed if you follow the rules.

Cultural, in which you succeed if you fit in as a team member.

With such differing motivations, individuals in the different organizations can have quite different "models of the world." They can have different perceptions of what constitutes system success. They almost certainly will have different imperatives that must be satisfied.

It is one thing to accommodate to true imperatives and another to identify them up front and early on. The imperatives of reasonable profit, following the rules, and cultural compatibility are understandable enough. But what about conflicting interests on contract types (fixed price, CPFF, CPIF, competitive bid, negotiated contract, fly before buy, etc.), on specifications (performance, functional, detailed, method, and "illities"), on client–supplier relations (adversarial, arms length, cooperative, partnership, team), and on perceptions of success (long term, short term, consequences of failure)?

Organization-oriented imperatives can result in difficult trade-offs in system architecture, design, and implementation.

Example:

Fixed-price contracts, by providing incentives to cost cutting, work against a system performing any better than absolutely required; hence, quality is at risk. But they do limit the cost risk to the customer. Hence, a product-oriented customer will favor them and a mission-oriented bureaucracy will resist them, based purely on organizational imperatives.

Example:

Performance specifications give the builder more flexibility, but make certification and acceptance much more contentious. Hence, engineers favor and contract administrators resist them.

Example:

Negotiated contracts and team relations usually produce better products, but raise the perception of collusion. The executive branch believes in them, whereas the legislative branch looks on them with deep suspicion.

Example:

Fly before buy and concurrency (of development and production preparations) are in direct conflict, pitting assured performance against expedited availability.

Therefore, and this time for reasons of organizational imperatives we once again observe that

No complex system can be optimum to all parties concerned.

As a consequence, organizations, like other complex systems, are the results of fit, balance, and compromise constrained by function and form. To be effective in supporting an organization, the architect must understand its functions, forms, and interfaces almost as well as those of the systems that support it. With such understanding comes the opportunity to relieve interorganizational stresses by diplomacy, understanding, neutrality, and, not least, by creative system design.

The situation is difficult enough when each organization is doing well what it can do best. But, from time to time, organizations are placed, or place themselves, in situations where it may be very difficult to do well. Indeed,

The strengths of an organization in one context can be its weaknesses in another.

Or

Given a successful organization with valid criteria for success, there are some things it can not do—or at least not do well.

Or

Being good at one thing does not automatically mean being good at something else.

This heuristic should be no surprise. Organizations, like machines, are specialized. In the process of specialization, other functions are downrated in priority or deliberately omitted. A hammer is a poor screwdriver and vice versa. Some of the more common incompatibilities:

Example:

Government bureaucracies are notoriously poor at predicting whether their research results can be developed into profitable products—whether it is the British government in electronics or NASA in Shuttles and LANDSATs. The idea that the government labs will be effective in a competitive world is a contradiction in terms—those labs exist, appropriately, to perform public-service missions assigned to them only, that is, they are structured for a monopolistic world.

Example:

Don't expect a bureaucracy to be "businesslike" or a bottom-line company to do too well at following "the rules." They can try, but it is counter to their organizing principles and functions.

Example:

Don't expect a "do your own thing" company, typical of the early entrepreneurial stage of many high-tech hardware companies, to do very well in producing major systems.

Example:

Don't expect a systems house to be other than conservative or to be successful at producing component hardware.

Example:

Don't expect a mission-oriented nonprofit organization to convert easily to a for-profit product-oriented one.

Example:

A highly entrepreneurially-oriented company will have difficulty in a highly regulated market. The entrepreneur wants to change things; the regulator must control them.

The architect should expect trouble whenever the client suggests or asks for system functions inconsistent with organizational imperatives. At the very least, the architect should make sure that the inconsistencies are understood before proceeding very far into conceptual design.

ORGANIZATIONS AS STRUCTURES

The two organizational structures of most importance to the architect are the client's and the user's. The client's structure is important because it affects system-acquisition decisions. The user's structure is important because it affects how well the system will perform. If the structures are awkward and cumbersome, acquisition decisions and system performance will be as well. If they match, superior performance should result.

Four kinds of structures are seen in the aerospace/electronics field: line-staff, pyramid, matrix, and segmented-ring.

The *line-staff* structure (Figure 13–1) originated in military systems and soon thereafter became a standard structure for many organizations, both civil and military. It represents both a functional division of labor and a flow diagram for authority, responsibility, and official communications. Its elements are intended to be relatively independent unless specifically interconnected. Communications between elements that are not interconnected are minimal and are often discouraged. In the military, it defines the "chain of command." It takes special orders to bypass a level, that is, to "skip echelon." It is an orderly

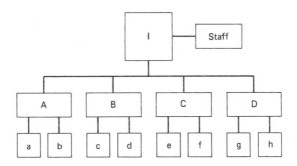

Figure 13–1. Line-staff structure.

structure and works best in static or preplanned situations. Its greatest dilemma is that only the top of the organization (**I**) is in a position to know and act upon anything and everything that goes on—and yet doing so can overwhelm the top executive. Delegation of authority is common, but carries with it the risk of loss of control. The most common solutions to this dilemma are to use a staff to gather and condense information for the boss and a council (**I** plus A, B , C and D) to coordinate decision making.

From the architect's perspective, the only individual in a line-staff client organization that can give final approval to an architecture is the top executive, although lower-level managers can, and do, disapprove some elements. But only the top executive is in a position to know "the whole story" and to see the big picture. There is, therefore, a strong incentive to design a system architecture in accordance with what the top executive seems to want. The situation has obvious dangers of which both the top executive and the architect should be aware.

A line-staff structure in a client bureaucracy tends to be liberal at the top and conservative at the bottom, a direct consequence of the ability to make rules at the top (where they are called guidelines) and the imperative not to violate (or make) rules at the bottom. On the other hand, a line-staff structure in a bottom-line supplier organization tends to be conservative at the top—profit margins are too small to be otherwise—but liberal at the bottom—engineers work better with few restraints.

The result, on structural grounds alone, can be serious differences between client and supplier at both the top and bottom of their organizations. Middle management in both usually sorts things out.

Pyramidal organizations (Figure 13–2) have several origins. They resemble line-staff structures in retaining a hierarchy of levels, but they treat each level as a stable platform, a freely intercommunicating entity. Line-staff structures, as noted, discourage that intercommunication. The incentives in a pyramidal structure are to reach consensus at each level. There is also an implication that anyone at the lowest level can communicate with anyone at the next higher level, presumably on a subject having concurrence at the originating level. The same implication holds for downward communication. Each level thus tends to self-stabilize and to solve "the whole problem" at its level. In this sense, the pyramidal structure resembles software and biological hierarchies, with each

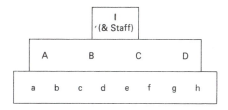

Figure 13–2. Pyramid structure.

level the foundation for higher-level functions. Each level, of course, has to be self-organizing, but that also means that each level most easily solves the problems that come up at that level.

Pyramidal structures are still relatively rare and of small scale. They are found in quality circles, university departments, ad hoc research teams, and small entrepreneural collectives. They have been suggested by some observers as a structure more atuned to the knowledge age than is the line-staff structure. Whether that is true or not, pyramids do represent a sharply different information transfer structure from line-staff structures.

Matrix structures (Figure 13-3) came about when single organizations, constructed along line-staff functional lines, tried to handle several independent projects at the same time, with each project needing the same functions to be performed. For example, a system manufacturer, organized according to engineering disciplines, might want to manufacture several different systems (e.g., aircraft, missiles, spacecraft, communication systems, etc.). Each system project (P-1, P-2, and P-3) would need structural, mechanical, electrical, and electronic subsystems, and hence would have to go to divisions A, B, C, and D to obtain them. One solution would be to give each project an A, B, C, and D, but that is often inefficient.

The structural problem with the matrix is that subordinate levels are confronted with two lines of authority: their own vertical line authority and the horizontal project authority. The inherent conflicts between the legitimate missions of the functional organization and of the projects then appear in force at the lower levels (e.g., a and i), which have to decide which mission is more important at the moment. The de facto decision is often determined by the source of the money to pay for the requested tasks. In Figure 13-3, the money comes

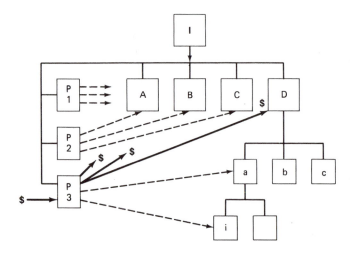

Figure 13-3. Matrix structure.

from project P-3, which, to complicate the situation, receives it directly from outside sources, bypassing the chief executive of the organization.

Sending the money through **I**, however, is not necessarily better since that permits **I** to make the mission-versus-institution choice, overruling P-3.

The key to matrix success clearly is in maintaining a proper balance between the conflicting interests of institutional and project management. There is sufficient common ground to achieve balance, given understanding all around. Managers of both the institution (**I**) and the project (P) want the system to succeed. P is the source of funds that **I** needs to operate. **I** is an efficient source of expertise and facilities for P. And neither P nor **I** wants the inherent organizational tensions to devolve to their subordinate units.

The matrix can also exist in a rotated form, where the projects are along the top and the technical disciplines on the side. Both arrangements have their pros and cons. Reorganizing by a 90° rotation can be traumatic.

Matrix organizations are most prominent in supplier organizations, but they can and do appear in user organizations as well, for example, in multiservice unified commands, in logistics and repair depots, in communications networks, and in contract-supported operations.

For most complex systems, the user structure that the system must support and the builder structure that will be needed will be matrices.

The system may fit into a user matrix in several ways. It may be in a projectlike position (e.g., an aircraft) needing support (logistics, communications) from institutional elements. Or it might be an institutional element itself (a communications network) with a number of users. In either case, a system in a matrix will find itself in a situation of conflicting interests. To operate successfully, it must provide some mechanism for alleviating, if not resolving, the conflicts inherent in matrixed (shared) facilities and support.

The *segmented-ring* structure (Figure 13-4) is a variation on the pyramid but with an important psychological difference. There is no implication of

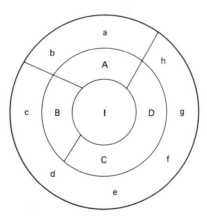

Figure 13-4. Segmented-ring structure.

higher and lower levels. Instead there is the perception of focus, of centering on some function that surrounding echelons support. In a builder organization, the center would be manufacturing, not the chief executive. Depending upon where the segment lines are drawn, differing degrees of knowledge transfer are indicated.

For example, in Figure 13-4, C and D work closely, A works more closely with a and b than with c through h, but works equally with B, C, and D. There are at least three channels from c to **I,** and so on. It is reported that some Japanese manufacturing firms operate along these lines. Some command and control operations are structured this way.

A physical realization example of a segmented ring is a spacecraft command center, where **I** consists of a small group facing a set of consoles, directly monitoring and controlling the craft. Supporting **I** are remote echelons of support specialized for individual spacecraft subsystems communicating through with **I** through their consoles. Many of the consoles have access on demand to selected information on all other consoles.

Figure 13-5, the so-called Venn diagram, is another way of showing what organizational relationships should occur if the corresponding system relationships are to be matched. Seven elements of a launch vehicle–payload combination are shown, so arranged that their disks overlap to the extent that their functions influence each other. Guidance and control affects, and is affected

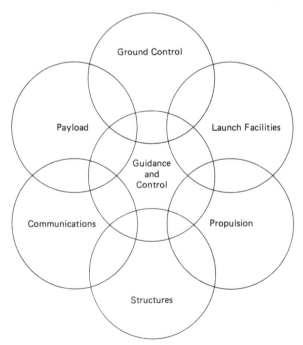

Figure 13-5. Functional (Venn) diagram.

by, all of them. Propulsion, on the other hand, overlaps with launch facilities, structures, and guidance and control but connects to the others only indirectly through guidance and control. (Engineers in the launch-vehicle business will recognize why guidance and control specialists most easily become systems engineers.) In this illustration, the guidance and control function is not the center of the universe in the same sense that I of Figure 13-4 was the focus for all support. It is in the center because of its multiple connections with other elements. It can be seen in the figure that there are double overlaps, the one between propulsion, structures, and guidance and control in the lower right corner being an important one.

The value of such Venn diagrams is in the thinking process required to draw them. It forces a consideration of interrelationships based not on a functional organization chart, but on the technical characteristics of the system elements to be built and operated. In this illustration, for example, it clearly is going to be important to keep the guidance and control organization "in the middle of things" technically, physically, and managerially.

Figure 13-6 illustrates two human interrelationships, of many, that exist in any organization—power centers and friends. The **bold** blocks are power centers, parts of the organization that, from expertise or criticality or force of personality, have more influence than the others.

The dashed lines show two kinds of friendships—between individuals on the left and as a network on the right. The network, with power center B reporting directly to **I,** is in a preferred position. A, a, and f are at a disadvantage. The relationship between A and b can be difficult.

The purpose of Figure 13-6 is to recognize that organization charts are, at best, incomplete models of how organizations actually operate. They indicate *official* interrelationships, and, in that sense, it is important that they be reasonably complete. They act as needed guidelines for all concerned, including the architect. System architectures are necessarily based on them, not on friendships, power centers, or other informalities. The latter are too weak as a foundation for a system design; unfortunately, if unrecognized, they can be strong enough to cripple that design without being accountable for the results. But in

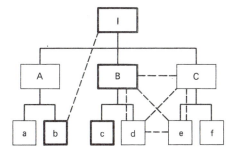

Figure 13-6. Power centers and friends.

all fairness, friendships sometimes are the only reason some poorly structured organizations or systems work at all.

ORGANIZATIONS AND THEIR COMMUNICATIONS SYSTEMS

When companies are small, their organization charts are little more than sketches showing only the aggregation and division of labor among individuals. Art Raymond (1951), describes how the DC-1 was conceived and built; engineering was in the loft and the shop was on the ground floor. All the engineers were in continuous contact with those building the planes. Close proximity of all parties meant free and informal communication. Organization charts no doubt were brought out only to help outsiders understand who did what.

But as organizations and systems become more complex and as operations are dispersed all over the country and world, the boxes become buildings and the lines become communications systems. The organization charts become constrained by the ability to communicate. Military organizations and doctrines, in particular, historically have reflected the limitations of runners, messengers on horseback, line-of-sight signaling, and the physical separation of fleets and armies from headquarters. Though global voice and data communications are now ubiquitous and inexpensive, organizations have been slow in changing their structures to reflect the radical changes in available communications.

Clearly, in today's complex world, the capability of an organization for communications and coordination depends upon the design of its communications system. And the use of the system reflects the intended command and control of the organization.

As a result, the structures of the organization and its communications system are often much alike. Physical communications links interconnect organizational units just like the reporting lines on a line-staff organization chart. Computer memories and security provisions are partitioned to correspond with organizational authority and responsibility.

Communications system architects, therefore, need to know not only what the client's organization chart looks like, *but the rationale that created it as well.*

For example, a frequent communications design error is to provide, or offer to provide, extensive communications among all elements of a corporation. But as we saw at the start of this chapter, a common heuristic for the design of management structures is that of minimum communications between elements, that is, to provide maximum delegation to relatively autonomous units. The heuristic indicates that as organizations grow, they would fractionate into self-standing units, minimizing the number of mandatory interactions. Were this not to occur, and if all parts of the organization had to interact with all others—as the founders did in the early years—then the number of interactions and associated communications capabilities would increase roughly as the square of the number of people involved. The organization would face data overload. To avoid that overload, organizations fractionate through delegation, often moving off site in the process. The remote subordinate units, in becoming more autonomous, will develop internal support units (e.g., finance, accounting, security, sales), reducing the need for communications to what had been external corporate support. Thus, growing organizations do not necessarily require proportionately greater communications capability. In fact, they may actively resist it.

Minimal communications tend to keep some order in the directing of, and reporting by, an organization. A case in point: the military services obtain their communications support both from a defensewide communications system and from tactical networks of their own. The single most important function of that support is the command and control of the forces. A very strict, disciplined, organizational chain of command exists for force control. Few would have it otherwise. As one result, the chains of command of the different services are separate, with a few exceptions at a very high level (the Unified and Specified Commands).

The question for a defense communications architect, therefore, is should the service networks be physically independent? For years the answer was affirmative. Indeed, it was virtually mandated that direct communications should not even be possible between units that were not organizationally connected, even to the point that incompatible frequencies and protocols were used by the different services for essentially the same functions, for example, aircraft and air-to-ground communications.

Then during the early 1970s, it began to be realized that few modern operations were for a single service; virtually all operations since World War II required joint participation by two or more services in the same area at the same time. Under such conditions, separate communications meant that two combat units from different services could not communicate with each other directly, a serious problem in combat and one that was costing lives. Yet, having everyone talking with everyone else, having the chain of command bypassed, and having no record of who had talked to whom and when would be chaotic.

A better architectural solution probably would have been a physical network that permitted communications between all parties, but with procedures and access controls that prevented misuse of the channels. As Secretary of Defense Elliott Richardson put it at the time, "One should distinguish between use and abuse of a telecommunications system" and design accordingly. In practice, however, the services' value judgments continued to be that command and control imperatives outweighed communications possibilities and defense communications remained largely unchanged.

An example with a quite different outcome: universities and company research laboratories tend to be organized pyramidally, that is, horizontal communications are much more voluminous than vertical communications. The favored research networks are local-area networks (LANs) and the ARPANET, neither of which are hierarchical and parts of which are packet switched—a technique that makes monitoring and control quite difficult except at the end points. Not surprisingly, both networks were originated and designed by the research community to match its organizational structure—or lack thereof.

The lesson that communications system architectures should be matched to organizational ones rather than vice versa is not unique to communications. The reason is that organizational structures are made up of people and not things.

It was assumed in the United States some years ago in the architecting of buildings that a change in architecture, in time, would produce desired behavioral changes in the people that used those buildings. Better architectures—and the meaning of "better" was as defined by the clients and architects—would produce better human behavior. As the subsequent construction and use of multiple high-rise low-income housing demonstrated, behavioral changes did occur, but not in the directions anticipated. For example, crime increased dramatically. The lesson learned:

It is easier to match a system to the human one it supports than the reverse.

The reverse can produce unexpected and even contrary human behavior. The response of one system to changes in the other is complex. The interdependencies are difficult to model. In general, change is more likely to propagate from organization to support than in the other direction. By the same token, to affect a change in a support system will probably require a prior change—or an agreement to change—in the human one.

ORGANIZATIONAL DYNAMICS AND SYSTEMS ARCHITECTING

Architecting is a dynamic process. Ideas must be generated. Models and specifications must be created. Decisions must be made and agreements reached. And all in a timely manner and in the right order.

The difficulty is that this whole process must be accomplished through human organizations, which have their own characteristic time constants and channels—their own dynamics. And unless understood by the architect, these structural dynamics can lead to needless frustration, tactless complaints, and sharply reduced cooperation. Well understood, dynamics can be major assets, their constraints mitigated and even used to advantage.

For example, in a hierarchical organization, the amount of forwarded communications decreases in going through each level. If this did not occur, all levels would be swamped with unnecessary material. The decrease is perhaps a factor of 10 through each level. By no means does all information go every-where, a fact the architect needs to remember whether in architecting communi-cations links or trying to obtain the necessary human-value judgments to keep the architecting process on schedule.

There is a flip side to the need to keep information flow at a manageable level. The top level in a multilevel level organization will hear only a small frac-tion of what is happening at the lowest level, and the lowest level will hear only a correspondingly small fraction of what is going on at the top. (In a seven-level hierarchy, the reduction can be a factor of a million!) An oft heard *sociological* demand, therefore, is for "more and better communications" to offset this in-herent structural problem. The natural focus of complaints is middle manage-ment, the "gatekeepers" of information control, who in the seven-level company know only 0.1% of what is going on at either the top or bottom.

It is not easy to decide what information to pass along nor how to con-dense and reexpress what has been received. Computers may do this according to established rules, but not humans in human situations. This decision process, and its vagaries, is well demonstrated in the game of "pass along." A message is whispered from one game player to the next around a circle. By the time the message reaches the originator, it is deficient in critical details, unrecognizable to the point of hilarity, or far from the original intent.

In the real world, the results are more often tragic than humorous. Mili-tary orders are progressively reinterpreted through a chain of command, despite very high-quality, very responsive communications, command, and control sys-tems. A warning becomes an order to attack and destroy. A request for quick confirmation of orders becomes an occasion for agonizing reappraisal and fatal delay. In a world of recriminations for taking action, verbal direction is not executed pending written instructions and valuable time is lost. System dynam-ics slows to a crawl.

But it is unfair to berate the decision makers for what are failures in the structure. Decisions take time, sometimes far more than one would think. Con-sider the problem of obtaining the go-ahead for an idea requiring N approval signatures. Each level, with its different inputs and environment, has a different picture of the world. The decision must make sense in each world. Let's be op-timistic and say that the necessary time to consider a serious proposal takes on average only a half day. Then, assuming that the decisions are made that do not stop the proposal in its tracks,

The time in days, T, to obtain an approval requiring N signatures is approximately $T = 2^{N/2}$.

Thus, though each step takes only a half day, 12 signatures will require about three years. The equation can be derived empirically or by modeling the decision process as a series of proposals and "return to the drawing board" steps to accommodate new inputs from each signatory. Curiously, the equation is the same as for a random walk.

A closely related heuristic (Deitchman, 1971) is

The probability of implementing new ideas depends on the number of persons in the chain leading to their implementation and on the probability that each person understands and retransmits that idea.

For example, if each probability is independent and equal to p less than 1.0, then if there are N people in the chain, the probability of implementation is p^N, which becomes vanishingly small very quickly if the individual probabilities are only so-so. Others have speculated that if it takes more than 3 years to gain acceptance of an idea (or roughly 12 approvals), forget it.

The coordination process has been modeled by several authors (Brooks, 1982; Tausworthe, 1976) with a general result quite similar to that for systems in general, that is, calling for elements to be as independent of each other as possible and for minimizing the number of elements as far as possible (keep it simple). Tausworthe then comes up with a perhaps unexpected conclusion about the dynamics of coordination:

A team producing at the fastest rate humanly possible spends half its time coordinating and interfacing.

Both the Brooks and the Tausworthe models conclude that adding even one member to an optimum-size team *increases* the total time the project will take. Both models concerned software development, but would seem to be more broadly applicable.

The indicated delays and breakdowns in achieving approval can be avoided, but only by short-circuiting the approval chain, for example, by reaching simultaneous consensus of several signatories working together, or relegating some of the signatories to observer or lesser status. One rather draconian method of doing this is to call on Pareto's law as applied to organizational dynamics:

Pareto's law: 80% of the useful work in an organization is accomplished by 20% of the people.

Or, perhaps its questionable overextension:

Only 20% of the signatures really count.

But if the number of signatures or factors can be reduced by a factor of 5 using Pareto's law by concentrating on the most important 20%, then the costs on time and energy can be reduced by a factor of 32. The trick, of course, is to pick the right 20%. Leaving out one that is, or is perceived to be, critical can abort the whole process.

Yet there is a method behind this law. Sequential certifications, approvals, and signatures are only really useful if each brings to the process additional information, perspective, or insights. Those that do not or cannot should be eliminated, not excluding those at the top. I had the opportunity as the chief executive officer of the 4300-person seven-level Aerospace Corporation to edict that no approval document should require more than three signatures, mine included. Carrying out the edict, of course, meant extensive delegation and consideration of what each signature actually added (other than rank) to the process. The results were remarkable. The number of approval documents crossing my desk dropped from several a day to a few per month. The documents I did see clearly required the approval and perspective of the CEO and I studied them carefully as a consequence. No "stacks of papers to sign" each day. As as far as I could tell, the company worked better than ever before, the true signatories felt more responsible, and morale increased. The company wit was quick to point out that everyone knew all along the CEO was part of the 80%.

One of the more frustrating characteristics of decision systems is their inertia—the resistance to change—that characterizes any complex structure. But inertia is an unavoidable result of purposeful organizations. It minimizes the effects of sudden shocks and crisis-induced proposals. But it can impede progress. A useful key in dealing with it is to consider a physical analogy: a massive object cannot be moved instantaneously from one place to another and only with an infinite force can it be given an instantaneous increase in velocity. But even a small force produces acceleration (the second derivative of position with time). Applied consistently over enough time, the result can be dramatic changes in velocity, momentum, and, in due course, position. Thus:

When faced with resistance to positional change, remember that instantaneous changes are impossible, but anyone can work the second derivative.

Useful second-derivative forces are long-range plans, long-range budgets, changes in hiring practice, proposals requiring no up-front funding, time-phased reorganizations with little happening for some time, provisional agreements "in principle," confidence-building measures, free trials, ad hoc teams, and discussion groups. Most of these cost very little and require few approvals. Some even pass unnoticed at the time. But over time, the resultant changes can be dramatic. Constant acceleration, after all, produces change proportional to time squared.

Still another way of shortening decision times is to change the decision procedure. Changes in procedure to make progress, according to Congressman Les Aspin (circa 1976 at Stanford University), have a long and honorable legislative history. As he stated it, "It is very difficult for Congress to vote on matters of principle, but it can vote easily on changes in procedure. Progress is made by converting the former to the latter." Some examples of procedural action when substantive agreement is not possible:

- Agree to disagree and wait for events or new facts to change the picture
- Agree on a date by which a decision will be made, by arbitration if necessary
- Agree to escalate the decision to higher levels (with the corresponding risk of a decision no one will like)
- Agree in principle (authorization), but delay funding (appropriation) until next year
- Agree on issues of lesser substantive import as confidence-building measures toward further negotiations on major points of disagreement
- Establish a fact-finding committee with a deadline for response
- Expand the problem by bringing in other issues so that all parties, while not getting everything they wanted, get some of them

The substitution of procedural decisions for substantive ones, though brought to near-perfection by legislators, is just as valid a technique for architects struggling with the conflicting interests of clients, builders, users, government agencies, and the public.

It is also worth remembering that decision making is not without risk to the decision maker. An early management principle was that authority should go with responsibility. Its failing was that almost no individual involved with complex systems can control all the factors that make for success or failure. It is simply not possible to provide enough authority to guarantee that responsibilities can be met and success guaranteed within the resources provided. A spacecraft project manager has little control over the launch vehicle on which the project depends. The manager of a manufacturing division within a matrix, responsible for the quality of manufactured products, can never be given enough authority to demand product changes that cost more than the product can bear in the competitive market. Very few administrative organizations have sufficient resources to carry out, to everyone's satisfaction, the personnel and financial responsibilities assigned to them.

And the architect never has enough authority to guarantee success when so many other people make so many decisions affecting it. Yet if a system fails, the architect must bear part of the total responsibility along with everyone else. For the architect, it means not only understanding the personal risks, but also appreciating the pressures on other decision makers with whom the architect works.

The difference between responsibility and authority necessarily falls on the individual. There is nowhere else to put it. Thus,

Personal risk is proportional to the difference between responsibility and authority.

I leave it to management to work out how to compensate for that personal risk. I will add only one observation. From my experience, the greatest differences between responsibility and authority exist at the middle or project management level. At lower levels, neither are very great. At higher levels, there is an averaging over many projects.

SUMMARY

Organizations are systems, with specialized functions, form, dynamics, and behavior. None can be optimum to everyone, for all products, or for all functions.

The structures considered here were line-staff, pyramidal, matrix, and segmented-ring. The organizational types were bottom-line, bureaucratic, and cultural. Each structure and type is characterized by its own imperatives, management control, information-flow patterns, and technical systems to support it. It is essential that the systems architect understand these factors if a successful fit, balance, and compromise are to be achieved in system design, implementation, and operation.

RECOMMENDED READING

DEAL, TERRENCE E., and A. A. KENNEDY. (1982). *Corporate Cultures, The Rites and Rituals of Corporate Life.* Reading, MA: Addison-Wesley. This book shows the importance of corporate culture—business environment, values, heroes, rites, and rituals, and the cultural network—on the success of a company.

EPPEN, G. D., F. G. GOULD, and C. P. SCHMIDT. (1984). *Introductory Management Science,* 2nd Ed. Englewood Cliffs, NJ: Prentice Hall. See especially Chapters 1, 10, 15, 16, and 17; and Section 3.8. It introduces the reader to the concepts of mathematical models and heuristics to describe management decisions and actions.

LUTRIN, C. E. and A. K. SETTLE. (1980). *American Public Administration: Concepts & Cases,* 2nd Ed. Mountain View, CA: Mayfield. This is an introductory text on the origins, purposes, strengths, weaknesses, and characteristics of bureaucracies (in the structural rather than the pejorative sense). See especially Chapters 1 to 4, and 9.

PFIFFNER, JOHN M. and F. P. SHERWOOD. (1960). *Administrative Organization.* Englewood Cliffs, NJ: Prentice Hall. See especially Chapter Two, "Complexity of Organization: The Concept of Overlays." It shows how overlays of an organization chart can show other modes of interaction—sociometric, functional, decisional, and power centers.

RAYMOND, ARTHUR. (1951). *The Well Tempered Aircraft.* Royal Aeronautical Society, London.

RECHTIN, E. (March 1975). "Equations for Managers." *IEEE Spectrum* **12,** 3, 58–61. This is the source of a number of management heuristics in this text.

ROWE, ALAN J. (1988). *The Meta Logic of Cognitively Based Heuristics.* Los Angeles: University of Southern California School of Business Administration.

TAUSWORTHE, R. C. (1976). *"Simple Intuitive Models of Programming,"* Deep Space Network Progress Report 42-33, Jet Propulsion Laboratory, Pasadena, CA. This report derives the "maximum team production rate" law and the resultant partitioning principle. It generates models of productivity, documentation quality, and programming reliability, and shows their sensitivities to various parameters.

TO BROWSE, DEPENDING ON INTEREST

DEITCHMAN, S. J. (July–August 1971). "Implementation of New Ideas in Bureaucracies." *Operations Research,* letters to the Editor, **19,** 4, 989–90.

ROWE, ALAN J., R. O. MASON, and K. E. DICKEL. (1985). *Strategic Management & Business Policy, A Methodological Approach,* 2nd Ed. Reading, MA: Addison-Wesley. See especially Chapters 10 to 12. This is a text designed to enhance the reader's skill at strategic thinking, oriented toward business management.

14

PROFILE OF A
SYSTEMS ARCHITECT

The chapters to follow are written particularly for managers contemplating the establishment of systems architecting as an essential function of their organization. Effective systems architecting requires: (1) a management decision that the function is needed, (2) systems architects, and (3) an organizational structure within which the architects can function. The three conditions are closely coupled. None, including the first, is sensible without the others. Before making the decision of need, managers will first want to know what kind of people are these architects? Will they fit in? And where? How do I recognize a good architect when I see one? Do I have to search outside the organization or do I have people within it who can do the job?

Given reasonable answers to these questions, a practical approach to setting up architecting is to find one or more architects who can define the function in some detail; determine what is needed to do the function well; and *then* decide whether a commitment to architecting can and should be made.

THE BEHAVIORAL PROFILE

We saw in the previous chapter that architecting and managing have many things in common. So it is no surprise that good architects have many of the same behavioral characteristics as managers, although the mix may be different. Both must have three essential skills: human, technical, and conceptual. Managers, in general, are strongest in the first two, that is, they understand how to work with people and things to get a job done. Architects, in general, are strongest in the last two, that is, they have a good technical background and come up with workable ideas.

It is possible to be a very good manager with weak conceptual skills by knowing how to get ideas from others, although *top* managers more often than not are outstanding corporate strategists and conceptualists. It is occasionally possible to be a very good architect with limited human skills—there are some notorious examples—providing that the architect is well respected and is teamed with a good manager who can supply what the architect lacks.

But the absolutely essential attribute of the architect must be the ability to conceptualize, because that is the essence of architecting. It is even possible to have a weak technical background, as did Arthur Raymond of the DC-3, whose Harvard degree was in the humanities, as long as the overall system view comes naturally. A humanities degree encourages that perspective.

Behavioral scientists have long been challenged by the question of creativity. Is it teachable or is it present at birth? No doubt, like any talent, it is some of both. But how is it evidenced in architects and designers? Professor Mark Chignell of the University of Southern California in a recent interview with Jonathan Losk (1990) described what he found by questioning the practitioners in the field. From his observations, the personality traits of successful, creative systems architects are

1. Communication skills
2. A high tolerance for ambiguity
3. The ability to make good associations of ideas
4. The ability to work consistently at an abstract level
5. A level of technical expertise (level not specified)
6. A tempered ego; the opposite of arrogance
7. Leadership; gets the most out of others
8. The willingness to backtrack, to seek multiple solutions
9. The ability to build teams
10. Charisma
11. The ability to read people well
12. Self-discipline, self-confidence, a locus of control
13. A purpose orientation
14. A sense of faith or vision
15. Drive, a strong will to succeed
16. Curiosity, a generalist's perspective

If all those traits were found full strength in a single person, that would make the architect an astonishing individual indeed! They would equally well make for an astonishing manager. The supply is certainly limited.

Fortunately, the number of systems architects that are needed, even in a major company are few—at most, a handful per project. Indeed, many architects believe that the greatest architectures are the product of a single mind (Brooks, 1982) [Spinrad, 1989] or at least of a very small team.

THE FUNCTIONAL PROFILE

Focusing Chignell's behavioral list to a few essentials calls for a human-oriented perspective of the functions that systems architecting performs. As Spinrad sees it, architecting is

1. Top-level design—functional, physical, and operational, the partitioning of which can be very important (the "what")
2. Creative, *obsessive,* juggling of requirements, constraints, technology, costs, and standards (the "how") and
3. Creating enduring growth and change (the "why")

It is a world in which desirable functions conflict with each other. Standards conflict with sustainable commercial advantage. "Good" may be determined by a customer group undeterminable beforehand. Not only are there many variables, there are no simple trade-offs.

In this world, Spinrad continues, "a lot of right brain 'reasoning' goes on—a kind of gestalt process. Critical choices are often a matter of 'architectural taste.'"

From this description, being a creative architect in such an environment requires a strong combination, but not necessarily all in equal measure, of the following (from the Chignell list):

2. A high tolerance for ambiguity
4. The ability to work consistently at an abstract level
8. The willingness to backtrack, to seek multiple solutions
12. Self-discipline, self-confidence, a locus of control
13. A purpose orientation
14. A sense of faith or vision
15. Drive, a strong will to succeed
16. Curiosity, a generalist's perspective

Next only to creativity, the essential need in systems architecting is to maintain the integrity of the system from conception through operation. The long ride down the waterfall creates many opportunities for the system to diverge from the original purposes, functions, and form. The chief architect, more than anyone else, must maintain and strengthen that integrity, must intervene when it is threatened, must retain its options "to the last agonizing minute" (Spinrad, 1989), and must imbue the rest of the project with the values that were built into the client's judgments.

Maintaining system integrity demands a combination of

1. Communication skills
9. The ability to build teams
10. Charisma

of which the last two are largely dependent on the first. Important within communication skills are language, ideational fluency, critical-mindedness, and an ability to talk things out (Losk, 1990). Losk (1989) suggests a heuristic for the architect—one certainly evident in the best of them:

Don't ever stop talking about the system.

Architects, being obsessed with their system, as Spinrad notes, indeed never stop talking about it. As we will see in the next chapter, it is an important element of their continuing creativity—a form of peer review. There may be such people as reclusive architects, but their value in maintaining system integrity will be small indeed.

There is another reason for the architect's talkativeness: the difficulties of natural language—its imprecision and the ease of misunderstandings—leading to another Losk (1989) heuristic:

There's no such thing as immaculate communication!

The architect must, therefore, describe and redescribe the system to a long stream of people of many different perspectives and persuasions, just to keep the system on track.

So, for the manager looking for good architects, the first impressions on meeting one are likely to be of someone with a broad, systemwide point of view and a skill at communicating ideas. It should not take much to get a discussion going—if not a full scale lecture!— on past projects and lessons learned.

THE DEVELOPMENT OF A SYSTEMS ARCHITECT

Architectural creativity, like artistry, is a talent. Like natural language ability, it is a potential skill of the human brain. But only with development will it become evident and flourish. Only with education will there be understanding. And only with training will there be the skills needed to create fine works. All of these take time.

As with other professions, it takes about 10 years after graduation from college to acquire the knowledge and judgment necessary to head an architectural team. And those 10 years need to be well spent.

Consequently, few organizations can undertake the architecting of major complex systems from scratch any more than they can become an instant systems engineering house. The function must be developed and supported, with the usual first step being the recruiting of established professionals as a nucleus.

But product architects also are a major determinant through their products of the organization's purpose, image, and reputation. So, both to be effective as architects and to work in the best interests of the company, they must know the company well and be loyal to it. These two needs, technical ability and knowledge of the company, suggest that potential members of architectural teams be sought among the more entrepreneurial members of the technical staff who have had a few years experience in project or functional groups [Pieronek 1990].

Hundreds of years of experience in many kinds of organizations indicate that the most reliable method of development of architects is through mentoring and progressive increases in responsibility. The most difficult part of this process is to encourage creativity rather than stifling it. An overbearing chief architect can squelch junior architects all too easily by running a "pronouncement theory" shop. "Do it this way, because I say it is right." Risky as it may be, the junior architect must be allowed to learn by mistakes—correctable ones, one would hope. The tensions between competing requirements, the unboundedness of systems, the limits of heuristics, and the jolts of reality must be *felt,* not passively observed. Figure 7-1 only partially describes the pressures, tensions, and implied judgments of architecting.

The commitment to systems architecting, even more than to engineering as a whole, is long-term—decades. The development of the architectural team takes time. Projects take years *and the architect must stay with the project,* certainly through system certification and acceptance. And one would hope that each chief architect would carry out more than one project for the company during a long career.

THE ORGANIZATIONAL POSITION OF THE ARCHITECT

Architecting is context-dependent, which means that what it creates depends on the environment within which it operates. System context, technological possibilities, client needs, and organizational commitment all play a part. Consequently, there is no single best location for architects in all organizations or for all system products. Architecting can be accomplished as part of systems engineering, as an activity of a specialized internal group, or by contract to an architectural firm.

It is clear enough, however, that the architects must be at a level where they can see systems as a whole—although what is a system to one part of the organization, may be a subsystem or supersystem to another. It is also clear that the architects must work directly with decision makers who can make effective value judgments, or the architecting process will stall out. Although architecting can be viewed as a staff function in that it does not make value judgments, it is in large part responsible for technical decisions and must have the direct or delegated authority to make or recommend them.

Some architects can be located almost anywhere—the sheer force of their personality and ideas will make them effective—but not junior architects under development, nor architects located too far from a base of support.

Some chief architects may also be project managers and thus easily located on an organization chart. Their small architectural team can be built from within the project or by bringing together specialists from throughout the company.

Or architecting can be done within a systems development group. The special need here is to recognize and alleviate the historical tensions between systems architects and systems engineers. Management needs to make sure that the essentiality of and the distinctions between them are understood by all. The systems architect is not, and should not be perceived as, a super systems engineer. If some systems engineers show the particular talent and interest needed to be systems architects, well and good, but an architect is not a promoted engineer. Conversely, an architect is not a "general engineer," modestly good at many things, but expert in none. It is a considerable simplification to say that architects are primarily concerned with function (why) and engineers with form (what), that architects propose alternates and engineers dispose of them, that architects tend to stand to one side and engineers tend to mix it up in a project, and that architects are right-brained and engineers left-brained—but there is a lot of truth in these distinctions.

Provided the position reflects these realities, it can and should be wherever management believes it can be most effective in conceptual design, in maintaining system integrity, and in system verification.

RECOMMENDED READING

CHIGNELL, MARK H. (1990). Interview by Jonathan Losk. (Losk, 1990.)

LOSK, JONATHAN. (1989). *A Profile of the System Architect.* Unpublished graduate report, University of Southern California, Los Angeles.

PIERONEK, T. (1990). *A Personal Essay, the Search for Future Architects.* Unpublished graduate report, University of Southern California, Los Angeles.

SPINRAD, ROBERT. (1989). *Systems Architecting.* Unpublished lecture at the University of Southern California, Los Angeles.

15

ASSESSING ARCHITECTING AND ARCHITECTURES

When choices must be made with unavoidably inadequate information, choose the best available and then watch to see whether future solutions appear faster than future problems. If so, the choice was at least adequate. If not, go back and choose again.—From Chapter 2

To be successfully managed, architecting like any other function needs to be assessed from time to time. The critical times for architecting are during the conceptual design phase and at certification, with progress reports on system integrity throughout the build phase.

THE CONCEPTUAL PHASE

The first indication of whether the architecting process is going well or not is the degree of trust and confidence observed between client and architect. For good architecting to take place, both must respect the roles of the other—the architect for the value judgments of the client and the client for the technical judgments of the architect.

Each must be willing and able to answer the questions of the other. The architect must determine the real underlying purposes of the client, purposes the client may not be able to articulate clearly in the beginning. The client must be given some appreciation of the performance, cost, and schedule of conceivable alternatives, the feasibility of which may be uncertain in the architect's mind. The ideas of both parties are necessarily provisional almost to the end of the conceptual design phase.

Therefore, unless the client and the architect can work closely and well together, it is best to get another architect, the sooner the better.

The next indication of progress is anything but rational. It is a feeling of satisfaction by client and architect together, expressible in many ways:

"This project feels good."

"Solutions are coming along faster than problems."

"Things are coming together nicely."

"Our ideas stood up very well to challenge today. There was no trouble at all in explaining the concept. We got a lot of good suggestions and came up with still more good ideas ourselves in the process."

A special form of challenge arises when specialists are added to the team to help resolve technical issues. The management equivalent of a system is a team; both are expected to produce more than the sum of their parts. The architectural team in particular reflects the system it is modeling. Team spirit is a measure of system cohesiveness. Therefore, do the specialists join up or just do their jobs? Is there technical synergism essential for a true system or is there technical provincialism by the specialists? Do the team members instinctively work together because the conceptual model encourages it or do they "work on assignment" or just carry out "work packages?" If the last, then charismatic chief architect or not, the conceptual model may not be a strong system design.

The next indicator is convergence. When architecting first begins, the number of conceivable alternates is often large, partly as a result of ill-structured purposes. By clarifying purposes, using heuristics, and imposing constraints (e.g., sociopolitical, client preferences, probable builders' skills), the number is reduced to a handful. Further reduction requires much more difficult priority and trade-off decisions.

Example:

The architect and the client cannot agree on the number of engines needed for an aircraft.

Example:

The architect and the sales staff (a surrogate for the customer) cannot agree on backward compatibility of a software package.

Example:

Two military services need to acquire air-to-air communications for their fighter squadrons. Each has a valid conceptual model, but the models' coding schemes differ. Each rejects the other's "for operational reasons."

At this point, the architecting stalls out, a new alternate is conceived, or new factors are brought in (e.g., flight demonstrations, software conversion packages, or a new mutually compatible coding scheme, respectively, in the previous examples). In the latter two cases, there can be a convergence to a solution. In the first case, the project may experience a series of abrupt decision reversals.

As one architect put it, "Convergence begins when there are no more 180s."

Another indicator of architecting progress is the status of cost modeling, a parallel activity with its own peculiarities. Client and architect, of course, are interested in cost and not just performance and schedule. But cost modeling is a discipline unto itself and both client and architect need to appreciate that fact. If system purposes and model configurations are at the ill-structured stage, then detailed cost estimations are worse than useless; they are actively misleading. Nonetheless, clients need to know whether projected costs will be "in the ball-park." An architect that offers an early cost estimate within a factor of less than 3 to 10 is either foolish or inexperienced or both.

Example:

In initial thinking about spacecraft, about the best that can be said is whether it might be in the $10M, $100M, $1B, or $10B class. But to claim that it will be $37.5M is deceptive. Or to choose between two designs on the basis of a 25% cost difference is a mistake.

Example:

In initial thinking about personal computer families, pick the classes of interest ($100, $1000, $10,000) first, avoiding niches that are traps. Then calculate technical risk. Until then, detailed cost models mean very little.

But as design proceeds, cost modeling can become more meaningful. Unfortunately, it is in the nature of the profession that all estimates are given to at least four significant figures. It would be better if the final bottom line for a near-finished conceptual model were no more precise than two significant figures, with a separate estimate of cost uncertainty. Even then, there will be items in the cost model for which there is not yet enough information to make an estimate and/or for which historical precedent does not exist. The estimates for these items are therefore "to be determined" (TBD). A useful indication of architecting progress thus can be

A measure of the status of a conceptual model is the number of TBDs remaining in its cost model. (Wheaton, 1989)

And, finally, as the conceptual model nears completion and the time comes to talk to potential implementers or to issue draft requests for proposals, a modified ulcer heuristic gives yet another indicator:

Conceptual design is nearing completion when prospective implementers of the system feel only moderately ill about accepting the performance estimates as acceptance requirements for the system they will be constructing. (Maier, 1988)

THE CERTIFICATION PHASE

From contract award to the builder to acceptance by the client, the primary responsibilities of the architect are to maintain system integrity, advise on responses to deviations therefrom, and to assure that acceptance criteria are met. The client and manager can expect continuing status reports on system implementation from the architect, particularly on discrepancies traceable to the conceptual design and on potential troubles ahead.

Most system designs will require modifications during implementation for a variety of practical reasons, some foreseen and some not. If the architecting has been well done, system options will exist in the design that can be used to resolve or eliminate the problems. The system design will be resilient to needed modifications.

Choosing the *best* modification or option, however, involves considerations of cause, cost, schedule, performance, system consequences, contract changes, and liability, among others. For the client to make the choice may require that the architect become deeply involved in design and process details. From the manager's viewpoint, an essentiality is the assurance that the architect has free access to all pertinent information, that is, an enabling clause in all outside contracts and an internal understanding of full cooperation with the architect. In practice, this access usually works to the benefit of all concerned. Denial of it by any unit or contractor is cause for concern by management. The one serious exception is the legitimate proprietary rights of a supplier.

Proprietary rights, particularly if they involve materials or processes, can be a serious obstacle to system quality and reliability. Particularly worrisome are unreported process changes made for what to the supplier seem good and sufficient reasons. But disclosing the changes means disclosing the material composition or process itself and that disclosure will be denied. Such changes are time bombs in the system, likely to go off unexpectedly and to be difficult to trace.

A more common denial of information is that from a subordinate unit that wants to solve its own problems, a situation typical of systems with virtually autonomous elements. In this case, **minimum communications** works against free access by the chief architect. Resolving the conflict of interests is up to management, not the architect. An unhappy architect, frustrated by lack of information, should be of serious concern to the manager. It indicates that system integrity can be at risk.

NOTABLY SUCCESSFUL SYSTEMS

One of the easiest ways of assessing ongoing architecting is to compare the system under development with the architectural successes and failures of the past. This section, therefore, begins with representative lists of widely acclaimed systems in which excellent architecting and design were major contributors to success. The selection criteria were as follows:

- An operational mission was accomplished exceptionally well, in a timely, reliable, and high-quality manner, and did so for many years.
- The justifications and objectives for the mission were clear.
- For the stated mission, the systems were life-cycle cost-effective.
- The systems were major, complex products in their own fields at the times of their conception and operation.
- A major quantative advance in systems architecture was accomplished.
- New technologies were incorporated, often for the first time.
- Unique trade-offs were made, producing new systemwide capabilities.

Usually, but not always, there were clearly identifiable architectural (or design) teams, although some were informal and ad hoc. Not all the systems met all the criteria to the same degree, but each has been widely acclaimed both within and outside its own mission area. Most were blessed with strong advocates and skilled administrators.

Aerospace Vehicle Architectures

Douglas Commercial Series (DC-3 et seq.)
Boeing Aircraft 707 Series
Lockheed U-2 reconnaissance aircraft
Lockheed SR-71 reconnaissance aircraft
McDonnell Douglas F-4 fighter aircraft series
General Dynamics F-16 fighter aircraft
Grumman F-14 carrier aircraft
McDonnell Douglas F-15 fighter aircraft
Lockheed Georgia C-130 cargo aircraft
McCready Gossamer man-powered aircraft series
Nutan ultralight home-built aircraft and the circumglobal Voyager
Minuteman ballistic missile series
China Lake Sidewinder air-to-air missile
Lockheed Polaris–Poseidon–Trident submarine-launched missiles
Martin Marietta Titan space launch-vehicle series
McDonnell Douglas Delta space launch-vehicle series
Von Braun/Chrysler Saturn space launch vehicles
Soviet Proton and Energia space launch vehicles

Spacecraft Architectures

Hughes Aircraft INTELSAT and commercial communication satellites
Langley/Boeing Lunar Orbiter spacecraft
JPL/Hughes Aircraft Surveyor lunar lander spacecraft
Ford Aerospace NATO and INTELSAT communication satellites
TRW FleetSatCom UHF tactical communications satellites
JPL Mariner interplanetary flyby spacecraft series
JPL Voyager Jupiter/Saturn/Uranus/Neptune flyby spacecraft
JSC/Grumman Apollo Lunar Excursion Module
NASA Infrared Astronomical Satellite (IRAS)
Soviet Venera (Venus landers and orbiters) spacecraft
Hughes Aircraft Company Venus Orbiter
Navy/Johns Hopkins Laboratory Transit position location satellites
NASA Skylab space station
Soviet space station series
Soviet Venera spacecraft

Information Systems Architectures

Bell Telephone System
INTELSAT global communications network
Xerox ETHERNET local area network
NASA/JPL Deep Space Network
Apple Macintosh personal computer series
Digital Equipment Corporation (DEC) VAX minicomputer series
IBM 360 mainframe computer series
Cray Supercomputer
Point of sale transaction systems
Automated teller banking systems
International financial transaction systems
TRW credit-rating system
Spreadsheet business management systems
FORTRAN software language
LISP artificial-intelligence software language
AT&T UNIX software language
Defense Advanced Projects Agency ARPANET

Industrial Systems Architectures

Original Ford Motor Company mass-production system
Modern computerized inventory systems
Electronic chip manufacturing foundries
MOSIS tailored chip brokerage system

Some systems have been omitted that demonstrably were successful in many ways. Others might well put them on their top lists. The Defense Satellite Communications System (DSCS) series has provided excellent, secure, but not inexpensive, satellite communications for the Department of Defense. Weather satellites, typically deficient in funding and lacking instruments to measure wind velocities, have been good cloud descriptors but poor weather predictors. LANDSAT, the remote resource-sensing satellite, is a technical success but an economic orphan.

The Space Transportation System (Shuttle) has been an astounding engineering success, but its stated objectives, justifications, and consequent system operational decisions were flawed, leading in the past to a marginal assessment. Reconstituted under more realistic objectives, its future is increasingly brighter; statistically, it now has one of the best flight records in launch-vehicle history. Classified systems, although acknowledged by all U.S. Presidents as extraordinarily successful, are not available for unclassified study. And, of course, new systems are coming on line all the time. The full GPS constellation, MILSTAR, the B-1, and B-2 bombers are examples.

When these examples were first presented to a group of practicing systems engineers, two important insights came to the fore. The first, understandably, was the definition of success. Publicly perceived success seemed to be measured against what had happened before, rather than on an absolute basis. If little had existed before, then an order of magnitude improvement was a dramatic success, even though that improvement in absolute magnitude was much less than what came after. Hence:

There's nothing like being the first success.

The second insight was that in a surprising number of cases, the first systems in a series were unsuccessful and/or when success did come, it came for reasons not originally stated. This was certainly true for the DC-1, which was seriously underpowered. The first NASA/JPL planetary spacecraft, the Lunar Ranger series, was plagued with launch and electronic failures; nonetheless, it demonstrated almost all the critical architectural features of the later and uniformly successful NASA/JPL Mariners, Vikings, and Voyagers. The LISA percursor to the Macintosh; the initial closed-architecture Macintosh; the underranged Polaris 1; the Ford Motor Company assembly line, which lacked a distribution system to make it practical; and the early Deep Space Network, which used off-optimum transmit and receive frequencies, are other examples.

But what seemed to make these early inadequacies into subsequent successes was a basically sound architecture that with the minimum number of sometimes fortuitous modifications, produced remarkable results. So, remember:

> **If at first you do not succeed, but the architecture is sound, try, try again. Success sometimes is where you find it.**

One of the best standards against which managers can measure well designed programs still remains Art Raymond's (1951) short list of critical ingredients:

1. Proper environment: Conducive work environment, funding, and customer relations
2. Good initial choice: What is needed versus what is possible
3. Excellence of detailed design
4. Thorough development and debugging
5. Follow through with assistance of operating personnel
6. Thorough exploitation
7. Correct succession: Properly timed introduction of the new model
8. Adaptiveness: Ability to cope with the unexpected

SOME PAINFUL SYSTEM ARCHITECTURAL FLAWS

The previous section provided goals. This one provides alerts of serious system trouble ahead. The most serious architectural flaws are those created during conceptual design and caused by lack of sufficient contact between client and architect. They are serious because so many subsequent design decisions flow from them.

- Ill-defined purposes with consequently poor resource allocations
- Inherently conflicting, but unresolved, priorities
- Poor definition of success
- Designed for a nonexistent market
- Incomplete consideration of social, political, and/or economic factors
- Too little consideration of opponent's response

Recovery from one of these flaws is sometimes possible. Recovery from two or more can be tantamount to starting over.

Next are conceptual flaws traceable to what seemed reasonable assumptions at the time. For example, they represented a consensus of top experts. The underlying cause of the resultant flaw, however, was a failure to recognize when a consensus was based on very little historical information and, therefore, should be hedged, that is, by technology risk reduction, by concurrent development of a backup element, or by provision of options or fallback positions. Examples:

- Overspecification of a critical subsystem, usually due to an overoptimistic assumption of technological readiness
- Systems overtaken by events and unable to adjust
- Systems technically or socially ahead of their time

Finally, there are flaws arising from incomplete or misunderstood acceptance criteria. They can produce serious conflict between the architect and the builder. Only the client can resolve the conflict, generally by adding resources or accepting lesser performance than anticipated. Two examples:

- Inadequate quality for the needs of the system
- Inadequate test data during development, acceptance, and deployment

Fortunately, the number of permanently flawed systems is much smaller than the number of subsequently successful ones. Then, as well, most of the fatally flawed systems were aborted before full-scale production or so seriously modified as to be unrecognizable. Although they could be listed, I choose not to because it is not usually apparent what clear and unambiguous lessons they teach. Most have multiple flaws in addition to architectural ones—management error, unstable funding, multiple or changing sponsors, nonrational sociopolitical factors, and the like—and disentangling them is seldom worth the effort. Between the two heuristics, **recovery from two unlikely** and **triage,** it is better to let them die in peace and work instead on systems that can be saved.

RECOMMENDED READING

BATES, JEFFERSON D. (1973). *Apollo 16.* City: NASA John F. Kennedy Space Center. This is a brief history of manned space flight followed by description of Apollo 16, the last, largest, and most complex of the Apollo missions.

BELLO, MARK. (1988). "A Comprehensive Approach to Space Shuttle Safety." *National Academy of Engineering News Report* **38,** 3, 6—9. This is a short summary of the National Research Council's report on the "Post-Challenger Evaluation of Space Shuttle Risk Assessment and Management."

BRODSKY, R. F. (ed.). (1979). *The Mission and Design of the Pioneer Venus Spacecraft System,* AIAA Professional Study Series. New York: American Institute of Aeronautics and Astronautics.

BURKE, J. D. (1980). *A Gossamer Condor and Albatross: A Case Study in Aircraft Design,* AIAA Professional Study Series. Pasadena, CA: AeroVironment Inc.

DROSTE, CARL S., and J. E. WALKER. (1980). *The General Dynamics Case Study on the F-16 Fly-by-Wire Flight Control System,* AIAA Professional Study Series. New York: American Institute of Aeronautics and Astronautics.

FUHRMAN, R. A. (September/October 1978). "The Fleet Ballistic Missile System: Polaris to Trident." *AIAA Journal of Spacecraft and Rockets* 15, 5, 265–86.

GUTERL, FRED. (November 1988). "Compact Disc." *IEEE Spectrum* 25, 11, 102–108. A remarkable combination of technology and architecture creates a new complex system in consumer electronics and data storage.

HALL, R. CARGILL. (1977). *Lunar Impact, A History of Project Ranger,* NASA History Series. Washington, DC: National Aeronautics and Space Administration.

HALL, R. CARGILL. (September-October 1980). "To Acquire Strategic Bombers, the Case of the B-58 Hustler." *Air University Review,* XXXI, 6, 3–20. "It was the only strategic bomber ever rejected by the organization it would serve."

HANLEY, ARTHUR. (April 1988). "X-Wing Faces a Tough Comeback." *Aerospace America,* 26, 4, 8–9. It describes system-level problems causing unacceptable cost growth.

IEEE. (October 1976). "A Special Issue: What Went Wrong?" *IEEE Spectrum,* 64, 10. This is a set of short histories on automated mail delivery, 3-D radar, pacemakers, NASA commercial satellites, electric power-grid blackouts, radio telescopes, and other electronic systems that failed to live up to promise.

LOVELACE, ALAN M. (Fall 1979). "Apollo and Shuttle—A Perspective." *The Bridge,* 9, 3, 20–22. A comparison by the then Deputy Administrator of NASA, pointing out, well before the first launch, that the Space Shuttle differed from the lunar program in that it lacked precisely the qualities most prominently associated with Apollo and its success.

MAIER, MARK W. (1988). *A Comparison of Four Theories of Architectural Design,* and *An Extension of Concepts and Heuristics in Modeling.* Unpublished graduate reports, University of Southern California, Los Angeles.

PICKERING, W. H. (1967). *Mariner–Mars 1964 Final Project Report.* Washington, DC: NASA Scientific and Technical Information Division. This is a report on the engineering and scientific aspects of the most complex of the Mariner flyby series.

RAYMOND, ARTHUR. (1951). *The Well Tempered Aircraft.* London: The Royal Aeronautical Society.

RENZETTI, N. A. (1987). *Goldstone Solar System Radar.* Pasadena, CA. Jet Propulsion Laboratory. This describes the architecture of a solar system radar.

RENZETTI, N. A., and A. L. BERMAN. (1981). *The Deep Space Network—An Instrument for Radio Science Research,* Pasadena, CA. Publication 80–93. Jet Propulsion Laboratory.

STIX, G. (November 1988). "1969 Moon Lander." *IEEE Spectrum* 25, 11, 76–82.

STEINER, J. E. (1978). *Case Study in Aircraft Design, the Boeing 727,* AIAA Professional Study Series. New York: American Institute of Aeronautics and Astronautics.

WHEATON, MARILEE. (May 1980). *Heuristics for Software Development and Cost Analysis.* El Segundo, CA: The Aerospace Corporation. Unpublished graduate report.

16

LOOKING TO THE FUTURE

UPCOMING COMPLEX SYSTEMS

The long historical trend toward increasingly complex systems is accelerating, driven by worldwide communications, surveillance, air transportation, and finance. What were once local markets became national ones, then regional ones, and now global ones. National boundaries to research, engineering, development, manufacturing, distribution, and servicing have all but disappeared; attempted protectionist measures instead usually have led to higher costs and measurable economic decline.

Transnational companies, those with no single country headquarters, are replacing international ones, complicating the influence of national governments on international and domestic commerce and on national security. The international sale of advanced defense systems, coupled with increasing political volatility of the customer nations, makes national security system planning and system acquisition much more complex.

In short, what had appeared as controllable boundaries have become permeable. Bounded socioeconomic systems have become complex megasystems. And as they expanded, so did the systems they required and built.

Technology, as it has many times before, is both enabling and ameliorating the increase in system complexity. The first essential, if more capable and complex systems are to work at all, is for increased reliability of the consituent elements. The necessary reliability has been largely provided by the development of microchips, tailored materials, error-correcting codes, advanced automotive and aircraft engines, and ultraquality techniques. The design and development of these elements, in turn, have been supported by better and better computer models.

Within the last decade or so, complex systems have been faced with another limitation, their command and control. Human operation of aerospace vehicles, air traffic control, communications networks, and even finance is simply too slow and error-prone for high-speed real-time control. It is now constrained to giving general directions. As a result, machine intelligence is increasingly being brought into play to link man with high-speed machines.

The systems showing the greatest rate of increase in capability, complexity, reliability, and intelligence are those in aerospace vehicles, spacecraft, space habitations, communications networks, information systems, and industrial and civil systems. A sampling of the complex systems entering or in concept development in these fields shows how much work lies ahead.

Aerospace Vehicles

Shuttle C	Advanced Launch System
Hypersonic Transport Plane	Cislunar transfer vehicle
Aerospace Plane	Low observable close air support

Spacecraft and Habitations

Space Station Freedom Block I	Space Station Freedom Block II
Lunar surface base	Mars orbital/surface base
Planetary exploration series	Undersea habitations
Strategic Defense Weapon System	

Communications and Information Systems

Global C^3I system

Megacomsats or equivalent cluster constellations

Integrated defense communications system

Strategic defense command and control system

National research and education communications network

Computer-aided software engineering and certification

Circumplanetary Communication/Navigation Infrastructures

Desktop publishing networks

Advanced public television

Image motion-detection radars and infrared sensors

Associated data bases

Industrial and Civil Systems

National civil infrastructure

Controlled-access highway networks

Flexible ultraquality manufacturing systems

Ultraquality nuclear-power networks

Space manufacturing

Intelligent global electric-power transfer networks

Electrical automobile complexes

Global research, engineering, manufacturing, distribution, and servicing complexes

DIRECTIONS FOR RESEARCH IN ARCHITECTING

By far the greatest amount of research in complex systems is done in support of system development, for example, that in materials, processes, communications, aerodynamics, computer engineering, and the basic sciences. The focus of this section is on a much more limited area, research in support of the architecting process itself.

Research on the normative approach to systems architecting is limited by the nature of the process. Values are decreed, which means that normative research is directed more toward history and commentary than toward the development of general architectural principles. Two areas of particular interest to modern systems architects are the history of technology and studies in reverse architecting. Both help develop the architect's sense of time and timing.

Research on the rational approach, particularly that pushing the boundaries outward from that of tightly structured problems into the ill-structured ones, should be particularly valuable. Rational processes, in general, are easily taught, understood, and exploited as extensions of system analysis and design. The concept of General Systems Problem Solvers (GSPS)—of treating systems as structures more or less independent of context—remains attractive in principle. Mathematical abstractions, from algebra and Boolean logic to predicate calculus, can be powerful languages for organizing creative thought. The revolution in communications created by one generalized equation, Claude Shannon's on channel capacity, is a case in point.

Research in the heuristic approach has generally been anecdotal, based on recollections of architects who often are unaware of how they conceive and create what they do. If they are aware, they may or may not be able to articulate their insights in succinct and memorable statements. Further, few systems architects have had the opportunity in their careers to work on, much less be the chief architect for, many major systems. The profile of the systems architect needs to be refined by careful behavioral science techniques based on more than a handful of interviews. The heuristics themselves need to be certified and organized, perhaps in several different ways. As indicated in Appendix A, what may be needed is an associative thesaurus that indicates which heuristics are near other heuristics and in which direction. Given pointers, the architect could more easily handle the interrelated system problems to which the heuristics apply. Michael Asato has successfully applied that idea to spacecraft design, generating a set of computer HYPERCARD™ diskettes for the purpose. In principle, both architecting and HYPERCARDing should work well together; both are inherently associative, a-logical, and "right-brained."

Research can also be productive in the challenges given in Part Two: ultraquality, purposeful opposition, a sense of time and timing, biological architectures and intelligent behavior, and economics and public policy. Each is at a frontier of systems architecting.

Research in machine intelligence, from biology to electronic simulations, opens up whole new possibilities for architecting. At the present, artificial intelligence seems overfocused on similarities with existing digital, von Neumann computers, and logical thought processes to the exclusion of associative, nonrational ones. But that is changing.

Computer modeling is potentially a far more potent architecting tool than it already is. The architect's problem is that very few "transfer models"—those that bridge between disciplines and/or processes—exist. With perhaps a few exceptions, attempts at computer-integrated manufacturing (CIM) have not been successful. They are plagued with problems of configuration control, updating, and certification. Industry is learning the importance of expeditious transfer from research to engineering to manufacturing—also of vital interest to systems architecting in maintaining system integrity in the process—but there are few transfer models or computer programs available to assist the process.

Along these lines, Benjamin W. Wah has suggested that the major difficulty in computers for symbolic processing lies in integrating designs with radically different knowledge representations, that is, the distributed representations of artificial neural networks and the declarative ones of standard computers. Knowledge representation and codifying how experts think are presently major obstacles to the effective use of expert systems; research along these lines could raise expert systems to the next higher level of machine intelligence.

And, finally, research is needed in the management of architecting, to carry our understanding of it to the same level as that of manufacturing and engineering. Its converse, the architecting of management, may have equally far-reaching possibilities, but has been little explored.

RECOMMENDED READING

BELL, GORDON C. (February 1988). "Gordon Bell Calls for a U.S. Research Network." *IEEE Spectrum* **25**, 2, 54–58.

CARD, MICHAEL F. (ed.). (October 1978). "Large Space Structures." *Aeronautics and Astronautics* **10**, 16, 23–59.

CHRISTIANSEN, DONALD. (ed.). (July 1986). "Special Issue on Verification and Arms Control." *IEEE Spectrum* **23**, 7, 33–80.

DAVIS, JOHN G., JR., and S. C. DIXON (July 1988). "Beyond Simulation." *Aerospace America* **26**, 7, 38–42. It describes the system problems generated by materials facing a new and rigorous environment for the first time when going into space, a particular problem for the national aerospace plane (NASP).

ERVIN, ROBERT D., and K. CHEN. (Winter 1988). "Toward Motoring Smart." *Issues in Science and Technology* **V**, 2, 92–97. The article describes intelligent vehicles on intelligent highways.

FEINSTEIN, JOSEPH. (October 1982). "Future Weaponry." *IEEE Spectrum* **19**, 10, 91–99. It contains sub-articles by William Perry and Samuel Tennant. Future directions for military space communications/navigation/surveillance systems are given with comments on survivability.

FRIEDMAN, HERBERT. (July 1986). "Space Age Lessons About Our Environment." *Aerospace America* **24**, 7, 28–30. July 1986. The value of space systems in monitoring changes in the geosphere and biosphere is explored.

KAPLAN, GADI. (October 1982). "Peace Efforts." *IEEE Spectrum* **19**, 10, 102–14. It contains articles by Robert W. Buchheim, Simon Ramo, Ivan A. Getting, and Donald Christiansen on the technical aspects of treaty making and verification.

MACCREADY, PAUL B. (Winter 1988). "Sunraycer Odyssey." *Engineering and Science* **51**, 2, 3–13. This is the story of the solar-powered car that won the race across Australia.

MARYNIAK, GREGG E. (1984). *Living Off the Land—The Use of Resources in Space for Future Civilian Space Operations.* Princeton, NJ: Princeton University. It describes futuristic thinking by the O'Neill group at the Space Studies Institute.

[NASA] Solar System Exploration Committee. (1983). *Planetary Exploration Through Year 2000, Parts One and Two.* Washington, DC: U.S. Government Printing Office.

National Academy of Engineering. (1988). *Cities and Their Vital Systems: Infrastructure Past, Present and Future.* Washington, DC: National Academy Press.

National Commission on Space. (1986). *Pioneering the Space Frontier.* New York: Bantam Books.

RIVARD, JEROME G. (October 1987). "The Automobile in 1997." *IEEE Spectrum* **24**, 10, 67–71. Integrated performance features, more luxuries and advanced diagnostics are possible through systems engineering. This is one of a series of articles in a special issue, "Our Wheels Go Global."

ZORPETTE, GLEN. (March 1988). "An Underwater Visit to Aquarius." *IEEE Spectrum* **25**, 3, 24–29. It presents a description of a high-tech underwater habitat with its autonomous life-support system, advanced sensing, and data-handling capability.

Appendices

A

HEURISTICS LIST

ORGANIZING THE HEURISTICS LIST

The text contains more than 100 heuristics and the reader could undoubtedly add many more. Memorizing the list, given the unboundedness of systems and their heuristics, is hardly worthwhile. It would be a poor mechanism for associative recall. Instead, heuristics need to be easily associated with their context and with each other. And the faster the recall, the better.

The following list suffers, as do all lists, in being linear, that is, one heuristic after another. In this case, they are given in the order of appearance in the text, which generally means in the order that an architect moving down a product waterfall might first encounter them.

But many of the heuristics apply throughout the long architecting process, and some of the later ones on the list need to be brought in early in conceptual design, for example, those associated with manufacturability, acceptance criteria, and testing. Heuristics, after all, reflect the architecting process itself, one that necessarily considers the system as a whole in both physical elements and time.

In principle, heuristics might be properly organized in a thesauruslike manner, of which HYPERCARD™ is a modern computerized version. In other words, along with each heuristic would be given pointers to other heuristics that were closely associated with it, though in different "directions." **KISS,** for example, would have **minimum communications, aggregation, too smart, sanity checks,** and **stable** as close relatives.

Still other taxonomies are possible, depending on the interests of the clients, architects, builders, and users. But for purposes of sequential listing in a book, a chapter-by-chapter listing is as good as any. To place the heuristics in context, page numbers are given after each heuristic. Some heuristics, in modified form, arise in several contexts, for example in systems architecting and management reorganization. When this occurs, more than one page reference follows the heuristic. To make recognition faster, key words are **bold faced.**

CHAPTER 1: THE SYSTEMS ARCHITECT

- **Murphy's Law,** "If anything can go wrong, it will." (19)
- **Keep It Simple, Stupid (KISS).** (19)

   Or

   Simplify. Simplify. Simplify. (19)

   Or

   Occam's Razor: "The **simplest** solution is usually the **correct** one." (19)

CHAPTER 2: ON BOUNDARIES AND INTERFACES

- **Relationships** among the elements are what give systems their **added value.** (29)
- The greatest **leverage** in system architecting is at the **interfaces.** (29, 107)
- The efficient architect, using contextual sense, looks for the **likely misfits** and designs the architecture so as to eliminate or minimize them. (30, 70)
- **Success** is defined by the **beholder,** not by the architect. (30)
- Choosing the appropriate **aggregation** of functions is **critical** in the design of systems. (39, 72, 76, 269)
- Except for good and sufficient reasons, **functional and physical** structuring should **match.** (40, 76)
- In **partitioning,** choose the **elements** so that they are as independent as possible, that is, elements with low external complexity and high internal complexity. (41, 76)

   Or

   In partitioning a distributed system, choose a configuration in which local activity is high speed and global activity is slow change. (41)

   Or

   In partitioning a system into subsystems, choose a configuration with **minimal communications** between the subsystems. (Aerospace systems) (33, 41, 147, 269)

   Or

Do not partition by **slicing** through regions where **high rates** of information exchange are required. (Computers) (41)

- Design the **elements** to make their performance as **insensitive** to unknown or uncontrollable **external** influences as practical. (42)
- The architecture of a **support** element must fit that of the system that it supports. (43)
- Sometimes, but not always, the best way to solve a difficult problem is to **expand** it. (45)
- **Extreme** requirements should remain under challenge throughout system design, implementation, and operation. (46)
- When confronted with a particularly difficult interface, try changing its **characterization.** (46)
- Once the architecture begins to take shape, the sooner contextual constraints and **sanity checks** are made on assumptions and requirements, the better. (48)

And

Build **reality checks** into **model-driven** development. (48)

- (Software version) In architecting a new software program, all the serious **mistakes** are made in the **first day.** (48)

Or

(Aerospace version) In architecting a new aerospace system, by the time of the first design review, performance, cost, and schedule will have been predetermined. One might not know what they are yet, but, to first order, all the critical assumptions and choices will have been made that determine those parameters. (48)

- When choices must be made with unavoidably inadequate information, **choose** the best available and then **watch** to see whether future solutions appear faster than future problems. If so, the choice was at least adequate. If not, go back and **choose** again. (49, 270, 295)
- Organize **personnel** tasks to minimize the time individuals spend **interfacing.** (51)
- Try to determine which **nodes** are most **error-prone.** (51)

CHAPTER 3: MODELING, SIMULATING, AND PROTOTYPING

- **Don't assume** that the **original statement** of the problem is necessarily the best, or even the **right,** one. (54)
- Work **forwards** and backwards.
  Generalize or specialize.
  Explore multiple directions based on partial evidence.
  Form **stable** substructures.

Use **analogies** and metaphors.
Follow your **emotions.** (26, 54)

- System structure should resemble functional structure. (54)
- From psychology: If the concepts in the mind of one person are very different from those in the mind of the other, there is no **common model** of the topic and no communication. (56)

Or

From telecommunications: The best receiver is one that contains an internal model of the transmitter and the channel. (56)

- **No** complex system can be **optimum** to all parties concerned, nor all functions optimized. (57, 269, 272)
- Amid a wash of paper, a **small number of documents** become critical pivots around which every project's management revolves. (58)
- **A model is not reality.** (58)
- **Before** the flight, it's **opinion. After** the flight, it's **obvious.** (59)
- In new missions and markets, **expect the unexpected.** (62)
- Design the structure with **good "bones."** (62)
- Watch out for the **intermediate** systems. They may be **traps** instead of useful system **niches.** (71)

CHAPTER 4: THE ARCHITECT'S KIT OF TOOLS

- The **efficient architect,** using contextual sense, **continually looks** for the likely **misfits** and redesigns the architecture so as to eliminate or minimize them. (77)
- **Contain excess energy** as close to the source as possible. (83)
- **The triage:** Let the dying die. Ignore those who will recover on their own. And treat only those who would die without help. (83)
- The greatest **dangers** are also at the **interfaces.** (89)
- Be sure to ask the question, "What is the **worst** thing that other elements could do to you **across** the interface? (89)
- **Unbounded limits** on element behavior may be **a trap** in unexpected scenarios. (89)
- Be prepared for **reality** to add a few **interfaces** of its own. (89)
- Complex systems will develop and **evolve** within an overall architecture much more rapidly if there are **stable intermediate** forms than if there are not. (91)
- Build in and maintain **options** as long as possible in the design and implementation of complex systems. You will need them. (93)

Or

- Hang on to the **agony of decision** as long as possible. (93)
- The **ulcer** heuristic: System performance is understood well enough when implementers of the system feel only moderately ill about accepting the **performance** estimates as **acceptance** requirements for the system they will be constructing. (94, 297)
- **Concept formulation** is complete when the **builder** thinks the system can be built to the client's satisfaction. (94)
- The **choice between** architectures may well depend upon which set of **drawbacks** the client can handle best. (95, 269)
- **Pause and reflect!** (95)

CHAPTER 5: INFORMATION SYSTEMS

- The greatest **leverage** in system architecting is at the **interface.** (29, 107, 132)
- Responses to indeterminate diagnoses:
  If it **ain't broke,** don't fix it.
  Let's **wait and see** if it goes away or happens again.
  It was just a **random failure.** One of those things.
  Just **treat the symptom.** Worry about the cause later.
  Fix everything that might have caused the problem.
  Your guess is as good as mine. (115)
- In introducing **technological and social change,** *how* you do it is often more important than *what* you do. (120, 270)
  Or
  If social cooperation is required, the **way** in which a system is **implemented** and introduced must be an **integral part** of its architecture. (120)
- Do not make an architecture **too smart** for its own good. (120)

CHAPTER 6: BUILDING THE SYSTEM

- An element "**good enough**" in a small system is unlikely to be good enough in a more complex one. (127)
- Within the same class of products and processes, the **failure rate** of a product is linearly **proportional** to its **cost.** (127)
- **Quality** cannot be tested in, it has to be **built in.** (129)
  Or
  High-quality, reliable systems are produced by high-quality architecting, engineering, design, and manufacture, not by inspection, test, and rework. (129)

- In correcting system **deviations** and failures, it is important that all the participants know not only *what* happened and *how* it happened, but *why* as well. (130)
- Next to interfaces, the greatest **leverage** in architecting is in aiding the **recovery from,** or exploitation of, **deviations** in system performance, cost, or schedule. (131)
- Just as a piece and its template must match, so must a system and the resources that make, test, and operate it. (132)

Or

The **product** and **process** must **match.** (132)

Or

A system architecture cannot be considered complete lacking a suitable match with the process architecture. (132)

- **Performance, cost, and schedule** cannot be specified independently. At least one of the three must depend on the others. (139)
- Schedule stretch is a system constant, the **rubber schedule** heuristic. (139, 203)

Or

The time to complete is proportional to the time spent. (139)

CHAPTER 7: SYSTEM TEST, ACCEPTANCE, AND OPERATIONS

- Regardless of what has gone before, the **acceptance criteria determine** what is actually built. (142)
- For a system **to meet** its acceptance **criteria** to the satisfaction of all parties, it must be **architected,** designed, and built to do so—no more and no less. (143)
- Qualification and acceptance **tests** must be both **definitive and passable.** (143)
- The **realities** at the end of the conceptual phase are **not the models, but the acceptance criteria.** (144)
- **Define** how an **acceptance** criterion is to be **certified** at the same time the criterion is established. (144)
- To be tested, a system must be **designed to be tested.** (144, 146)
- The **test setup** for a system is itself **a system.** (145)
- The **cost** to find and fix a **failed part** increases by an **order of magnitude** as that part is successively incorporated into higher levels in the system. (148)

Likewise

The least expensive and most effective place to **find and fix** a supply problem is **at** its **source.** (148)

- The first **quick look** analyses are **often wrong.** (152)
- **Recovery** from failure is not complete until a specific **failure mechanism,** *and no other,* has been shown to be the cause. (153)
- Chances for **recovery from a single** failure, even with complex consequences, are fairly **good. Recovery from two** or more independent failures is **unlikely** in real time and uncertain in any case. (153)
- Place **barriers** in the paths between **energy sources** and the elements the energy can damage. (154)
- **Knowing** a failure has occurred is **more important** than the actual failure. (154)
- The probability of failure is proportional to the weight of **brass** in the immediate vicinity. (154)

CHAPTER 8: ULTRAQUALITY—EXCELLENCE BEYOND MEASURE

- **Tally** the defects, **analyze** them, **trace** them to the source, make **corrections,** keep a **record** of what happens **afterwards,** and keep **repeat**ing it. (163)
- The **number** of problems encountered in development is **inversely related** to their **magnitudes.** (165)
- **Reducing failure rate** by each factor of **2** takes as much effort as the original development. (165)
- **Testing, without understanding** the multiple failure mechanisms to which a system is susceptible, can be both **deceptive and harmful.** (167)
- **Unless everyone** who needs to know **does know,** somebody, somewhere, will **foul up.** (172)
- Ultraquality systems and processes demand **ultraquality documentation—** complete but concise and **error-free.** (173)
- If being **absolute** is impossible in estimating system **risks,** then be **relative.** (177)
- **Fault avoidance** is **preferable** to fault tolerance in system design. **Fault tolerance,** when used, should be **specific** to fault type. (180)
- You cannot achieve **quality** . . . unless you **specify** it. (186)

CHAPTER 9: PURPOSEFUL OPPOSITION

- For every **system,** there will be at least one **countersystem.** (189)
- A **system optimized** for a particular situation is **unlikely to encounter** that situation. (190, 207, 254)

- **Wealth is knowledge** and knowing **how, where, when, and why** to use it. (78, 194)
- Sometimes the best way to **defeat** a system is to do so "**out of bounds.**" It may also be the best way to **preserve** it. (195)
- Don't get in a **zero-sum game** with the outside world. (196)
- What independent reviews are to quality, **red teams** are to **survival,** only more so. (200)

CHAPTER 10: A SENSE OF TIME AND TIMING

- **Predicting** the future may be **impossible,** but ignoring it is **irresponsible.** (207, 270)
- You cannot avoid **redesign.** It's a **natural** part of design. (215)

CHAPTER 11: BIOLOGICAL ARCHITECTURES AND INTELLIGENT BEHAVIOR

- Different architectures can generate **different behavior.** (217)
- The name of the game in efficient **sensing** is **contrast.** (228)
- For the best in **intelligent** behavior, the architectures of human and machine should be a **matched pair.** (239)

CHAPTER 12: THE COMPLEX WORLD OF ECONOMICS AND PUBLIC POLICY

- **Profit** is a matter of **definition** and **cost** is **not an absolute.** (256)
- **Competitiveness** is more a matter of **know-how** than know-what. (256)
- **Risk** is defined by the **beholder,** not the architect. (264)

CHAPTER 13: ON ORGANIZATIONS AND ARCHITECTURES

- **No** complex system can be **optimum** to all parties concerned. (57, 269, 272, 335)
- The **strengths** of an organization in one context can be its **weaknesses** in another. (273)

Or

Given a successful organization with valid criteria for success, there are some things it cannot do—or at least not do well. (273)

Or

Being **good at one thing** does not automatically mean being good at something else. (273)

- It is easier to **match** a system **to the human** one it supports than the reverse. (282)
- The time in days, *T,* to obtain an approval requiring *N* signatures is approximately $T = 2^{N-2}$. (283)
- The **probability** of implementing **new ideas** depends on the number of persons in the chain leading to their implementation and on the probability that each person understands and retransmits that idea. (284)
- A team producing at the **fastest rate** humanly possible spends **half** its time **coordinating** and interfacing. (284)
- **Pareto's law: 80%** of the useful work in an organization is accomplished by **20%** of the people. (284)

Or, perhaps,

Only 20% of the signatures really count. (284)

- When faced with resistance to positional change, remember that instantaneous changes are impossible, but anyone can work the **second derivative.** (285)
- **Personal risk** is proportional to the difference between **responsibility** and **authority.** (287)

CHAPTER 14: PROFILE OF A SYSTEMS ARCHITECT

- **Don't** ever **stop talking** about the system. (292)
- There's no such thing as **immaculate communication!** (292)

CHAPTER 15: ASSESSING ARCHITECTING AND ARCHITECTURES

- A measure of the **status** of a conceptual model is the number of **TBD's** remaining in its cost model. (297)
- **Conceptual design** is near **completion** when prospective implementers of the system feel only moderately ill about accepting the **performance estimates as acceptance requirements** for the system they will be constructing. (94, 297)
- There's nothing like being the **first success.** (301)
- If at first you do not succeed, but the architecture is sound, **try, try again.** Success sometimes is where you find it. (302)

B

REFERENCE TEXTS SUGGESTED FOR INSTITUTIONAL LIBRARIES

AGRAWAL, DHARMA P. *Advanced Computer Architecture*. Washington, DC: The Computer Society of the IEEE, 1986.

ALEXANDER, C. *Notes on the Synthesis of Form*. Cambridge, MA: Harvard University Press, 1964.

AUGUSTINE, N. R. *Augustine's Laws*. New York: AIAA, Inc., 1982.

ARBIB, M .A. *Brains, Machines, and Mathematics,* 2nd Ed. New York: Springer-Verlag, 1987.

ARBIB, M. A., *The Metaphorical Brain 2, Neural Networks and Beyond*. New York: John Wiley, 1989.

BACH, GEORGE LELAND. *Economics, An Introduction to Analysis and Policy,* 8th Ed. Englewood Cliffs, NJ: Prentice Hall, 1974.

BOORSTIN, DANIEL J. *The Discoverers*. New York: Vintage Books, 1985.

BOYES, J. L. (ed.) *Principles of Command and Control*. Washington, DC: AFCEA International Press, 1987.

BROOKS, F. P., Jr. *The Mythical Man-Month, Essays on Software Engineering*. Reading, MA: Addison-Wesley, 1982.

BURKE, J. D. *A Gossamer Condor and Albatross: A Case Study in Aircraft Design,* AIAA Professional Study Series. City: American Institute of Aeronautics and Astronautics, 1980.

DAVIS, S. M. *Future Perfect*. Reading, MA: Addison-Wesley, 1987.

DEAL, TERRENCE E., and A. A. KENNEDY. *Corporate Cultures, The Rites and Rituals of Corporate Life.* Reading, MA: Addison-Wesley, 1988.

DEUTSCH, M. S., and R. R. WILLIS. *Software Quality Engineering.* Englewood Cliffs, NJ: Prentice Hall, 1988.

EISNER, H. *Computer Aided Systems Engineering.* Englewood Cliffs, NJ: Prentice Hall, 1988.

EPPEN, G. D., F. J. GOULD, and C. P. SCHMIDT. *Introductory Management Science.,*2nd Ed. Englewood Cliffs, NJ: Prentice Hall, 1984.

FERNANDEZ, EDUARDO B., and T. LANG. *Software-Oriented Computer Architecture.* New York: The Computer Society of the IEEE, 1986.

FLOOD, R. L., and E. R. CARSON. *Dealing with Complexity, An Introduction to the Theory and Application of System Sciences.* New York: Plenum, 1988.

GAJSKI, D. D., V. M. MILUTINOVIC, H. J. SIEGEL, and B. P. FURHT. *Computer Architecture.* New York: The Computer Society of the IEEE, 1987.

GENESERETH, M. S., and N. J. NILSSON. *Logical Foundations of Artificial Intelligence.* Los Altos, CA: Morgan Kaufmann, 1987.

GERSTEIN, DEAN R., R. D. LUCE, N. J. SMELSER, and S. SPERLICH. (Eds.). *The Behavioral and Social Sciences, Achievements and Opportunities.* Washington, DC: National Academy Press, 1988.

GLEIK, JAMES. *Chaos.* New York: Penguin, 1987.

HALL, R. CARGILL. *Lunar Impact, A History of Project Ranger,* NASA History Series. Washington, DC: National Aeronautics and Space Administration, 1977.

HAYES, ROBERT H., S. C. WHEELWRIGHT, and K. B. CLARK. *Dynamic Manufacturing.* New York: The Free Press, 1988.

HOFSTADTER, D. R. *Gödel, Escher, Bach: An Eternal Golden Braid.* New York: Vintage Books, 1980.

JURAN, J. M., *Juran on Planning for Quality.* New York: The Free Press, 1988.

KLIR, G. J. *Architecture of Systems Problem Solving.* New York: Plenum, 1985.

KOSTOFF, SPIRO. *The Architect.* New York: Oxford University Press, 1977.

LANG, JON. *Creating Architectural Theory.* Van Nostrand Reinhold, 1987.

LEITES, NATHAN, and C. WOLF, JR. *Rebellion and Authority, An Analytic Essay on Insurgent Conflicts.* Chicago: Markham, 1970.

LEWIN, RONALD. *ULTRA Goes to War.* New York: McGraw-Hill, 1978.

LEY, WILLY, and W. VON BRAUN. *The Exploration of Mars.* New York: American Book- Stratford Press, 1956.

LUTRIN, C. E., and A. K. SETTLE, *American Public Administration: Concepts & Cases.* 2nd Ed. Palo Alto, CA: Mayfield, 1980.

MILLER, J. G. *Living Systems.* New York: McGraw-Hill, 1978.

MINSKY, M., *The Society of Mind.* New York: Simon and Schuster, 1986.

NADLER, G. *The Planning and Design Approach.* New York: John Wiley, 1981.

NAGLER, G. R. (ed.). *Naval Tactical Command and Control.* Washington, DC: AFCEA International Press, 1987.

NORMAN, DONALD A. *The Psychology of Everyday Things.* New York: Basic Books, 1988.

PARSAYE, K., and M. CHIGNELL. *Expert Systems for Experts.* New York: John Wiley, 1988.

PEARL, JUDEA. *Heuristics.* Reading, MA: Addison-Wesley, 1984.

PEÑA, WILLIAM. *Problem Seeking, An Architectural Programming Primer.* New York: Cahners Books International, 1977.

PFIFFNER, JOHN M., and FRANK P. SHERWOOD. *Administrative Organization.* Englewood Cliffs, NJ: Prentice Hall, 1960.

RESTAK, RICHARD M. *The Brain.* New York: Bantam Books, 1984.

ROWE, ALAN J., R. O. MASON, and K. E. DICKEL. *Strategic Management & Public Policy, A Methodological Approach,* 2nd Ed. Reading, MA: Addison-Wesley, 1985.

ROWE, P. G. *Design Theory.* Cambridge, MA: The MIT Press, 1987.

RUBINSTEIN, MOSHE F. *Patterns of Problem Solving.* Englewood Cliffs, NJ: Prentice Hall, 1975.

SIMON, H. A. *Sciences of the Artificial.* Cambridge, MA: The MIT Press, 1981.

SIMON, H. A., *Artificial Intelligence, Current Status and Future Potential,* the Charles H. Davis Lecture Series. Washington, DC: National Academy Press, 1985.

STEINER, J. E., *Case Study in Aircraft Design, the Boeing 727,* AIAA Professional Study Series. New York: American Institute of Aeronautics and Astronautics, 1978.

VERMURI, V. *Artificial Neural Networks: Theoretical Concepts.* New York: Computer Society Press, 1988.

VITRUVIUS (trans. by Morris Hicky Morgan). *The Ten Books on Architecture.* New York: Dover, 1960.

WARD, P. T., and S. J. MELLOR. *Structured Development for Real-Time Systems, Volume 1: Introduction and Tools.* Englewood Cliffs, NJ: Yourdon Press, 1985.

WEINBERG, GERALD M. *Rethinking Systems Analysis and Design.* New York: Dorset House, 1988.

WIDROW, BERNARD. *DARPA Neural Network Study, October 1987–February 1988.* Fairfax, VA: AFCEA International Press, 1988.

INDEX

AUTHOR INDEX

A

Adam, J. A., 201
Adelson, E. H., 122
Agrawal, D. P., 320
Alexander, Christopher, 50, 97, 320
Alkon, D. L., 242
Allen, Frederick, 26
Anninov, A., 97
Aoki, C., 242
Arbib, M. A., 240, 320
Ashley, Holt, 51
Augustine, N. R., 320

B

Bach, G. L., 265, 320
Bates, J. D., 303
Beam, Walter R., 26
Bell, G. C., 308
Bellman, K. L., 240
Bello, M., 303
Berman, A. L., 304
Bernstein, H., 186
Bickerton, D., 240
Blaauw, G. A., von, 27
Bloch, E., 265
Blockinger, R. A., 156
Boehm, B. W., 50
Bollman, V. S., 156
Booton, Richard C., Jr., 27
Boorstin, D. J., 213, 320
Boulding, K., 214
Boyes, J. L., 122, 320

Braun, W., von, 214, 321
Brodsky, R. F., 303
Brooks, Frederick P., Jr., 10, 22, 23, 24, 58, 72, 96, 233, 241, 284, 320
Brooks, H., 265
Brooks, R. A., 241
Burger, J. R., 122
Burke, J. D., 304, 320
Burt, P. J., 122
Bush, Vannevar, 122
Buzbee, B. L., 97, 122

C

Canty, Donald, 27
Card, M. F., 309
Carpenter, Robert, 27
Carson, E. R., 50, 72, 321
Chen, K., 309
Chignell, Mark H., 24, 73, 121, 294, 322
Chisvin, L., 242
Chol, D., 24
Christiansen, D., 186, 309
Chua, L. O., 97
Clark, K. B., 141, 321
Coates, J. F., 214
Compton, W. D., 140, 265
Conley, R. E., 122
Cooper, N. G., 96, 213
Corcoran, E., 187
Courtois, P. J., 51

D

Davis, J. G., Jr., 309
Davis, R., 121

323

SUBJECT INDEX